EU LAW IN CRIMINAL PRACTICE

EU LAW IN CRIMINAL PRACTICE

Edited by
Duncan Atkinson

Consultant Editors
David Perry qc
Valsamis Mitsilegas

OXFORD
UNIVERSITY PRESS

OXFORD

UNIVERSITY PRESS

Great Clarendon Street, Oxford, OX2 6DP,
United Kingdom

Oxford University Press is a department of the University of Oxford.
It furthers the University's objective of excellence in research, scholarship,
and education by publishing worldwide. Oxford is a registered trade mark of
Oxford University Press in the UK and in certain other countries

Published in the United States of America by Oxford University Press
198 Madison Avenue, New York, NY 10016, United States of America

British Library Cataloguing in Publication Data
Data available

Library of Congress Cataloguing in Publication Data
Data Available

ISBN 978-0-19-966425-2

FOREWORD

David Perry QC

In *Macleod v Attorney General for New South Wales* [1891] AC 455, Lord Halsbury LC famously asserted: 'All crime is local'. By this he meant that jurisdiction over a crime belongs to the country where it is committed. Lord Halsbury's dictum was not strictly true, even in the last decade of the nineteenth century and it is certainly not true today. Criminal justice systems have become more cosmopolitan, jurisdiction over crime has expanded and so too has international cooperation: no civilised State today could afford to adopt a policy of parochial insularity. These trends have been driven by the ease with which individuals move around the world and increasingly sophisticated communication technologies. The need for cooperation between neighbouring or contiguous States is nowhere more true than within the European Union, where freedom of movement is a fundamental principle.

This excellent and timely book is about the impact of the European Union on the administration of criminal justice in the United Kingdom. The subject matter is important, and increasingly so. There are over 130 criminal justice measures which impact upon the United Kingdom, and even if the Government decides to opt out of those criminal justice measures adopted under the Maastricht and Amsterdam Treaties, the influence of the Union on domestic criminal justice will continue to grow. The trends in this area are all one way. The domestic courts interpret Part 1 of the Extradition Act 2003 against the background of the Framework Decision of the European Arrest Warrant. Article 54 of the Convention Implementing the Schengen Agreement, which is intended to ensure that no one is prosecuted on the same facts in more than one Member State, has obvious implication for domestic criminal proceedings. Practitioners are likely to become more involved in proceedings before the Court of Justice as the scope for preliminary references by the national courts increases.

With admirable clarity the authors explain the European Union's growing involvement in criminal justice, the current institutions, legislative instruments and their current effect, and provide useful insights into what is likely to happen in the future. The glossary provides a succinct explanation of the key institutions and concepts.

The book provides a rich analysis of what is an increasingly important influence on the administration of criminal justice in the United Kingdom: which it is necessary for practitioners and advisers to understand if they are to move forward with confidence. The authors are to be congratulated for providing a guide to an area of law with which we must all become more familiar. With this book we will be well armed to make a positive contribution to the future of our own criminal law and for this we should be truly grateful.

ACKNOWLEDGEMENTS

I am very grateful to all of these members of chambers for the combination of zest and dedication that has brought this book to fruition. I should also mention with thanks another member of chambers, Katherine Hardcastle, who produced the glossary of EU terms that appears at the end of the book, and to the expert oversight of the project by David Perry QC and Professor Valsamis Mitsilegas. I am also very grateful for the efficiency, support, and enthusiasm of the editorial team at Oxford University Press, and of Eleanor Walter in particular.

CONTENTS

LIST OF COMMONLY USED ABBREVIATIONS

AFSJ	Area of freedom, security and justice (Title V, Part 3 of the TFEU)
CICA	Crime (International Cooperation) Act 2003
CISA	Convention implementing the Schengen Agreement
CJA	Criminal Justice Act 2003
CJEU	Court of Justice of the European Union
EAW	European Arrest Warrant
ECHR	European Convention on Human Rights and Fundamental Freedoms
ECtHR	European Court of Human Rights
EEW	European Evidence Warrant
EIO	European Investigation Order
OLAF	L'Office européen de lutte antifraude (European Anti-Fraud Office)
PACE	Police and Criminal Evidence Act 1984
TEC	Treaty of the European Economic Community (Treaty of Rome)
TEU	Treaty on European Union (Treaty of Maastricht)
TFEU	Treaty of the European Economic Community as renamed by the Treaty of Lisbon

LIST OF CONTRIBUTORS

About the Editors

Duncan Atkinson is a barrister at the Chambers of David Fisher QC and David Perry QC. He was appointed junior treasury counsel in 2009, and has an unrivalled practice, specializing in criminal litigation, homicide, fraud, terrorism, and regulatory work, public law, and inquests. He has been instructed in some of the most high profile, sensitive, and difficult criminal cases and inquests in recent years, including the trial of Levi Bellfield, the Royal Blackmail case, the 'fertiliser bomber' case, and the inquest into the Potter's Bar rail disaster, and has appeared as leading, sole, and junior counsel in cases of rape, public nuisance, blackmail, prison escape, corruption, conspiracy to pervert the course of justice, and prosecutions under the Official Secrets Act. He is the joint author of *Blackstone's Guide to the Criminal Procedure Rules* (2e, OUP, 2011), and a contributor to *Blackstone's Criminal Practice* (OUP), and *Fraud: Criminal Law and Procedure* (OUP).

David Perry QC (consultant editor) is joint head of chambers at the Chambers of David Fisher QC and David Perry QC. Described as a "phenomenally impressive" silk, David not only handles complex domestic cases but also advises overseas governments and is a top extradition expert. David was appointed silk in 2006 and is on the editorial board for *Blackstone's Criminal Practice*

Valsamis Mitsilegas (consultant editor) is Head of the Department of Law, Professor of European Criminal Law, and Director of the Criminal Justice Centre at Queen Mary, University of London. His expertise lies primarily in the area of EU law, in particular EU Justice and Home Affairs (including immigration, asylum and border controls, criminal law, police and judicial co-operation in criminal matters and the external dimension of EU action in these fields). Professor Mitsilegas provides regular advice to the UK Government and the Judiciary of England and Wales and is actively engaged with the legal profession as regards the impact of European Union law on the domestic legal system. He contributes a chapter on European Union law to *Blackstone's Criminal Practice*.

About the Contributors

Victoria Ailes was called to the bar in 2005 after taking her degree in Mathematics and Philosophy at Trinity College, Oxford. She was judicial assistant to Lord Rodger of Earlsferry and Lord Brown of Eaton under Heywood in 2007–8. She now acts in criminal matters, particularly those with an international or cross-jurisdictional dimension.

Michael Bisgrove is a barrister at the Chambers of David Perry QC and David Fisher QC. Following an undergraduate degree in neuroscience, Michael moved to London and converted to Law. He began his career at the Bar in 2006. From an initial general criminal practice, Michael developed an enthusiasm for public and regulatory law. In addition he has worked in large scale review and disclosure exercising on behalf of HMG. Michael has a keen interest in corporate misbehaviour and is now deepening and broadening his experience of financial regulation and financial crime both offshore and within England and Wales

Julian Blake studied Social and Political Sciences at the University of Cambridge before becoming a Fox International Fellow at Yale University, USA. In this position he researched and lectured in international relations and international security studies. He therefore has significant expertise in crimes that are international or multi-jurisdictional in nature. He practices in international crimes and torts, extradition, national security law and appeals from foreign jurisdictions to the Privy Council. Julian has been involved in some of the most high profile cases and investigations in recent years. This includes civil claims by former residents of Guantanamo Bay and the Gibson Inquiry into mistreatment of detainees post 9/11. He is currently instructed to represent the Government in a freedom of information appeal brought by the All Party Parliamentary Group on Extraordinary Rendition and a civil claim brought by two prominent Libyan political figures.

Alex Chalk appears as leader and junior in the most serious criminal cases, ranging from terrorism, to heavy fraud and homicide. Notable cases include the prosecution of six men accused of plotting acts of terrorism within the UK. He has also acted for the Crown in an Operation Trident double-murder case concerning street shootings in London.

Ranked in Chambers UK for his fraud work, Alex has appeared for the Serious Fraud Office as junior counsel in a multi-million pound advance fee fraud. He has also acted in a long-running prosecution brought by the Serious Organised Crime Agency. As defence counsel Alex has successfully acted for clients charged with grave offences, including murder, attempted murder and rape. As leading counsel Alex has prosecuted the long-running election fraud trial of three candidates standing to become local councillors. He has advised in other cases involving alleged breaches of electoral law, including offences under the Representation of the People Act 1983.

James Chegwidden is a barrister at 6KBW College Hill. Called in 2008, he practises in employment law, general civil claims, regulatory law and human rights. He was the recipient in 2010 of the Peter Duffy Scholarship for human rights scholarship at Lincoln's Inn and thereafter spent time working at the European Court of Human Rights, Strasbourg as an *avocat stagiaire* in the UK Division. James's experience in European rights jurisprudence includes applying ECHR guideline judgments in EU and Council of Europe states (Cyprus and Turkey), reported cases involving the application of EU directives (*Ségor v Goodrich Actuation Systems* (2012), and appeals. Additionally, he has provided pro-bono advocacy and assistance to individuals and charities on rights issues, including in 2012 a delegation to the United Nations Human Rights Committee on children's rights to bodily autonomy. James is a member of the Lawyers' Secular Society and the Human Rights Lawyers' Society, and a contributor to *The Proceeds of Crime* (Mark Sutherland Williams ed).

Annabel Darlow is a barrister specialising in criminal law with a particular emphasis on appellate work and serious fraud. She was appointed Crown Court Recorder in 2009 and Standing Counsel to the Department for Business, Innovation and Skills in 2012.

Rosemary Davidson is a barrister at 6KBW College Hill and was called to the bar in 2004. She has a BA in jurisprudence from Balliol College, Oxford and an LLM in Public Law and Human Rights from University College, London. She practises in public law and human rights, with particular specialisms in extradition and immigration. She has written extensively on extradition, including being the co-author and assistant editor of *The Extradition and Mutual Legal Assistance Handbook* (OUP, 2010).

Richard Evans is a barrister who was called to the Bar in 2008. He specialises in general crime, extradition and health and safety. He studied law at Jesus College, University of Cambridge and Université Panthéon-Assas, Paris II.

Jacob Hallam read history at Corpus Christi College Cambridge. He specialises in cases involving serious crime for both defence and prosecution, on his own, as junior counsel, or as a leading junior in Crown and appellate courts. Since 2007, his work has primarily centred on cases of homicide, many of which have involved aspects of international law. In addition to his work in the criminal courts, Jacob has developed an expanding practice in advisory work, judicial review, extradition and libel law. Jacob is an experienced advocate, and a member of the faculty of advocacy teachers at Gray's Inn.

Will Hays is a barrister at the Chambers of David Perry QC and David Fisher QC. He practises in criminal law, public law and related areas. As well as prosecuting and defending serious crime in the Crown Court, Will has a particular expertise in restraint and confiscation, having appeared as junior in the Supreme Court on three occasions in matters concerning confiscation. He also appears in civil matters, including proceedings for civil recovery and judicial review. He is regularly instructed to appear in the Tribunals in matters ranging from immigration to VAT. Will is appointed to the Attorney General's C Panel for civil and EU work.

Christopher Hehir is a barrister at 6KBW College Hill, practising in criminal law. He studied law at Merton College, Oxford and received his BA (Jurisprudence) in 1988. Christopher was called to the Bar in 1990, and was appointed a Recorder of the Crown Court in 2009.

Paul Humpherson studied and subsequently taught law at Worcester College, Oxford, before moving to London to study for the Bar. He was called by Gray's Inn in 2010 and has practised as a criminal barrister for the last two years from 6KBW College Hill. Over that time Paul has prosecuted and defended in a wide range of criminal cases, and has begun to develop expertise in regulatory law and financial crime.

Paul Jarvis was called to the Bar in 2001. He practises in the areas of national and international crime, in particular cross-border crime including fraud, insider dealing, market abuse, bribery, corruption and money-laundering. He also acts and advises in cases concerning trademark and copyright offences and other areas where EU legislation plays a key role such as environmental crime. He is recommended by *Chambers & Partners* as a leading junior barrister in the area of crime

Ben Lloyd is a barrister at 6KBW College Hill, practising in extradition, criminal law, public law and related areas. He has appeared in extradition cases before the UK Supreme Court and is experienced in litigation involving the application of EU law. He was called to the Bar in 2004.

Dan Pawson-Pounds is a barrister at 6KBW College Hill, having served in the British Army before being called to the Bar. He practises in criminal law, regulatory law, public law and related areas. He has wide experience of prosecuting and defending a range of grave offences in the Crown Court and advises a number of government departments in relation to war crimes, potential human rights abuses and other international criminal offences. He also has experience of corporate criminal investigations

Adam Payter is a barrister at 6KBW College Hill, specialising in extradition, professional discipline and financial, regulatory and corporate criminal investigations. Prior to joining Chambers, Adam worked at Liberty in 2009 and he is now an elected member of Liberty's Policy Council. He previously worked at the United Nations International Criminal Tribunal for the former Yugoslavia. From 2008–2011, Adam sat as a Justice of the Peace. He was called to the bar in 2008.

Simon Ray is a member of 6KBW College Hill and is ranked as a leading junior barrister with considerable expertise in serious and complex criminal litigation. He specialises in financial crime, corruption and corporate offending and in recent years has been instructed in cases in the Supreme Court and the House of Lords.

Alistiar Richardson is a barrister at 6KBW College Hill, specialising in financial and corporate crime. Alistair has particular expertise in asset forfeiture. He has also lectured internationally on mutual legal assistance, extradition and criminal law, and provides advice to overseas governments in these areas

Esther Schutzer Weissman studied classics at Oxford before converting to law. She completed her pupillage with David Perry QC, assisting in cases in Strasbourg, before becoming a tenant specialising in serious crime and international financial crime. Esther has been in high-profile cases such as *R v Ibori* and *SFO v Nadir*, as well as doing a selection of administrative law cases (judicial review of decisions to offer no evidence, judicial review of a decision not to hold an inquest, appeals arising out of the UN Refugee Convention and on the meaning of the Extradition Act). Esther was appointed to the Special Advocates Panel in 2009 and is a Treasury Counsel monitoree. She previously spent three months working at the ECHR in Strasbourg and is the contributing editor to the criminal section of Article 6 in European Human Rights Law.

Mark Weekes graduated in 1997 from Trinity College, Oxford with a degree in Modern History, after which he completed the CPE at the University of Westminster (1998) and BVC at Inns of Court School of Law (1999). He was called to the Bar (Lincoln's Inn) in 1999. Mark was a pupil at, and has always practised from 6KBW College Hill. He has prosecuted and defended in the Crown Court and Court of Appeal in a wide variety of cases and also regularly deals with extradition, public law and and confiscation matters. Mark is currently instructed as part of the Special Prosecution Team investigating systemic governmental corruption in the Turks and Caicos Islands following the suspension of the government there in 2009.

Sarah Whitehouse graduated from St Andrews University and became a banker for 8 years before converting to law. She was called to the Bar in 1993 and was appointed Treasury Counsel in 2006. She was appointed to the Attorney General's list of Special Advocates in 2009. She is ranked as a leading junior (band 1) by Chambers & Partners and was criminal Junior Barrister of the Year in 2012. She appears on a regular basis in the Court of Appeal and prosecutes and defends in a wide variety of criminal cases including terrorism, murder, sexual offending, and fraud. She is a Grade A advocacy tutor at Lincoln's Inn.

TABLE OF CASES

EUROPEAN COURT OF HUMAN RIGHTS

IRELAND

UNITED KINGDOM

TABLE OF LEGISLATION

UNITED KINGDOM

TABLE OF TREATIES, CONVENTIONS, AND INSTRUMENTS

INTRODUCTION

The relationship between the UK and Europe has long been a matter of controversial debate, and the impact of the European Union is felt in a great many aspects of our daily lives. It is not the intention of this book to enter that debate. Rather, this book seeks to provide clear, practical assistance to those engaged in criminal law in this country as to how the increasing role of the EU impacts on them and their clients.

The law of the European Union ('EU law') effects the national criminal law of the UK in two different but complementary ways.[1] First, because EU law takes precedence over national law, EU law affects the interpretation of domestic criminal law. Secondly, the EU has an increasing role in regulating areas that had previously been regarded as the sole preserve of the English criminal law. As part of that process, EU law can oblige national legislators to introduce new rules into their domestic criminal law. There are many examples of this having occurred, which can be categorised[2] as:

(a) measures intended to influence substantive criminal law, such as Framework Decisions on terrorism,[3] drug-trafficking,[4] cybercrime,[5] money laundering,[6] and people smuggling;[7]
(b) measures intended to influence national criminal procedure, such as the Framework Decisions on the standing of victims in criminal proceedings[8] and the status of convictions;[9]
(c) police cooperation measures, such as the Prüm system for the exchange of information contained in fingerprint, DNA, and vehicle registration databases[10] and the operation of police and judicial cooperation agencies such as Europol and Eurojust;
(d) mutual recognition measures such as the European Arrest Warrant[11] and the Framework Decision on the mutual recognition of freezing orders.[12]

The methods by which the EU can legislate in the field of criminal law were transformed dramatically by the coming into force of the Treaty of Lisbon in 2009. As a result of that Treaty, the EU is set to take a greater role in the 'area of freedom, security and justice'.[13] Examples of this are already apparent, such as Directives guaranteeing the minimum rights of suspects during a police investigation[14] and addressing people trafficking,[15] and the proposed

---

[1] See Professor John Spencer QC, 'EU Criminal Law—The Present and the Future?' in *Constitutional Order of States? Essays in EU Law in Honour of Alan Dashwood* (Oxford: Hart Publishing, 2011)

[2] Using the categorisation contained in the Centre for European Legal Studies paper 'Opting Out of EU Criminal Law: What is Actually Involved?' by Hinarejos, Spencer, and Peers (September 2012).

[3] Council Framework Decision 2002/475/JHA of 13 June 2002.

[4] Council Framework Decision 2004/757/JHA of 25 October 2004.

[5] Council Framework Decision 2005/222/JHA of 25 February 2005.

[6] Council Framework Decision 2001/500/JHA of 26 June 2001.

[7] Council Framework Decision 2002/946/JHA of 28 November 2002.

[8] Council Framework Decision 2001/220/JHA of 15 March 2001.

[9] Council Framework Decision 2008/675/JHA of 24 July 2008.

[10] Prüm Decision [2008] OJ L 210/1.

[11] Council Framework Decision 2002/584/JHA of 13 June 2002.

[12] Council Framework Decision 2003/577/JHA of 22 July 2003.

[13] The heading to Title V of Part 3 of the TFEU.

[14] Directives 2010/64/EU and 2012/13/EU.

[15] Directive 2011/36/EU.

and far-reaching new investigative tool contained in the proposed Directive for a European Investigation Order. For all these reasons, EU law has an importance for criminal practitioners in the UK and that importance will only increase in the future.

The Opt-Out

It might be thought that this will change if the present Government follows through on its 'current thinking'[16] and opts out of all pre-Lisbon police and criminal justice measures. Article 10(4) of Protocol No. 36 to the EU Treaties, as amended by the Treaty of Lisbon, provides that the UK may give notice that it no longer accepts 'the acts of the Union in the field of police co-operation and judicial co-operation in criminal matters which have been adopted before the entry into force of the Treaty of Lisbon' at any time up to six months before the end of the transitional period. That period expires on 1 December 2014, and thus the UK Government would have to give the requisite notice by 31 May 2014. Under the terms of the Protocol, this would be an all-or-nothing move, in the sense that the UK 'cannot pick and choose the measures from which we wish to opt out. We can only opt out *en masse* and then seek to rejoin individual measures.'[17]

In February 2012, 100 MPs signed a letter to the *Daily Telegraph* in which they urged the Government to exercise this opt-out. They argued, 'the EU Commission's ambitions for a pan-European code of Euro Crimes highlight how Europe should be about co-operation rather than control. We need practical co-operation to fight terrorism, drugs, human trafficking and other cross-border crimes—not harmonisation of national criminal laws. We do not wish to subordinate UK authorities to a pan-European Public Prosecutor. We do not want to see British police forces subjected to mandatory demands by European police under the European Investigation Order. We have deep concerns about the operation of the European Arrest Warrant for our citizens.' They concluded: 'we should maintain our national standards of justice and democratic control over crime and policing—but let other nations integrate more closely if they wish.'

In a paper issued by the Centre for European Legal Studies (CELS),[18] Alicia Hinarejos, John Spencer, and Steve Peers point out that the logic of this argument is flawed. Of the measures the signatories to this letter identified, the position of European Public Prosecutor does not yet exist and the European Investigation Order has not yet been introduced. Neither, therefore, is a pre-Lisbon measure on which the opt-out would operate. Whilst the European Arrest Warrant would be affected by the opt-out, there are indications that this is one of the measures that the Government would seek to rejoin if the opt-out is exercised. In the course of questioning about her statement,[19] the Home Secretary appeared to acknowledge that the Government's objective would be to amend the European Arrest Warrant rather than to repeal it. Moreover, the CELS paper argues 'of all the "mutual recognition" measures that

---

[16] As the Rt Hon Theresa May, Secretary of State for the Home Department described the Government's stance in her statement to the House of Commons on 15 October 2012 (Hansard, cols 34–5).

[17] Rt Hon Theresa May, Secretary of State for the Home Department described the Government's stance in her statement to the House of Commons on 15 October 2012.

[18] Centre for European Legal Studies paper 'Opting Out of EU Criminal Law: What is Actually Involved?' by Hinarejos, Spencer, and Peers (September 2012), para. 16.

[19] Hansard, col 39.

were agreed under the Maastricht regime this is in practice the most important; and because of this, it is at least possible that, if the Protocol 36 opt-out were exercised, the practical necessities of law enforcement would force the UK to opt back into it.'

The CELS paper goes on to argue that the opt-out would be a counterproductive move because it would, in a variety of other areas in addition to the European Arrest Warrant, cut the UK off from the benefits it at present derives from mutual cooperation and mutual recognition, and the benefits that UK citizens derive from a consistency of law across the Union in a variety of cross-border areas. For example, if the UK opted out of the various measures that secure mutual recognition of judgments[20] 'the natural consequence of opting out of these mutual recognition instruments would be that other Member States would no longer be under an EU obligation to automatically enforce decisions or orders stemming from UK courts.'[21]

Although the Home Secretary has said that the 'current thinking' of the Government is to take advantage of the opt-out, that does not represent a settled position and she declined to say which measures the UK would then seek to opt back into. It follows that at the time that this book goes to press the measures that it addresses remain in force. Moreover, many of the EU measures from which the exercise of Protocol No. 36 would allow the UK to withdraw have been enacted into UK law and the Framework Decisions on which those pieces of UK statute and regulation are based would remain of value to the UK courts in their interpretation. In addition, a number of other significant EU measures would be unaffected by the opt-out because they post-date the Treaty of Lisbon. These include the Charter of Fundamental Rights, Directives in relation to the rights of suspects[22] and of victims,[23] and the proposed European Investigation Order. It follows that while the reader needs to be aware of the potential opt-out, the vast majority of the content of this book will remain of value even if the 'current thinking' of the Government becomes its final position.

Structure of the Book

The Chambers of David Fisher QC and David Perry QC is experienced in the application of EU law in the criminal context, and various members of these chambers have contributed sections to the text, focusing on different areas in which EU law has a role in criminal litigation.

In Part I, EU criminal law is put into context. In the overview, Michael Bisgrove and Paul Jarvis seek to provide the necessary background knowledge for the reader to put the later chapters into appropriate context by addressing the formation and development of the EU and the route to the Lisbon Treaty through earlier agreements such as the Maastricht Treaty. Paul Jarvis then goes on, in Chapter 2, to provides a necessary overview of the Treaty of Lisbon, and particularly Title V: Area of Freedom, Security & Justice, and of the Framework

---

[20] Framework Decisions on mutual recognition of fines (2005/214/JHA of 24 February 2005), mutual recognition of confiscation orders (2006/783/JHA of 6 October 2006), mutual recognition of judgments and probation decisions (2008/947/JHA of 27 November 2008) and mutual recognition of judgments (2008/909/JHA of 27 November 2008).

[21] CELS paper, para. 85.

[22] Directives 2010/64/EU and 2012/13/EU.

[23] <http://ec.europa.ev/justice/police/crim/victims/doc/con_2011_275_En.pdf>.

Decisions and other legislative instruments by which EU criminal law was enacted before that Treaty altered the landscape.

Part II of the book considers various aspects of pre-trial procedure for criminal cases in the UK by reference to the impact of EU procedures and Framework Decisions. The focus is on the EU measures that are engaged in the relevant area and how those can be addressed in the UK context. In Chapter 3, Sarah Whitehouse, Victoria Ailes, Alex Chalk, James Chegwidden, and Jacob Hallam consider the doctrine of mutual recognition and the various mechanisms under EU law by which evidence is obtained or matters proved. These include existing measures such as freezing orders and measures that may never come into force such as European Evidence Warrants. This is an area in which new measures are due to be implemented shortly, such as European Investigation Orders, and the book aims to prepare practitioners for how to deal with these when they come into effect.

In Chapter 4, Rosemary Davidson considers the very significant impact that the EU has achieved in the sphere of extradition, as a result of the Framework Decision on the European Arrest Warrant. The aim of that Framework Decision was to replace existing systems of extradition within the Union with a much simplified system, which the UK sought to implement through Part 1 of the Extradition Act 2003. Whilst the Review of the United Kingdom's Extradition Arrangements undertaken by the Rt Hon Sir Scott Baker, David Perry QC, and Anand Doobay[24] recommended a number of revisions to the present scheme, its conclusion was that 'the European Arrest Warrant has improved the scheme of surrender between Member States of the European Union and that broadly speaking it operates satisfactorily.'[25] To the same effect, a spokesman for the Crown Prosecution Service in 2009 described the European Arrest Warrant as the 'most effective mutual recognition tool introduced' and told the House of Commons Justice Committee that its impact was 'greatly simplifying and speeding up extradition within the EU since its introduction'.[26] Whilst, therefore, the possibility of the Government opting out raises a question mark as to the future of the European Arrest Warrant, its importance in the meantime, and the possibility that the Goverment will opt back into its operation, justifies its consideration here.

In Part III of the book, consideration is given to various ways in which EU measures and particularly Framework Decisions have in impact on post-arrest proceedings in UK courts. In Chapter 5, Chris Hehir, Adam Payter, Paul Humpherson, and Annabel Darlow consider the various procedural safeguards by which EU legislation and related documents, including some Council of Europe material, have sought to protect the rights of suspects, defendants, and victims. These include the Charter of Fundamental Rights of the European Union and the Road Map[27] which aimed 'to set common minimum standards as regards certain procedural rights applying in criminal proceedings throughout the European Union.' This also includes application of the doctrine of double jeopardy in EU law. In Chapter 6, Daniel Pawson Pounds, Will Hays, Simon Ray, Ben Lloyd, Alistair Richardson, Richard Evans, and Mark Weekes consider the substantive offences that the

---

[24] Presented to the Home Secretary on 30 September 2011.
[25] Scott Baker Review, para. 1.9.
[26] House of Commons Justice Committee, Justice Issues in Europe, Seventh Report of Session 2009–2010, HC 162-I.
[27] [2009] OJ C 295/01.

EU has enacted and which now form part of UK law. The majority of these would fall foul in the EU Framework Decision guise of the opt-out, but would at least in the immediate term remain on the UK statute book.

Finally, Esther Schutzer-Weissman and Julian Blake address preliminary references to the European Court of Justice, which represent another way in which UK practitioners can become involved in EU law.

Duncan Atkinson

Part I

CONTEXT

1

HISTORY AND BACKGROUND

A. Overview

Over the past six decades, the economies and laws of Europe have become increasingly integrated. Following the end of the Second World War, a number of treaties created discrete communities which, over time, have overlapped and merged. This process has led to the creation of the European Union and, most recently, the ratification of the Treaty of Lisbon. **1.01**

This chapter summarises the creation and development of European Union law, from its origins in the 1950s as a trio of international communities to its present day structure. It traces the treaties that have shaped the powers and influences of the EU and outlines the changing relationship between EU law and national law. The purpose of this history is to provide the practitioner with the essential background to an understanding of the types of EU law now in operation, and the various areas in which EU law now has an impact on criminal law and practice in England and Wales. The rest of the book will explain the present state of EU criminal law in these areas, against this background. **1.02**

B. The Formation and Development of the European Union

The European Coal and Steel Community

The process of European integration began in the aftermath of the Second World War. In 1951 France, Germany, Italy, Belgium, the Netherlands, and Luxembourg signed the Treaty **1.03** of Paris that established the European Coal and Steel Community (ECSC). The signatories agreed to organise their heavy industry under common management, establishing a common market in coal and steel. The purpose was to create a binding integration such that none could wage war against another.

1.04 The Treaty of Paris created four institutions—a High Authority, an Assembly, a Council, and a Court of Justice. The High Authority was made up of representatives from each of the six governments, its role being to implement the aims of the Treaty. The Assembly was made up of delegates from the national parliaments and had a supervisory and advisory role. The Council was made up of one representative from each government and had some decision-making powers. The Court of Justice, which has evolved into the institution that continues to operate today, is described in more detail in Chapter 2.[1]

The Treaty of Rome

1.05 Following the perceived success of the ECSC, efforts were made to deepen the integration of the six founding members by developing a European Defence Community (EDC) and a European Political Community. However, although the Treaty to establish the EDC was signed in 1952, it was never ratified, in part due to fears over loss of sovereignty. Without the EDC, the idea of the political community also fell away.

1.06 The next effective step in European integration was the drafting and implementation of the Treaty establishing the European Economic Community (TEC) or the Treaty of Rome in 1957, which created two further communities: the European Economic Community (EEC) and the European Atomic Energy Community (Euratom).[2]

1.07 The participants in the Treaty of Rome were the same six countries that had formed the ECSC. The communities shared their Court and Assembly with the ECSC, but had their own executive bodies.

1.08 The purpose of Euratom was to oversee the peaceful development of atomic energy. The EEC was intended to develop a common market between the six countries. This included the abolition of tariffs between the countries and the encouragement of undistorted competition within the community. Unlike the EDC, the goals of Euratom and the EEC were to foster economic integration and development.

The Merger Treaty

1.09 The Merger Treaty (Treaty of Brussels) in 1965 led to a consolidation of institutions between the three communities. The executive bodies of the ECSC and Euratom were subsumed into the Commission of the EEC and the Council of the EEC. The communities remained legally separate and were collectively known as the European Communities. Thus the common institutions were the Court of Justice and the Parliamentary Assembly, and now the Commission and the Council.

Growth of the union

1.10 The membership of the European Communities began to expand. The UK had initially declined to join the Communities, instead establishing the European Free Trade Association

---

[1] Chapter **2.22**.
[2] The Treaty of Lisbon renamed the TEC the Treaty on the Functioning of the European Union (TFEU), and references to it using that acronym will be seen in the text that follows.

(EFTA), however, in 1961 the UK sought to join the European Communities. The first membership application was rejected; a second application was also rejected in 1967. Finally, in 1973, the UK was permitted to join, along with Denmark and Ireland. At the same time, Norway applied for membership. However, a national referendum was against accession, meaning that Norway did not accede.

Further expansion of the membership occurred with the acceptance of Greece's application in 1981 and the applications of Spain and Portugal in 1986. In the meantime Greenland, which had gained a measure of independence from Denmark, voted to leave the Communities. **1.11**

Austria, Finland, and Sweden—all members of EFTA—had adopted a position of neutrality during the Cold War. This position was incompatible with membership of the European Communities, where a common security and foreign policy was developing. However, the passing of the Single European Act (which made trade between EFTA and the EEC more difficult), combined with the ending of the Cold War, gave impetus to their desire to accede. In 1995, the three countries joined, following successful referenda. A second referendum in Norway again resulted in the country not joining the Communities. **1.12**

Enlargement continued apace in 2004, when a further ten countries acceded to the Communities (which had by now become the European Union). These countries, eight from Eastern Europe and two Mediterranean, were less economically developed than the existing members, but represented a substantial increase in the number of people. In 2007 Romania and Bulgaria, which were not considered ready in 2004, acceded to the Union. Croatia is expected to accede in 2013. **1.13**

The Maastricht Treaty: the formation of the European Union

In parallel with geographic development, political and structural development continued. Signed in 1992, the Treaty on European Union (TEU), also known as the Maastricht Treaty, created the European Union on 1 November 1993. **1.14**

The objectives of the Maastricht Treaty were set out in its opening provisions: **1.15**

> The Union shall set itself the following objectives:
>
> - to promote economic and social progress which is balanced and sustainable, in particular through the creation of an area without internal frontiers, through the strengthening of economic and social cohesion and through the establishment of economic and monetary union, ultimately including a single currency in accordance with the provisions of this Treaty;
> - to assert its identity on the international scene, in particular through the implementation of a common foreign and security policy including the eventual framing of a common defence policy, which might in time lead to a common defence;
> - to strengthen the protection of the rights and interests of the nationals of its Member States through the introduction of a citizenship of the Union;
> - to develop close co-operation on justice and home affairs . . . [3]

The Maastricht Treaty established a 'three-pillar' structure within the EU. Each pillar was a sphere of influence, or a set of policy areas. The first was the European Community Pillar. In essence, this consolidated the policy areas circumscribed by the EEC, Euratom, and the ECSC. The second and third were new areas of cooperation between the Member States. **1.16**

---

[3] Article B TEU.

The second pillar was the Common Foreign and Security Policy pillar. The third was the area of Justice and Home Affairs. Collectively, the three pillars fell under the umbrella of the European Union.

1.17   The three-pillar structure was the result of a tension between the wish, on the one hand, to extend the EEC into the coordination of foreign, military, and criminal justice policy and, on the other hand, the desire of Member States to retain national control of areas deemed sensitive or essential to national security. The mechanisms by which decisions in each area would be taken and effected were therefore different.

The first pillar

1.18   The European Community Pillar had legal personality, consisting of the EC, the ECSC, and Euratom. The ECSC expired in 2002 and its functions were absorbed into the EC. The first pillar's areas of competence dealt with economic, social, and environmental policies. This pillar was supranational in character, governed as it was by the supranational institutions of the Council, the Commission, Parliament, and Court of Justice.

The second pillar

1.19   The Common Foreign and Security Policy Pillar dealt with foreign policy and military matters. This pillar involved the community institutions, particularly the Council. However, due to the perception that these areas were vital to national sovereignty, national governments retained substantial control. Decisions were made intergovernmentally rather than supranationally, in that Member States consulted with each other within the Council with a view to coordinating their actions.

The third pillar

1.20   Justice and Home Affairs (later changed to Police and Judicial Cooperation in Criminal Matters (PJCC)), brought together cooperation in the fight against crime. Again, this pillar operated intergovernmentally. When established by the Maastricht Treaty, this area included asylum, immigration, and visa policies as well as judicial cooperation and police cooperation. It also included cooperation in the areas of drug and people trafficking, terrorism, fraud, and organised crime. Under Maastricht, the means of legislating to effect decisions was the 'joint action'. A joint action would be adopted where objectives of the Union would be better achieved by the Member States working together rather than individually.

1.21   Subsequently, the matters falling within the third pillar were reduced by the Treaty of Amsterdam (signed in 1997) and the Treaty of Nice (signed in 2001). These moved asylum, immigration, and visas into the first pillar, and thus placed them under the supranational governance of the EU institutions, leaving to the third pillar the area of police and judicial cooperation in criminal matters. It therefore remains the Maastricht pillar of more relevance to a criminal practitioner in relation to EU law pre-dating the Treaty of Lisbon.

1.22   The Amsterdam Treaty replaced 'joint action' with the legislative instrument of 'Framework Decisions'. Framework Decisions required Member States to achieve a particular result, but did not specify the mechanism by which they must do so. They could be proposed by a Member State or by the Commission, and adopted by decision of the Council.

C. The Case for Change

By the early twenty-first century, membership of the Union had grown from six States to **1.23**
27. Political and legal integration had broadened and deepened. However, the structure of
the Union was piecemeal. Only the first pillar had legal personality and decision making—
heavily reliant on unanimity—became slower and more difficult.

The Amsterdam Treaty had not effectively addressed the necessity for institutional reform. **1.24**
The Nice Treaty made some changes, for example extending the use of majority voting,
however, these changes did not go far enough and an increasing detachment of the Union
from its citizens became apparent. There was a growing need to make the European Union
democratically legitimate.

In 2001, the European Council set out a vision for the future of the European Union. The **1.25**
Laeken Declaration stated that:

> The Union needs to become more democratic, more transparent and more efficient. It also has
> to resolve three basic challenges: how to bring citizens, and primarily the young, closer to the
> European design and the European institutions, how to organise politics and the European
> political area in an enlarged Union and how to develop the Union into a stabilising factor and
> a model in the new, multipolar world.

The process of drafting an instrument to effect this vision began in 2001. The Treaty **1.26**
Establishing a Constitution for Europe was drafted, abolishing the pillar structure and
replacing it with a single entity. Cooperation in criminal matters was to be incorporated in
the supranational decision-making process.

However, the development of the Union was set back by the refusal of the citizens of France **1.27**
and the Netherlands to accept the treaty. There followed a period of reflection, after which
negotiations on a new 'Reform Treaty' began. They resulted in a text which is intended to
reflect many of the aims of the constitutional treaty and address the problems faced by the
European Union. This treaty, the Lisbon Treaty, came into force on 1 December 2009.

D. The Effect of the Lisbon Treaty

The Lisbon Treaty is a revisionary treaty affecting the Treaty of Rome (TEC)—which is renamed **1.28**
the Treaty on the Functioning of the European Union—and the Maastricht Treaty (TEU). In
addition to changes to the decision-making process, the most significant change is the abolition
of the three-pillar structure and the consolidation of all aspects of the European Communities
into the legal personality of the European Union, on which competencies are conferred.

The Treaty of Lisbon came into force on 1 December 2009[4] and in so doing brought about **1.29**
fundamental changes to the rules governing the competence of the EU institutions in

---

[4] [2007] OJ C 306. While the ratification of the Treaty was not greeted warmly by some in the UK, the *Daily Express* went further than most of the Treaty's detractors by running the headline: 'BRITAIN: THE END'. See T.C. Hartley, *The Foundations of European Union Law* (Oxford: Oxford University Press, 2010), 10. For a general overview of the Treaty provisions see Paul Craig, *The Lisbon Treaty: Law, Politics and Treaty Reform* (OUP, 2010) and by the same author 'The Treaty of Lisbon: Process, Architecture and Substance' (2008) 33 ELRev 137.

criminal justice matters. The process of 'legislating' in all matters, including those formally falling within the category of police and judicial cooperation, now falls under the first pillar mechanisms.

Areas of competence

1.30 Instead of the earlier pillar structure, areas of policy are divided into competencies which are either exclusive to the European Union, shared, or supporting.

1.31 The exercise of Union competencies is restricted by the principles of conferral, proportionality, and, other than in areas of exclusive competence, subsidiarity. The principle of subsidiarity provides that the Union may only intervene where it would be more effective than the Member States. It is discussed in more detail in Chapter 2. The principle of conferral is that the competencies of the European Union are voluntarily conferred by its Member States. The Union will only act within the limits of those competencies to obtain the objectives set out therein. Conferral and proportionality apply equally to areas of exclusive competence and shared competence.

Areas of exclusive competence

1.32 Areas of exclusive competence are those in which the Union has exclusive competence to make Directives and conclude international agreements when provided for in a Union legislative act. These include the common fisheries policy, customs policies, and the establishment of competition rules necessary for the functioning of the internal market. The Member States' role is limited to applying those acts.

Areas of shared competence

1.33 Areas of shared competence are predominantly those in which the Member States cannot exercise competence where the Union has done so. However, where the Union has not acted, or has decided not to act, Member States may exercise their competence.

1.34 Included within the area of shared competence is the area of freedom, security, and justice (AFSJ).

Areas of supporting competence

1.35 Within the areas of supporting competence, the Union can only support, coordinate, or supplement the policies of Member States. It has no legislative power in these fields. These areas include culture, tourism, and health.

Area of Freedom, Security, and Justice

1.36 After the coming into force of the Treaty of Lisbon, all rules governing justice and home affairs cooperation within the EU were merged into Title V of Part 3 of the TFEU, which is headed 'Area of Freedom, Security & Justice' (AFSJ).[5]

1.37 The Treaty of Lisbon divides the AFSJ into policies relating to border control, immigration, and asylum; judicial cooperation in civil matters; judicial cooperation in criminal matters; and police cooperation. Those aspects of the area relating to criminal cooperation were

---

[5] For the background to and development of the notion of a AFSJ, see Estella Baker, 'The European Union's "Area of Freedom, Security and (Criminal) Justice" Ten Years On' [2009] Crim LR 833.

previously contained within the third pillar. The aspects relating to civil cooperation and border control had originally been contained within the third pillar following the Maastricht Treaty, but had moved into the first pillar following the Treaty of Amsterdam.

The goal of judicial cooperation in criminal matters is to create a common area where each Member State can trust their fellow Member States to apply certain minimum standards of justice. The cooperation is based on the mutual recognition of judgments and judicial decisions. **1.38**

In areas where cross-border cooperation is necessary, the Union can establish rules relating to matters such as the admissibility of evidence and the rights of defendants. The Union can also establish minimum rules regarding the definition of cross-border crimes and the sanctions applicable to them. These crimes include trafficking of people or drugs; money laundering and fraud; and organised crime. **1.39**

In general, where the EU institutions legislate in accordance with the competences gifted to them under the Treaties, that legislation will either be directly enforceable in each Member State (Regulations) or oblige each Member State to implement it into its national law (Directives). However, where that competence falls within the AFSJ, any legislation will *not* have those effects as far as the UK and Ireland are concerned unless they 'opt in' to that legislative process. In that respect, Article 2 of Protocol No. 21 to the TFEU provides: **1.40**

> no measure adopted pursuant to [Title V], no provision of any international agreement concluded by the Union pursuant to that Title, and no decision of the Court of Justice interpreting any such provision or measure shall be binding upon or applicable in the United Kingdom or Ireland; and no such provision, measure or decision shall in any way affect the competences, rights and obligations of those States; and no such provision, measure or decision shall in any way affect the Community or Union *acquis* nor form part of Union law as they apply to the United Kingdom or Ireland.

Denmark has a similar 'opt-in', although the circumstances in which it may be exercised are different and are set out in Protocol No. 22. To date, the UK has opted in to a number of proposed Directives and not opted in to the proposed Directive on preventing and combating trafficking in human beings and protecting victims, which is set to replace Framework Decision 2002/629/JHA. **1.41**

In addition to the opt-in contained in Protocol No. 22, the UK negotiated an 'opt-out', which is contained in Protocol No. 36. This measure allows the UK Government to decide, by May 2014, whether the UK should continue to be bound by the approximately 130 police and criminal justice measures adopted prior to the entry into force of the Treaty of Lisbon which would all become subject to the jurisdiction of the Court of Justice of the EU.[6] **1.42**

Title V contains five Chapters and 23 Articles, running from Article 67 to Article 89. The Chapters are headed 'General Provisions' (see **1.44**), 'Policies on Border Checks, Asylum and **1.43**

---

[6] In the recent Centre for European Legal Studies (CELS) working paper *Opting Out of EU Criminal Law: What is Actually Involved?* (September 2012), the authors address the commonly held views that the opt-out in Protocol No. 36 would enable the UK to excise the influence of EU law in matters of police and criminal justice and would have no adverse impact on the UK. They argue that both of these views are wrong. They conclude that, if the opt-out were to be exercised, the UK would still be bound by those measures enacted post-Lisbon. Furthermore, the measures opted out of would include some—including the European Arrest Warrant—the loss of which could pose a risk to law and order.

Immigration', 'Judicial Cooperation in Civil Matters', 'Judicial Cooperation in Criminal Matters' (see **1.55**), and 'Police Cooperation' (see **1.69**).

General provisions

1.44   Article 67 embraces the objectives of the EU by setting out how it intends to preserve the area of freedom, security, and justice created by the TFEU. As far as is relevant to this chapter, the provisions of Article 67 are as follows:

    1. The Union shall constitute an area of freedom, security and justice with respect for fundamental rights and the different legal systems and traditions of the Member States.

    …

    5. The Union shall endeavour to ensure a high level of security through measures to prevent and combat crime, racism and xenophobia, and through measures for co-ordination and co-operation between police and judicial authorities and other competent authorities, as well as through the mutual recognition of judgments in criminal matters and, if necessary, through the approximation of criminal law.

    6. The Union shall facilitate access to justice, in particular through the principle of mutual recognition of judicial and extrajudicial decisions on civil matters.

1.45   Article 67(1) acknowledges the EU's continuing commitment to the protection of what the TFEU describes as fundamental rights. The meaning of that expression is considered briefly in the context of the Charter of Fundamental Human Rights later in this chapter (see **1.71**) and in more detail in Chapter 5.

1.46   Moreover, whereas Article 67(1) highlights the EU's stated respect for the different legal systems and traditions of the Member States, that can be contrasted with the final words of Article 67(3) where the EU makes plain its willingness to harmonise the criminal laws of the Member States 'if necessary'. There is, therefore, a tension between the EU's willingness to leave the Member States alone to make their own criminal laws and its desire to approximate criminal laws across all Member States in order to preserve the AFSJ.

1.47   The EU's aims, as expressed in Article 67(3), are remarkably broad. They include measures to combat *all* crime and measures to coordinate action between the police and judicial authorities of the Member States in the prevention, detection, and prosecution of crime. In this regard, the concept of 'mutual recognition' features heavily both in Article 67(3) and elsewhere in Title V.

1.48   'Mutual recognition' was first raised as an ideal at the Cardiff Council in June 1998.[7] The following year, the Tampere European Council conclusions referred to mutual recognition as 'the cornerstone of judicial co-operation in criminal matters'.[8] This conclusion led to the proposal to abolish the system of extradition that existed at that time and advance instead a system based on the principles of mutual recognition. Those proposals crystallised into the Council Framework Decision 2002/584/JHA of 13 June 2002 on the European Arrest Warrant and surrender procedures between Member States. The Extradition Act 2003 implemented that Framework Decision into UK law (this topic is addressed in more detail

---

    [7] Presidency Conclusions, Cardiff, 15–16 June 1998, para 39: 'The European Council underlines the importance of effective judicial co-operation in the fight against cross-border crime. It recognises the need to enhance the ability of national legal systems to work closely together and asks the Council to identify the scope for greater mutual recognition of decisions of each others' courts.'
    [8] 15–16 October 1999, paras 33–7.

in Chapter 4). Since then, there have been a number of Framework Decisions introduced under the old 'third pillar' where mutual recognition has played a significant role[9] (see Chapter 6).

Mutual recognition obliges the courts of one Member State to recognise and enforce the **1.49** decisions of the court of another Member State, without reviewing the basis on which those decisions were made. This approach assumes that the domestic laws of the Member States are broadly similar but in some respects they could not be more different.[10] In recognition of these differences, there are a limited number of grounds on which the domestic courts can refuse to recognise the decisions of the courts of other Member States, and these include *ne bis in idem* (double jeopardy) and the existence of some immunity or privilege vesting in the person who is the subject of the decision.[11]

Turning to Article 67(4), it may at first blush seem that this Article applies only to civil mat- **1.50** ters but the better view[12] is that references to 'access to justice' should include access to justice in the field of criminal law too. This would include, for example, the provision of public funding and victims' rights. Thus, another of the EU's aims under the aegis of the AFSJ is to ensure access to the criminal courts of the Member States for those who need it (victims) or those who have it foisted upon them (defendants).

Article 68 goes on to provide that the body responsible for coordinating the EU's efforts to **1.51** give legislative form to the laudable aims in Article 67 will be the European Council which 'shall define the strategic guidelines for legislative and operational planning within the area of freedom, security and justice'. It should be noted, however, that as the initiative for leg- islation in this area will come in the main from the Commission, it is important for the Commission to set out its own legislative agenda. It last did this in the form of the Stockholm Programme in 2010.[13]

Article 69 stresses that where the EU introduces measures under Chapter 4 (Judicial **1.52** Cooperation in Criminal Matters) and Chapter 5 (Police Cooperation) of Title V, the national parliaments of the Member States, when enacting legislation to implement those measures, must 'comply with the principle of subsidiarity'.

The remaining Articles of Chapter 1 of Title V deal with a variety of matters including the **1.53** adoption of measures for collaboration between the Commission and the Member States in the 'objective and impartial evaluation of the implementation of the Union policies' referred to in Title V (Art. 70), the creation of a standing committee within the Council 'in order to ensure that operational co-operation on internal security is promoted and strengthened

---

[9] Council Framework Decisions 2003/577/JHA (on the execution in the EU of orders freezing property or evidence), 2005/214/JHA (on financial penalties), 2006/783/JHA (on confiscation orders), 2008/909/JHA (judgments imposing custodial sentences), and 2008/947/JHA (on probation decisions).

[10] See T. Spronken, G. Vermeulen, D. de Vocht, and L. van Puyenbroeck, 'EU Procedural Rights in Criminal Proceedings', Report for the Institute for International Research on Criminal Policy at the University of Ghent, 2009, which focused on the differing approaches taken by the Member States to the provision of information to suspects about their rights and entitlements.

[11] For more on the perils and pleasantries of mutual recognition see S. Peers, 'Mutual Recognition and Criminal Law in the EU: Has the Council Got it Wrong?' [2004] CMLR 5. Mutual recognition receives more detailed analysis in Chapter 5.

[12] S. Peers, *EU Justice and Home Affairs Law*, 3rd edn (Oxford: Oxford University Press, 2011), 50.

[13] See Chapter 5.

within the Union' (Art. 71), the retention of the responsibility on the part of Member States to safeguard their own internal security (Art. 72), the discretion of Member States to engage between themselves in 'such forms of co-operation and co-ordination as they deem appropriate' for safeguarding national security (Art. 73), the adoption of measures by the Council to 'ensure administrative co-operation between the relevant departments of the Member States in the areas covered by' Title V (Art. 74), the creation of 'a framework for administrative measures with regard to capital movements and payments' in pursuit of the prevention and combating of terrorism and related activities (Art. 75), and the means by which acts referred to in Chapters 4 and 5 of Title V shall be adopted.

1.54 Of these, Article 71 is noteworthy because shortly after the Treaty of Lisbon came into force, the Council established a committee known as COSI, or the Standing Committee on Internal Security. Its stated purpose is to develop, monitor, and implement the Internal Security Strategy for the EU.

Judicial Cooperation in Criminal Matters

1.55 This Chapter of Title V of the TFEU is likely to be of most significance to the criminal practitioner. Within that Chapter, the most important provisions are Article 82, which underlines the centrality of mutual recognition to judicial cooperation, and Article 83, which permits the EU to establish minimum rules for the definition of criminal offences. Each of these Articles therefore repays some examination here.

Article 82

1.56 The text of Article 82 is as follows:

1. Judicial co-operation in criminal matters in the Union shall be based on the principle of mutual recognition of judgments and judicial decisions and shall include the approximation of the laws and regulations of the Member States in the areas referred to in paragraph 2 and in Article 83.

   The European Parliament and the Council, acting in accordance with the ordinary legislative procedure, shall adopt measures to:
   (a) lay down rules and procedures for ensuring recognition throughout the Union of all forms of judgments and judicial decisions;
   (b) prevent and settle conflicts of jurisdiction between Member States;
   (c) support the training of the judiciary and judicial staff;
   (d) facilitate co-operation between judicial or equivalent authorities of the Member States in relation to proceedings in criminal matters and the enforcement of decisions.

2. To the extent necessary to facilitate mutual recognition of judgments and judicial decisions and police and judicial co-operation in criminal matters having a cross-border dimension, the European Parliament and the Council may, by means of directives adopted in accordance with the ordinary legislative procedure, establish minimum rules. Such rules shall take into account the differences between the legal traditions and systems of the Member States.

   They shall concern:
   (a) mutual admissibility of evidence between Member States;
   (b) the rights of individuals in criminal procedure;
   (c) the rights of victims of crime;
   (d) any other specific aspects of criminal procedure which the Council has identified in advance by a decision; for the adoption of such a decision, the Council shall act unanimously after obtaining the consent of the European Parliament.

Adoption of the minimum rules referred to in this paragraph shall not prevent Member States from maintaining or introducing a higher level of protection for individuals.

3. Where a member of the Council considers that a draft directive as referred to in paragraph 2 would affect fundamental aspects of its criminal justice system, it may request that the draft directive be referred to the European Council. In that case the ordinary legislative procedure shall be suspended. After discussion, and in case of a consensus, the European Council shall, within four months of the suspension, refer the draft back to the Council, which shall terminate the suspension of the ordinary legislative procedure.

Within the same timeframe, in case of disagreement, and if at least nine Member States wish to establish enhanced cooperation on the basis of the draft directive concerned, they shall notify the European Parliament, the Council and the Commission accordingly. In such a case, the authorisation to proceed with enhanced cooperation referred to in Article 20(2) of the Treaty on European Union and Article 329(1) of this Treaty shall be deemed granted and the provisions on enhanced cooperation shall apply.

The bedrock of judicial cooperation between the Member States is mutual recognition, as foreshadowed by Article 67(3). In order to facilitate the type of mutual recognition envisaged by Article 82(1), the EU institutions are empowered to use the ordinary legislative procedure (the detail of which is discussed in Chapter 2) to 'establish minimum rules' concerning those areas listed in Article 82(2). It is clear that adoption of minimum rules at EU level does not prevent the Member States from passing legislation that provides for 'a higher level of protection for individuals'. In other words, the Member States cannot act in such a way as to water down the EU measures but they can enhance them, as long as the enhancement is to the advantage of the citizen and not the State. **1.57**

Article 82(3) contains what is commonly referred to as the 'emergency brake' procedure, which can also be seen in Article 83(3). The rationale for the inclusion of this procedure was a concern expressed by various Member States that in the field of criminal law, the EU may use its new competence to introduce measures that would be alien to their national systems.[14] **1.58**

It seems from the wording of Articles 82(3) (see **1.56**) and 83(3) (see **1.61**) that it is for any given Member State to decide whether the proposed EU legislation 'would affect fundamental aspects of its criminal justice system'. It remains to be seen whether any challenge could be made to the Court of Justice (CJEU) in respect of the decision of a Member State to refer a draft proposal to the Commission on the basis that in fact that proposal did not affect a fundamental aspect of its criminal justice system. As one commentator has noted, if the CJEU cannot occupy such a role, then the mechanisms enshrined in Articles 82(3) and 83(3) 'results in a permanent veto by a Member State, which has the effect of blocking common Union legislation in the area.'[15] **1.59**

Even if the actions of one Member State can veto an EU legislative proposal, Articles 82(3) and 83(3) allow the Member States to engage in what is described as enhanced cooperation provided at least nine of them wish to do so. Ordinarily, whenever Member States want to engage in enhanced cooperation Article 329 TFEU obliges them to submit a request to the Commission, which will then draft a proposal for the Council in the **1.60**

---

[14] See E. Herlin-Karnell, *The Constitutional Dimension of European Criminal Law* (Oxford: Hart Publishing, 2012), chs 2 and 4.

[15] Andre Klip, *European Criminal Law: An Integrative Approach*, 2nd edn (Antwerp: Intersentia, 2012), 37.

terms sought and it is then for the Council to authorise the use of enhanced cooperation. Under Articles 82(3) and 83(3), however, authorisation is deemed to have been granted under Article 329 where the Member States notify their intentions to the European Parliament, the Council, and the Commission. Once that has been done, there is no impediment to those Member States going it alone by seeking to adopt the draft EU legislation as between themselves.

Article 83

1.61   The text of Article 83 is as follows:

1. The European Parliament and the Council may, by means of directives adopted in accordance with the ordinary legislative procedure, establish minimum rules concerning the definition of criminal offences and sanctions in the areas of particularly serious crime with a cross-border dimension resulting from the nature or impact of such offences or from a special need to combat them on a common basis.

     These areas of crime are the following: terrorism, trafficking in human beings and sexual exploitation of women and children, illicit drug trafficking, illicit arms trafficking, money laundering, corruption, counterfeiting of means payment, computer crime and organised crime.

     On the basis of developments in crime, the Council may adopt a decision identifying other areas of crime that meet the criteria specified in this paragraph. It shall act unanimously after obtaining the consent of the European Parliament.

2. If the approximation of criminal law and regulations of the Member States proves essential to ensure the effective implementation of a Union policy in an area which has been subject to harmonisation measures, directives may establish minimum rules with regard to the definition of criminal offences and sanctions in the area concerned. Such directives shall be adopted by the same ordinary or special legislative procedure as was followed for the adoption of the harmonisation measures in question, without prejudice to Article 76.

3. Where a member of the Council considers that a draft directive as referred to in paragraph 2 would affect fundamental aspects of its criminal justice system, it may request that the draft directive be referred to the European Council. In that case the ordinary legislative procedure shall be suspended. After discussion, and in case of a consensus, the European Council shall, within four months of the suspension, refer the draft back to the Council, which shall terminate the suspension of the ordinary legislative procedure.

     Within the same timeframe, in case of disagreement, and if at least nine Member States wish to establish enhanced cooperation on the basis of the draft directive concerned, they shall notify the European Parliament, the Council and the Commission accordingly. In such a case, the authorisation to proceed with enhanced cooperation referred to in Article 20(2) of the Treaty on European Union and Article 329(1) of this Treaty shall be deemed granted and the provisions on enhanced cooperation shall apply.

1.62   Article 83(1) sets out the competence of the EU institutions to establish minimum rules concerning the definition of criminal offences in the area of 'particularly serious crime with a cross-border dimension'. It goes on to list the areas that satisfy this test but adds that on the 'basis of developments in crime', the Council may adopt a decision that identifies other areas of crime that also satisfy this test. In other words, the list is not exhaustive and may be added to in the future by unanimous decision of the Council acting with the consent of the European Parliament.

1.63   In much the same way, Article 83(1) allows the EU institutions to define sanctions in those areas. Thus, the competence of the Commission to propose measures in accordance with the ordinary legislative procedure extends to defining the elements of criminal offences on the list and setting out the sanctions for those who commit offences on the list. These are two different competencies. If a criminal offence already exists in the national law of the Member States the EU can legislate in such a way as to oblige the Member State to impose a certain type of penalty on those who commit that offence.

It is interesting to note that Article 83(1), like Article 82(2), empowers the EU institutions **1.64** to 'establish minimum rules' within the fields covered by those Articles, but whereas Article 82(2) (see **1.56**) contains the proviso that the Member States can introduce 'a higher level of protection for individuals', Article 83(1) does not do so and it therefore seems that the Member States are not bound to consider the welfare of the individual when deciding on the precise wording of the criminal offences they are obliged to enact.

It is not at all clear what the expression 'minimum rules' is intended to mean in the context of **1.65** a competence that allows the EU institutions to create new criminal offences. One tentative suggestion is that the 'minimum rules' requirement exists to ensure that the Member States cannot make it harder for national prosecutors to convict alleged offenders of the offence created by the Directive although they can make it easier. If this suggestion ultimately proves to be correct then it is unlikely that the Member States would be permitted to add elements but they *may* be able to replace one element with another where the substituted element increases the prospect of conviction.[16]

There is nothing in Article 83 to suggest, however, that the competence of the EU institu- **1.66** tions extends beyond the creation of new criminal offences and the imposition of sanctions. In other words, the EU institutions do not have the competence to seek to define the general part of the criminal law of the Member States.

Article 83(3) contains the same 'emergency brake' as set down in Article 82(3). The language **1.67** of both Articles is exactly the same and so the process of applying the brake will also be the same.

Articles 84, 85, and 86

Of the remaining Articles within this Chapter of Title V, Article 84, should be noted. Article **1.68** 84 authorises the European Parliament and the Council, in accordance with the ordinary legislative procedure, to 'establish measures to promote and support the action of Member States in the field of crime prevention, excluding any harmonisation of the laws and regulations of the Member States.'

Police Cooperation

Within the area of police cooperation, the Union can legislate in the field of the collection **1.69** and exchange of information and evidence. There is also provision for the establishment of joint investigative teams and for the conduct of operational action by Europol.

Article 87 obliges the EU to 'establish police cooperation involving all the Member States' **1.70** competent authorities, including police, customs and other specialised law enforcement services in relation to the prevention, detection and investigation of criminal offences.'

---

[16] See Andre Klip, *European Criminal Law: An Integrative Approach*, 2nd edn (Antwerp: Intersentia, 2012), 166–8.

In order to achieve this, the European Parliament and the Council, acting in accordance with the ordinary legislative procedure, may establish measures concerning the following: (a) the collection, storage, processing, analysis, and exchange of relevant information; (b) support for the training of staff, and cooperation on the exchange of staff, on equipment, and on research into crime detection; and (c) common investigative techniques in relation to the detection of serious forms of organised crime.

1.71 The primary agency through which this cooperation is encouraged is Europol, the role and powers of which are discussed in Chapter 2[17] and whose future, though still uncertain, will be crafted by the European Parliament and the Council under Article 88.

Effect of the Charter of Fundamental Human Rights

1.72 In 1999, the EU Council began the process of formulating a comprehensive statement of the social, political, civil, and economic rights of EU citizens. The draft of the Charter of Fundamental Human Rights was approved by the European Parliament and the Commission in 2000. The Charter was based on the fundamental freedoms recognised in the European Convention on Human Rights.

1.73 The legal status of the Charter had for a long time been unclear. The EU, without legal personality, was unable to sign up to the Charter, therefore, although carrying substantial political weight, the Charter's legal force was in doubt.

1.74 Following the entry into force of the Lisbon Treaty, the EU became a signatory to the Charter. The Lisbon Treaty confers on the Charter the same legal force as the Treaties. It applies to the EU institutions and, in the implementation of EU laws, to Member States.

1.75 However, under Protocol No. 30, the Charter does not extend the ability of the European Court and the UK courts to find that laws of the UK are inconsistent with the Charter. In particular, the Charter does not create any additional justiciable rights under national law. This is intended to be an opt-out provision to prevent the incorporation of the Charter into UK national law.[18] Both the Charter and its status in the UK as a result of Protocol No. 30 are further addressed in Chapter 5.

E. Other Treaties Affecting Criminal Procedure in England and Wales

1.76 It is not only the law of the European Union that impacts on the criminal law of England and Wales. There are a number of other treaties with other supranational organisations which have effected national legislation and procedure.

Council of Europe

1.77 The Council of Europe (which is entirely distinct from the institutions of the European Union) was formed in 1949 and comprises 47 Member States. The stated aim of the Council is to achieve greater unity between its members for the purpose of safeguarding and realising the ideals and principles which are their common heritage, and to facilitate their economic and social progress.

---

[17] Chapter 2.44.
[18] For further discussion of the limits of the opt-out, see Chapter 5 and *R (On the application of S) v Secretary of State for the Home Department* [2010] EWHC 705.

Rather than ceding sovereignty to Council institutions and surrendering to extra-national legislation, members of the Council of Europe commit themselves to policy decisions through conventions. **1.78**

The most significant impact of the Council has been the formulation of the European Convention on Human Rights and the creation of the European Court of Human Rights. A large number of less prominent conventions have also been entered into, including the Convention on the International Validity of Criminal Judgments, the Convention on the Transfer of Sentenced Persons, the Convention on Action against Trafficking in Human Beings, and the Criminal Law Convention on Corruption. **1.79**

The United Nations

The United Nations was founded in 1945 and now comprises over 190 Member States. The UN is responsible for the creation of the International Court of Justice. In a similar way to the Council of Europe, the UK can be bound by decisions of the UN by committing itself to conventions. Such conventions include the International Convention for the Suppression of the Financing of Terrorism, the UN Convention Against Transnational Organized Crime, and the UN Convention against Corruption. **1.80**

Individually negotiated treaties

In addition to treaties and conventions mediated by international organisations, the UK Government may enter into individually negotiated treaties with other countries or groups of countries. **1.81**

F. Conclusion

The common thread running through all the areas in which international cooperation is entered into is that they cannot be tackled by one nation alone. Crime is no longer solely a national concern; it crosses jurisdictions and borders with ease. It is therefore necessary for countries to adopt universal standards and to cooperate in the investigation and prosecution of criminal acts. **1.82**

The European Union, and the Area of Freedom, Security and Justice, seeks to integrate the criminal justice systems of the Member States in order to facilitate the effective prosecution of cross-border crime and to provide assured minimum protections for defendants. As the EU legislates in these areas, it is likely that the criminal courts of the UK will see evidence adduced as a result of European law, arguments premised on European jurisprudence, and crimes prosecuted which have their origin not in an Act of Parliament, but in European legislation. **1.83**

2

INSTITUTIONAL FRAMEWORK AND LEGISLATIVE INSTRUMENTS

A. Overview

2.01 The purpose of this chapter is to describe the various institutions of the European Union and the extent to which they can influence the form and content of EU law. The chapter will also consider the types of legislative measure that can be introduced by the EU institutions, the legal significance of those measures, and how they can be recognised and enforced before the domestic courts of the UK. It is essential for criminal practitioners to have an understanding of the way in which EU law is made that so they can determine in any given case whether the rights or obligations created by a provision of EU law apply, either directly or indirectly, and therefore understand how that provision may be of assistance to the party they represent.

2.02 EU law impacts on the national criminal law of the UK in two different but complementary ways:[1]

(a) First, EU law affects the way in which the English courts interpret domestic criminal law. EU law takes precedence over national law and so where a provision of domestic criminal law is in conflict with a directly enforceable rule of EU law, the former has to be interpreted in such a way as to make it compatible with the latter. If the two instruments cannot be reconciled in this way then the rule of EU law will 'nullify'[2] the rule of domestic criminal law.

---

[1] See Professor John Spencer QC, 'EU Criminal Law—the Present and the Future?' in *Constitutional Order of States? Essays in EU Law in Honour of Alan Dashwood* (Oxford: Hart Publishing, 2011).
[2] See Professor John Spencer QC, 'EU Criminal Law—the Present and the Future?' in *Constitutional Order of States? Essays in EU Law in Honour of Alan Dashwood* (Oxford: Hart Publishing, 2011).

(b) Secondly, EU law can oblige national legislators to introduce new rules into their domestic criminal law. The body of European 'legislation' that sets out these obligations can be referred to as EU criminal law. The methods by which the EU can legislate in the field of criminal law was transformed dramatically by the coming into force of the Treaty of Lisbon. It is the nature of that transformation that is considered later in this chapter. It is worth noting, however, that whilst there is no reason why EU law should not oblige national legislators to de-criminalise behaviour, every provision of EU law introduced in the last two decades has been designed to extend rather than to restrict the number of criminal offences on the statute books of the Member States.

Aside from the ability of the EU to impose legislative obligations on the Member States **2.03** in a 'vertical' way, a number of institutions exist within the EU to encourage greater cooperation between the Member States in the field of criminal law, thus also giving EU criminal law a 'horizontal' dimension. It follows that not only can the EU tell Member States what type of changes they must make to their domestic criminal laws but it can enhance the effectiveness of those changes once introduced by informing and coordinating the activities of the Member States in the prevention and prosecution of cross-border crime.

B. Institutional Framework

The Treaty of Lisbon was not a third stand-alone Treaty and nor was it a consolidating Treaty, **2.04** but rather it amended both the TEC (the Treaty of Rome) and the TEU (the Maastricht Treaty). The TEC was renamed the Treaty on the Functioning of the European Union (TFEU, or in some commentaries, TOFU) and all references in the former TEC and the TEU to the 'Community' or 'European Community' were replaced with references to the 'Union'. The Treaty of Lisbon therefore signalled the final transformation of the European Community into the EU.[3]

This section is concerned with the institutional structure of the EU after the Treaty of Lisbon **2.05** came into force. Article 13 TEU identifies the institutions of the EU as follows:

(1) ...the Union's institutions shall be: the European Parliament, the European Council, the Council, the European Commission (hereinafter referred to as the 'Commission'), the Court of Justice of the European Union, the European Central Bank, the Court of Auditors.

(2) Each institution shall act within the limits of the powers conferred on it by the Treaties and in conformity with the procedures, conditions and objectives set out in them. The institutions shall practice mutual sincere co-operation.

The roles and responsibilities of the European Central Bank and the Court of Auditors falls **2.06** outside the scope of this work but the other institutions, to a greater or lesser extent, play a significant role in the development of EU criminal law and so it is appropriate to consider them here.

---

[3] See the Treaty of Lisbon (Changes in Terminology) Order 2011 (SI 2011/1043) for details of how existing UK legislation has been amended to adopt the new terminology (in force 22 April 2011) (Criminal Law Week 2011, vol. 14, para. 31). The history of the earlier treaties and their evolution leading to the Treaty of Lisbon is addressed in Chapter 1.

Legislative institutions

2.07 The institutions of the EU that have legislative competence are the Commission, the European Parliament, and the Council. The European Council is not a legislative body but it serves to direct the political development of the EU and so to that extent it is involved indirectly in the legislative process.

The Commission

2.08 The Commission lies at the heart of the EU. Based in Brussels, it comprises one representative from each of the Member States appointed by the Member States with the approval of the European Parliament. The representatives of the Member States are required to be independent of the Member States themselves and to act only in the best interests of the EU. The Commissioners therefore operate outside the narrow national interests of the Member State that appointed them.

2.09 The role of the Commission is enshrined in Article 17(1) TEU in these terms:

> It shall promote the general interest of the Union and take appropriate initiatives to that end. It shall ensure the application of the Treaties, and of measures adopted by the institutions pursuant to them. It shall oversee the application of Union law under the control of the Court of Justice of the European Union.

2.10 In the fulfilment of that role, Article 17(2) TEU provides that the Commission has the sole right to propose the form and content of EU legislation under 'the ordinary legislative procedure' set down in Articles 289(1) and 294(2) TFEU. This procedure begins with the Commission drafting a proposal for a new EU measure. This draft will then be sent to the national governments of the Member States which will discuss it and suggest alterations. Once there is general agreement between the Commission and the national governments about the content of the draft, the Commission will submit it to both the European Parliament and the Council. The European Parliament will look at it first. During the 'first reading', the draft can be amended before being forwarded to the Council. If the Council approves the draft in that form then it will be adopted and become law. If the Council does not approve then the draft can be bounced back to the European Parliament for reconsideration at which time there will be a 'second reading'. The European Parliament then has three months in which to adopt the Council's rival suggested form. If it does not act in that time the Council's version will become law. The procedure becomes even more complicated where the Council and the European Parliament continually act to remove or supplement the other's alterations, or where the Commission seeks to make amendments of its own while that process is ongoing. Generally, though, however long the process takes, the end result often represents a compromise arrived at between the EU institutions as to the content of the measure under consideration.

2.11 The Commission is also responsible for ensuring that the Member States comply with their obligations under EU law generally and, more specifically, that they implement EU legislation where implementation is required. If the Commission determines that a Member State is in default of its obligations then it can bring infringement proceedings before the Court of Justice of the European Union pursuant to Article 258 TFEU.

The European Parliament

2.12 The citizens of the Member States elect representatives to sit in the European Parliament as MEPs. Elections are held every five years. The more populous the Member State, the more seats there will be in the European Parliament for their MEPs, up to a maximum of 96 for any one Member State. Article 14(2) TEU provides that the total number of seats in the European Parliament cannot exceed 750. The European Parliament sits in Strasbourg, although meetings of its committees are sometimes held in Brussels and its Secretariat is based in Luxembourg.

By virtue of Article 231 TFEU, the European Parliament acts on the will of the major- **2.13** ity of its members. Under the ordinary legislative procedure, therefore, once the European Parliament has received a draft proposal from the Commission it will decide by a simple majority whether to approve it. It does not follow, however, that the European Parliament is powerless unless and until the Commission floats a legislative proposal in its direction. If the European Parliament feels that the Commission really ought to be proposing legislation in a certain area, it can extend just such an invitation to the Commission. Of course, the Commission can spurn that invitation if its wishes to, but if it does so it must give reasons for its refusal.

In addition to the ordinary legislative procedure, Article 289 TFEU also recognises the **2.14** existence of the 'special legislative procedure'. This arises in specific cases provided for by the Treaties and involves the adoption of EU legislation by the European Parliament with the participation of the Council, or vice versa. This procedure does not require the Commission to have advanced any legislative proposal first and so vests in the European Parliament and the Council a power to legislate without the involvement of the Commission.

The European Parliament has a range of additional powers outside these legislative pro- **2.15** cedures. One of the most important for present purposes is that by virtue of Article 218(6)(a)(ii) TFEU, it must agree on EU accession to the European Convention for the Protection of Human Rights and Fundamental Freedoms (ECHR). The consequences of accession are considered in Chapter 5.

The Council

The Council used to be known as the Council of Ministers. It consists of the representa- **2.16** tives of the governments of the Member States. The identity of that representative will vary depending on the issue being considered by the Council. Where that issue falls within the competence of a particular minister in a national government, that minister will generally be the representative of that government on the Council when the issue is considered. The Presidency of the Council rotates between the Member States equally.

As mentioned earlier, the Council's role under the ordinary legislative procedure is jointly **2.17** to adopt, along with the European Parliament, the Commission's legislative proposals. The Council can act by a simple majority of its members except where the Treaties provide otherwise, in which case the Council must either adopt what is known as QMV (qualified majority voting) or reach unanimity.

Where QMV is required, the vote of each member of the Commission is weighted to reflect **2.18** the size and influence of his or her Member State. This means that the 'Big Four' of Germany, France, Italy, and the UK each have 29 votes with the other Member States having less and some having much less. Malta, for example, has the least number of weighted votes with three. All told, the total number of votes is 345, meaning that a qualified majority is 255, being about 74 per cent of the total votes.

2.19 The significance of QMV lies in the fact that the representative of the UK Government on the Council will be unable unilaterally to block the joint adoption of proposals from the Commission even where those proposals may be controversial at the domestic level. If, however, the UK representative was not the only objector then they could, pursuant to Article 3(3) of Protocol No. 36 TFEU, request verification of the fact that those Member States who comprise the qualified majority have a combined population in excess of 62 per cent of the EU's total population. If verification is not forthcoming, the vote will fail. This modification of the QMV system works to ensure that generally a coalition of smaller States cannot overcome the will of the larger States.

2.20 As with the European Parliament, the Council also has the power to invite the Commission to advance legislative proposals and, under the special legislative procedure, it can adopt legislation in conjunction with the European Parliament and without the Commission's involvement.

The European Council

2.21 The European Council is comprised of the Heads of State of the Member States as well as the President of the Council and the President of the Commission. According to Article 15(1) TEU, the European Council is responsible for providing the EU 'with the necessary impetus for its development and shall define the general political direction and priorities thereof'. The European Council is, therefore, a political body and not a legislative one. Its role is to set the political agenda for the EU and it does so by a process of 'consensus' amongst its members, except where the Treaties stipulate that its decision making must take on a different form.

Judicial institutions

2.22 In one guise or another, the judicial institutions of the EU have been in existence since the early 1950s. Article 19(1) TEU now identifies these judicial institutions as the Court of Justice, the General Court, and specialised courts. Somewhat confusingly, this collection of institutions is referred to in the TEU as the Court of Justice and so at first glance it may not be obvious whether a reference to the Court of Justice is a reference to that specific court or to the collection of courts mentioned in Article 19(1).

The Court of Justice

2.23 The Court of Justice (hereafter CJEU) comprises one judge from each Member State. Sir Konrad Schiemann, formerly a judge of the Court of Appeal, has been the UK's appointee since 8 January 2004. In addition to the justices, the CJEU also comprises eight Advocates-General whose role in most cases is to submit an Opinion to the Court on any matter in issue before it. The justices and the Advocates-General serve for renewable periods of six years. The justices elect one of their number to serve as the President of the CJEU for a renewable period of three years.

2.24 The CJEU sits in Luxembourg, in contrast to the European Court of Human Rights which sits in Strasbourg. The CJEU is organised into chambers, normally comprising three or five justices, to hear individual cases. The Court can sit as a Grand Chamber of 13 judges, chaired by the President, where it feels that a case is sufficiently complex to warrant it or where a Member State of another institution of the EU requests it. In cases of the utmost importance, the CJEU can convene a chamber with every justice sitting to hear the case.

The CJEU will reach its decisions by a simple majority, although the decision reached will **2.25** not disclose how many justices went one way and how many the other. A single judgment will be handed down; there will be no dissenting judgments, and so outwardly at least the judgment will give the impression of unanimity on the part of the justices even where there were strong dissenters behind the scenes. In theory, every judgment of the CJEU carries equal weight regardless of the number of judges who sit on the case. In reality, however, where the CJEU convenes as a Grand Chamber it can and sometimes does seek to overrule previous decisions of the Court.

The CJEU's role within the EU is to ensure the uniform interpretation and application of **2.26** EU law. In order to fulfil that role, the CJEU has a number of different jurisdictions that it can occupy. In particular, these include:

(a) *Enforcement proceedings against a Member State* The Commission may take action before the CJEU against Member States that have failed to fulfil their obligations under the Treaties. In such a case, the CJEU will decide whether that failure has been made out and, if so, the Member State will need to act quickly in order to bring its domestic law in line with EU law.
(b) *Reviews of EU legislative acts* EU institutions and Member States may petition the CJEU to review the legality of any legislative acts of, inter alia, the Council, the Commission, the European Parliament, and the European Council, except as far as the last two institutions are concerned, this jurisdiction extends only to acts 'intended to produce legal effects vis-à-vis third parties' (Art. 263 TFEU).
(c) *Preliminary references from national courts* Under Article 267 TFEU, the CJEU can make preliminary rulings on references from national courts. This procedure will be invoked by the national court where the correct interpretation of EU law is relevant to its decision on the merits of the case before it. This is the means by which it is most likely that criminal practitioners will find themselves before the CJEU. It is addressed in detail in Chapter 7.

The General Court

The General Court used to be called the Court of First Instance (CFI). Like the CJEU, it **2.27** comprises one judge appointed from each Member State for a renewable term of six years. Its composition to hear individual cases and its procedures are similar in most respects to the CJEU. Article 256(1) TFEU provides that the General Court has jurisdiction 'to hear and determine at first instance', inter alia, proceedings for the review of legislative acts of the EU institutions. This jurisdiction seems to overlap with the same jurisdiction enjoyed by the CJEU but there is one significant difference. The jurisdiction of the General Court to review the legality of legislative acts is confined to applications made by certain individuals, whereas the CJEU's comparable jurisdiction is exercisable at the request of EU institutions and the Member States.

An individual here means any natural or legal person where the EU legislative act is addressed **2.28** to that individual or where it 'is of direct and individual concern to them, and against a regulatory act which is of direct concern to them and does not entail implementing measures' (Art. 263 TFEU). Thus, if a citizen of a Member State satisfies the definition in Article 263 TFEU and believes that there are grounds to challenge the lawfulness of a piece of EU legislation then his application for review should be made to the General Court and not to the CJEU.

2.29   Where the General Court reviews an EU legislative act on petition from a qualifying individual, its decision can be appealed to the CJEU but only on a point of law and even then only in relation to arguments on the law that were advanced before the General Court.

Specialised courts

2.30   Article 257 TFEU authorised the creation of certain specialised courts the decisions of which will be subject to appeal to the General Court. To date, only one specialised court has been established and that is the Civil Service Tribunal.

Administrative bodies

2.31   The purpose of this section is to explain the functions of those EU institutions that have a role to play in coordinating the actions of the Member States in the field of criminal law to ensure that the objectives of the EU in maintaining an area of freedom, security, and justice are met. This section will also consider the future of these institutions in the wake of the Treaty of Lisbon and, in particular, whether Article 86 TFEU has paved the way for the eventual introduction of a European Public Prosecutor.

OLAF[4]

2.32   L'Office européen de lutte antifraude (OLAF), or the European Anti-Fraud Office, is formally attached to the Commission and, as its name suggests, it exists to investigate fraud. A Commission Decision in April 1999[5] formally established OLAF as the successor to the Task Force for the Coordination of Fraud Prevention. Its powers are set out in Regulation (EC) No. 1073/1999, Article 1(3) of which obliges OLAF to:

> conduct administrative investigations for the purposes of fighting fraud, corruption and any other illegal activity affecting the financial interests of the European Community [and] investigating to that end serious matters relating to the discharge of professional duties such as to constitute a dereliction of the obligations of officials and other servants of the Communities . . .

2.33   The Director of OLAF is obliged by the provisions of the Regulation to be independent of the Member States and the institutions of the EU in the sense that he must not take any instructions from them, although he is required to make regular reports to the European Parliament, the Council, the Commission, and the Court of Auditors on the progress of ongoing OLAF investigations. This requirement of independence is highly dubious given that OLAF is formally attached to one of the very institutions that it is not supposed to be influenced by. There is clear scope for a conflict of interest, for example in a case where OLAF is called upon to investigate allegations of fraud within the Commission itself. The role of OLAF is considered in more detail in Chapter 5.[6]

Europol[7]

2.34   The European Police Office (Europol) was created in 1998. It comprises the Management Board, the Director, the Financial Controller, and the Financial Committee. The Management Board in turn comprises one representative from each Member State, and each representa-

---

[4] See Constantine Stefanou, Simone White, and Helen Xanthaki, *OLAF at the Crossroads: Action against EU Fraud* (Oxford: Hart Publishing, 2011) and Valsamis Mitsilegas, *EU Criminal Law* (Oxford: Hart Publishing, 2009), 210–19.

[5] [1999] OJ L 136, 31.05.1999, p 20.

[6] Chapter **5.198**.

[7] Valsamis Mitsilegas, *EU Criminal Law* (Oxford: Hart Publishing, 2009), 161–87.

tive has one vote. Europol is essentially an agency for the furtherance of police cooperation between the Member States. Its purpose is now set out in Article 88 TFEU in these terms:

1. Europol's mission shall be to support and strengthen action by the Member States' police authorities and other law enforcement services and their mutual cooperation in preventing and combating serious crime affecting two or more Member States, terrorism and forms of crime which affect a common interest covered by a Union policy.

2. The European Parliament and the Council, by means of regulations adopted in accordance with the ordinary legislative procedure, shall determine Europol's structure, operation, field of action and tasks. These tasks may include;

   (a) the collection, storage, processing, analysis and exchange of information, in particular that forwarded by the authorities of the Member States or third countries or bodies;

   (b) the coordination, organisation and implementation of investigative and operational action carried out jointly with the Member States' competent authorities or in the context of joint investigative teams, where appropriate in liaison with Eurojust.

   These regulations shall also lay down the procedures for scrutiny of Europol's activities by the European Parliament, together with national Parliaments.

3. Any operational action by Europol must be carried out in liaison and in agreement with the authorities of the Member State or States whose territory is concerned. The application of coercive measures shall be the exclusive responsibility of the competent national authorities.

Further legislation on the structure, operation, field of action, and tasks of Europol is expected in 2013, but until then Europol's role is governed by a third-pillar Council Decision adopted in 2009.[8] Under that instrument, its main tasks are effectively as set out in Article 88(2)(a) and (b). **2.35**

Eurojust[9]

If Europol exists to facilitate police cooperation then Eurojust's mandate is to facilitate judicial cooperation. Eurojust was established in 2002 but its purpose is now set down in Article 85 TFEU as follows: **2.36**

1. Eurojust's mission shall be to support and strengthen coordination and cooperation between national investigating and prosecuting authorities in relation to serious crime affecting two or more Member States or requiring a prosecution on common bases, on the basis of operations conducted and information supplied by the Member States' authorities and by Europol.

   In this context, the European Parliament and the Council, by means of regulations adopted in accordance with the ordinary legislative procedure, shall determine Eurojust's structure, operation, field of action and tasks. These tasks may include:

   (a) the initiation of criminal investigations, as well as proposing the initiation of prosecutions conducted by competent national authorities, particularly those relating to offences against the financial interests of the Union;

   (b) the coordination of investigations and prosecutions referred to in point (a);

   (c) the strengthening of judicial cooperation, including any resolution of conflicts of jurisdiction and by close cooperation with the European Judicial Network.

   These regulations shall also determine arrangements for involving the European Parliament and national Parliaments in the evaluation of Eurojust's activities.

2. In the prosecutions referred to in paragraph 1, and without prejudice to Article 86, formal acts of judicial procedure shall be carried out by the competent national officials.

---

[8] [2009] OJ L 121/27. See Chapter 1 for an explanation of the three pillars.
[9] Valsamis Mitsilegas, *EU Criminal Law* (Oxford: Hart Publishing, 2009), 187–209.

2.37 Further legislation on the structure, operation, field of action, and tasks of Eurojust is expected in late 2012, but until then Eurojust's role, like that of Europol, is governed by a third-pillar Council Decision adopted in 2009.[10] The future of Eurojust is highlighted by Article 86 TFEU, which provides that in order to 'combat crimes affecting the financial interests of the Union', the Council, via the means of the special legislative procedure, 'may establish a European Public Prosecutor's Office (EPPO) out of Eurojust'. Article 86(2) states that the EPPO:

> shall be responsible for investigating, prosecuting and bringing to justice, where appropriate in liaison with Europol, the perpetrators of, and accomplices in, offences against the Union's financial interests . . . It shall exercise the functions of prosecutor in the competent courts of the Member States in relation to such offences.

2.38 The idea for a European Public Prosecutor was first canvassed in the *Corpus Juris* project,[11] which was a set of rules devised by leading academics to improve the criminal law protection of the EU's financial interests. If the creation of the EPPO comes to pass, it will have extensive powers to investigate and prosecute a wide range of criminal offences 'affecting the financial interests of the Union'. This will include the power to function as a prosecution agency in the domestic courts of the Member States in place of existing national prosecutors, such as the Crown Prosecution Service. Eurojust is further addressed in Chapter 5.[12]

C. Legislative Instruments

Introduction

2.39 This section will consider the types of measure by which the EU institutions can legislate in the field of criminal law, the effects of those measures, and how they fall to be applied and interpreted by national courts.

2.40 As outlined earlier, the competence of the EU to legislate derives from the Treaties, which are essentially the manifestations of the will of the Member States. In that sense, it is the Member States that confer jurisdiction on the EU institutions to make laws. It should be borne in mind, however, that that jurisdiction is limited by the terms of the Treaty by which it is conferred. If the EU institutions act outside the competence afforded to them by the Treaties then in all likelihood the CJEU would strike down any measures they introduce as being outside their jurisdiction to act.

2.41 In one sense, then, the Treaties are the equivalent of UK Acts of Parliament (primary legislation) and any measures introduced by the EU institutions in the exercise of the competences bestowed on them by the Treaties are the equivalent of statutory instruments (secondary legislation).

Treaties

2.42 It is important to note here that in addition to creating the powers that enable the EU institutions to legislate, the Treaties also contain binding rights, liabilities, obligations, and restric-

---

[10] Council Decision 2009/492/JHA of 16 December 2008.
[11] *Corpus Juris: Introducing Penal Provisions for the Purpose of the Financial Interests of the European Union* (Paris: Editions Economica, 1997).
[12] Chapter **5.129**.

tions, which can collectively be described as laws, which apply directly in the Member States without the need for any implementing legislation by national parliaments.

The most well known of these laws are the four freedoms enshrined in the TFEU: free move- **2.43** ment of persons, goods, services, and capital. These freedoms have been key to the creation of the single market and are jealously guarded by the TFEU, which will permit of no restrictions to them unless those restrictions can be objectively justified.[13]

In the UK, the European Communities Act 1972 was passed in order to make the law of the **2.44** Treaties enforceable in the domestic courts. Without this Act, the Treaties, as international organs negotiated between the UK executive and the governments of the other Member States, would not have bound the domestic courts to apply EU law. Section 1(2) defines what is meant by 'the Treaties'. This includes the Treaty of Lisbon but it does *not* include Title VI of the Treaty of Maastricht 1992, which first introduced the 'third pillar' and gave rise to various Framework Decisions in the field of criminal law. This exclusion seems to have been overlooked in much of the case law. Its significance is considered later in this chapter in the context of the UK Supreme Court's decision in *Assange v The Swedish Prosecution Authority*.[14]

Section 2(1) of the 1972 Act reads as follows: **2.45**

> All such rights, powers, liabilities, obligations and restrictions from time to time created or arising by or under the Treaties, and all such remedies and procedures from time to time provided for by or under the Treaties, as in accordance with the Treaties are without further enactment to be given legal effect or used in the United Kingdom shall be recognised and available in law, and be enforced, allowed and followed accordingly; and the expression 'enforceable Community right' and similar expressions shall be read as referring to one to which this subsection applies.

Of course, references to the 'Community' should now be read as references to the 'Union'. **2.46** This section provides that EU law as enshrined in the Treaties or as set out in certain forms of secondary legislation passed pursuant to powers bestowed on the EU institutions by the Treaties has direct effect. Moreover, the section makes it clear that EU law will determine whether a piece of secondary legislation has direct effect. The circumstances in which such a determination will be made are considered later in this chapter (see 2.72).

Section 2(4) of the 1972 Act provides that 'any enactment passed or to be passed, other than **2.47** one contained in this Part of this Act, shall be construed and have effect subject to the foregoing provisions of this section', which includes section 2(1) and the recognition of direct effect. Taken together, these provisions require the subordination of UK law, including Acts of Parliament, to directly enforceable EU law. Thus, EU law is supreme but only because the UK Parliament has legislated for it to be supreme. If there ever came a time when the UK Parliament did not want EU law to take precedence over a domestic statute then clear words could be inserted into the statute to that effect.[15] Should this situation ever come to pass, then in all likelihood this would amount to a repudiation of the Treaties and doubtless

---

[13] Andre Klip, *European Criminal Law: An Integrative Approach*, 2nd edn (Antwerp: Intersentia, 2012), 80 et seq.

[14] [2012] UKSC 22, [2012] 2 WLR 1275. This important decision receives more detailed analysis at **2.110**.

[15] This is by no means a universally accepted proposition. Some commentators maintain that the UK Parliament cannot simply restore to itself powers that it has voluntarily surrendered to the EU.

the Commission would take action against the UK, although it is highly unlikely that this situation would ever arise. As Lord Denning MR noted in *Macarthys Ltd v Smith*:[16]

> If the time should come when Parliament deliberately passes an Act with the intention of repudi-ating the Treaty or any provision in it or intentionally of acting inconsistently with it and says so in express terms then I should have thought it would be the duty of the our courts to follow the statute of our Parliament. I do not however envisage any such situation...Unless there is such an intentional and express repudiation of the Treaty it is our duty to give priority to the Treaty.[17]

2.48 The doctrine of the supremacy of EU law means that where a domestic measure has been introduced that violates directly effective EU law, the national courts will disapply it, although the domestic measure will remain in force. Where a domestic measure does not per se violate directly effective EU law, but action taken by the executive in furtherance of that measure does, then similarly the national courts must act to annul that action.

2.49 The CJEU in Case 106/77 *Amministrazione delle Finanze dello Stato v Simmenthal SpA*[18] expressed that proposition in these terms:

> Every national court must in a case within its jurisdiction, apply Community law in its entirety and protect rights which the latter confers on individuals and must accordingly set aside any provision of national law which may conflict with it, whether prior to or subsequent to the community rule. Accordingly any provision of a national legal system and any legislative, administrative or judicial practice which might impair the effectiveness of community law by withholding from the national court having jurisdiction to apply such law the power to do everything necessary at the moment of its application to set aside national legislative provi-sions which might prevent community rules from having full force and effect are incompatible with those requirements which are the very essence of community law. This would be the case in the event of a conflict between a provision of community law and a subsequent national law if the solution of the conflict were to be reserved for an authority with a discretion of its own, other than the court called.

2.50 In *Fleming (t/a Bodycraft) v Customs and Excise Commissioners*,[19] Lord Walker endorsed the conclusion in *Simmenthal* by reference to the 1972 Act:

> It is a fundamental principle of the law of the European Union...recognised in s.2(1) of the European Communities Act 1972, that if national legislation infringes directly enforceable Community rights, the national court is obliged to disapply the offending provision. The provision is not made void but it must be treated as being (as Lord Bridge of Harwich put it in *R v Secretary of State for Transport, ex parte Factortame* [1990] 2 AC 85, 140):
>
> > 'without prejudice to the directly enforceable Community rights of nationals of any Member State of the EEC'.

2.51 It follows from Lord Walker's comments in *Fleming* that a domestic measure that violates directly enforceable EU law in one case may not necessarily do so in another. The CJEU made this same observation in Case C-264/96 *Imperial Chemical Industries v Colmer*,[20] when it said:

> when deciding an issue concerning a situation which lies outside the scope of Community law, the national court is not required, under Community law, either to interpret its legislation in

---

[16] [1979] 3 All ER 325.
[17] At 329.
[18] [1978] ECR 629, paras 21–3.
[19] [2008] UKHL 2, [2008] 1 WLR 195, para. 24.
[20] [1998] ECR I-04695, para. 34.

a way conforming with Community law or to disapply that legislation. Where a particular provision must be disapplied in a situation covered by Community law but the same provision could remain applicable to a situation not so covered, it is for the competent body of the state concerned to remove that legal uncertainty insofar as it might affect rights deriving from Community rules.

The disapplication of a UK statute that created a criminal offence in that case occurred at **2.52** the end of the long-running saga of publican, Karen Murphy, who sought to beam Premier League football matches into her establishment via the means of a genuine Greek decoder device thereby avoiding the need to buy a similar device from Sky and paying a far heftier subscription for its use. She was charged with two offences contrary to section 297(1) of the Copyright, Designs and Patents Act 1988.[21] Ms Murphy was convicted at the magistrates' court and again on appeal to the Crown Court but she then appealed by way of case stated to the Divisional Court. The argument on that appeal focused on whether the broadcast she had received via her Greek decoder had been 'provided from a place in the United Kingdom'. She argued, relying on a number of EC Directives, that because the footage had been beamed via satellite from the UK to Greece and then from Greece to her decoder, the place of the broadcast was Greece and not the UK. The Divisional Court held that the Directives offered little assistance in the correct interpretation of the Act and went on to find that because 'the programme which is the subject of the charge came into existence' in the UK the elements of the offence were made out. [22]

At the very end of the judgment, the court alluded to two arguments that had not been **2.53** advanced before it, namely whether the prosecution of Ms Murphy had infringed any of the four freedoms guaranteed under the Treaties or the EU rules on anti-competitive practices. As to the former, the court observed that as 'the rights we have discussed are essentially territorial in nature, it is unclear to us how there can be a relevant free movement case.'[23] In fact, clarity was to come some years later.

In the intervening period Ms Murphy sought to use these arguments in what a differently **2.54** constituted Divisional Court described as 'the second part of an appeal by way of case stated'.[24] This time, the appellant relied on Directive 98/84/EC (the Conditional Access Directive), which obliged Member States to approximate their laws against the use of 'illicit devices which give access to protected services' but not in a way that restricted the provision of protected services 'which originate in another Member State'. Her argument was simple: given that she was using a genuine (and not an illicit) Greek decoder that she had bought from a supplier in Greece, to prosecute someone in her position under the Act 'would be to restrict the free movement of conditional access devices and/or the provision of protected services, contrary to both [the Directive] and the underlying free movement provisions of the EC Treaty itself.'[25] Accordingly, the decision to prosecute her having been taken in breach of EC law (as it then was), her convictions should be set aside. The Divisional Court decided, for various reasons, to make a preliminary reference to the CJEU on this point.

---

[21] Which reads: 'A person who dishonestly receives a programme included in a broadcasting or cable programme service provided from a place in the United Kingdom with intent to avoid payment of any charge applicable to the reception of the programme commits an offence and is liable on summary conviction to a fine not exceeding level 5 on the standard scale.'
[22] *Murphy v Media Protection Services Ltd* [2008] 1 WLR 1869, para. 37.
[23] *Murphy v Media Protection Services Ltd* [2008] 1 WLR 1869, para. 45.
[24] *Murphy v Media Protection Services Ltd* [2008] EWHC 1666 (Admin).
[25] *Murphy v Media Protection Services Ltd* [2008] EWHC 1666 (Admin), para. 26.

2.55 In its judgment of 4 October 2011, some three years later, the CJEU considered the free movement provisions by then contained in Article 56 TFEU. The Court noted that Article 56

> requires the abolition of all restrictions on the freedom to provide services, even if those restrictions apply without distinction to national providers of services and to those from other Member States, when they are liable to prohibit, impede or render less advantageous the activities of a service provider established in another Member State where it lawfully provides similar services.[26]

2.56 The Court had no hesitation in finding that as the 1988 Act effectively prohibited foreign decoder devices from being imported into and used in the UK, this amounted to a restriction on the freedom to provide services, which would infringe Article 56 TFEU unless it could be objectively justified. The Court made it clear that a restriction can only be justified if it 'serves overriding reasons in the public interest, is suitable for securing the attainment of the public interest objective which it pursues and does not go beyond what is necessary in order to attain it'[27] and concluded that no objective justifications existed in this case.[28] Accordingly, the Court held:

> In light of all the foregoing the answer to the questions referred is that, on a proper construction of Article 56 TFEU, that article precludes legislation of a Member State which makes it unlawful to import into and sell and use in that State foreign decoding devices which give access to an encrypted satellite broadcasting service from another Member State that include subject-matter protected by the legislation of that first State.[29]

2.57 The Court also held that on the same facts there had been a restriction on competition as prohibited by Article 101 TFEU. The case came back before the Divisional Court.[30] Stanley Burnton LJ took stock of the CJEU's ruling and held that by virtue of the directly effective provisions of Article 56 TFEU, section 297(1) of the 1988 Act 'under which the appellant was convicted, cannot be applied to the appellant's use of the card in question'.[31] It followed that the appellant was wrongly convicted and so her appeal against conviction was allowed and those convictions quashed.[32]

2.58 The *Murphy* case is but one example of how, in the field of domestic criminal practice, EU law could have a significant role where the prosecution of suspected offenders risks infringing any directly enforceable provisions, such as the four freedoms. It demonstrates that the application of EU law can be very fact-specific. It also follows from the decision of the CJEU in that case that section 297(1) itself was not incompatible with directly enforceable EU law although its use on the facts of this case was. In another case, where a prosecution under that section does not engage EU law, there is no reason to suppose that the doctrine of 'direct effect' will play any part in determining its ultimate disposal.

---

[26] Joined Cases C-403/08 and C-429/08 [2011], para. 85.
[27] Joined Cases C-403/08 and C-429/08 [2011], para. 93.
[28] Joined Cases C-403/08 and C-429/08 [2011], para. 124.
[29] Joined Cases C-403/08 and C-429/08 [2011], para. 125.
[30] [2012] EWHC 259 (Admin).
[31] [2012] EWHC 259 (Admin), para. 9.
[32] The saga did not in fact end there because in a further judgment ([2012] EWHC 529 (Admin)), the Divisional Court had to deal with the issue whether the parties costs should be determined under the civil costs regime or the criminal costs regime. The court favoured the latter.

Competence

Where the Member States confer competence on the EU institutions to legislate in a par- **2.59**
ticular area via a Treaty provision, it does not follow that the Member States will have surrendered their own legislative competence unless the Treaties make that clear. One obvious
area where the EU has exclusive competence to legislate is in the field of common policy as
set out in Article 3 TFEU. In contrast, Article 4(2) TFEU sets out those areas where the EU
and the Member States share competence. These include the area of freedom, security, and
justice, which itself includes crime and criminal justice.

Where the EU and the Member States share competence to legislate then both can introduce **2.60**
binding acts, although it would make little sense for the EU and the Member States to legislate in the same area at the same time, for obvious reasons. Article 2(2) TFEU circumvents
this difficulty by stating that where competence is shared in this way, the Member States 'shall
exercise their competence to the extent that the Union has not exercised its competence' and
shall 'exercise their competence to the extent that the Union has decided to cease exercising
its competence'. This means that the EU can take the first bite of the cherry when it comes
to introducing legislation in a particular area of its shared competence but if it chooses not
to take a bite at all then the Member States can do so.

Subsidiarity and proportionality

In deciding whether to take that first bite, by Article 5(3) TEU, the EU must determine **2.61**
whether 'the objectives of the proposed action cannot be sufficiently achieved by the Member
States'. This is known as the principle of subsidiarity. Thus, if the objective of the proposed
EU legislative can be achieved at the national level without a pan-European initiative, then
the EU should leave it to the Member States to legislate. The principle of subsidiarity, therefore, serves to protect the sovereignty of the Member State and ensure that EU legislation is
only enacted when it is clearly necessary.

Article 5(4) TEU goes on to provide that where the EU has the competence to legislate and **2.62**
decides that it needs to do so, the content and form of that legislation must be such as is necessary to achieve the objectives of the legislation and no more. This is known as the principle
of proportionality.

Article 69 TFEU provides that the national parliaments of the Member States must ensure **2.63**
that any legislative initiatives emanating from the EU comply with the principles of subsidiarity and proportionality. Moreover, by virtue of Article 2 of the Protocol on the Application
of the Principles of Subsidiarity and Proportionality, annexed to the Treaty of Lisbon, the
EU must consult widely before drafting any legislative measures in order to ensure that the
views of the Member States are taken into consideration at an early stage in the legislative
process. National parliaments have a period of two months in which to raise objections to
any proposed measure if they feel that the measure offends the principle of subsidiarity. If
one-third of the national parliaments object, then the proposal will be bounced back to the
Commission for it to be reviewed (the 'yellow card'). If, however, a *majority* of national parliaments object, and national governments and MEPs agree, then the proposal can be struck
down (the 'orange card').

Secondary legislation

This section deals with the various forms of secondary legislation that exist both under the **2.64**
Treaty of Lisbon (see **2.65**) and under the old third pillar (see **2.102**) insofar as those latter

measures are still relevant to domestic practitioners. As later chapters will explore pre-Lisbon framework decisions of relevance to criminal practitioners in various areas of law and procedure as well as post-Lisbon legislation, it is necessary to understand the operation of secondary legislation both before and after the change wrought by that Treaty.

Post-Lisbon

2.65 Section 1 of Chapter 2 of Title 1 to Part Six of the TFEU is headed 'The Legal Acts of the Union', and Article 288 thereunder provides that in the exercise of the EU's competences, 'the institutions shall adopt regulations, directives, decisions, recommendations and opinions'. Each will be considered in turn.

Regulations

2.66 In the exercise of the EU's criminal competence, it is unlikely that the Regulation will be an oft-used legislative device. There are examples of Regulations adopted pre-Lisbon that created criminal offences as a necessary adjunct to their primary purpose, such as Regulation 338/97 on the Protection of Species of Wild Fauna and Flora by Regulating Trade therein, but post-Lisbon no draft Regulations have been either proposed by the Commission or adopted by the European Parliament/Council.

2.67 By Article 288 TFEU, a Regulation has general application and 'shall be binding in its entirety and directly applicable in all Member States'. Thus, once a Regulation is adopted at EU level, there is no need for Member States to pass any domestic legislation for its implementation.

Directives

2.68 Directives will be the main form of EU secondary legislation in the area of criminal law and procedure. In contrast to Regulations, Directives are not directly applicable and so Member States will need to implement them into their national law. Article 288 TFEU provides that a Directive 'shall be binding, as to the result to be achieved, upon each Member State to which it is addressed, but shall leave to the national authorities the choice of form and methods.'

2.69 The TFEU does not stipulate how the Member States must implement a Directive (whether by the introduction of primary or secondary legislation or in some other way, such as a Code of Practice[33]) or what form that national measure must take (e.g. whether the measure created is criminal or civil in nature), provided the result envisaged by the Directive is achieved. The situation is different where the Directive itself prescribes the type of legal measure that must be used by the Member States in order to implement it in national law.

2.70 In the UK, section 2(2) of the European Communities Act 1972 makes provision for the ways in which the UK can implement EU law, such as Directives. This can be achieved by primary legislation, or by Order in Council, or 'by order, rules, regulations or schemes' made by a minister or department designated for that purpose. In either of the latter scenarios, the implementing measure must take the form of a statutory instrument and it must have parliamentary approval before it becomes law.

---

[33] The CJEU have taken the view, however, that some types of implementing measure will not suffice. In Case 102/79 *Commission v Belgium* [1980] ECR 1473, a ministerial circular purporting to set aside the rules of national law that stood against the result envisaged by the Directive was an insufficiently robust measure. The Court held that whatever steps the Member States take to implement the Directive those steps must actually and effectively remove any offending rules of national law and not merely declare them to be no longer in force.

Each Directive will state the period during which the Member States must implement it into **2.71** their national law. The implementation period for most Directives is around two years. If, by the end of that period, the Directive has not been implemented or it has been implemented imperfectly, the Commission can take action against the Member State before the CJEU, as has been discussed earlier.

Direct Effect If the implementation of a Directive does not occur either satisfactorily or at **2.72** all by the end of the implementation period then the Directive may have direct effect, in the same way as Treaties and Regulations. This means that individuals who stood to benefit from the provisions of the Directive once implemented may, under certain circumstances, be able to rely directly on the Directive in the national courts.

As mentioned earlier in this chapter, it will be for EU law to determine whether an unimple- **2.73** mented Directive has direct effect. The CJEU in Case C-319/97 *Criminal proceedings against Antoine Kortas*, gave guidance on when Directives will be directly enforceable:

> whenever the provisions of a Directive appear, so far as their subject-matter is concerned, to be unconditional and sufficiently precise, they may be relied upon before national courts by an individual against the State where that State has failed to implement the Directive in national law by the end of the period prescribed or where it has failed to implement the Directive correctly. [34]

In order to have direct effect, therefore, the Directive must be unconditional and suffi- **2.74** ciently precise. In Joined Cases C-246/94, C-247/94, C-248/94 and C-249/94 *Cooperativa Agricola Zootecnica S. Antonio and Others v Amministrazione delle finanze dello Stato*,[35] the CJEU considered the meaning of those expressions:

> A community provision is unconditional where it sets forth an obligation which is not qualified by any condition, or subject, in its implementation or effects, to the taking of any measure either by the Community institution or by the Member States. Moreover, a provision is sufficiently precise to be relied on by an individual and applied by a national court whether it sets out an obligation in unequivocal terms.

As one commentator has noted, this amounts to a feasibility standard: 'if the provision lends **2.75** itself to judicial application, it will almost certainly be declared directly effective; only where direct effect would create serious practical problems is it likely that the provisions will be held not to be directly effective.'[36]

An obvious distinction needs to be drawn here between rights and obligations. Where the **2.76** Directive was intended to grant a right to individuals and those rights are directly effective then the national courts should afford those rights to the individual concerned. One example might be where the Directive affords the individual some procedural right, such as the right to consult a lawyer or to have an interpreter present during questioning. If the State refuses to enact those rights into domestic law then the courts must act to ensure that the individual has the benefit of his or her directly effective entitlements under the Directive once the implementation period has expired. If the national courts are only seized of the individual's case after those rights have been denied to him then they may have to act to exclude any evidence gathered in violation of those rights.

---

[34] [1999] ECR I-3143, para. 21.
[35] [1996] ECR I-4373, paras 18 and 19.
[36] T.C. Hartley, *The Foundations of European Union Law* (Oxford: Oxford University Press, 2010), 214, himself quoting the view of Advocate-General van Gerven in Case C-128/92 *Banks* [1994] ECR 1–1209.

2.77 By contrast, where the Directive was intended to impose obligations on individuals (e.g. by creating a new criminal offence), it would be wrong for the defaulting Member State to prosecute anyone for that offence because such action would offend the maxim *nullum crimen sine legem*.[37] On the other hand, where the Directive provides that certain activities should no longer be criminal (an unlikely event) and the Member State refuses to pass de-criminalising legislation, no individual should be prosecuted for committing the national criminal offence that offends the intended result of the Directive.

2.78 As at the date of writing, although Directives have been adopted pursuant to the increased competence of the EU institutions in criminal matters under the Treaty of Lisbon, the implementation periods have not expired and so there are presently no directly enforceable Directives in this field.

2.79 **Indirect Effect**   If national legislation is introduced during the implementation period that successfully achieves the results set down by the Directive, that does not mean the Directive is no longer relevant to domestic criminal practitioners.

2.80 Where a UK statute has been enacted in order to give effect to the results the Directive was intended to achieve, but the terms of the Act are ambiguous or unclear or otherwise require interpretation, can practitioners look to the Directive for assistance? The short answer is, yes. In the context of Framework Decisions, the CJEU in *Criminal proceedings against Pupino*[38] held:

> 43. In the light of all the above considerations, the court concludes that the principle of interpretation in conformity with Community law is binding in relation to framework decisions adopted in the context of Title VI of the Treaty on European Union. When applying national law, the national court that is called on to interpret it must do so as far as possible in the light of the wording and purpose of the framework decision in order to attain the result which it pursues and thus comply with article 34.2(b) EU.

2.81 Although the terminology used by the Court of Justice belongs to the pre-Lisbon era, the duty of conforming interpretation espoused in *Pupino* is alive and well in the post-Lisbon world. The duty requires the courts of the Member States to take a broad view of their domestic measures in situations such as that under consideration in order to ensure alignment between the laws of those Member States which have sought to implement the Directive. This broad view may require the national courts to walk away from the established rules of statutory construction and towards more communitarian rules. In the *Assange* case, Lord Mance put it in these terms:

> [the] legal duty of conforming interpretation has been understood by United Kingdom courts as requiring domestic courts where necessary to depart 'from a number of well-established rules of construction': *Pickstone v Freemans plc* [1989] AC 66, 126B, per Lord Oliver of Aylmerton; and 'to go beyond what could be done by way of statutory interpretation where no question of Community law or human rights is involved': *Test Claimants in the FII Group Litigation v Revenue and Customs Comrs* [2010] EWCA Civ 103 [2010] STC 1251, paras 97 and 260, per Arden LJ ... Pursuant to the resulting duty, domestic courts may depart from the precise words used, e.g. by reading words in or out. The main constraint is that the result must 'go with

---

[37] The maxim is derived from Art. 49(1) of the Charter of Fundamental Rights, which provides that 'No one shall be guilty of any criminal offence on account of any act or omission which did not constitute a criminal offence under national law or international law at the time when it was committed...'

[38] Case C-105/03 [2006] QB 83.

the grain' or 'be consistent with the underlying thrust' of the legislation being construed, that is, not 'be inconsistent with some fundamental or cardinal feature of the legislation': *Vodafone 2* [*v Revenue and Customs Comrs*] [2009] EWCA Civ 446, [2010] Ch 77, [2009] STC 1480, para 38, per The Chancellor, and *Test Claimants in the FII Group Litigation*, para 97, per Arden LJ, in each case citing *Ghaidan v Godin-Mendoza* [2004] 2 AC 557.[39]

How far beyond the common law rules of statutory construction can the UK courts go? It is **2.82** one thing to say that the terms of the Directive can be taken into account in deciding what an ambiguous provision of the implementing statute means, but quite another to suggest that clear words of the Act should be read out in order to arrive at a text that fits more neatly with the language of the Directive, but that seems to be the view the higher courts have taken. There are, however, limits to just how far the terms of a UK statute can be stretched. In *Vodafone 2*,[40] referred to by Lord Mance in *Assange* (see earlier), it was held that if the duty of conforming interpretation might lead a court to interpret an Act in such a way as to do violence to a 'cardinal feature of the legislation' then that would be a step too far. This means that whilst the national courts can bend the terms of a statute to fit the contours of the Directive, they cannot break them.

In a similar vein, the CJEU in *Pupino* noted: **2.83**

47. The obligation on the national court to refer to the content of a framework decision when interpreting the relevant rules of its national law ceases when the latter cannot receive an application which leads to a result compatible with that envisaged by that framework decision. In other words, the principle of interpretation in conformity with Community law cannot serve as the basis for an interpretation of national law *contra legem*.

The reference to *contra legem* in that passage is important. It means that indirect effect can- **2.84** not do what direct effect cannot do and impose obligations on individuals. In other words, if the implementing legislation falls to be interpreted by reference to the provisions of the Directive, that exercise cannot result in the national court taking the view that the individual should be in a worse position than he was in before the terms of the Directive were considered.

In the area of customs law, there are examples of cases where Directives have been used to **2.85** interpret secondary legislation passed in order to implement them. One such example is *White & Others*,[41] where the four unconnected appellants had all been convicted of being involved in smuggling tobacco products into the UK for resale. Confiscation orders were made against all four under the relevant legislation. The issue on appeal was the extent to which each had benefitted from their criminal conduct given the roles they carried out in furtherance of the smuggling operation.

In order to decide whether they had benefitted, the Court of Appeal had to consider whether **2.86** each had become personally liable to pay the excise duty on the tobacco products because the evasion of that duty amounted to a pecuniary advantage that was capable of being a benefit for the purposes of the confiscation regime. Under the relevant UK statutory instrument, duty became chargeable once the goods reached the excise duty point and the person responsible for paying that duty was the importer and any person who caused the goods to

---

[39] [2012] UKSC 22, para. 203.
[40] *Vodafone 2 v Revenue and Customs Comrs* [2009] EWCA Civ 446, [2010] Ch 77, [2009] STC 1480.
[41] [2010] EWCA Crim 978.

reach that point. The court held that consideration of the relevant Directive did not alter this interpretation as the terms of the Directive itself compelled much the same result.

2.87 Of course, before any criminal practitioner can seek to pray in aid before the national courts the interpretative value of a Directive, they will need to know that the contentious provision of national law that features in their case was introduced in order to implement a Directive. This may not be obvious in any given case. Although Member States are obliged to state that EU law has been implemented when they introduce new legislation, that rule is not always followed.

2.88 Looking to the future, it is likely that any Directive emanating from Europe in the exercise of the competences bestowed on the EU institutions in criminal matters by the Treaty of Lisbon will receive more widespread publicity than would have previously been the case, and so criminal practitioners who subscribe to current awareness publications will probably be alert to any changes to national legislation that will flow from the Directive. Where, however, the relevant Directive was passed before the Treaty of Lisbon came into force, the only way of knowing whether the domestic offence under consideration was created in response to such a Directive, and hence whether the rule of conforming interpretation may come into play, will be to do a little detective work. This would involve finding out when the domestic offence was created and by what instrument and to consult the Official Journal of the European Union for the two-year period before the domestic enactment to see if there is any relevant Directive. That will be a time-consuming task but it could also be very fruitful.

2.89 *R v Budimir; Interfact Ltd v Liverpool City Council*[42] is a good example of a case where knowledge of the relevant Directive came too late. The applicants were convicted of offences contrary to the Video Recordings Act 1984 committed between 2004 and 2007. Unbeknown to them at the time, the Technical Standards Directive, Council Directive 83/189/EEC, which had been adopted on 28 March 1983, required the Member States to notify to the Commission 'any draft technical regulation', meaning any provision of national law in the field of technical regulations as defined by the Directive. Failure to notify would make the provision of national law unenforceable against the individual. It was not until August 2009, after the applicants had been convicted, that the UK Government notified the Commission that the offences under the 1984 Act satisfied this definition. Clearly, had the applicants been aware of the existence of the Technical Standards Directive at the time they were prosecuted they could have sought to bring any criminal proceedings to a halt. Instead, and in light of this notification, the applicants sought on appeal to argue that their convictions should now be set aside. The logic of their argument would have meant that every conviction under the 1984 Act from the time of its implementation to the date of notification should also have been set aside. The Administrative Court was alive to the ramifications that could follow from such a finding. Instead, the court held that the failure to notify did not render the offence-creating provisions of the 1984 Act a nullity under EU law and so it was very much a matter for the national courts to determine what effect that failure would have at the national level. The court held that in the absence of any injustice to the applicants, and there was none, their convictions should remain.

2.90 Notwithstanding the outcome of the Administrative Court's decision in *Budimir*, the lesson here is that whilst domestic criminal proceedings may, at first blush, appear to have nothing

---

[42] [2010] EWHC 1604 (Admin), [2011] QB 744, [2011] Crim LR 142.

whatsoever to do with EU law, further analysis may just reveal an argument based on EU law that could win the day, as it ultimately did in the *Murphy* case and would have done in the *Budimir* case.

Decisions, Recommendations, and Opinions

Decisions differ from Directives in that they can be addressed to individuals as well as to **2.91** Member States. Decisions can have direct effect in much the same way as Directives and subject to the same limitations when they pertain to criminal law. Recommendations and Opinions, on the other hand, do not have direct effect and nothing further need be said about them here.

Pre-Lisbon

Under the third-pillar regime laid down by the Maastricht Treaty (see Chapter 1), the forms **2.92** of secondary legislation were Framework Decisions, Decisions, Common Positions, and Conventions.

Framework Decisions

Framework Decisions, like Directives, are binding as to the result to be achieved but each **2.93** Member State is left to determine itself the method and form of any implementing measure. The main difference between Framework Decisions and Directives is that whereas the latter have direct effect, the former do not. Thus, a failure on the part of a Member State to enact legislation to give effect to the objectives of a Framework Decision within the implementation period will not entitle individuals who might otherwise have benefitted from the rights the Framework Decision sought to give them to invoke the terms of the Framework Decision before the national courts (in contrast, see 2.72 for an analysis of legislation with direct effect).

Framework Decisions were clearly intended to introduce harmonising measures through- **2.94** out the EU and so to that extent they were the most significant third-pillar measure in the EU's arsenal. Much of what follows in this section of the chapter applies to all third-pillar measures but given the importance of Framework Decisions, it is appropriate to deal with this discussion here.

As mentioned earlier in this chapter, in respect of first-pillar acts the Commission has **2.95** the power to bring infringement proceedings before the CJEU against any Member State that fails to implement those acts where implementation is required. The power to bring infringement proceedings against Member States that fail to implement third-pillar acts was limited to situations where the Member States themselves had accepted the juris-diction of the CJEU to hear such complaints. This created the rather anomalous situa-tion whereby Member States in breach of their obligations to implement a Framework Decision could decline to afford jurisdiction to the Commission to prosecute them for their failure.

Now that the third pillar has been swept away, this anomaly will not arise for any legisla- **2.96** tive acts introduced by the EU in the wake of the Treaty of Lisbon, but what about those third-pillar acts adopted before that Treaty came into force? The Lisbon Treaty Protocol on Transitional Provisions provides that after 1 December 2014, which will be five years after the Treaty came into force, all third-pillar measures will be treated in the same way as first-pillar measures and so the actions of the Member States will be subject to the scrutiny of the CJEU whether they want it or not. During that period, however, the position will remain that the Commission will have no power to bring infringement proceedings against Member States in respect of the implementation of third-pillar measures unless the Member States consent.

2.97 One caveat ought to be noted here. Article 10 of the Transitional Protocol provides that where a third-pillar act is amended after the Treaty of Lisbon has come into force, 'The amendment...shall entail the applicability of the powers of the institutions...as set out in the Treaties with respect to the amended act for those Member States to which that amended act shall apply.' Therefore, if the EU institutions amend a Framework Decision, the legislation as amended will become, in effect, a first-pillar instrument entitling the Commission to take action against defaulting Member States without first needing their permission. It remains to be seen what an 'amendment' means within the context of Article 10. It has been suggested that the interpretation most consistent with the objectives of the EU should be taken, in which case any alteration to the legislation that is more than *de minimis* ought to suffice.[43]

2.98 Article 10(4) of Title VII of Protocol No. 36 to the TFEU provides that at least six months before the expiry of the five-year period the UK 'may notify to the Council that it does not accept' that the third-pillar instruments should be treated as first-pillar instruments from 1 December 2014. This is known as the UK's 'opt-out'. Once the UK has made this notification, all third-pillar instruments in the field of police cooperation and judicial cooperation adopted before the Treaty of Lisbon came into force 'shall cease to apply to it' as from 1 December 2014 but this will not be the case where there has been an amendment to any third-pillar measure of the type considered earlier. If the UK chooses to exercise its opt-out, there will be consequences. In particular, the Council, acting by QMV, may determine that the UK should 'bear the direct financial consequences, if any, necessarily and unavoidably incurred as a result of the cessation of its participation in those acts.' Of course, the UK can always change its mind and opt back in to individual third-pillar measures, but whether it is allowed to do so will depend on either the Commission or the Council.

2.99 If the UK decided to exercise the 'opt-out', the consequences, of course, would be more than just financial. Taking the EU's Framework Decision on the European Arrest Warrant as an example, if the UK opted out then from 1 December 2014 this Framework Decision would no longer apply to the UK. This would mean that requests for extradition between the UK and the other Member States would be governed not by the terms of the Framework Decision but by the regime as it existed before the Framework Decision was adopted at EU level. There are other examples although, where the Framework Decision established an entirely new regime, there would be no old regime to fall back on. That could leave the UK in a legal 'no man's land'. The UK Government will no doubt need to think long and hard in these circumstances before activating the opt-out.[44]

---

[43] S. Peers, 'Finally "Fit for Purpose"? The Treaty of Lisbon and the End of the Third Pillar Legal Order' (2008) YEL 47.

[44] For further analysis of the position see Professor John Spencer's article 'Opting Out of EU Criminal Justice', *Archbold Review*, 7 August 2012, as well as a paper issued by the Centre for European Legal Studies (CELS), and available on its website, entitled 'Opting Out of EU Criminal Law: What is Actually Involved?'. The section of the Introduction to this book headed 'The Opt-Out' considers the CELS paper and offers an up-to-date analysis of the Government's current thinking on this subject.

It may be assumed that as long as third-pillar acts continue to apply to the UK, the national **2.100** courts will be bound by the same duty of conforming interpretation discussed in relation to Directives. After all, *Pupino* itself was a case decided before the Treaty of Lisbon came into force. The UK courts have readily acknowledged this duty when considering the provisions of the Extradition Act 2003, as discussed later in this book (Chapter 4), and the extent to which they should be seen as viewed through the prism of the Framework Decision that led to its enactment. As far as Directives and Framework decisions are concerned, it seems to be the position that the duty of conforming interpretation applies equally to legislation designed to implement both. Or at least it did until the decision of the UK Supreme Court in *Assange v The Swedish Prosecution Authority*.[45]

In his dissenting judgment in *Assange*, Lord Mance drew a distinction between the duty of con- **2.101** forming interpretation and the presumption of the common law that the Framework Decision under consideration 'gave effect to the United Kingdom's international obligations fully and consistently'.[46] The presumption of consistency, being a canon of construction must, he argued, 'yield to contrary parliamentary intention'[47] and so if Parliament deliberately intended to legislate for a result that was at odds with the UK's international obligations, the courts would be bound to interpret the statute in light of that intention even if it meant the UK would thereby be in breach of those obligations. Lord Hoffmann in *R v Lyons*,[48] put it in this way:

> Parliament may pass a law which mirrors the terms of the treaty and in that sense incorporates the treaty into English law. But even then, the metaphor of incorporation may be misleading. It is not the treaty but the statute which forms part of English law. And English courts will not (unless the statute expressly so provides) be bound to give effect to interpretations of the treaty by an international court, even though the United Kingdom is bound by international law to do so. Of course, there is a strong presumption in favour of interpreting English law (whether common law or statute) in a way which does not place the United Kingdom in breach of an international obligation.

For Lord Mance, the duty of conforming interpretation and the ratio of the decision in **2.102** *Pupino* do not apply to Framework Decisions because they fall outside the provisions of the European Communities Act 1972, and so the courts of the UK are not bound by decisions of the CJEU as to their meaning or effect. He summarises his view as:

> The framework decision, the Court of Justice's decision in *Pupino* and the European legal principle of conforming interpretation are not therefore part of United Kingdom law under the 1972 Act. The only domestically relevant legal principle is the common law presumption that the Extradition Act 2003 was intended to be read consistently with the United Kingdom's international obligations under the framework decision on the European arrest warrant. But this presumption is subject always to the will of Parliament as expressed in the language of the Act read in the light of such other interpretative canons and material as may be relevant and admissible.[49]

On the facts of the *Assange* case, therefore, whilst the Framework Decision itself fell to be **2.103** interpreted by reference to *Pupino*, the Extradition Act 2003 did not. In Lord Mance's judgment, therefore, the only question that mattered was what Parliament intended the words 'judicial authority' in the Extradition Act 2003 to mean and the answer was clear: the warrant

---

[45] [2012] UKSC 22, [2012] 2 WLR 1275.
[46] At para. 201 and referring to *Bennion's Statutory Interpretation*, 5th edn (London: LexisNexis, 2008), sections 182 and 221.
[47] *Bennion's Statutory Interpretation*, 5th edn (London: LexisNexis, 2008), sections 182 and 221.
[48] [2002] UKHL 44, [2003] 1 AC 976, para. 27.
[49] [2012] UKSC 22, para. 217.

had to be issued by a court, judge, or magistrate[50] and this was so even though the CJEU would hold that the terms of the Framework Decision would suggest otherwise. This was another example, in Lord Mance's view, of the will of Parliament taking precedence over the UK's international obligations.

2.104 Lady Hale agreed with Lord Mance's conclusions about the inapplicability of the duty of conforming interpretation in cases where a statute enacting a Framework Decision falls to be interpreted. Lord Phillips, with whom Lords Walker, Brown, Kerr, and Dyson agreed, appears to have agreed with Lord Mance's analysis regarding the inapplicability of the duty of conforming interpretation but ultimately concluded that the UK courts should, in any event, seek to interpret the Extradition Act 2003 in conformity with the Framework Decision. Lord Phillips said:

> I have read with admiration Lord Mance's analysis of the effect of the decision in *Pupino* and I accept, for the reasons he gives, that it does not bind this court to interpret Part 1 of the 2003 Act, in so far as this is possible, in a manner that accords with the Framework Decision. I consider, none the less, that it is plain that the Court should do so. This is not merely because of the presumption that our domestic law will accord with our international obligations. As Lord Mance himself acknowledges at para 201 of his judgment Part 1 of the 2003 Act was enacted in order to give effect to the Framework Decision. The immediate objective of that Decision is to create a single uniform system for the surrender of those accused or convicted of the more serious criminal offences. That objective will only be achieved if each of the Member States gives the same meaning to 'judicial authority'. If different Member States give different meaning to those two words, that uniformity will be destroyed. In these circumstances it is hard to conceive that Parliament, in breach of the international obligations of this country, set out to pass legislation that was at odds with the Framework Decision. It is even more difficult to conceive that Parliament took such a course without making it plain that it was doing so. For this reason it is logical to approach the interpretation of the words 'judicial authority' on the presumption that Parliament intended that they should bear the same meaning in Part 1 of the 2003 Act as they do in the Framework Decision.[51]

2.105 Lord Brown was similarly minded and observed:

> even were the *Pupino* imperative not in play (which now appears may well be the correct view), the general presumption that the United Kingdom legislates in compliance with its international obligations would produce the same result.[52]

2.106 In a similar tone, Lord Kerr said:

> It had been assumed that the decision of the Court of Justice of the European Union in Criminal proceedings against *Pupino* (Case C-103/03) [2006] QB 83 would require national courts, in applying national law which purported to give effect to the Framework Decision, to do so in a manner that will 'attain the result which it pursues' (para. 43). Lord Mance has now authoritatively demonstrated that this is not the case. But of the proposition that the 2003 Act was enacted in order to give effect to the Framework Decision there can be no doubt. The domestic law presumption that Parliament did not intend to legislate contrary to the United Kingdom's international obligations under the Framework Decision may not be as strong in terms of injunctive force as the *Pupino* prescription but it is nevertheless a factor of considerable potency in determining the proper interpretation to be given to the 2003 Act.[53]

---

[50] [2012] UKSC 22, para. 266.
[51] [2012] UKSC 22, para. 10.
[52] [2012] UKSC 22, para. 98.
[53] [2012] UKSC 22, para. 112.

The dissenting minority (Lord Mance and Lady Hale) would have allowed the appeal on the basis that although the result the Framework Decision was designed to achieve was the recognition in domestic law that public prosecutors could issue EAWs, the use of 'judicial authority' in the Extradition Act 2003 was clearly intended by Parliament to go against that result by providing that *only* courts and their officers can issue EAWs. The majority seem, on the face of it, to have accepted Lord Mance's conclusion that the duty of conforming interpretation does not arise where the UK courts are called upon to construe an Act of Parliament that implements a Framework Decision but even applying the common law canon of construction identified by Lord Mance, the outcome on the facts of the *Assange* case is the same as if the duty did apply, namely that the Extradition Act 2003 should be interpreted in such a way as to ensure compatibility with the aims of the Framework Decision. Hence, the majority view that 'judicial authority' within the Extradition Act 2003 includes a Public Prosecutor. **2.107**

The effect of the decision of the Supreme Court in *Assange*, therefore, is difficult to discern. It may be simply a matter of form over substance whether a domestic court seeking to interpret a statute that implements a Framework Decision looks to the duty of conforming interpretation and the decision in *Pupino*, on the one hand, or the rule of statutory interpretation expounded by Lord Mance, on the other, especially if the result of undertaking either exercise will lead to the conclusion that the statute has to be interpreted in such a way as to give effect to the aims of the EU instrument.[54] **2.108**

Either way, if the UK decides not to 'opt out' of the transitional arrangements discussed earlier then from 1 December 2014 the duty of conforming interpretation will undoubtedly apply because Framework Decisions will be treated like other first-pillar instruments (including Directives). **2.109**

Decisions

Where the EU wanted to introduce a legislative measure that did *not* envisage the approximation of the laws of the Member States, then a Decision would be preferred to a Framework Decision. One example is the Decision of 6 December 2001 that extended the mandate of Europol to cover some serious forms of international crime. Decisions are binding on the Member States but they do not have direct effect. **2.110**

Conventions

Whereas the Treaty of Amsterdam in 1997 first introduced the Framework Decision and the Decision as forms of EU secondary legislation, the Convention was created by the Treaty of Maastricht some five years earlier. Conventions only enter into force when every Member State has ratified them. This can take a very long time, so long in fact that some Conventions that were introduced in the 1980s and 1990s have not been ratified to this day. **2.111**

Common Positions

Common Positions were really just expressions of the EU's approach to matters of pan-European concern. One example is Common Position 97/661 of 6 October 2007 on negotiations in the Council of Europe and the OECD in relation to corruption. Common Positions were therefore not legislation as such. **2.112**

---

[54] In the first case to refer to the decision of the UK Supreme Court in *Assange*, the Administrative Court in *Stopyra v Poland* [2012] EWHC 1787 (Admin) held, at para. 31, that following *Assange*, 'it is clear that a UK court should interpret the [Extradition Act] 2003 ... so far as possible consistently with the Framework Decision.'

Part II

PRE-TRIAL

3

EVIDENCE ACQUISITION

A. Overview

Article 67(3) TFEU states that   **3.01**

> The Union shall endeavour to ensure a high level of security through measures for coordina-
> tion and cooperation between police and judicial authorities and other competent authorities,
> as well as through the mutual recognition of judgments in criminal matters and, if necessary,
> through the approximation of criminal laws.

The Member States of the European Union have been energetic in seeking to cooperate and   **3.02**
coordinate in this field:

> Co-operation in criminal matters is an area in which the European Union has been an
> extremely active legislator. Since the Treaty on European Union paved the way for criminal

legislation, hundreds of Conventions, Joint Actions, Common Positions, Recommendations, Resolutions, Decisions and Framework Decisions have been adopted.[1]

3.03 Such diligence has not, however, resulted in a vast array of practical means by which Member States can make use of simple procedures to obtain evidence for use in criminal proceedings. There has, nonetheless, been some progress and this chapter examines the measures which are available to the appropriate authorities in EU Member States to assist them in gathering evidence in criminal investigations. Section B[2] deals with the development from cooperation by means of mutual legal assistance (MLA) into that of mutual recognition. Sections F and G set out the arrangements for obtaining evidence in two discrete areas of criminal proceedings:

- criminal convictions; and
- DNA and fingerprint evidence.

3.04 Progress in adopting fully integrated measures in EU law began slowly. There has been very limited 'approximation of criminal laws'[3] and even the 'mutual recognition of judgments in criminal matters' did not become a reality until 1998. The result has been described by one academic as 'a legal hotchpotch, difficult for practitioners to grasp and undoubtedly resulting in an under-use of the instruments adopted by the Council.'[4] Pace has increased over the past 15 years, however, and the instruments described in this chapter are a result of the developments that have taken place. A brief summary of the key developments follows.[5]

3.05 The Treaty of Amsterdam of 1997 made cooperation in criminal matters, and the approximation of the Member States' criminal laws, the main issues within the so-called 'third pillar' of the TEU (the Maastricht Treaty). It set for the first time an objective of creating a European Criminal Justice Area. This justice area has been described as one where courts sitting in different States can implement the necessary judicial decisions, without borders presenting any obstacles and where 'judicial decisions circulate unhindered, as do persons, capital and goods'.[6]

3.06 In 1998, the UK assumed the Presidency of the EU. It was apparent that there were barriers to cooperation between Member States in the field of criminal law. In its role as President, the UK proposed that mutual recognition principles should be applied so that Member States would accept the validity of decisions from the courts of other Members without the need for procedural uniformity. The Presidency concluded in Cardiff on 15 and 16 June 1998. One of its decisions was that 'The Council . . . recognises the need to enhance the ability of national systems to work closely together and asks the Council to identify the scope for greater mutual recognition of decisions of each other's courts.'[7] This provided the impetus for the developments which followed.

---

[1] Andre Klip, *European Criminal Law: An Integrative Approach*, 2nd edn (Antwerp: Intersentia, 2012), 335–6.

[2] At para. 3.10.

[3] e.g. Council Directive 91/308/EEC prohibits money laundering across all EU Member States.

[4] Nadja Long, 'Development of an EU Criminal Justice Area: Study', at <http://www.europarl.europa.eu/studies>.

[5] The evolution of the EU through the various treaties on which it is based is discussed in more detail in Chapter 1.

[6] Nadja Long, 'Development of an EU Criminal Justice Area: Study', at <http://www.europarl.europa.eu/studies>.

[7] Doc. SN 150/1/98 REV 1, para. 39, at <http://www.consilium.europa.eu/uedocs/cms_data/docs/pressdata/en/ec/54315.pdf>.

On 15 and 16 October 1999, the European Council met in Tampere, Finland. The purpose **3.07** of the meeting was to promote the creation of an area of freedom, security, and justice in the EU. The meeting concluded with an agreement to further 'a genuine European judicial space with measures such as better access to justice in Europe and mutual recognition of judicial decisions and an EU-wide fight against crime.'[8]

In 2000, the EU Mutual Legal Assistance Convention (MLA Convention) became the **3.08** instrument regulating cross-border criminal investigations. It was implemented into domestic law in the UK by the Crime (International Co-operation) Act 2003, which establishes a framework for dealing with outgoing and incoming requests from other Member States, and indeed worldwide. The regime created by the MLA Convention was relaxed. As we shall see later, it has become permissive rather than obligatory and relies upon voluntary engagement and willing cooperation by Member States.

In 2002, a Framework Directive[9] created the European Arrest Warrant (EAW) and ushered **3.09** in the first mechanism representing a shift from mutual legal assistance to mutual recognition.[10] In 2008, a further Framework Decision[11] set up, with effect from January 2011, the European Evidence Warrant (EEW), which in effect provided for the automatic recognition of Member States' search warrants in other States. To confirm the arrival of this new form of cooperation, mutual recognition was given the force of Treaty law by the Treaty of Lisbon of 2010, in which Articles 67(3) and 82(1) explicitly state that the principle of mutual recognition shall be the basis of EU cooperation in criminal matters.

In fact, EEWs are yet to come into use, and may never now do so. In April 2010, seven **3.10** Member States launched a proposal for its replacement with the European Investigation Order (EIO). Both the EEW and EIO are addressed in this chapter (in Sections C and D respectively) so that the practitioner is equipped for all eventualities and if, as looks likely, the EIO does replace the EEW, its evolution and the flaws in the EEW which the EIO seeks to rectify, may be appreciated.

B. Mutual Legal Assistance

Introduction

The term 'mutual legal assistance' refers to formal cooperation between sovereign States in **3.11** criminal investigations and proceedings. Most typically, this constitutes requests between countries made by Letters of Request (sometimes known as Letters Rogatory), for the authorities in one country to gather and provide evidence to the authorities in another. It may be distinguished from informal or administrative assistance, which involves the sharing of information for intelligence and investigative purposes.

As noted earlier, the principal instrument regulating such cooperation within the EU is the **3.12** MLA Convention of 2000. However, this was introduced against the background of an existing framework for cooperation within the Council of Europe. The Council of Europe's

---

[8] Tampere European Council, 15–16.10.99, Conclusions of the Presidency.
[9] Council Framework Decision 2002/584/JHA of 13 June 2002 [2002] OJ L 190/1.
[10] EAW is addressed in detail in Chapter 4.
[11] Council Framework Decision 2008/978/JHA of 18 December 2008 [2008] OJ L 350/72.

European Convention on Mutual Assistance in Criminal Matters 1959[12] was the first modern multilateral agreement in this field. All signatories to the 2000 Convention have also signed the 1959 Convention, and the latter remains in force, supplemented by Protocols in 1978 and 2001, as an important backdrop to the EU measures.

3.13 As a result of the early introduction and success of the 1959 Convention and the introduction of cooperation in criminal matters by the TEU, the EU has comparatively recently overtaken the Council of Europe as the primary driver of cooperation amongst its Members.

3.14 The EU Mutual Assistance Convention of 2000 acknowledges and expressly extends the 1959 Convention, rather than purporting to rival or replace it. In turn, the Council of Europe has sought to reflect developments within the EU: when the EU Council was drawing up the EU Convention, the Council of Europe was simultaneously preparing the second Protocol to its own convention.[13] Deliberate steps were taken to ensure that they closely reflected one another. In some cases, the provisions are identical. In other cases, the second Protocol follows the provisions found in the Schengen Convention. This is, therefore, an instance in which the EU has sought to converge with and enhance the work of the Council of Europe.

3.15 Given that it was introduced against the background of an existing system, the 2000 Convention does not seek to establish a comprehensive regime. Rather, it was intended to develop and modernise the existing provisions of the 1959 Convention; both by making them quicker and more flexible, and by extending the range of circumstances in which assistance could be granted. However, many forms of assistance (including straightforward requests for the gathering and sharing of evidence) are adequately covered in the 1959 provisions and are therefore not dealt with at all in the EU instruments. One example of this is where a request is made between countries in which both the 1959 and 2000 Conventions have been ratified. In such a case, both are cited in the request regardless of the measure sought, since the 2000 Convention also contains provisions of general application no matter what the type of assistance sought.

3.16 The 2000 Convention was signed by Member States on 29 May 2000 in Strasbourg. All signatories to the 2000 Convention also signed the 1959 Convention. Both Conventions have been enhanced by subsequent Protocols which supplement and amend them.[14] Together they provide an important backdrop to EU mutual agreement measures. When dealing with any particular request, the versions of the Conventions used by the Member States are the most recent ones ratified by both States.

3.17 Although the 2000 Convention was established by Council act and is only open to signature by EU Member States, it is a free-standing legal instrument and does not depend for its force on the wider legal framework of the EU. In this sense, it operates on the same basis as any other regional agreement for MLA. Participating countries are treated as trusted but independent and sovereign nations bound by their obligations under the Convention. There is no attempt at harmonisation of applicable laws and no attempt to achieve mutual recognition of domestic orders. Even in the field of restraint and confiscation, where the

---

[12] ETS No. 030: hereafter the 1959 Convention.
[13] 2001 Protocols to the 1959 Convention.
[14] The 1959 Convention by Protocols in 1978 and 2001, and the 2000 Convention by a Protocol in 2001.

international trend is for legislation recognising and executing the orders of foreign courts, no such attempt has been made.

It follows that the 2000 Convention depends entirely upon implementation by Member States for its effect, principally in the form of legislation. In fact, many of the provisions of the 2000 Convention are permissive rather than obligatory in any event, providing a framework for willing cooperation and encouraging bilateral or ad hoc agreements. There is no obligation under the 2000 Convention to provide any particular assistance sought. The duty to assist is therefore to be read across from the 1959 Convention, which the 2000 Convention inherits by implication: **3.18**

> The Parties undertake promptly to afford each other, in accordance with the provisions of this Convention, the widest measure of mutual assistance in proceedings in respect of offences the punishment of which, at the time of the request for assistance, falls within the jurisdiction of the judicial authorities of the requesting Party.[15]

Moreover, even when read together with the 1959 Convention and its Protocols, the 2000 Convention does not pretend to bring uniformity to procedures between its parties. It seeks to recognise and facilitate the application of other multilateral (but not pan-EU) agreements, including the Schengen Agreement and Benelux Treaty. It also repeatedly reinforces its support for bilateral agreements and non-treaty-based arrangements. Under Article 1(2), the Convention does not affect the application of 'more favourable' provisions in other agreements. This is intended to ensure that the agreement which facilitates the closest degree of cooperation may be relied on. However, the 2000 Convention is unlikely to displace the provisions of any external agreement providing stronger safeguards for individuals affected by a request. **3.19**

Direct transmission

One respect in which the 2000 Convention does reflect the trust between EU Member States is in its approach to the transmission of requests between authorities. Under most MLA treaties,[16] assistance is afforded between Central Authorities. The role of a Central Authority varies; in some cases it may be limited to acting as a clearing house for Letters of Request; in others it takes a deeper role in the making or drafting of outgoing requests for assistance and executing the requests it receives. The purpose of a Central Authority is ultimately diplomatic, and where a request is received for evidence to be transferred between countries pursuant to a typical MLA treaty, the evidence acquired would typically be returned in a diplomatic bag. **3.20**

Under the 2000 Convention, the formality of the system of Central Authorities is to some extent circumvented. Article 6(1) provides that requests for mutual assistance are to be made directly between 'judicial authorities with territorial competence for initiating and executing them', and should be responded to through the same channels. In addition, under Article **3.21**

---

[15] 2000 Convention, Art. 1(1), as amended by the Second Additional Protocol of 2001, which added the word 'promptly'. Not all EU Member States have signed the Second Additional Protocol.

[16] Though not the 1959 Convention, which provided by default for communication between Ministries of Justice, albeit at the instance of judicial authorities, and only expressly acknowledged the concept of a Central Authority in its Second Additional Protocol of 2001. In practice, States have always been able to designate an appropriate recipient for requests to replace the Ministry of Justice, and most European Central Authorities form part of the Ministry of Justice of the relevant country in any event.

6(5), there is provision for direct communication from a judicial or Central Authority of one State to a police or customs authority in another. This applies to MLA in respect of joint investigations, covert investigations, and controlled deliveries, and is intended to reduce formality in those cases in which there is likely to be a high level of communication and cooperation between those in each jurisdiction actually responsible for executing the request.

3.22 The 2000 Convention also provides, under Article 3(1), for assistance in relation to certain proceedings brought by administrative authorities which may give rise to proceedings before criminal courts. This enables assistance to be provided, for example, in respect of an *Ordnungswidrigkeit* (a fine which is imposed by an administrative authority but which may give rise to an appeal to the criminal courts) under German law. Under the 1959 Convention, assistance would only be available once a case concerning an *Ordnungswidrigkeit* had reached the appeal stage.

3.23 A 'judicial authority' is not defined under the 2000 Convention, but its use reflects the model of cooperation between judicial authorities in extradition proceedings. The idea that requests for the exchange of evidence should be made between courts rather than prosecuting authorities seems an odd one from the perspective of a common law system. In most common law jurisdictions, responsibility for receiving and arranging the execution of requests lies with the office of the Attorney General or the national prosecutions body. The 'judicial authority' approach arises from the inquisitorial system in which far greater control over the investigation of cases is given to the courts. It therefore makes sense for judges or examining magistrates to direct requests for assistance from outside their jurisdiction just as they direct investigative measures within their own jurisdictions. European countries differ as to whether they regard prosecutors as a judicial or administrative authority.

3.24 The UK has made a number of declarations in accordance with Article 24 of the 1959 Convention as to the entities which it considers to be judicial authorities for the purpose of executing outgoing requests. These include not only the magistrates' courts, the Crown Court, and the High Court but also a number of prosecuting authorities, including the Director of Public Prosecutions, the Attorney General, and several government departments. These are all considered judicial authorities under the 2000 Convention, and hence able to make requests directly.

3.25 The position differs in relation to incoming requests. The UK was granted the right (together with Ireland, the EU's other common law jurisdiction) to declare under Article 6(3) of the 2000 Convention that any requests and communications sent to it must be sent via its Central Authorities. The reason for this being that it does not consider its prosecution authorities to be 'geared' to receiving requests directly from overseas prosecutors.[17] The position in the UK is further complicated by the fact that it has separate Central Authorities for each of its jurisdictions,[18] although requests are also accepted directly in appropriate cases by HM Revenue and Customs.

---

[17] Explanatory Memorandum for the Convention on Mutual Assistance in Criminal Matters between the Member States of the European Union (Cm 5229).

[18] Within the Home Office for England and Wales, the Crown Office for Scotland, and the Northern Ireland Office for Northern Ireland. Independent Central Authorities also exist for Gibraltar, Guernsey, Jersey, and the Isle of Man.

Procedural requirements

Another key difference between the Conventions is the presumption introduced by Article **3.26** 4 of the 2000 Convention that assistance should be provided in accordance with the formalities and procedures indicated by the requesting country, save to the extent that these were contrary to the fundamental principles of law of the requested country. Under the 1959 Convention, the presumption had been that the law of the requested Member State would prevail. Although this did not necessarily cause problems when evidence was shared between the civil law systems of Western Europe, where there are comparatively few hurdles to the admissibility of evidence, it was sometimes difficult for the UK to secure admissible evidence.

Nevertheless, the principle remains that it is for the country receiving the request to arrange **3.27** for its execution and to make any necessary decisions as to how best to do so. The presence of officials from the requesting State to assist with the process is, however, encouraged. Although there have since been moves towards mutual recognition of, for example, search orders,[19] under the Convention all such authorities are to be obtained by the requested State.

Refusal of requests

The 1959 Convention contains comparatively limited grounds on which countries may **3.28** refuse to assist.[20] These are set out in Article 2:

(a) if the request concerns an offence which the requested Party considers a political offence, an offence connected with a political offence, or a fiscal offence;
(b) if the requested Party considers that execution of the request is likely to prejudice the sovereignty, security, public order or other essential interests of its country.

The text of Article 2 of the Convention leaves these grounds for refusal to the discretion of **3.29** Member States. It would not, for example, be a breach of international law for a country to provide assistance in relation to a political offence. Moreover, in some cases it may actually be in the interests of the accused that the assistance is provided.

The provision on political offences considered under Article 2 of the 1959 Convention is **3.30** effectively nullified by the 2001 Protocol to the 2000 Convention, which provides that for the purposes of MLA between Member States, *no* offence may be regarded as a political offence, an offence connected with a political offence, or an offence inspired by political motives.

The provision on fiscal offences is also reversed in respect of those countries that have signed **3.31** the 1978 Protocol to the 1959 Convention, Article 1 of which provides that countries shall not refuse assistance 'solely on the ground that the request concerns an offence which the requested Party considers a fiscal offence'. This provision is replicated in Article 8 of the 2001

---

[19] See Section D: European Evidence Warrants.
[20] Compare e.g. Art. 4 of the UN Model Treaty on Mutual Assistance in Criminal Matters, adopted by UN General Assembly Resolution 45/117, which is the template for many bilateral treaties. Consideration was given to including similar provisions to Art. 4, such as refusal if a prosecution is for the purpose of punishing a person for his race, religion, nationality, or political opinions. However, it was decided that this was unnecessary given the shared values and traditions of the European countries.

Protocol to the 2000 Convention, and, in contrast to the 1978 Protocol, no reservations are permitted.[21]

Dual criminality

3.32 There is an ongoing international debate about the need for a requirement of dual criminality (ie the requirement that the conduct under investigation be criminal in the requested State as well as in the requesting State) in the context of MLA. Some countries feel that issues of principle arise, both in the form of disagreements with other countries in some instances as to the conduct which should be criminal and in the form of a distaste for giving force to foreign law within their own borders. However, in other cases it may be a frustrating technicality which delays or thwarts compliance with requests that both States are keen to see executed. Moreover, it is arguable that the request for MLA is the wrong stage in the criminal process at which to impose safeguards for the suspected person, particularly where the assistance sought may be provided without coercive measures.

3.33 Within Europe, moreover, there is a closer approximation of fundamental values which makes the abolition of dual criminality more attractive. As a result, even as originally drafted in 1959, the Council of Europe Convention provided for dual criminality to be a ground for refusal of a request only in the case of search and seizure. This was on the basis that this was a coercive measure for which provision was made, and that more stringent safeguards were appropriate. Where dual criminality was applied by one State, other States were permitted to declare that they would also apply it reciprocally.

3.34 The EU has grappled with the issue of dual criminality but failed, in the event, to make significant progress. A provision in the 2001 Protocol to the 2000 Convention providing for the abolition of the dual criminality requirement was dropped. Instead, a declaration was entered into the minutes of the Council at the adoption of the Protocol, recording that the debate had not allowed for the establishment of a definitive position on that question. In the meantime, the Protocol extended the dual criminality requirement to cover the newly introduced provisions dealing with assistance relating to bank accounts, although this measure was also covered by a separate protection in the form of a minimum penalty threshold or (if this was not met) a list of offence categories. The provisions of the 2000 Convention relating to controlled deliveries ('shall take place in accordance with the procedures of the requested Member State') have also been interpreted as entitling the requested State to insist on dual criminality.

3.35 The 2001 Protocol to the 2000 Convention does attempt to deal with the biggest problem with dual criminality, which is that it is sometimes assumed that parity is required between the elements of criminal offences on both sides. This approach tends to make cooperation impossible even where the conduct under investigation would be criminal in both countries. Article 8 provides that:

> If a Member State has made the execution of a request for search and seizure dependent on the condition that the offence giving rise to the request is also punishable under its law, this condition shall be fulfilled, with regard to offences referred to in paragraph 1, if the offence corresponds to an offence of the same nature under its law.

---

[21] Article 11.

Spontaneous exchange of information

The EU has introduced provisions encouraging countries to pass information in the absence   **3.36**
of a specific request. This first appeared in the Schengen Implementation Convention (Art.
46) and is now replicated in the 2000 Convention (Art. 7). The intention is that where the
competent authorities of one Member State become aware of an offence falling within the
jurisdiction of another, or of evidence relating to such an offence, it should pass any relevant
information unprompted. There is no obligation to do so, but the attempt to encourage this
reflects the closer cooperation considered appropriate in the area of freedom, security, and
justice.

Confidentiality

It is generally appropriate to keep the existence of a request for assistance confidential.   **3.37**
Requesting States may require this under Article 25 of the 2001 Protocol to the 1959
Convention, although if agreement cannot be reached on confidentiality the request may
be refused.

Under Article 18 of the 2000 Convention, Member States are specifically required to keep   **3.38**
confidential any information provided in response to a request for assistance with interception of telecommunications. Under Article 4 of the 2001 Protocol, Member States are also
required to ensure that banks do not disclose the fact that information has been transmitted
or that an investigation is being carried out following a request for banking information.

There is no statutory bar to the disclosure of the existence of a request in the UK, although   **3.39**
the UK Central Authority will usually keep requests confidential. The courts have held that
there are circumstances in which fairness requires that the gist of the Letter of Request is provided or an interested person is invited to make representations.[22] A suspect will, of course,
become aware of a request upon execution in certain types of case (e.g. where searches are
conducted). Irrespective of how a person who is the subject of a request becomes aware of it,
if he or she raises any legal objection the material should not be forwarded until the question
has been resolved.

In addition to the confidentiality requirements, it was also thought necessary in drafting the   **3.40**
2000 Convention to make specific provisions in relation to data protection given the inclusion in the Convention of certain methods of investigation which are not exclusively judicial. These are found in Article 23. They limit the use to which personal data (but not other
information) communicated under the Convention can be put. Although they provide some
protection to data subjects, it is in fact less than arises under the prohibition on collateral use
under some bilateral treaties.

Implementation

The 2000 Convention, together with the UK's other MLA treaties and obligations, are given   **3.41**
effect in domestic law by the Crime (International Cooperation) Act 2003 (CICA). CICA
largely replaced the UK's prior legislation in relation to MLA, and in addition to the 2000
Convention and its 2001 Protocol, implements the 2003 Framework Decision on the

---

[22] *R (Evans) v Director of the Serious Fraud Office* [2003] 1 WLR 299; *R (Abacha) v Secretary of State for the Home Department* [2001] EWHC 787 (Admin).

execution in the EU of orders freezing property or evidence adopted by the Council of the EU on 22 July 2003.[23]

3.42 The structure of the Act is to make general provision for both incoming and outgoing requests, but also to restrict some matters to 'participating countries'. Participating countries are those with whom particular provisions apply under treaties, particularly the 2000 Convention and 2001 Protocol, which require legislative effect. 'Participating countries' have always included all EU Member States, and are gradually being increased as other countries enter into MLA treaties with the UK or EU.

3.43 The principal legislative provision governing a request for evidence to be provided to the UK by another State (whether under the 2000 Convention or any other international instrument) is section 7 of CICA. Requests may only be made directly by certain named prosecuting authorities.[24] Other prosecuting authorities and defendants must apply to a court to request evidence for their use in the proceedings on their behalf. In all cases, it is an essential precondition that the authority making the request (whether the court or a prosecuting authority directly) is satisfied of two matters:

(a) that an offence has been committed or that there are reasonable grounds for suspecting that an offence has been committed; and

(b) that proceedings in respect of the offence have been instituted (if the request is made directly by a prosecuting authority, then by that authority) or that the offence is being investigated.

Section 7(3)(c) makes clear that a person suspected of an offence may only apply to a court to request assistance if proceedings have been instituted against him.

3.44 Section 9 of CICA provides that evidence received under a request for assistance may not, once provided, be used for 'any purpose other than that specified in the request' without the consent of the overseas authority;[25] however, the Court of Appeal held in *BOC Ltd v Barlow* that an earlier version of this provision restricted use only in criminal proceedings.[26]

3.45 The principal provisions governing requests for assistance by other States (including EU Member States) in obtaining evidence from within the UK are found in Part 1 Chapter 2 of CICA. The bodies which may request assistance are set out in section 13. They include courts and prosecuting authorities in any country outside the UK, any other authority in such a country which appears to the relevant territorial authority to have the function of making requests for assistance, and appropriate international bodies.

3.46 Upon receipt of a request, the first question is whether the statutory conditions for the grant of assistance are met. These vary depending on the nature of the request. In the case of a request for assistance in obtaining evidence to be received by a court in the UK, for example,

---

[23] See Section C: Freezing Orders.

[24] Set out in the Crime (International Cooperation) Act 2003 (Designation of Prosecuting Authorities) Order 2004 (SI 2004/1034), as amended. They include the principal prosecution authorities in each jurisdiction (including the Serious Fraud Office), the Attorneys General, and various government departments.

[25] With consent, however, there is no limitation on use: see e.g. *Magnetic Services Limited v HMRC* [2009] UKFTT 391 (TCC).

[26] [2002] QB 537. The court was considering s. 3 of the Criminal Justice (International Cooperation) Act 1990, now replaced by s. 9 of CICA.

the conditions are found in sections 13 and 14 of CICA. In accordance with these sections the request must be made by a competent body in connection with certain types of proceedings set out in section 14(1). Furthermore, in most cases the authority considering the request must be satisfied that an offence under the law of the requested State has been committed or there are reasonable grounds for suspecting that it has, and that an investigation or proceedings are being conducted in the requesting State (s. 14(2)). If the relevant statutory conditions are not met, the request must be returned. The second question is whether to comply with the request for assistance. This is at the discretion of the territorial authority, although it must take into account any Treaty ground for refusal (which will include the provisions of Arts 2 and 5 of the 1959 Convention). There is an obligation to act lawfully, rationally, and in a procedurally fair way when considering the discretion to assist. A person affected by the grant of assistance may challenge it by way of judicial review.

Particular forms of assistance

Most frequently, a request will simply be for evidence to be obtained in the requested State for **3.47** the purpose of criminal proceedings in the requesting State. Providing for this was the core purpose of the 1959 Convention. It also covers matters such as the voluntary transfer of witnesses (including those in custody), search and seizure, and judicial records. It is beyond the scope of this work to examine the provisions of the 1959 Convention in detail, save where they interrelate with the 2000 Convention. However, there are a number of respects in which the 2000 Convention and the 2001 Protocol have enhanced and added to these basic provisions.

Sending and service of procedural documents

Article 5 of the 2000 Convention makes provision for service of procedural documents on **3.48** individuals within other Member States by direct postal transmission. This is the default approach to service within Europe. The exceptions set out in the Convention cover a range of situations in which service by post may be ineffective either practically in the requested State or legally in the requesting State. In those circumstances only, they may be sent via the competent authorities of the requested Member State (but there is no reference to any involvement by judicial or Central Authorities).

This extends the 1959 Convention, which made provision in Article 7 for the service of writs **3.49** and records of judicial verdicts. This process is to be carried out by the requested State, and proof of service returned to the requesting State if so required. It is plain that the summoning of witnesses, including expert witnesses, is subsumed within the term 'service of writs', and that this provision may therefore be used to attempt such a measure. However, according to long-standing international custom, witnesses are completely free *not* to go to a country making a request unless they choose to do so. In accordance with this rule, Article 8 provides that there shall be no penalty, punishment, or restraint as against such witnesses unless they are re-served after voluntarily entering the requesting country, regardless of anything which may be written in a summons.

Part 1, Chapter 1 of CICA regulates those cases where direct service is not used. Section 1 of **3.50** CICA provides for the Secretary of State to serve process on behalf of a foreign government, so that it can assist in those rare cases in which direct postal transmission is not appropriate. However, unless another form of service, such as personal service, is specifically requested, the UK will give effect to a request for service on behalf of a foreign government by sending it via recorded delivery post.

3.51   A person upon whom foreign process or other documents are served is not put under any obligation under the law of the UK as a result, regardless of the method of service and the involvement of the authorities of the UK in effecting transmission. Section 2(3) of CICA provides that any foreign process served by the UK which requires a person to appear as a party or attend as a witness in a foreign court must contain a notice to the effect that:

(a)   service of the document does not impose any obligation to comply under the law of the relevant part of the UK;

(b)   the recipient may wish to seek advice as to the possible consequences of failing to comply under the law of the foreign country; and

(c)   under that law he may not be entitled to the same rights and privileges as he would have in similar circumstances in the relevant part of the UK.

3.52   Sections 3–6[27] of CICA provide that a court may serve process in criminal proceedings in the UK on a person outside the UK, either by direct post or by Letter of Request. The statute makes it clear that there is no obligation upon the overseas recipient to comply and no sanction (e.g. the risk of proceedings for contempt of court) for failing to do so. The process may, however, subsequently be re-served on the person in question in the UK in the event of his return and the usual consequences for non-compliance will then follow.

Transfer of persons in custody

3.53   Article 11 of the 1959 Convention makes provision for the attendance of persons in custody to appear as witnesses in the requesting State, usually with their consent. This is to be distinguished from prisoner transfer agreements, where the purpose of the transfer is to enable the prisoner to serve his sentence in his own country, and from extradition. Article 9 of the 2000 Convention supplements this by providing for a separate but related category of assistance: transfer of serving prisoners to assist in investigations. The provisions ensure that the period while the prisoner is abroad is counted towards his sentence, and the transfer requires the agreement of the competent authorities. It also permits countries to make a declaration that they will only effect voluntary transfers.

3.54   These provisions are given effect by sections 47 and 48 of CICA where the purpose of the transfer is to assist in an investigation within the EU. For the personal appearance of witnesses to give evidence, the provisions of the Criminal Justice (International Cooperation) Act 1990 remain in force. Transfer of prisoners under both Acts is conditional on the prisoner's consent, and the UK has therefore made the required declaration under the 2000 Convention.

Hearing of persons in custody

3.55   One of the more pioneering aspects of the 2000 Convention was provision for witness testimony to be given not in person but via live telephone or video link between Member States. The provisions also appear in nearly identical form in the 2001 Protocol to the 1959 Convention. The two conventions take nearly identical approaches:

(a)   requests should only be made where it is not desirable or possible for the witness to appear in the requesting State in person,[28] and the request should set out the reasons for this;[29]

---

[27]   Sections 3 and 4 applicable to England and Wales and Northern Ireland; ss. 5 and 6 applicable to Scotland.

[28]   2000 Convention, Art. 10.1; 2001 Protocol, Art. 9.1.

[29]   2000 Convention, Art. 10.3; 2001 Protocol, Art. 9.3.

(b) the witness is summoned to attend by the judicial authority of the requested State;[30]

(c) the hearing is conducted directly by the requesting State in accordance with its own procedures,[31] but a judicial authority of the requested State is present with the witness during the hearing and is responsible for ensuring the identification of the person to be heard and respect for the fundamental principles of law of the requested State;[32]

(d) the witness may claim any right not to testify which he or she would have in either State;[33]

(e) hearings involving a suspect or accused may only be carried out with his or her consent;[34]

(f) telephone hearings may only take place with the consent of the witness;[35]

(g) other measures for the protection of the witness may be agreed;[36] and

(h) the requested State must be in a position to bring proceedings for any refusal to testify or false testimony.[37]

3.56 In relation to outgoing requests, these provisions have been implemented in England and Wales by section 32 of the Criminal Justice Act 1988 for the purposes of trials on indictment, and in the Youth Court, appeals to the Criminal Division of the Court of Appeal and hearings of references, under section 9 of the Criminal Appeal Act 1995.[38] Section 32(3) has the effect of applying section 1 of the Perjury Act 1911 to the overseas witness. Procedural rules as to interpreters and record-keeping are found in the Criminal Procedure Rules, rule 32.6-32.8.

3.57 In relation to incoming requests, the relevant provisions are found in sections 30 and 31 of CICA. The Secretary of State will nominate a court in which the witness is to be heard,[39] and the law of perjury and contempt of court applies as though the evidence is given in proceedings in this country.[40] The court will intervene where it considers it necessary to safeguard the rights of the witness, who is not to be compelled to give any evidence which he could not be compelled to give in proceedings in the relevant part of the UK or which prejudices the security of the UK.[41]

Controlled deliveries

3.58 The Schengen Convention first introduced provisions for controlled deliveries in relation to drug trafficking. The 2000 Convention expands this to apply to an illicit consignment relating to any criminal offence. Unusually, despite the general approach of the Convention, controlled deliveries are to be carried out in accordance with the law and under the direction of the requested State.

---

[30] 2000 Convention, Art. 10.4, 2001 Protocol, Art. 9.4.
[31] 2000 Convention, Art. 10.5(c), 2001 Protocol, Art. 9.5(c).
[32] 2000 Convention, Art. 10.5(a), 2001 Protocol, Art. 9.5(a).
[33] 2000 Convention, Art. 10.5(e), 2001 Protocol, Art. 9.5(e).
[34] 2000 Convention, Art. 10.9; 2001 Protocol, Art. 9.8.
[35] 2000 Convention, Arts 11.2 and 11.6; 2001 Protocol, Arts 10.2 and 10.6.
[36] 2000 Convention, Art. 10.5(b); 2001 Protocol, Art. 9.5(b).
[37] 2000 Convention, Art. 10.8; 2001 Protocol, Art. 9.7.
[38] In Scotland, TV link evidence can be used in cases prosecuted on indictment: Criminal Procedure (Scotland) Act 1995.
[39] Crime (International Cooperation) Act 2003, s. 30(3).
[40] Crime (International Cooperation) Act 2003, s. 30(4).
[41] Crime (International Cooperation) Act 2003, Sch. 2, paras 5 and 9(1)–(3).

3.59   There is no specific legislation in the UK dealing with controlled deliveries across UK borders, although they can be arranged by liaison with the Serious Organised Crime Agency (SOCA) and/or HM Revenue and Customs.

Joint investigations

3.60   The provisions for joint investigations reflect the recognition in Article 30 TEU of the importance of cooperation between law enforcement agencies.[42] There is no need, in principle, for a basis in international law for such investigations, and officers from EU Member States did regularly work alongside one another before the provisions were introduced. However, the provisions provide a helpful framework within which joint teams can be established.

3.61   Joint teams are established with a leader from the country in which they operate, but with seconded members from one or more other countries; there is no limit to the number of countries that may be involved. They operate under the law of the host nation, and seconded officers may be delegated tasks under this law by agreement between the relevant competent authorities. Information may be shared and used with relative freedom for the purposes of the investigation.

3.62   Where such joint teams are established, it is appropriate that foreign officers should be treated as far as possible in the same way as domestic officers for the purposes of criminal liability, and Articles 15 and 16 of the 2000 Convention cover this. The UK has made detailed amendments to its legislation to extend appropriate provisions relating to the police to officers who are serving as part of an 'international joint investigation team'. For example, the offence of assaulting officers in the execution of their duty has been extended to cover foreign officers participating in a team in the UK[43] and the relevant bodies may be liable for the acts of such officers.[44] It is notable that what gives rise to these safeguards under the domestic legislation is simply the fact that the joint investigation is established under the auspices of the 2000 Convention under the leadership of a constable.

Covert investigations

3.63   While there are many forms of covert investigation, Article 14 of the 2000 Convention covers only the assumption of covert or false identities by officers. The provision is deliberately flexible, and even allows for a Member State to make a request for a foreign undercover officer to be sent into its territory as well as for permission to deploy its own. The principal safeguards are the requirement (again, by way of exception to Art. 4) that the operation be carried out under the law of the requested State and the requirement that both States agree.

Telephone intercept

3.64   Article 18 of the 2000 Convention covers the provision of telephone intercept material.

3.65   With what may at first appear to be over-complication, the Convention provides for interception to take place either for immediate transmission or for recording and subsequent transmission, and for the interception to take place when the subject of the interception:

> (a) is in the requesting Member State and technical assistance is needed from the requested Member State to carry out the interception;

---

[42]   See also Eurojust in Chapter 2.
[43]   Police Act 1996, s. 89.
[44]   Police Act 1996, s. 88; Serious Organised Crime and Police Act 2005, ss. 28–30.

(b) is in the requested Member State, and his telecommunications can be intercepted there; and

(c) is in a third Member State.

The confusion is compounded by the fact that many published versions of the 2000 Convention contain 'requesting' in error for 'requested' in paragraph (b).[45] However, the principles become clear when it is appreciated that the fact that a telecommunication takes place wholly or partly within a particular country does not necessarily mean that that country is necessarily able either in principle or in practice to carry out an interception. Under the Convention, assistance is to be sought from whichever State can provide it, and there is separate provision for notification of the jurisdiction where the person whose communications are intercepted is physically located.[46] **3.66**

Although material resulting from UK-based interception of telephone communications does not represent admissible evidence in criminal proceedings in the UK, telephone intercept material is relied on in many other jurisdictions. The Regulation of Investigatory Powers Act 2000 contains provision for the necessary interception warrant to be authorised for the purposes of a request.[47] Particularly stringent provisions exist to reflect the sensitive nature of such assistance: a request for interception may be refused where the requested measure would not be taken in a similar national case,[48] and under domestic legislation the Secretary of State is required to ensure that restrictions are in place which would prevent disclosure in proceedings overseas which would not be made in the UK.[49] **3.67**

Banking information

The 2001 Protocol to the 2000 Convention deals principally with banking information. This is always an area of difficulty because of the disinclination of banks for it to be known that they are disclosing information about their customers, and because of the computer-based nature of the data. It is also the case that few EU member countries have a centralised register of bank accounts held, so that even identifying an account is typically a laborious process. **3.68**

Article 1 of the Protocol confronts this problem, in that it obliges Member States to 'take the necessary measures to determine, in answer to a request, whether a particular suspect holds any bank accounts. There is no requirement that this should be done by means of a centralised register. The means of execution is left to be determined by the Member States. Article 2 covers the provision of 'particulars' of bank accounts, and is not limited to those held by suspects. **3.69**

Article 3 contains an innovative measure which enables Member States to monitor banking operations in one or more foreign bank accounts for a specified period. The monitoring need not be real-time and may, for example, be daily or weekly, but the details are left to be agreed between States. **3.70**

Part 1, Chapter 4 of CICA ('Information about banking transactions') implements this Protocol in relation to both incoming and outgoing requests within 'participating' States **3.71**

---

[45] Compare the Explanatory Report on the Convention of 29 May 2000, which contains the correct text.
[46] 2000 Convention, Art. 20(2).
[47] Regulation of Investigatory Powers Act 2000, ss. 5(3)(c) and 6(2)(j). Competent authorities of requesting States are persons to whom disclosure is permitted: s. 19(2)(a).
[48] 2000 Convention, Art. 18.5(b).
[49] Regulation of Investigatory Powers Act 2000, s. 15(7)(b).

(EU Member States and other States designated by Parliament). Orders are available in relation to 'serious criminal conduct' as defined in the Protocol and may be for information or monitoring. Dual criminality is required. It is an offence under section 42 of CICA to disclose the existence of a request for these forms of assistance.

C. Freezing Orders

Background

3.72 Following the increase in cross-border criminality within the EU, criminal groups have taken to hiding and investing proceeds of crime in Member States other than the one in which the crime was committed. To deprive criminals of their illicit gains, the EU has adopted measures for asset recovery in criminal matters which require international judicial cooperation. One such measure is Council Framework Decision 2003/577/JHA[50] which was adopted on 22 July 2003 to deal with the execution of orders freezing property or evidence.

Scope

3.73 The Decision[51] establishes rules by which a Member State shall automatically recognise and execute in its territory a freezing order issued in criminal proceedings by a judicial authority of another State.[52] It applies to orders issued for the purpose of securing evidence or the subsequent confiscation of property in cases falling under one of 32 listed criminal offences, provided that they are punishable under the law of the Member State issuing the order by a maximum term of imprisonment of at least three years.

3.74 For cases outside these listed offences, the State in which the order is to be executed will subject its recognition and enforcement to one of two conditions. The first is that the criminal acts for which the order was issued constitute an offence under the law of that State, and the second is that the acts for which the order was issued constitute an offence which, under the laws of the State, allow for such freezing.[53]

3.75 In accordance with Directives laid down in the Framework Decision, a freezing order (together with the relevant accompanying certificate) is transmitted when it is served by a judicial authority in one State on the competent authority in another State by means capable of producing a written record allowing the executing State to establish its authenticity.[54]

3.76 Any order issued by one Member State on another must be recognised without further formality and necessary measures for its immediate execution[55] taken except in situations where any measures to be taken are contrary to the fundamental principles of law in the executing State.[56] Once a freezing order has been granted, property which is the subject of the order shall remain frozen in the executing State until that State has responded to requests

---

[50] [2003] OJ L 196/45, pp 44–55.

[51] Council Framework Decision 2003/577/JHA.

[52] Council Framework Decision 2003/577/JHA, Art. 1.

[53] Council Framework Decision 2003/577/JHA, Art. 3. Under conditions laid down in Art. 39(1) of the EU Treaty the Council may decide at any time after consultation with the European Parliament to add other categories of offence to the list of 32.

[54] Council Framework Decision 2003/577/JHA, Art. 4 (transmission of freezing orders).

[55] Council Framework Decision 2003/577/JHA, Art. 5 (recognition and immediate execution).

[56] Council Framework Decision 2003/577/JHA, Art. 7 (grounds for non-recognition or non-execution) and Art. 8 (grounds for postponement).

made in accordance with requirements set out in Article 10(1)(a) or (b) of the Framework Decision.[57]

Implementation

Member States were required to comply with the provisions of the Framework Decision **3.77** before 2 August 2005.[58] However, as at 23 November 2010, there was no information regarding the position in one State, 22 States had implemented the Framework Decision, and three States had begun the process of introducing the framework into legislation. With regard to the position in the UK, those parts of the Framework Decision relating to the freezing of evidence had been implemented and work was being done to implement those parts dealing with the freezing of property.[59]

The future

The European Commission in its report assessing the implementation of Article 14 of the **3.78** Framework Decision noted that there were several omissions and misinterpretations of the Framework Decision within national laws. Further, some implementing laws were made with no reference to the Framework Decision, because they had been adopted to implement some other instrument of international law. It also noted that some of the provisions lacked clarity and lacked coherence with existing laws.[60] As such, it deemed the implementation of Council Framework Decision 2003/577/JHA unsatisfactory.[61]

To address these identified issues, reduce disparities in approaches to implementation, har- **3.79** monise laws, and lay the foundation for future work in this area, the European Commission on 12 March 2012 proposed a draft Directive[62] setting out a minimum set of rules for Member States. It is intended that this new Directive will facilitate mutual trust and effective cross-border cooperation in the enforcement of the freezing and confiscation of criminal assets.[63]

European Union freezing orders: to be or not to be...

The UK European Scrutiny Committee on 18 April 2012, after due consideration welcomed **3.80** the aim of the draft Directive to ensure minimum standards across the EU in this area. It acknowledged that for most part the UK broadly complies with or exceeds the requirements of the draft Directive. It, however, also noted that there were elements of the draft Directive

---

[57] Council Framework Decision 2003/577/JHA, Art. 6 (Art. 10(1)(a) refers to evidence and requires that transmission be accompanied by a request for the evidence to be transferred to the State that issued the freezing order; Art. 10(1)(b) deals with assets and holds that transmission of assets shall be accompanied by a request for confiscation requiring either enforcement of a confiscation order in the issuing State or confiscation in the executing State and subsequent enforcement of any such order).

[58] Council Framework Decision 2003/577/JHA, Art. 14.

[59] See 16921/10 COPEN 268 EJN 69 EUROJUST136.

[60] See Communication from the Commission on Proceeds of organised crime—Ensuring that 'crime does not pay', COM(2008) 766 final of 20.11.2008.

[61] Report from the Commission of 22 December 2008 based on Article 14 of the Council Framework Decision 2003/577/JHA of 22nd July 2003 on the execution in the European Union of orders freezing property or evidence, COM(2008) 885 final of 22.12.2008.

[62] Proposal for a Directive of the European Parliament and of the Council on the freezing and confiscation of proceeds of crime in the European Union, COM(2012) 85 final of 12.03.2012.

[63] Proposal for a Directive of the European Parliament and of the Council on the freezing and confiscation of proceeds of crime in the European Union, para. 1.

which differed from the approach taken by the UK and areas which may be difficult to implement.

3.81 These highlighted issues and potential problem areas include:

(a) changes which may be required in domestic legislation to ensure that there are powers to freeze and confiscate 'instrumentalities' as defined in Article 2 of the draft Directive (instrumentalities include any property used or intended to be used to commit a criminal offence);

(b) the extent of the criminal offences covered in Article 2(6);

(c) a clarification of the meaning and intention of the terms in Article 4(1) as well as the rationale for exclusion in Article 4(2);

(d) the provision in Article 7 which stated that in urgent cases assets could be frozen prior to obtaining a court order, this a clear contradiction with UK law which requires a court order to freeze property in all cases, regardless of urgency;

(e) the implications of Article 8 on safeguards for the legal aid budget; and

(f) a clarification of whether Article 9 includes value-based confiscation which is the basis of the UK's confiscation regime.

3.82 The UK was granted a three-month period, which expired on 14 June 2012, to decide whether to opt in to the new Directive.[64] What the future holds remains to be seen. However, the issue of whether the UK opts in is one of great debate and subject to informal consultations with SOCA, the Crown Prosecution Service, and the Association of Chief Police Officers.

D. European Evidence Warrants

Introduction

3.83 The EEW[65] was created by a Framework Decision[66] adopted on 18 December 2008. It represents the single biggest step away from the 'soft', optional regime of mutual assistance, towards a 'hard', compulsory system of mutual recognition of judicial requests in the field of cross-border search and seizure.

3.84 If it comes into force, and most Member States including the UK have failed to incorporate it into domestic legislation, it will be an important tool for litigators seeking to gather evidence from abroad.

3.85 It is generally considered, however, to be a flawed measure. It adds to, rather than replaces, the existing mutual assistance regime, thereby creating confusion. Additionally, it has so many caveats (e.g. it cannot be used to ask for a statement to be taken) that its usefulness is limited.

3.86 Pressure is building from certain Member States for the EEW to be superseded by a wide-ranging measure which will sweep aside the existing mutual assistance regime, and allow only for limited grounds for non-recognition. The terms of a so-called European Investigation Order are under active consideration, as part of a process that the UK opted in to in July 2010.[67]

---

[64] European Scrutiny Committee, Sixty-Third Report.

[65] Whilst the EEW is an important measure of which practitioners need to be aware, there is every possibility that it may never come into force.

[66] Council Framework Decision 2008/978/JHA of 18 December 2008.

[67] EIOs are discussed at Section E.

The road to the European Evidence Warrant

The European Evidence Warrant, like the European Arrest Warrant, forms part of a wider **3.87** programme to move beyond the principle of mutual assistance to one of mutual recognition between Member States in the field of criminal law. It is a reaction to the perceived slowness and inefficiency of the mutual assistance regime.

The origins of this measure lie in the Treaty of Amsterdam,[68] which inserted an Article 31 **3.88** into the Treaty on European Union. It provided that:

Common action on judicial cooperation in criminal matters shall include:

(a) facilitating and accelerating cooperation between competent ministries and judicial or equivalent authorities of the Member States in relation to proceedings and the enforcement of decisions;
(b) facilitating extradition between Member States;
(c) ensuring compatibility in rules applicable in the Member States, as may be necessary to improve such cooperation;
(d) preventing conflicts of jurisdiction between Member States;
(e) progressively adopting measures establishing minimum rules relating to the constituent elements of criminal acts and to penalties in the fields of organised crime, terrorism and illicit drug trafficking.

Proposals to achieve these ends were set out in the conclusions of the special meeting of the **3.89** European Council in Tampere in 1999.[69] The Council concluded that mutual recognition should become the 'cornerstone of judicial co-operation in both civil and criminal matters within the Union',[70] adding that the principle should apply 'both to judgments and to other decisions of judicial authorities'.

The Council also considered that the principle of mutual recognition of judgments should **3.90** extend to pre-trial orders, 'in particular to those which would enable competent authorities quickly to secure evidence and to seize assets which are easily movable.' It further proposed that evidence lawfully gathered by one Member State's authorities should, in principle, be admissible before the courts of other Member States.[71]

The Commission was urged to adopt a programme of measures to achieve these ends, and **3.91** further the principle of mutual recognition. Steps have been taken to implement this agenda, and the Council agreed upon a mutual recognition programme. The programme included a list of 24 measures, which led to the Framework Decisions on the EAW,[72] freezing orders,[73] and the EEW.

The Tampere Programme was further developed by the Hague Programme at the European **3.92** Council of 4–5 November 2004, which urged the completion of the programme of measures to implement the principle of mutual recognition, issuing an 'action plan' to that effect.[74]

---

[68] Signed on 2 October 1997. See also Chapter 1.
[69] [1999] OJ L 176/17, paras 32–52; <http://www.europarl.europa.eu/summits/tam_en.htm>.
[70] See point 33, Tampere European Council, 15–16.10.99, Conclusions of the Presidency.
[71] Tampere European Council, 15–16.10.99, Conclusions of the Presidency, para. 36.
[72] Council Framework Decision 2002/584/JHA [2002] OJ L 190/1. EAWs are dealt with in Chapter 4.
[73] Council Framework Decision 2003/577/JHA [2003] OJ L 196/45. See Section C.
[74] Council and Commission Action Plan implementing the Hague Programme on strengthening freedom, security and justice in the European Union [2005] OJ C 198, 12.8.2005.

3.93 The EEW was first proposed in 2003, but it was not until 18 December 2008, after difficult negotiations[75] that a Framework Decision[76] was finally adopted. It took effect from 19 January 2011.

The European Evidence Warrant

3.94 The EEW Framework Decision applies to criminal and not civil cases. It does not replace the existing mutual assistance procedures, and merely runs alongside them. Paragraph 25 of the EEW preamble states:

> The EEW should coexist with existing mutual assistance procedures, but such coexistence should be considered transitional until, in accordance with the Hague Programme, the types of evidence-gathering excluded from the scope of this Framework Decision are also the subject of a mutual recognition instrument, the adoption of which would provide a complete mutual recognition regime to replace mutual assistance procedures.

3.95 The Framework Decision was adopted under Article 31 TEU. If it ever comes into force[77] it will create a compulsory regime requiring Member States to give automatic recognition to each other's search warrants, without further formality if the offence which forms the basis of the EEW is one of 32 serious offences. Article 11 states that:

> The executing authority shall recognise an EEW, transmitted in accordance with Article 8, without any further formality being required and shall forthwith take the necessary measures for its execution in the same way as an authority of the executing State would obtain the objects…

3.96 The relaxed regime of the 2000 Convention is replaced with deadlines for cooperation. Unless there are grounds for postponement under Article 16, the executing authority must take possession of the objects, documents, or data 'without delay' and 'no later than 60 days after the receipt of the EEW by the competent executing authority'.[78]

3.97 In order to ensure the admissibility of the evidence obtained, the authorities of the executing State are obliged to comply with the formalities and procedures set down by the authorities of the issuing States provided that they are not contrary to fundamental principles of law in the executing State.

3.98 The principle of dual criminality[79] (that an offence in the issuing State must also be an offence in the executing State) is disapplied in respect of 32 offences[80] (including terrorism, human trafficking, money laundering, armed robbery, rape, arson, murder, serious bodily harm) and any offence carrying a maximum penalty of over three years' imprisonment.

3.99 However, on further examination it becomes clear that there are several important limits on the scope of the EEW. Perhaps most significantly it can only be issued to obtain evidence

---

[75] Political agreement was not easy to achieve. e.g., the Netherlands sought a partial application of the territoriality principle to permit refusal to comply with an EEW where the relevant offence was committed wholly or partially in the Netherlands.

[76] Council Framework Decision 2008/978/JHA of 18 December 2008 [2008] OJ L 350/72.

[77] Statutory provisions to enable implementation of the EEW are set out at s. 92 of the Criminal Justice and Licensing (Scotland) Act 2010 (not yet in force), but there are no equivalent provisions under English law. It has not been adopted in most Member States as a result of ongoing negotiations for its replacement.

[78] Council Framework Decision 2008/978/JHA, Art. 15(3).

[79] Dual criminality is addressed at **3.31**.

[80] Council Framework Decision 2008/978/JHA, Art. 14. However, Germany has secured the right to issue a declaration to reimpose the double criminality principle in certain circumstances.

that already exists and is directly available in the form of objects, documents, or data. Article 4 expressly excludes requests to conduct interviews, take statements, take bodily samples such as DNA or fingerprints, or conduct analyses of existing objects, documents, or data. Although already existing, they are not 'directly available' without further investigation or examination. Secondly, the EEW prohibits requests for interception of communications, monitoring of bank accounts, or even seizure of communications data retained by providers in the executing State.[81]

3.100 Recognition or execution of the EEW may be refused within 30 days of receipt in the executing State if:

(a) its execution would infringe the *ne bis in idem* principle;[82]
(b) in certain cases specified in Article 14(3) the EEW relates to acts which would not constitute an offence under the law of the executing State;
(c) execution is not possible with the measures available to the executing authority in the specific case;
(d) there is an immunity or privilege under the law of the executing State that makes its execution impossible;
(e) it has not been validated by the relevant authority in the issuing State when so required;
(f) the criminal offence is considered under the law of the executing State to have been committed wholly or significantly within its territory, or outside the territory of the issuing State and the law of the executing State does not permit legal proceedings to be taken in respect of such offences where they are committed outside that State's territory;
(g) it would harm national security interests; and
(h) the form is incomplete or incorrectly drafted.

3.101 The fact that recognition or execution of an EEW may only be subject to the double criminality bar in limited circumstances can lead to curious results. It means, for example, that in theory an abortion clinic in a Member State in a country where abortion is legal could be searched for evidence on the basis of an EEW from a country where abortion is illegal.

E. European Investigation Orders

The history of the European Investigation Orders proposal and its adoption by the United Kingdom

3.102 The position created by the adoption of the EEW as regards the obtaining of evidence is generally viewed as confusing and untidy.[83] Several regimes work alongside each other, and mix the principles of mutual admissibility and mutual recognition. There are several overlapping measures,[84] and different instruments apply to different types of evidence. For example, a

---

[81] Council Framework Decision 2008/978/JHA, Art. 4(2)(e).
[82] This is subject to the Art. 14 caveat set out earlier. See also Chapter 5 for consideration of this principle.
[83] The Green Paper on obtaining evidence in criminal matters from one Member State to another and securing its admissibility, issued by the Commission of the European Communities states that the existing rules are 'burdensome and may cause confusion among practitioners' (COM(2009) 624 final, p. 4).
[84] e.g. the requirement for the requested State to carry out a request in accordance with the formalities and procedures indicated by the issuing State is found in para. 15 of the preamble to the EEW Framework Decision, and also Art. 4 of the 2000 Convention.

Member State seeking to obtain a suspect's computer, bank statements, and mobile phone records may need to proceed under three different regimes.[85]

3.103 In reaction to some of these perceived problems of the mutual recognition system, a Green Paper on obtaining evidence in criminal matters from one Member State to another and securing its admissibility was published on 11 November 2009, establishing the long-term goal of a 'comprehensive system for obtaining evidence in cross-border cases'.[86]

3.104 The formal birth of the proposal for an EIO regime was on 29 April 2010, when seven Member States launched in Brussels an initiative for a Directive on the subject.[87]

3.105 In addition, in the 2010–2014 'Stockholm Programme—An open and secure Europe serving and protecting citizens' the European Council observed that 'the existing instruments in this area constitute a fragmentary regime' and stated that a 'new approach is needed, based on the principle of mutual recognition but also taking into account the flexibility of the traditional system of mutual legal assistance.' The European Council then invited the Commission to:

> Propose a comprehensive system, after an impact assessment, to replace all the existing instruments in this area, including Council Framework Decision 2008/978/JHA of 18 December 2008 on the European Evidence Warrant for the purpose of obtaining objects, documents and data for use in proceedings in criminal matters, covering as far as possible all types of evidence and containing deadlines for enforcement and limiting as far as possible the grounds for refusal.[88]

3.106 Before the Commission had itself acted, in April 2010 a group of seven Member States[89] tabled their own proposal for a Directive[90] regarding a European Investigation Order in criminal matters.

3.107 The adoption of the proposal by the UK came some months later, in July 2010. The Home Secretary announced to Parliament on the date of opt-in that the 'existing draft is not perfect' and promised to inject a proportionality test and also sufficient dual criminality tests into the measure in order to protect the UK administration from facing the investigation of trivial

---

[85] The computer could be requested pursuant to an EEW (it is an existing 'object'); the bank records could be requested under the Protocol to the Convention on Mutual Legal Assistance 2000; the mobile phone records could be requested under the Convention on Mutual Legal Assistance 2000.

[86] Issued by the Commission of the European Communities, COM(2009) 624, at p. 5 states that the solution to the present difficulties

> would seem to lie in the replacement of the existing legal regime on obtaining evidence in criminal matters by a single instrument based on the principle of mutual recognition and covering all types of evidence. Compared with the scope of application of the Framework Decision on the European Evidence Warrant, this new instrument would also cover evidence that—although directly available—does not already exist, such as statements from suspects or witnesses or information obtained in real time, such as interception of communications or monitoring of bank accounts. It would also include evidence—although already existing—is not directly available without further investigation or examination, such as analyses of existing objects documents or data or obtaining bodily material, such as DNA samples or fingerprints. The present consultation is aimed at confirming the validity of this approach.

[87] [2010] OJ C 165/22.

[88] At p. 39.

[89] Austria, Bulgaria, Belgium, Estonia, Slovenia, Spain, and Sweden.

[90] <http://register.consilium.europa.eu/pdf/en/10/st09/st09288-ad01.en10.pdf>.

cases or being required to collect evidence of conduct which in the UK is not criminal under domestic law.

The current status of the European Investigation Orders

The draft Directive remains a draft. However, since the initial proposal a number of Member **3.108** States have taken positions on the proposal. Denmark has opted out. Like the UK, Ireland has chosen to participate in the proposal.

The proposal was widely criticised, including by the Commission itself, for its lack of any **3.109** impact assessment or consultation process before being sent to Brussels.[91]

After long negotiations at the Council, a partial general approach on the first 18 Articles of **3.110** the draft Directive and Article Y (costs) was agreed in June 2011. Various improvements were made to the text, including the inclusion of the proportionality test promised by the Home Secretary upon the UK's opt-in, the prevention of forum-shopping by prosecuting agencies, double-jeopardy, dual criminality, and territorial safeguards.

The draft text was reviewed by the Justice and Home Affairs Council meeting on 13–14 **3.111** December 2011[92] and, pending the approval of the Member States' delegations, it will be this text which the European Parliament considers in its 2012 session.

The reconfiguring of mutual recognition

As explained in Section B, the infrastructure for MLA and that of mutual recognition are **3.112** separate and the two systems for cross-border cooperation sit side by side. Because the EIO regime is designed as a further extension of the mutual recognition principle for use in Europe among Member States, its effect will be on the way in which mutual recognition works, and not on MLA which will continue to function as before for those States outside the EU. The effect on mutual recognition will, however, be great.

First, the proposal would repeal Council Framework Decision 2008/978/JHA establish- **3.113** ing the EEW. Secondly, it would replace the corresponding provisions of the Schengen Convention (as between participating EU Member States), the EU Convention on Mutual Assistance, and also the relevant provisions of the Council of Europe's Mutual Assistance Convention and its Protocols. The Framework Decision on freezing orders[93] would also be substituted by it as concerns the freezing of evidence.

This would represent a considerable consolidation and, on one view, simplification of the **3.114** mechanisms at work in mutual recognition. Of course, it would not simplify the landscape completely, because those provisions repealed or substituted would be only as to Member States opting in to the EIO Directive. Those which do not would remain on the current foot- ing. As such, providing that some Member States decline to opt in (and some, e.g. Denmark, already have so declined), there will necessarily be more than one system in place for cross- border European evidence-gathering, which detracts somewhat from the notion that pro- ceeding with the EIO proposal will simplify matters. In the short term, it will not.

---

[91] JUST/B/1/AA-et D(2010) 6815, p 7, Fundamental Rights Agency opinion, Vienna, 14 February 2011, p 15.
[92] See Press Release, European Council, Justice and Home Affairs, 13–14 December 2011, 18498/11.
[93] [2003] OJ L 196/45. Also see Section C.

Key provisions of the European Investigation Orders Directive

3.115 The goal of the proposed Directive is to allow Member States that have opted in to apply the principle of mutual recognition to a further area of the criminal process—namely, criminal investigations. Whereas currently, recognition applies to Arrest Warrants[94] and Evidence Warrants,[95] this would go further and include the investigative stage. Under the Directive, participating Member States would agree to carry out investigations at the request of another Member State on the basis of mutual recognition, namely, on the basis that such orders for investigation would be automatically treated as valid and executable by the receiving State, with only limited grounds for refusal to carry out such investigations.

3.116 The scope of the EIO is for criminal proceedings 'brought by, or that may be brought before, a judicial authority in respect of a criminal offence under the national law of the issuing State' (Art. 4), but this may also extend to administrative proceedings brought by the government where there is a criminal dimension (Art. 4(b)).

3.117 Thanks to an amendment to the original version, the issue of an EIO depends on a proportionality test (Art. 5(a)(1)). That test requires the issuing authority to satisfy itself that the EIO is 'necessary and proportionate' and that the investigative measure could have been ordered under the same conditions in a similar domestic case. This was designed to inject some restrictions on overuse of the power, and to prevent forum-shopping by prosecutors using the EIO to gain an unfair advantage from differences between the procedural systems of other participating States.

3.118 Time limits are a feature of the new proposal. The investigation must be conducted 'with the same celerity and priority as for a similar national case' (Art. 11(1)). More specifically, receiving States are required to acknowledge receipt of an EIO within 30 days and carry out the said investigation within 90 days. The more streamlined system is designed to make legal cooperation faster and more efficient, guaranteeing a more timely system of delivering justice.

3.119 The issuing State may request that its agents assist with the execution of the EIO in the receiving State (Art. 8(3)). Such a request must be complied with, subject to national security and the fundamental principles of law of the receiving State. In so assisting, foreign agents will be required to act within the laws of the receiving State, by which they will be bound. The agents will have no law enforcement powers, except to the extent agreed by the receiving State and subject to its laws.

3.120 The grounds for non-execution of an EIO are limited (Art. 10), but include national security concerns; protecting immunities or privileges established in the receiving State (e.g. those related to press freedom); the principle of proportionality, whether the possible offences being investigated would, if charged, satisfy the test of dual criminality in both sending and receiving States; the rule against double jeopardy; and, where coercive measures are concerned, the principle of territoriality in the issuing State.

3.121 Article 13 ensures that proper remedies are in place for any affected party to challenge the investigative measure in question on a level equivalent to that of a similar domestic case, and

---

[94] See Chapter 4.
[95] See Section D.

information must be provided about such remedies. Challenge of the reasons behind the issuing of the EIO is, however, limited to the issuing State only.

Article 19 provides for the temporary transfer of persons in custody in order to have an inves- **3.122** tigative measure carried out which would require his presence in the territory of the issuing State, as long as the person 'shall be sent back within the period stipulated by the executing state' (Art. 19(1)). The executing State may refuse transfer if the person concerned does not consent or if transfer is likely to prolong his detention.

On the question of costs, it is, perhaps unfairly, the executing party which is required to foot **3.123** the bill for the investigation (Art. Y(1)), however, where costs will be 'exceptionally high', it may consult with the issuing party as to how to share such costs (Art. Y(2)).

Evidence subject to a European Investigation Order

The draft Directive does not define the extent of the investigative measures covered by the **3.124** EIO regime, stating only in its recitals that 'the EIO has a horizontal scope and therefore applies to almost all investigative measures'. This means that investigation would include, as a start, the taking of witness statements and questioning of suspects, witnesses, third parties, or victims; interception evidence of phones and other communication media; and the taking of bodily samples or biometric data. The monitoring of banking systems and activity is the subject of special protection in the draft as requiring further safeguards (Arts 23–5).

As has been observed, the proportionality test injected into the proposal via an amendment **3.125** in 2011 means that the evidence intended to be gained under an application for an EIO must have been capable of being similarly gained had the case been a purely domestic one. This narrows somewhat the scope of potential evidence that could be caught by an EIO and protects the measure against misuse.

Extraterritorial investigation and enforcement: new powers

One truly seismic change which would be brought about in European cross-border assist- **3.126** ance by the EIO scheme is how, for the first time, law enforcement officers would be permitted to conduct investigations *directly in another Member State* where an EIO has been issued. The provisions, found in Article 8(3) of the proposed Directive, set out how such a scheme would work. The State issuing the EIO may 'request' that one or several agencies of the issuing State 'assist in the execution of the EIO in support to the competent authorities of the executing State'. That 'request', however, is one that the executing State cannot, under Article 8(3), refuse unless the assistance is contrary to the fundamental principles of law of the executing State or harms its security interests. As such, the 'request' is really more of a requirement save in exceptional circumstances.

Some safeguards are injected into the scheme by way of recital 11, which states that a State **3.127** in receipt of such a request can set 'conditions as to the scope and nature of the attendance of the authorities of the issuing State'. A further safeguard added to the revised draft is that foreign agents assisting the executing State will be bound by the law of the executing State and that visiting foreign officials will 'not have any law enforcement powers' in the territory of the executing State (Art. 3a).

With the additional safeguards in place, it would appear that the role of foreign officials in **3.128** investigation of offences and execution of EIOs will be limited to 'assisting' the executing State, and cannot be a self-standing investigation in its own right. That said, the prospect of foreign officials taking part in *any* domestic investigation has alarmed some,[96] who cite the fact that visiting agents of a foreign State will not be familiar with the rules on how law enforcement officials of the executing State conduct investigations and will not have had the same training as their colleagues in the executing State., Therefore they will be at risk of breaching domestic procedures and potentially affecting the fairness of the investigation and/or the ensuing trial. This criticism would probably be met by those in favour of the EIO scheme with the suggestion that any restriction on the involvement of foreign officials could be stipulated in advance by the executing State as per recital 11. One such restriction could be a requirement of advance training by the officials involved as to domestic law and procedure in the host country.

3.129   Where an issuing authority is present in the territory of the executing State, and is assisting the execution of the EIO, it may also issue a further EIO directly to the executing State (Art. 7(2)). This would allow the gathering of further evidence by a State if the first EIO did not facilitate what was desired. Although there is nothing specific to apply the proportionality test to this second EIO under Article 5, it is to be expected that the same test will apply to any subsequent EIO as did to the first.

Problems and challenges

3.130   The EIO proposal has generated a number of critiques relating to more familiar vexed questions affecting not only EIOs but cross-border criminal law systems generally.

The spectre of overuse

3.131   The fear of overuse of the EIO scheme, whereby one State might routinely and frequently issue EIOs to other participating States, with the result that the systems of other participating States become clogged with the requirements to comply with the zealous 'over-user', is a common one. It derives, in large part, from the experience gained from the execution of EAWs over the last decade, where certain countries, largely as a result of differing legal systems and the limited discretion provided for in some States as to whether to bring a public prosecution, have issued far more EAWs to other States than anticipated, thus placing a severe burden on executing States which have then been required to comply with the EAW under the principle of mutual recognition. As an indicator of the level of the burden, the UK, which issues around 200 EAWs per year, now receives between 3,000 and 6,000 EAWs from other States.

3.132   The problem of overuse has been addressed—partially at least—by the inclusion of the proportionality test in Article 5, which will add a new and defensible protection against abuse. However, the protection is partial only, as the revised Article 5a states that the proportionality test is to be carried out by the issuing State, and only 'exceptionally' by the executing State. It is not impossible to imagine a position where one State's analysis of proportionality differs routinely from another's, putting, perhaps, the 'exceptional' nature of the review by the executing State under strain.

Double jeopardy

3.133   This is less of a problem now than when the text was as at its first public draft, and contained no provision enshrining the *ne bis in idem* principle.[97] That has now been inserted into

---

[96]   C. Heard and D. Mansell, 'The European Investigation Order: Changing the Face of Evidence Gathering in EU Cross-Border Cases', Fair Trials International (2011), unpublished, p 5.

[97]   See discussion of this principle in Chapter 5.

Article 10(1), allowing for a State to refuse the EIO on the basis that it would constitute double jeopardy. However, that ground of refusal will not apply where the issuing State 'provides an assurance that the evidence transferred as a result of an execution of an EIO shall not be used to prosecute a person whose case has been finally disposed of in another Member State for the same facts.' As has been observed, though one might reasonably wonder why such an investigation is needed in the first place, especially when it is undertaken by the same State which has already conducted a trial of the relevant person for the same facts. The potential for needless (and possibly vexatious) further investigation is thus still, under the amended Article 10, very real.

Dual criminality

The requirement of dual criminality has, likewise, been achieved in the revised version of **3.134** the proposal, although it was absent in the initial draft. The current version of Article 10(1) permits a State to refuse to execute an EIO if the EIO 'concerns facts that do not constitute a crime or offence under the national law of the executing State'.[98]

Use by defence as well as prosecution

At present, the EIO is silent on the question of use of an EIO by the defence to gather **3.135** exculpatory evidence in another State. This is a failing which makes the measure appear to be only a prosecutor's tool. Although there is nothing currently prohibiting a State requesting exculpatory evidence under an EIO, this is not explicit in the text, which arguably should provide a specific means by which a defence party can approach the court for such an order. At present, the MLA systems of numerous jurisdictions already do this for defence applications, and given that the EIO regime would effectively abolish such systems, it would as currently drafted, have the effect of reducing, rather than protecting, the rights of the defence.

'Fishing expeditions'

Linked with the concern about overuse is the concern that EIOs will be used as a fishing **3.136** expedition simply to find more material, only in this case with the added force of mutual recognition obliging the executing State to implement the investigation desired.

This was, from the outset, curtailed in respect of information on individuals' bank accounts, **3.137** which is the subject of special protection under Article 23. Any EIO for such information is required to 'state why [the requesting State] considers that the requested information is likely to be of substantial value for the purpose of the investigation into the offence' (Art. 23(6)(a)).

Curiously, this specific requirement is absent elsewhere. On the contrary, there is no explicit **3.138** right to refuse an EIO on the basis that the evidence sought has no apparent relevance to the alleged crime. There is, thus, the potential that UK agencies will have to carry out investigations of tenuous relevance to the charge concerned. The only provision which might be of assistance to courts in preventing that from happening is a wide interpretation of the new Article 5a, which could see a legitimate basis of refusal on the basis that any fishing expedition is, by its nature, not proportionate in its scope. However, this is a matter for interpretive development by courts if/when the regime comes into force, rather than anything helpful within the proposed text itself.

---

[98] See also **3.32** for discussion of dual criminality.

Privacy and data protection

3.139 Although recital 17a of the proposed Directive states that 'personal data processed, when implementing this Directive, should be protected in accordance with the provisions on the protection of personal data processed in the framework of police and judicial cooperation in criminal matters and with relevant international instruments in this field', the EIO regime does not set out those provisions. It also does not make any specific provision for the minimum duties on State agencies as far as evidence gathering, storage, analysis, and transfer is concerned. The question of prevention of loss, misuse, or contamination of sensitive evidence such as DNA or bodily samples, banking records, and other personal details is something on which the EIO is silent. This leaves defendants or other affected persons in difficulty when attempting to ensure the proper use of their private data. As there is no requirement in the draft Directive for record-keeping throughout the duration of criminal proceedings, no court or defence team will necessarily be able to assess whether correct procedures were followed in relation to the collection and storage of evidence.

3.140 Furthermore, once a case is concluded, there is no provision within the proposal to insist on the destruction or return of evidence obtained abroad, nor indeed provisions as to retention periods generally. It is thus not prohibited, under the new scheme, for material collected to remain available for future use by States' Parties which have collected evidence subject to an EIO well after a trial is over or discontinued, is tempered by Article 17a's reminder, but not insistence, that international and other agreements already in place about the protection of data should apply.

The implications for practitioners

3.141 While still a proposal, the EIO Directive will have no impact on the criminal practitioner in the UK. Despite the UK's adoption of the proposed Directive, the measure does not come into force until it is passed into law by the organs of the EU. Unless and until it does, the MLA structure currently in place for cross-border investigations continues.

F. Obtaining Evidence of Convictions Abroad

Introduction

3.142 Obtaining evidence of convictions recorded elsewhere in the world is probably the area in which interstate cooperation is most frequently called upon by those practising in the criminal courts. This is particularly true in the UK, where, because of its status in international trade, the influx of migration (both from within the EU and outside it) and also its popularity as an international tourist destination, it is a frequent occurrence that a defendant has foreign origins or has resided in other nation States for significant periods of time. Knowing the criminal (or non-criminal) history of such a defendant is thus important at numerous stages—for bail applications, at the trial stage,[99] and, more obviously, at the sentencing and confiscation stage if a conviction is ultimately recorded.

3.143 Obtaining a record of convictions for offences in the UK is a relatively simple matter but the same is not true for overseas convictions where the relevant record may be in the exclusive possession of other States. There is no single EU-wide, let alone worldwide, register of criminal convictions and interstate cooperation is thus required.

---

[99] For the purposes, e.g., of bad character or tendency evidence.

Within the EU, assistance was formerly provided under the 1959 Council of Europe and **3.144**
2000 EU Conventions (see Section B: Mutual Legal Assistance). However, improving the
procedure for obtaining evidence of foreign convictions among other Member States has
been the subject of several legislative measures over the last decade. The UK has, as a consequence, also enacted legislation to provide a uniform means of requesting evidence from
abroad, as well as simplifying the way in which European convictions are to be accepted by
the courts of other Member States in their own proceedings.

Obtaining conviction records: the 2005 Directive

Articles 13 and 22 of the 1959 Convention provide the principal source for the exchange **3.145**
of criminal records specifically, and require (a) the provision of conviction details between
Member States upon the furnishing of a request[100] and (b) the provision to a Member State of
conviction details when one of that State's nationals is convicted in another Member State.[101]
The request provisions closely track the familiar principle of MLA, by which a requested
Member State would be under an obligation to assist a requesting Member State whenever
a formal request was issued.

However, the process identified in the 1959 Convention was not without its problems. **3.146**
The obligation to provide mutual assistance was couched in general terms only and did
not descend to the practical detail of how the request process would occur. First of all, a
State seeking to find a defendant's conviction history often had difficulty identifying which
Member States might possess information about that defendant's prior convictions; secondly, the Convention did not establish the practical means of obtaining the information;
and, thirdly, even where a request generated results, it was often a challenge to understand
those results, which required not only expert translation but an understanding of the criminal law system of the requested country.

The UK Central Authority for the Exchange of European Criminal Records

In order to improve the situation, the European Council passed a Framework Decision[102] in **3.147**
2005 on the exchange of information extracted from the criminal record.[103] This Decision
repeated the requirement of Article 22 of the 1959 Convention of notification to a Member
State when one of its nationals is convicted in another Member State. It also provided for a
ten-day turnaround in responding to requests from other States for a person's convictions
history. As a result of that Directive, the UK in 2006 established the UK Central Authority
for the Exchange of Criminal Records (commonly abbreviated as UKCA-ECR), to process
requests from other Member States and to request them from others on behalf of the UK.

Where a criminal record is sought from another EU State, the answer lies now with UKCA- **3.148**
ECR, which is the principal portal emitting and receiving requests for criminal records. The
Central Authority has a team of specialist translators to assist with understanding a criminal
conviction record, and maintains links with the relevant contacts in each Member State
to make record exchange easier and smoother, thus solving some of the problems with the
former system.

---

[100] 1959 Convention, Art. 13.
[101] 1959 Convention, Art. 22.
[102] 2005/876/JHA.
[103] [2005] OJ L 322/33.

Further progress

3.149 Subsequent to this, two Directives in 2009[104] have now paved the way for the creation of an EU-wide network of criminal convictions called the European Criminal Records Information System (ECRIS). The Directives require all countries to set up a Central Authority (as the UK had already previously done) with the task of managing requests and provision of criminal record information to other Member States. They also describe the structure for the electronic exchange of information extracted from criminal records between Member States. ECRIS is a decentralised information technology system based on the criminal record databases in Member States, and consists of a software program that allows exchanges of information between the national databases and a common communication infrastructure. Secondly, the Directives create a standardised European format of transmission of information on convictions. The idea behind the standardised format is for Member States to be able to categorise the type of offence for which a defendant has been convicted and link that to the equivalent offence within the requesting State's domestic criminal law. The standardised format provides for two reference tables of categories of offence and categories of sanction which should facilitate the automatic translation and enable the mutual understanding of the information transmitted by using a system of codes. Member States are to refer to these tables when transmitting information on the offence giving rise to the conviction and information on the content of the conviction.

Proving European convictions in a UK court: the previous position

3.150 Prior to 2009, the manner of proving an EU conviction in a UK criminal court was, as for all foreign convictions, governed by section 7 of the Evidence Act 1851: namely, by way of a sealed or certified copy of the judgment from the foreign court concerned, or the judge personally. This was, however, not always easy and there were inequalities in the manner in which a conviction recorded in the EU could be treated compared with domestic convictions—for example, a UK conviction created a presumption that the accused committed that crime in any future proceedings, even where its relevance was only to show disposition,[105] whereas this presumption would not apply to convictions outside the UK. The case of *Kordasinski*[106] is an example of the Court of Appeal's treatment of the previous law.

3.151 This could not remain the position in light of Article 82 TFEU. The Article's purpose was to give force to the principle of mutual recognition in the area of the judgments and decisions of courts of other Member States in criminal matters. The Article legislated that 'judicial cooperation in criminal matters in the Union shall be based on the principle of mutual recognition of judgments and judicial decisions and shall include the approximation of the laws and regulations of the Member States' in certain specified areas. Further, the TFEU mandated that the European Parliament and the Council shall 'lay down rules and procedures for ensuring recognition throughout the Union of all forms of judgments and judicial decisions'.

3.152 Council Decision 2008/675/JHA has now addressed taking account of convictions in the Member States in the course of new criminal proceedings. That Framework Decision makes it mandatory for EU convictions to be 'taken into account to the extent previous national

---

[104] Primarily, reference here is to Directive 2008/675/JHA.
[105] See PACE 1984, s. 74(3).
[106] [2006] EWCA Crim 2984.

convictions are taken into account, and that equivalent legal effects are attached to them as to previous national convictions, in accordance with national law.'[107] This obligation applies where 'information has been obtained under applicable instruments on mutual legal assistance or on the exchange of information extracted from criminal records.'[108]

The Coroners and Justice Act 2009

The UK's response to the 2008 Framework Decision[109] was to pass the Coroners and Justice   **3.153**
Act 2009. The Act, which came into force in 2010, represents the current practice on the use of EU convictions in the UK context.

Section 144 and, by it, Schedule 17, set out the main new provisions: **3.154**

(a) section 73 of the Police and Criminal Evidence Act (PACE) 1984 to include EU convictions, and establishes a more simplified means of proving any conviction or acquittal from an EU court (Sch. 17, para. 13);
(b) foreign convictions (whether or not within the EU) can be used for the purposes of bad character evidence where the conviction relates to an offence of the same description and the offence concerned would have been an offence in the UK at the time of the new trial (Sch. 17, para. 1);
(c) EU convictions are now included as relevant offences for the purposes of the no-bail rule for homicide/rape offenders being tried on new charges of the same category (Sch. 17, para. 3); and
(d) EU convictions are to be considered equivalent to domestic convictions for the purposes of considering allocation and sentence (Sch. 17, paras 4–12).

The new and easier means of proving a foreign conviction or acquittal is via a 'certificate,   **3.155**
signed by the proper officer of the court where the conviction or acquittal took place, giving details of the offence, of the conviction or acquittal, and of any sentence' (Sch. 17, para. 13). This exists as an additional route of proving a foreign conviction and does not replace the Evidence Act 1851 or other means of proving a conviction, although it is likely to be popular as it is somewhat easier to achieve.

Specialist proceedings may mandate their own means of proving foreign convictions. For   **3.156**
the purposes of extradition proceedings, the fact of a conviction overseas may be proved by a properly certified copy of the court record.[110] Proof of foreign convictions in asset recovery proceedings under the Proceeds of Crime Act 2002 was considered in the case of *Asset Recovery Agency v Virtosu*.[111]

Inculpation and exculpation: the two-way operation of the scheme

It should be noted that the new scheme, as set out in section 73 of PACE 1984 is able to   **3.157**
be employed to show the guilt but also the innocence of a defendant, for example to show previous good character or an acquittal overseas. This change is of significance to defence practitioners, since historically requests for information of previous convictions was largely a prosecutor's domain. A defendant is, of course, unable to gain access to the relevant

---

[107] Council Framework Decision 2005/876/JHA, Art. 3(1).
[108] Council Framework Decision 2005/876/JHA, Art. 3(1).
[109] Council Framework Decision 2008/675/JHA.
[110] Extradition Act 1989, Sch. 1, para. 12 and *Re Mullin* [1993] Crim LR 390.
[111] [2008] EWHC 149 (QB).

conviction information in the same way as the prosecution, and so such information, if not already available and disclosed, will have to be requested either by the prosecution itself (if it is happy to do so after being requested by the defendant or the court), or, if unwilling, by way of a Letter of Request from the judge hearing the case under section 7 of CICA.

Assessment of the new scheme

3.158 The scheme clearly has both its advantages and disadvantages. It provides an easier and more streamlined manner in which to prove and use EU convictions in a UK court, and a system which can operate to the benefit both of the prosecution and the defence. The unequal treatment of domestic and foreign convictions, as well as the heavier requirements imposed under the Evidence Act 1851, were significant obstacles to the proper use of EU convictions in domestic criminal trials in the UK and, to the extent that that has disappeared, the new scheme is a good one. Additionally, the maintenance of the double criminality rule wherever EU convictions are used means that the scheme affords a minimum rights protection.

3.159 In practice, however, there may be a number of difficulties with implementing the scheme. First, any certificate of conviction/acquittal will have to be authenticated by a 'proper officer' of the court who recorded the conviction, and it may be that this is not entirely clear in the case of some Member States, leading to potential challenge by one party or another as to the authenticity of the certificate. Questioning the legitimacy of the certificate will, however, quite possibly be of only limited effect, as some commentators have noted,[112] given that with the onset of mutual recognition the tendency is to recognise the authenticity of the overseas document rather than query the making of it, as has been the experience in extradition proceedings concerning requests to surrender under EAWs.

3.160 A second question will be whether judges are sufficiently confident, in the context of bad character evidence, to decide that an offence is of the 'same description' as a UK offence currently being tried, when the description of the offence depends on translation and the context of a different legal system. If judges are reticent to do so (and possibly rightly), then it will mean that the use of EU convictions as bad character will be rather limited. Even where they are used, the admission of the bare certificate of conviction is unlikely to be sufficient to show bad character in areas such as propensity evidence because ordinarily the facts of the offence would also have to be known. It would take time to obtain and translate such information.

3.161 More generally, delay in obtaining sufficient details about the EU conviction for any reason, is likely to be a basis for arguing that the interests of justice require that the EU conviction is not taken into account in the UK trial. This is especially likely to occur when a defendant is in custody. Of course, this will be mitigated by the eventual implementation of the ECRIS system but, at present, such delays are to be anticipated as an unfortunate reality of the operation of the scheme.

G. The Prüm Decision

3.162 The Prüm Treaty was signed on 27 May 2005 between Belgium, Germany, France, Spain, Luxembourg, the Netherlands, and Austria. The purpose of the treaty was to enhance

---

[112] Jodie Blackstock, *EU Criminal Procedure* (London: Justice, 2011), 31.

cooperation between the signatories by providing for automatic searching or comparison of databases in each country covering DNA, fingerprints, and vehicle registration information.

Through Council Decision 2008/615/JHA on the stepping up of cross-border cooperation **3.163** (the Prüm Decision), the effect of the treaty was extended to all 27 Member States of the EU. Members were required to implement the decision by August 2011. Unfortunately, the technical challenges and expense involved have meant that a large number of countries, including the UK, had still not done so at the time of writing.

In relation to DNA, the data that must be made available is reference data, consisting of the **3.164** non-coding part of the DNA and of a reference number that does not enable an individual to be identified. Searches are performed by comparing DNA profiles, but only with respect to individual cases and on a hit or no hit basis. If the search produces a match, the reference data is automatically provided; if it does not, the EU Member State which has conducted the search may be obliged to create one.

A similar approach is adopted in relation to fingerprints (through 'automated dactyloscopic **3.165** identification systems'). Again, reference data will consist only of the dactyloscopic data and a reference number, and the search is conducted on a hit or no hit basis.

In both cases, formal MLA may still be required to obtain fuller details or other information **3.166** relating to the reference data. However, this approach will substantially reduce the time currently taken in international cooperation in such matters.

There is also provision for online searches of vehicle databases, using a full vehicle registration **3.167** number or chassis number only.

For the UK, the precursor to implementation was the introduction of the Protection of **3.168** Freedoms Act 2012. This adopts across the UK the model previously in use only in Scotland of permitting profiles to be deleted from the National DNA Database in certain circumstances. The UK Government is likely to create a separate 'shadow' Prüm database, which will contain only DNA data which the UK wishes to make available for automatic search by other Member States. It may not, for example, share the DNA of those who have not been convicted of any offence or who have been convicted of minor offences only.

The Home Office has also said that it does not intend to implement the Prüm Decision **3.169** in full during the current spending review period (2011–2015) given its limited budget, although it will work on the DNA and vehicle registration aspects during the latter part of that period.[113] Should the UK exercise its threatened opt-out under Protocol 36 to the Lisbon Treaty, it will be relieved of the obligation to implement it at all.

---

[113] Letter James Brokenshire MP to Lord Roper, Chair of the European Union Committee of the House of Lords, 7 February 2011.

4

EXTRADITION

A. Overview

4.01 At the heart of EU extradition law is the European Council Framework Decision of 13 June 2002 on the European arrest warrant and the surrender procedures between Member States (Framework Decision on the EAW).[1] This abolished formal extradition procedures within the European Union and replaced them with a system of surrender between European judicial authorities. This system is based on the twin principles of judicial cooperation and mutual trust that characterise European criminal law as a whole. The Framework Decision on the EAW was enacted into UK law by Part 1 of the Extradition Act 2003 (the 2003 Act).

4.02 The purpose of this chapter is not to act as a guide to UK extradition law but instead to provide UK criminal and extradition practitioners with an understanding of the key principles of EU law that underpin Part 1 of the 2003 Act and guide its interpretation in the domestic courts.

B. The Framework Decision on the European Arrest Warrant

Background

4.03 The European Arrest Warrant (EAW) was the outcome of the increased focus on cooperation in criminal matters brought about by the Treaty of Amsterdam which came into force on 1 May 1999 (see Chapter 1 for a historical overview).

4.04 The groundwork for the EAW was laid at the meeting of the European Council in Tampere, Finland on 15 and 16 October 1999 at which it was decided that formal extradition

---

[1] 2002/584/JHA of 13 June 2002.

procedures within the EU should be abolished and replaced by a system of fast-track extradition for accused persons and the surrender of persons convicted and sentenced.[2] This system was to be based upon the principle of mutual recognition which the European Council endorsed as the 'cornerstone of judicial cooperation in both civil and criminal matters within the Union'.[3]

The European Council resolved to implement the principle of mutual recognition by means **4.05** of a programme of measures to be adopted by December 2000. The outcome of this programme and its subsequent timetable was that on 13 June 2002 the European Council adopted the Framework Decision on the EAW.

The legal framework

The legal foundation for the Framework Decision on the EAW was provided by the Treaty of **4.06** Amsterdam which inserted Articles 31(1)(b) and 34(2) into the Treaty on European Union (TEU).[4] Article 31(1)(b) provided that common action on judicial cooperation in criminal matters 'shall include . . . facilitating extradition between Member States'. Article 34(2) introduced the Framework Decision as a legislative instrument available for use by the European Council in the area of police and judicial cooperation in criminal matters.

The preamble to the Framework Decision on the EAW makes it clear that its purpose was to **4.07** facilitate the EU's objective of becoming an area of freedom, security, and justice by abolishing extradition procedures and replacing them with a system of surrender between judicial authorities.[5] Essentially, this amounted to a recognition that the free movement of criminal judicial decisions within the EU was a necessary corollary of the free movement of persons if criminals were to be prevented from using their Treaty rights in order to escape justice. The preamble also expressly recognised that such a system would need to be predicated on a high degree of confidence between Member States.[6]

The Framework Decision imposes an obligation on Member States, based on the principle **4.08** of mutual recognition, to execute any EAW issued to it without enquiring into the evidence behind the prosecution in the issuing Member State.[7] In addition, it contains provision for the minimum sentence thresholds of offences in respect of which an EAW may be issued,[8] double criminality,[9] mandatory and optional grounds for refusing an EAW,[10] and guarantees in relation to trials in absence, life sentences, and the temporary surrender of nationals.[11]

---

[2] European Council Document 200/1/99 of 16 October 1999, paras 33 and 35.
[3] European Council Document 200/1/99 of 16 October 1999, para. 33.
[4] Both of the provisions were repealed by the Lisbon Treaty and do not appear in the Treaty on the Functioning of the European Union. Framework Decisions adopted prior to the entry into force of the Lisbon Treaty are subject to the transitional arrangements contained in Protocol No. 36 to the Lisbon Treaty.
[5] Preamble to the European Council Framework Decision of 13 June 2002 on the European arrest warrant and the surrender procedures between Member States into national law, recital 5.
[6] Preamble to the European Council Framework Decision of 13 June 2002 on the European arrest warrant and the surrender procedures between Member States into national law, recital 10.
[7] Article 1(2); *Office of the King's Prosecutor, Brussels v Cando Armas and Anr* [2006] 2 AC 1, HL, para. 52.
[8] Article 2(1).
[9] Article 2(2).
[10] Articles 3 and 4. In relation to double jeopardy (Art. 3(2)) see Chapter **5.166**.
[11] Article 5. See also consideration of trial in absence at Chapter **5.188**.

It also specifies the formal requirements of an EAW,[12] the procedural requirements for their transmission,[13] and time limits.[14]

4.09 From the perspective of the requested person, the Framework Decision provides for certain individual rights,[15] provisions in relation to bail,[16] consent to surrender,[17] the right to a hearing,[18] and the doctrine of speciality.[19]

The key features of the Framework Decision on the European Arrest Warrant

Legal effect of Framework Decisions

4.10 Framework Decisions bind Member States as to the result to be achieved but leave national authorities free as to the method of implementation.[20] In the UK the method of implementation of the Framework Decision on the EAW was Part 1 of the Extradition Act 2003.

4.11 In *Criminal Proceedings Against Pupino*, the Court of Justice of the European Union (CJEU) held that there was an obligation on Member States to interpret national legislation, as far as possible, in conformity with the Framework Decision on the EAW.[21] Although this Decision is not binding on the UK courts, there is a common law presumption that Parliament would not intend to legislate contrary to the international obligations of the UK. In *Assange v Swedish Prosecution Authority*, the Supreme Court described this presumption as having 'considerable potency' in determining the proper interpretation of the 2003 Act.[22]

Transfer not extradition

4.12 The purpose of the Framework Decision on the EAW was to replace the extradition arrangements within the EU with a new simplified system of surrender designed to remove the delay and complexity that was inherent in the previous system.[23] In order to achieve this, the role of the executive in the extradition process was replaced with cooperation between judicial authorities. Although the drafters of the 2003 Act opted to retain the term 'extradition', the case law of the CJEU has made it clear that 'the move from extradition to the European Arrest Warrant constitutes a complete change of direction'.[24]

Mutual trust

4.13 Central to the functioning of the EAW is the principle of mutual trust. Recital 10 of the Preamble to the Framework Decision on the EAW states that the 'mechanism of the European arrest warrant is based on a high level of confidence between Member States'.

---

[12] Article 8.
[13] Articles 9 and 10.
[14] Article 17.
[15] Article 11.
[16] Article 12.
[17] Article 13.
[18] Article 14.
[19] Article 27. The doctrine of speciality refers to the rules restricting the right of the requesting State to deal with the requested person for offences other than those contained in the EAW after he has been surrendered.
[20] *Criminal Proceedings Against Pupino* [2006] QB 83; *Dabas v High Court of Justice in Madrid* [2007] 2 AC 31, HL.
[21] *Criminal Proceedings Against Pupino* [2006] QB 83; *Dabas v High Court of Justice in Madrid* [2007] 2 AC 31, HL.
[22] *Assange v Swedish Prosecution Authority* [2012] 2 WLR 1275, SC.
[23] European Council Framework Decision of 13 June 2002 on the European arrest warrant and the surrender procedures between Member States into national law, recital 5 and Art. 31.
[24] *Advocatenvoor de Wereld VZW v Leden van de Ministeraad* [2007] 3 CMLR 1, paras AG41–6.

This principle is derived from Article 82 of the Treaty on the Functioning of the European **4.14**
Union (TFEU) which makes it clear that judicial cooperation in criminal matters is to be
based on the principle of the mutual recognition of judgments and judicial decisions. The
effect of this principle is that a judgment in one Member State, such as a criminal conviction
and sentence, shall be recognised in all other Member States of the EU. Conceptually, the
basis of this cooperation is not that the separate interests of Member States happen to coin-
cide in this area, but rather that the interests of Member States in recognising and executing
criminal judgments across the EU are the same.[25] In other words, as Lord Bingham stated in
Dabas v High Court of Justice, Madrid:

> The important underlying assumption of the Framework Decision is that member states,
> sharing common values and recognising common rights, can and should trust the integrity
> and fairness of each other's judicial institutions.[26]

Nature of proceedings

The European Court of Human Rights (ECtHR) has consistently held that extradition pro- **4.15**
ceedings do not constitute the determination of a criminal charge within the meaning of
Article 6 of the European Convention on Human Rights (ECHR).[27] This approach has
also been endorsed before the CJEU.[28] The ECtHR has also held that decisions regarding
the entry, stay, and deportation of an alien (which includes extradition proceedings) do not
concern a determination of his civil rights so as to engage the civil limb of Article 6.[29]

In *Pomiechowski v District Court of Legnica, Poland* the Supreme Court drew a distinction **4.16**
between nationals and non-nationals as far as the civil limb of Article 6 in extradition proceedings is concerned. The court held that, unlike non-nationals, nationals who were subject
to extradition proceedings had a civil right to remain in their country of nationality that fell
within Article 6(1).[30]

As a general rule, Article 5 ECHR does not apply to extradition proceedings, with two lim- **4.17**
ited exceptions. The first is that a person may challenge the lawfulness of his detention in
the extradition context as in any other, although that does not mean the court has power to
review the underlying decision to expel or extradite.[31] The second is where there is an abuse
of process so that the detention and the extradition proceedings as a whole stand and fall
together.[32]

Extradition offences

An extradition offence is an offence in respect of which extradition may be sought. Article **4.18**
2(1) of the Framework Decision on the EAW sets down the basic procedural requirements
of an extradition offence. These are that the offence be punishable in the requesting State

---

[25] *Advocatenvoor de Wereld VZW v Leden van de Ministeraad* [2007] 3 CMLR 1, paras AG43, 45.
[26] [2007] 2 AC 31, HL, para. 4.
[27] *H v Spain* (1983) 37 DR 93; *EGM v Luxembourg* (1994) 77B DR 144.
[28] *Advocatenvoor de Wereld VZW v Leden van de Ministeraad* [2007] 3 CMLR 1, para. AG105 (per
Advocate-General Colomer).
[29] *Maaouia v France* (2000) 33 EHRR 1037; *Mamatkulov and Askarov v Turkey* (2005) 41 EHRR 494.
[30] *Pomiechowski v District Court of Legnica, Poland* [2012] 1 WLR 1604, SC.
[31] *Chahal v United Kingdom* (1997) 23 EHRR 413; *MT (Algeria) v Secretary of State for the Home Department*
[2010] 2 AC 110, HL.
[32] *R (Kashamu) v Governor of Brixton Prison* [2002] QB 887; *Fuller v Attorney General of Belize* [2011] UKPC
23, PC; *Pomiechowski v District Court of Legnica, Poland* [2012] 1 WLR 1604, SC.

with either a maximum sentence of at least 12 months' imprisonment (in cases in which the requested person is accused of the offence), or where a sentence of four months' imprisonment has been imposed (in cases in which the requested person has been convicted of the offence).

4.19 One of the most significant and controversial changes introduced by the Framework Decision on the EAW was the decision to dispense with the traditional extradition law concept of dual criminality[33] in relation to certain offences. Dual criminality requires the conduct in respect of which extradition is sought to amount to a criminal offence under the law of both the requesting and the requested States. The origins of the rule lie in the principle of reciprocity in international law, and the belief that assistance in enforcing the criminal laws of foreign States should only be given in relation to conduct deemed to be criminal under a State's domestic criminal law.[34]

4.20 Article 2(2) of the Framework Decision on the EAW sets down a list of 32 offences known as 'the Framework List' in respect of which the requirement of dual criminality is dispensed with. These offences are all classified as extradition offences as long as they are punishable under the law of the issuing Member State with a maximum sentence of at least three years.[35] The Framework Decision permits but does not require Member States to retain the dual criminality requirement in respect of offences that are not included in the Framework List.[36] As a result, it was the view of Advocate-General Colomer in *Advocaten voor de Wereld VZW v Leden van de Ministeraad* that, unlike previous extradition arrangements, the EAW system was not based on the principle of double criminality.[37]

4.21 In *Advocaten* the applicant argued that the definition of the offences in the Framework List were so vague as to breach the principle of legality as they were not sufficiently precise to allow a person to know, at the time an act was committed, whether or not it constituted a criminal offence.[38] The Court held that the definition of any offence and its penalty included in an EAW would be defined not by the Framework List but by the law of the issuing State. In addition, all Member States were subject to the requirements under Article 1(3) of the Framework Decision on the EAW and Article 6 TEU to respect fundamental rights and legal principles, including the principle of legality.

4.22 The applicants also argued that the distinction between Framework List offences in respect of which the requirement of dual criminality was excluded, and non-Framework List offences in respect of which the principle might be retained, amounted to an infringement of the principles of equality and non-discrimination.[39] The Court found that the combination of the inherent gravity of the offences on the Framework List, and the requirement of a minimum sentence threshold of three years, meant that they were all offences that as a matter of public policy ought to be criminal in every Member State and therefore the dispensation of

---

[33] Also known as double criminality.

[34] 'A Review of the United Kingdom's Extradition Arrangements', Presented to the Home Secretary on 30 September 2011, paras 35–6.

[35] European Council Framework Decision of 13 June 2002 on the European arrest warrant and the surrender procedures between Member States into national law, Art. 2(2).

[36] European Council Framework Decision of 13 June 2002 on the European arrest warrant and the surrender procedures between Member States into national law, Art. 2(4).

[37] [2007] 3 CMLR 1, para. AG 85.

[38] [2007] 3 CMLR 1, para. 48.

[39] [2007] 3 CMLR 1, para. 55.

the double criminality requirements in respect of each of them was objectively justified.[40] This judgment has been criticised for its brevity and its superficial treatment of the issues.[41]

Other criticisms of Article 2(2) of the Framework Decision on the EAW include the fear that **4.23** a person may be extradited from the UK for an offence that does not amount to criminal conduct in this jurisdiction, for example if abortion or assisted suicide were to be included within the definition of 'murder' on the Framework List. This concern is voiced by Lord Scott in his (dissenting) judgment in *Dabas*:

> There has been no harmonisation of the criminal laws of the European Union member states and, I believe, no widespread enthusiasm for any such harmonisation. So the possibility of surrender for prosecution in relation to conduct that would not be criminal in the requested state is a very live one.[42]

However, within the UK the risk of this is limited by the provisions of the 2003 Act that **4.24** provide that the Framework List is only applicable to conduct that occurred in the requesting State and no part of which occurred in the UK.[43] There is therefore no possibility of a person being extradited for conduct undertaken legally in the UK but which happens to contravene laws abroad.

Fundamental rights

The ECHR is the most familiar reference point for fundamental rights in UK domestic law **4.25** owing to its implementation through the Human Rights Act 1998. It plays a key role in domestic extradition proceedings as a result of the requirement in section 21 of the 2003 Act that extradition be refused where the judge decides that it would not be compatible with the person's Convention rights.

The Charter of Fundamental Rights and Freedoms of the European Union ('the Charter') **4.26** was signed on 7 December 2000. Its purpose was to codify into one text the existing rights and freedoms within the EU. The Charter receives more detailed analysis in Chapter 5.

The Charter was formally acknowledged by Article 6 TEU which recognises the rights, **4.27** freedoms, and principles set out in the Charter and deems it to have the same legal value as the European Treaties.[44] However, Article 1 of Protocol No. 30 expressly provides that nothing in the Charter provides justiciable rights applicable in the UK except insofar as already provided for under UK law. The CJEU has held that this Protocol does not call into question the applicability of the Charter in UK law and nor does it exempt the UK from the obligation to comply with its provisions.[45]

Article 4 of the Charter prohibits torture and cruel and degrading treatment in similar terms **4.28** to Article 3 ECHR, providing that:

> No one shall be subjected to torture or to inhuman or degrading treatment or punishment.

---

[40] [2007] 3 CMLR 1, paras 53 and 57.
[41] See e.g. F. Geyer, 'European Arrest Warrant: Court of Justice of the European Communities: Judgment of 3rd May 2007, Case C-303/05; *Advocaten voor de Wereld VZW v Leden van de Ministerraad*' (2008) 4(1) ECLR 149.
[42] *Dabas v High Court of Justice in Madrid* [2007] 2 AC 31, HL, para. 59.
[43] Extradition Act 2003, ss. 64(2) and 65(2).
[44] Article 6(1).
[45] *NS v Secretary of State for the Home Department* [2012] 2 CMLR 9.

4.29 Article 19 of the Charter makes express provision for extradition. Article 19(1) prohibits collective expulsions, and Article 19(2) states:

> No one may be removed, expelled or extradited to a State where there is a serious risk that he or she would be subjected to the death penalty, torture or other inhuman or degrading treatment or punishment.

4.30 The Framework Decision on the EAW itself states that nothing in it shall modify the obligation on Member States to respect fundamental rights as enshrined in Article 6 TEU. However, there is no express power to refuse extradition on the basis that it would be inconsistent with the requested person's fundamental rights. This apparent gap in protection is bridged in the UK context by section 21 of the Extradition Act 2003. In addition, the CJEU in *NS v Secretary of State for the Home Department* held that Article 4 of the Charter prohibited removal to another Member State where there were substantial grounds for believing that there was a real risk of inhuman or degrading treatment within the meaning of that provision.[46]

4.31 There is an ever-present tension between the principle of mutual trust under the Framework Decision on the EAW and the obligation on States to respect fundamental rights. This tension is reflected in the following observations of Scott Baker LJ in the case of *Hilali*:[47]

> It seems to us that the courts should give great weight to the fact that Spain is a western democracy, subject to the rule of law, a signatory of the European Convention of Human Rights and a party to the Framework Decision; it is a country which has and which applies the same human rights standards and is subject to the same international obligations as the United Kingdom. These surely are highly relevant matters which strongly militate against refusing extradition on the grounds of the risk of violating those standards and obligations.

4.32 The CJEU in *NS* considered this tension and held that any presumption that other Member States would respect fundamental rights had to be rebuttable in order to be consistent with the obligations under the Charter.[48]

Proportionality

4.33 Proportionality is a core principle of EU law set out in Article 5(1) TEU which states that the 'use of Union competences is governed by the principles of subsidiarity and proportionality'. Article 5(4) TEU provides:

> Under the principle of proportionality, the content and form of Union action shall not exceed what is necessary to achieve the objectives of the Treaties.

4.34 In EU law proportionality is usually considered as consisting of two or three elements depending on how the stages are analysed, all of which include an assessment of whether the measure is suitable to achieve the objectives claimed as its justification, whether a less intrusive measure is available, and whether the impact of the measure is disproportionate to its aims. The latter two factors are usually treated as part of a balancing exercise.[49]

---

[46] *NS v Secretary of State for the Home Department* [2012] 2 CMLR 9, para. 106.

[47] *Hilali v The Central Court of Criminal Proceedings Number 5 of the National Court, Madrid* [2006] EWHC 1239 (Admin).

[48] *NS v Secretary of State for the Home Department* [2012] 2 CMLR 9, paras 99 and 104.

[49] A. O'Neil, *EU Law for UK Lawyers* (Oxford: Hart Publishing, 2011), para. 2.138; F. T. Tridimas, 'Proportionality in Community Law: Searching for the Appropriate Standard of Scrutiny' in E. Ellis (ed.), *The Principle of Proportionality in the Laws of Europe* (Oxford: Hart Publishing, 1999), 68; *Rau v European Economic Community* [1988] 2 CMLR 704, 734–5 and 750–1.

In the context of rights, the ECtHR also views proportionality as a key principle of law, but **4.35** uses a simpler and less rigid test than that applied by the CJEU. The ECtHR assesses proportionality by balancing the measure under challenge and its aim with the individual right that is said to be infringed. In addition, the ECtHR applies certain other key doctrines and principles such as the margin of appreciation, and the requirements of a 'pressing social need' and 'particularly serious reasons' to justify an interference.[50]

In practice the UK courts have adopted a more structured approach, similar to the EU law **4.36** test, in relation to proportionality in the context of fundamental rights. That test is:[51]

- whether the legislative objective is sufficiently important to justify limiting a fundamental right;
- whether the measures designed to meet the legislative objective are rationally connected to it; and
- whether the means used to impair the right or freedom are no more than is necessary to accomplish the objective.

Article 49 of the Charter is entitled 'Principles of legality and proportionality of criminal **4.37** offences and penalties'. Article 49(3) provides:

> The severity of penalties must not be disproportionate to the criminal offence.

The principle of proportionality may apply in extradition cases in the context of human **4.38** rights law when a Convention right is engaged. However, its applicability in the context of EU extradition law is less clear.

In Germany, where the principle of proportionality has a strong grounding in domestic **4.39** law, the courts have applied Article 49(3) of the Charter to decisions under the Framework Decision on the EAW in order to permit the courts to conduct an assessment of whether extradition was proportionate given the seriousness of the offence in question and any sentence that had been, or might be, imposed.[52]

The Framework Decision on the EAW does not include any requirement of proportionality **4.40** in relation to extradition offences. However, the European Council in its *Council Handbook on How to Issue a European Arrest Warrant* has encouraged Member States to consider proportionality before deciding to issue a warrant by considering factors such as the seriousness of the offence, the possibility of detention, and the likely penalty. The *Handbook* states:

> The EAW should not be chosen where the coercive measure that seems proportionate, adequate and applicable to the case in hand is not preventive detention. The warrant should not be issued, for instance, where, although preventive detention is admissible, another non-custodial coercive measure may be chosen . . . or one which would imply the immediate release of the person after the first judicial hearing.[53]

---

[50] See e.g. *Handyside v United Kingdom* (1979–80) 1 EHRR 737, paras 87–9; *Smith and Grady v United Kingdom* (2000) 29 EHRR 493, paras 87–9.

[51] *De Freitas v Permanent Secretary of Ministry of Agriculture, Fisheries, Lands and Housing* [1999] 1 AC 68, PC at 80; *R (Daly) v Secretary of State for the Home Department* [2001] 2 AC 532, HL.

[52] 1 Ausl 1302/99; 1 Ausl (24) 1246/09. These cases are summarised in J. Vogel and J. R. Spencer, 'Proportionality and the European Arrest Warrant' [2010] Crim LR 210, and 'A Review of the United Kingdom's Extradition Arrangements', Presented to the Home Secretary on 30 September 2011, paras 5.131–5.136.

[53] Council 17195/1/10 REV 1 COPEN 275 EJN 72 EUROJUST 139, p 14.

4.41 In *Assange v Swedish Prosecution Authority* the Supreme Court considered criticisms that EAWs were being issued for trivial offences by certain Member States and concluded that:

> The scheme of the EAW needs to be reconsidered in order to make express provision for consideration of proportionality. It makes sense for that question to be considered as part of the process of issue of the EAW. To permit proportionality to be raised at the stage of execution would result in delay that would run counter to the scheme.[54]

4.42 In Article 8 ECHR cases the court may consider the seriousness of the offence(s) in an EAW as part of the proportionality exercise.[55] In *HH v Deputy Prosecutor of the Italian Republic of Genoa* Lady Hale stated that an Article 8 proportionality check was not required before an EAW could be issued, but that there must be 'some relationship of proportionality between the offending and the consequences'.[56] The extent to which an individual can rely on proportionality arguments in relation to the seriousness of the offence(s) in an EAW in a context other than Article 8 is unclear. The Charter applies in the UK in relation to the implementation of EU law which includes the Framework Decision on the EAW.[57] It is, therefore, possible that the UK courts may be persuaded to adopt proportionality arguments in similar terms to those accepted by the German courts. However, as can be seen from *Assange*, insofar as such arguments add an additional layer of complexity and delay to the EAW system they will be treated with caution.

C. The Implementation of the Framework Decision on the European Arrest Warrant in the UK

4.43 The Framework Decision on the EAW was enacted into UK law by Part 1 of the Extradition Act 2003, although the drafters chose not to adopt the exact language of the Framework Decision. The 2003 Act provides a statutory roadmap of the issues that the judge at the extradition hearing must consider which are as follows:

- whether the offences in the EAW constitute extradition offences within the meaning of the 2003 Act;[58]
- whether there are any bars to extradition;[59]
- whether in conviction cases the conviction occurred in the person's presence and, if not, whether there are sufficient safeguards in place to allow the person's extradition;[60]
- whether the requested person's extradition would be compatible with his rights under the European Convention on Human Rights.[61]

4.44 Although Part 1 of the 2003 Act largely reflects the provisions of the Framework Decision on the EAW there are three key differences. First, the 2003 Act has retained the terminology of 'extradition' rather than that of 'surrender' used in the Framework Decision. Secondly, the

---

[54] [2012] 2 WLR 1275, SC, para. 90.
[55] *Norris v Government of the United States of America (No. 2)* [2010] 2 AC 487, SC, paras 32, 63, 91, 109, and 114; *HH v Deputy Prosecutor of the Italian Republic of Genoa* [2012] UKSC 25, SC, paras 45, 91–2, 133, 146, and 148.
[56] [2012] UKSC 25, SC.
[57] *NS v Secretary of State for the Home Department* [2012] 2 CMLR 9.
[58] Extradition Act 2003, ss. 10, 64, and 65.
[59] Extradition Act 2003, ss. 11–19A.
[60] Extradition Act 2003, s. 20.
[61] Extradition Act 2003, s. 21.

UK has retained a double criminality requirement for Framework List offences where part of the offence occurred in the UK.[62] Thirdly, the 2003 Act includes a number of grounds for refusing extradition that do not derive from the Framework Decision. These are the bars of extraneous considerations,[63] passage of time,[64] hostage-taking considerations,[65] and onward extradition,[66] and the human rights test in section 21.[67]

The UK courts have repeatedly emphasised the obligation to interpret the 2003 Act in con-   **4.45**
formity with the terms of the Framework Decision on the EAW. Thus, in *Cando Armas* the House of Lords highlighted the twin assumptions that, first, Parliament did not intend the 2003 Act to be inconsistent with the Framework Decision and, secondly, while Parliament might provide for a greater measure of protection than the Framework Decision required, it did not intend to provide for less.[68]

This approach can be seen running through the seven Part 1 extradition cases that have   **4.46**
appeared before the House of Lords and the Supreme Court on points of procedure.[69] In those cases, the court has consistently interpreted the 2003 Act in conformity with the Framework Decision and in a manner that facilitates rather than hinders extradition within the EU. The court has repeatedly emphasised the aim of the Framework Decision in removing the complexity and delay that was inherent in the previous extradition system,[70] the need for a broad internationalist approach,[71] and counselled against interpreting the 2003 Act so as to impose additional formalities not found in the Framework Decision that might frustrate the objective of speedy surrender between EU States.[72]

The proposed opt-out

In a statement to the House of Commons on 15 October 2012, the Home Secretary indi-   **4.47**
cated the Government's intention to opt out of all pre-Lisbon police and criminal justice measures, including the EAW. She stated that the Government proposed to negotiate with the European Commission and other Member States to opt back in to 'those individual measures that it is in our national interest to rejoin'. During the ensuing debate, the Home Secretary would not be drawn on which measures the Government would seek to opt back into,[73] although in relation to the EAW she said that 'A number of issues have been raised in this House and elsewhere about the proportionality issue in relation to the European arrest warrant'.[74] The Home Secretary confirmed that she expected transitional arrangements to be

---

[62] Extradition Act 2003, ss. 64(2) and (4), 65(2) and (4).
[63] Extradition Act 2003, s. 13.
[64] Extradition Act 2003, s. 14.
[65] Extradition Act 2003, s. 16.
[66] Extradition Act 2003, ss. 18 and 19.
[67] Extradition Act 2003, s. 21.
[68] *Office of the King's Prosecutor, Brussels v Cando Armas and Anr* [2006] 2 AC 1, HL, para. 8.
[69] *Office of the King's Prosecutor, Brussels v Cando Armas and Anr* [2006] 2 AC 1, HL, para. 8; *Dabas v High Court of Justice in Madrid, Spain* [2007] 2 AC 31, HL; *Pilecki v Circuit Court of Legnica, Poland* [2008] 1 WLR 325, HL; *Caldarelli v Judge for Preliminary Investigations of the Court of Naples, Italy* [2008] 1 WLR 1724, HL; *Louca v Public Prosecutor, Bielefeld, Germany* [2009] 1 WLR 2550, SC; *Assange v Swedish Prosecution Authority* [2012] 2 WLR 1275, SC; *Pomiechowski v District Court of Legnica, Poland* [2012] 1 WLR 1604, SC.
[70] *Pilecki v Circuit Court of Legnica, Poland* [2008] 1 WLR 325, HL.
[71] *Caldarelli v Judge for Preliminary Investigations of the Court of Naples, Italy* [2008] 1 WLR 1724, HL.
[72] *Dabas v High Court of Justice in Madrid, Spain* [2007] 2 AC 31, HL.
[73] Hansard HC Deb, 15 October 2012, vol 551, col 35.
[74] Hansard HC Deb, 15 October 2012, vol 551, col 38.

available in the period between the mass opt-out and opting back in to individual measures and that it was proposed that this period would be as short as possible.[75]

4.48   At the time of writing, the consequences of any opt-out are unclear. What is clear is that the UK requires some form of extradition arrangement with the rest of Europe, not least to avoid becoming a safe haven for fugitive criminals. One possible outcome would be for the UK to opt back into the Framework Decision on the EAW, either in its current form, or a renegotiated version. As outlined earlier, the concerns relating to proportionality voiced by the Home Secretary are also recognised by the European Council in its Handbook on *How to Issue a European Arrest Warrant* and attempts to renegotiate the existing Framework Decision to reflect those concerns may be welcomed by some Member States.

4.49   A second, more radical, outcome would be not to opt back into the EAW. In principle, this would not leave the UK entirely without extradition relations within Europe given that it remains a signatory to the European Convention on Extradition 1957, along with all the other EAW Member States. The wording and structure of the Extradition Act 2003 are such that little amendment to the legislation would be required: the Government could simply re-designate the current EAW States as 'Category 2' territories to allow the UK to continue to extradite to and from those States. In legal terms, there would be a number of key differences in an extradition process under the 1957 Convention and Part 2 of the 2003 Act. First, the decision to certify the extradition request at the beginning of the process would lie with the Secretary of State.[76] Secondly, the judge at the extradition hearing would consider whether the offence requested was an extradition offence and would need to be satisfied that dual criminality was established in respect of all the offences contained in the request (as the Framework list would not apply).[77] Thirdly, the judge would only consider whether the bars of double jeopardy, extraneous considerations, passage of time, and hostage-taking considerations applied,[78] as well as human rights issues, but the questions of the death penalty, speciality and prior extradition, or transfer from another territory or the International Criminal Court would lie with the Secretary of State.[79] Finally, the decision to extradite would also lie with the Secretary of State.[80]

4.50   However, although the legal picture outlined is capable of being relatively neat, there may be a number of practical difficulties with either attempting to renegotiate the current EAW, or choosing not to opt back in at all. The first is that other Member States may not be willing or able to renegotiate the terms of the current Framework Decision.[81] Equally, those States may for political or legal reasons be unwilling to have extradition relations with the UK outside the Framework Decision on the EAW. This would leave the UK in the uncomfortable position of being unable to extradite suspected or convicted criminals to certain parts of Europe, and being unable to seek the return of such persons to the UK. Furthermore, extradition

---

[75]   Hansard HC Deb, 15 October 2012, vol 551, col 38.
[76]   Extradition Act 2003, s. 70.
[77]   Extradition Act 2003, s. 78(4)(b).
[78]   Extradition Act 2003, s. 79.
[79]   Extradition Act 2003, s. 93.
[80]   Extradition Act 2003, s. 93.
[81]   One of the causes of the proportionality issue in relation to the EAW is that certain States have a statutory obligation to prosecute all offences, and to issue EAWs in relation to them, irrespective of their gravity. Those States may be unable to agree to a proportionality-based amendment to the current Framework Decision because of the constraints of their own domestic legal provisions.

under the 1957 Convention is undoubtedly slower and more cumbersome than extradition under the EAW scheme. Finally, the UK may no longer have access to the European Schengen Information System which is a highly effective database used by Member States to locate fugitive criminals.

It remains to be seen what (if any) change to the EAW will materialise in practice. It is clear, however, that if the Government proceed to opt out of the Framework Decision on the EAW, care will be required to ensure the continued effectiveness of the UK's extradition arrangements within the EU. **4.51**

PART III

POST ARREST

5

PROCEDURAL SAFEGUARDS: THE RIGHTS OF SUSPECTS, DEFENDANTS, AND VICTIMS

A. Overview

5.01 The concept of mutual legal recognition has been the primary method by which integration in justice matters has been developed in the EU.[1] It is based upon common trust (or comity) among Member States in one another's criminal justice systems. As increased freedom of movement and the European Arrest Warrant (EAW) scheme have led to greater numbers of EU citizens facing criminal proceedings in foreign countries, concern has been expressed about the varying degrees of protection of the fundamental rights of defendants and victims in some Member States. This has led to growing calls for harmonisation of procedural safeguards in order to ensure that minimum standards exist across the EU.

5.02 The process of harmonisation has been piecemeal. This chapter seeks to provide a comprehensive guide to the sources of procedural safeguards for both defendants and victims. As a result of the increased EU competence in the area of justice following the Treaty of Lisbon, along with harmonisation initiatives already underway, it is ever more important that practitioners are aware of these protections.

5.03 There are also significant benefits to be derived from relying on EU law in criminal litigation.[2] First, the supremacy of EU law means that primary and subordinate legislation which is declared incompatible with directly effective EU law must not be applied by the national courts.[3] This can be contrasted with protections afforded by the European Convention on Human Rights (ECHR)—under section 4 of the Human Rights Act 1998 (HRA 1998) a national court can only make a declaration of the incompatibility of the primary legislation with ECHR rights.

5.04 Secondly, the scope and coverage of EU law rights is potentially more extensive than that afforded by ECHR rights. For example, Article 47(2) of the Charter[4] corresponds to the Article 6(1) ECHR right to a fair trial, but it is not limited to criminal trials and the determination of civil rights and obligations and criminal charges. This could be of significance in practice where individuals do not enjoy the protection of Article 6(1) ECHR, for example in extradition and immigration proceedings.

5.05 Thirdly, awards of compensation may be more readily available for damage suffered as a result of a Member State implementing EU legislation in breach of fundamental rights than for a breach of a claimant's ECHR rights. Under EU law, the question when considering an award of damages is whether the damage suffered is sufficiently serious. [5] In contrast, damages under section 8 of the HRA 1998 are discretionary and, in practice, are awarded rarely. EU law also allows a claim for damages to be made for a failure to introduce primary legislation. Again, this can be contrasted with the position under section 6(6) of the HRA 1998, which prohibits such a challenge.

---

[1] See Art. 82(1) TFEU. Articles 2, 3, and 67(1) TFEU provide that the EU constitutes an area of freedom, security, and justice, founded on the values of the rule of law and respect for human rights.

[2] See Kieron Beal and Tom Hickman, '*Beano* No More: The EU Charter of Rights After Lisbon' [2001] JR 113.

[3] See Case 6/64 *Costa v ENEL* [1964] ECR 585; Case 106/77 *Simmenthal II* [1978] ECR 629; Case C-106/89 *Marleasing* [1990] ECR I-7321; Case C-213/89 *Factortame* [1990] ECR I-2433.

[4] The Charter of Fundamental Rights of the European Union [2000] OJ C 364/01.

[5] See Joined Cases C-6 and 9/90 *Francovich and Bonifaci v Italy* [1991] ECR I-5357; Case C-392/93 *R v HM Treasury, ex p British Telecommunications plc* [1996] ECR I-1631; Case C-127/95 *Norbrook Laboratories v Ministry of Agriculture, Fisheries and Food* [1998] ECR I-1531.

The primary sources of EU criminal procedural safeguards are the fundamental rights as contained within the ECHR, the Charter, and the general principles of the EU law as developed by the jurisprudence of the Court of Justice of the European Union (CJEU). Following the Treaty of Lisbon, negotiations are underway for the EU to become a signatory to the ECHR. This significant development raises the prospect of individual complaints about EU institutions (including the CJEU) being made before the Strasbourg Court. Previously, the ECHR and Strasbourg's jurisprudence were applied indirectly as they were considered to constitute part of the general principles of EU law. **5.06**

Procedural safeguards have also been developed through secondary EU law, the most significant of which is the Roadmap.[6] The Roadmap, introduced in December 2009 to replace the 2004 draft Framework Decision on procedural rights, sets out six measures to be implemented for the development of equivalent standards of basic procedural rights across Member States. This means that defendants will benefit from the rights contained in the measures regardless of whether the criminal offence has a cross-border or EU aspect.[7] **5.07**

The areas covered by the six measures include matters of translation and interpretation; the provision of information and communication with others on arrest; legal advice and legal aid; safeguards for vulnerable defendants; and pre-trial detention. The list of measures is non-exhaustive and the Roadmap encourages the Council to consider the possibility of introducing other procedural rights in the future. Recently, progress has gathered momentum. In 2010, the first Directive arising out of the Roadmap concerning the right to interpretation and translation in criminal proceedings was adopted by the European Parliament and Council.[8] Subsequently, in March 2012, a Directive on the right to information in criminal proceedings was adopted.[9] The UK has indicated its willingness to opt in to each of these measures. **5.08**

However, the UK's position in relation to the 2011 proposed Directive on the right of access to a lawyer and to communicate on arrest[10] is less clear, having initially opted out because of concerns about the breadth of the rights proposed. For example, the Directive proposed that an accused should have a right to have a lawyer present at every stage of an investigation, including from the outset at the police station, regardless of the seriousness of the offence. The concern was that the proposed Directive would confer rights on defendants which went far beyond the protections afforded by the Article 6 case law of the European Court of Human Rights (ECtHR). It remains to be seen whether following further negotiations the UK will support this particular measure. The rights identified in the Roadmap in relation to detention and pre-trial investigation also raise issues, which are addressed in this chapter, of funding in cross-border cases (Section E) and pre-trial supervision (Section F). **5.09**

The power to take the legislative steps required for the Roadmap is now enshrined in Article 82(2) TFEU (set out at **1.55**). That provision expressly contemplates the establishment of further rules (in the character of Directives) to facilitate mutual recognition of judgments **5.10**

---

[6]   Resolution of the Council of 30 November 2009 on a 'Roadmap' for strengthening procedural rights of suspected or accused persons in criminal proceedings [2009] OJ C 295/01. The Roadmap is addressed in Section D.

[7]   Caroline Morgan, 'Where are We now with EU Procedural Rights?' [2012] EHRLR 427.

[8]   2010/64/EU.

[9]   PE-CONS 78/11.

[10]   COM 2011/1054.

and judicial decisions, and police and judicial cooperation in criminal matters having a cross-border dimension in relation to certain areas:

(a) the mutual admissibility of evidence between Member States;

(b) the rights of individuals in criminal proceedings;

(c) the rights of victims of crime; and

(d) any other specific aspects of criminal procedure which the Council has identified in advance (achieved by a unanimous decision of the Council, having the consent of the European Parliament).[11]

5.11 In the coming years it is to be expected that the EU will develop further rules for the protection of individual rights. This chapter also examines several other discrete areas in which EU law already has significant relevance to defendants in criminal proceedings including jurisdictional issues (Section G) and double jeopardy (Section H), in relation to both of which the principle of *ne bis in idem* is engaged, trial *in absentia* (Section I), data protection (Section J), and specific issues relevant to OLAF investigations (Section K).

5.12 Article 82(2) also envisages the establishment of minimum rules to protect the rights of victims of crime. There has already been significant progress in this area since the landmark CJEU case of *Cowan v Trésor*[12] established that victims have rights to compensation regardless of their nationality. The 2001 Framework Decision[13] established standards to ensure that victims are informed, involved, and supported despite residing in a different Member State to where the crime was committed. Despite such progress, it is recognised that further work is needed. More recent developments include the European Protection Order, a measure that will allow an individual protected under the law in one Member State, for example by a restraining order, to apply for similar protection if they move to a different Member State. There is also a proposed new Framework Decision, which will expand and replace the rights set out in the 2001 counterpart, including providing victims with a right to review decisions not to prosecute.[14]

B. The European Union and the European Convention on Human Rights

5.13 At present, the EU itself is not a party to the ECHR. This means that the EU and its institutions are not bound by the ECHR and the Strasbourg jurisprudence. The enforcement of fundamental rights within the EU is provided for by a separate legal jurisdiction with the CJEU as its highest court. The CJEU has applied the ECHR and the ECtHR's case law indirectly, as part of the general principles of EU law.[15] In addition, all Member States are parties

---

[11] If a member of the Council considers that a draft Directive would affect fundamental aspects of the criminal justice system, it may request that the draft is referred to the European Council (Art. 82(3) TFEU). In those circumstances, the ordinary legislative procedure is suspended. Within four months, the European Council shall refer the draft Directive back to the Council in order that the ordinary legislative procedure is resumed. In the case of disagreement, a minimum of nine Member States may establish enhanced cooperation on the basis of the draft Directive (Art. 329(1) TFEU).

[12] [1989] ECR 195.

[13] 2001/220/JHA.

[14] In July 2012, following the Court of Appeal case of *R v Killick* [2011] EWCA Crim 1608, which referred to the proposed Directive, the CPS announced that guidance on the right of review for victims will be issued.

[15] See Art. 6(3) TEU.

to the ECHR and are obliged to respect ECHR rights in their application and interpretation of EU law.

Following the coming into force of the Treaty of Lisbon on 1 December 2009, Article 6(2) **5.14** TFEU imposed an obligation on the EU to accede to the ECHR. The legal basis for EU accession is provided by Article 59(2) ECHR, as amended by Protocol No. 14, which came into force in June 2010. This means that the ECHR, as interpreted and applied by the ECtHR, and the ECtHR's external judicial mechanism will apply to EU acts. Therefore, an individual will be able to seek redress before the ECtHR in relation to an infringement of the ECHR by an EU institution or by a Member State implementing EU law.

Negotiations for the terms on which the EU will accede to the ECHR are ongoing. As at **5.15** the time of writing, the EU Steering Committee for Human Rights, advised by a working group of seven Member States and seven non-Member States, has passed to the Committee of Ministers a set of draft legal instruments to implement the accession.[16] The most important of these instruments is the draft Agreement on the Accession of the European Union to the ECHR (the draft Accession Agreement). Once finalised, it is expected that the opinions of the Parliament and the two European Courts will be sought before the Committee of Ministers adopts a final accession agreement to be ratified by all parties to the ECHR and the EU. The future relationship between the Courts in Luxembourg and Strasbourg is not yet clear, though some indication of the issues involved was given in a joint statement of the Presidents of the Courts, dated 27 January 2011.

One of the key issues identified in the joint statement concerns the distinction between direct **5.16** and indirect actions. Direct actions are defined as individual applications directed against measures adopted by EU institutions subsequent to the EU accession to the ECHR. On the other hand, indirect actions are described as individual applications against acts adopted by the authorities of the Member States for the application or implementation of EU law.

In relation to direct actions, the joint statement of the Presidents of the European Courts notes **5.17** that Article 35(1) ECHR will require individuals to exhaust domestic remedies. This means that applicants to the ECtHR will first have to refer their complaint to the EU Courts.

In relation to indirect actions, the situation is more complicated. An applicant will have to **5.18** refer the matter to the domestic courts of the Member State concerned. The domestic courts may, or in some cases must, refer a question to the EU Courts for a preliminary ruling on the interpretation or validity of the provision of EU law under consideration, pursuant to Article 267 TFEU. It is conceivable that a situation could arise where the domestic court did not make a preliminary reference. The ECtHR could then be required to adjudicate on a matter concerning EU law without the EU Courts having had the opportunity to consider the complaint. The joint statement suggests that a procedure should be put in place to allow for the EU Courts to consider the case before the ECtHR conducts its external review.

The key points in the draft Accession Agreement are as follows: **5.19**

(a) the draft Accession Agreement provides for a co-respondent mechanism whereby EU Member States and the EU can request to be a co-respondent party in ECtHR cases concerning EU law;

---

[16] CDDH-UE (2011)16.

(b) in relation to the point identified in the joint statement of the European Courts, the draft Accession Agreement provides for the possibility of the EU Courts making an assessment of the compatibility of EU law under the accelerated procedure of the CJEU;

(c) not all Member States have ratified the six additional Protocols to the ECHR. As a result, accession to the ECHR does not mean that the EU will be automatically bound by the Protocols. The draft Accession Agreement sets out that the EU will initially ascend to the first Protocol (including the protection of possessions and the right to education amongst others) and Protocol No. 6 (abolition of the death penalty). It is expected that the EU will have to take separate decisions whether to become a party to each of the other Protocols;

(d) there will be an EU judge elected to the ECtHR who will have the same responsibilities and status as the other judges; and

(e) the Accession Agreement will come into force three months after ratification by all Council of Europe Member States and by the EU.

C. The Charter of Fundamental Rights of the European Union

Background

5.20 On 3 and 4 June 1999, the European Council proposed a Convention to 'establish a Charter of fundamental rights in order to make their overriding importance and relevance more visible to the Union's citizens.' The Charter was to enshrine the fundamental rights and freedoms as well as basic procedural rights guaranteed by the ECHR, general principles of EU law, and fundamental rights that pertain only to EU citizens. The economic and social rights contained in the European Social Charter and the Community Charter of the Fundamental Social Rights of Workers (Art. 136 TEC) were also to be taken into consideration.[17]

5.21 On 2 October 2000, the Convention, consisting of representatives of the Heads of State and governments, national parliaments, the European Parliament, and the Commission, met and adopted a draft Charter of Fundamental Rights of the European Union. On 13 and 14 October 2000, the European Council unanimously approved the Charter. Shortly afterwards, on 14 November 2000, the European Parliament gave its agreement and the approval of the European Commission followed on 6 December 2000.

5.22 On 7 December 2000, the Presidents of the European Parliament, the European Council, and the European Commission signed the Charter on behalf of their institutions. The Charter was described as 'combining in a single text the civil, political, economic, social and societal rights hitherto laid down in a variety of international, European or national sources...' The question of how the Charter was to be given legal force, however, was expressly left open.[18] At the outset at least, the Charter was no more than a political declaration[19] but it was not long before Advocates-General and the CJEU began to refer to the Charter rights.[20]

---

[17] Annex IV, Conclusions of the Cologne Presidency, 3–4 June 1999.

[18] Conclusions of the Nice Presidency, 7–10 December 2000.

[19] In 2000, the UK Government insisted that the Charter would not be incorporated into the EU Treaties and the then Europe Minister, Keith Vaz MP said that it would be no more legally binding than a copy of the *Beano* or the *Sun*, see George Jones and Ambrose Evans-Pritchard, 'European Summit Charter on Rights "No More Binding than the *Beano*"', *Daily Telegraph*, 14 October 2000.

[20] See e.g. Case C-173/99 *BECTU v Secretary of State for Trade and Industry* [2001] ECR I-4881 per Advocate-General Tizzano; Case T-54/99 *Max.mobil Telekommunikation Service GmbH v Commission* [2002] ECR II-313, GC; Case C-275/06 *Productores de Música España (Promusicae)* [2008] ECR I-271, CJEU.

The Charter was also a significant point of reference in domestic proceedings before the **5.23** Lisbon Treaty came into force. For example in *R (A, B, X and Y) v East Sussex County Council*,[21] Munby J noted that,

> The Charter is not at present legally binding in our domestic law and is therefore not a source of law in the strict sense. But it can . . . properly be consulted insofar as it proclaims, reaffirms or elucidates the content of those human rights that are generally recognized throughout the European family of nations, in particular the nature and scope of those fundamental rights that are guaranteed by the Convention.[22]

The Charter was subsequently amended as a result of the negotiations for the abandoned **5.24** European Constitution and further amended ahead of the Lisbon Treaty. On 12 December 2007, in Strasbourg, the amended Charter was proclaimed and formally signed by the Presidents of the European Parliament, the Council, and the Commission. Following the coming into force of the Lisbon Treaty on 1 December 2009, Article 6(1) TFEU gave the Charter force as a matter of EU law.

Scope of the Charter

Article 6(1) of the Lisbon Treaty declares that the Charter will have the same legal value as **5.25** the Treaties. The Charter, therefore, has direct legal effect.

Article 51(1) of the Charter addresses its application to the institutions of the EU, to bodies **5.26** established under EU law, and to Member States. Notably, the Charter rights are justiciable and can be relied on by practitioners in two limited situations. First, when challenging the legislative and executive acts of EU institutions and, secondly, when Member States implement EU law,[23] although, in some cases, this is purportedly subject to further caveats (see further **5.32** on application to the UK, Poland, and the Czech Republic). Articles 51(2) and 6(2) of the Lisbon Treaty make plain that the Charter does not extend the competencies of the EU.

A recent reference for a preliminary ruling by the Administrative Court in Sofia, *Anton* **5.27** *Vinkov v Nachalnik Administrativno-nakazatelna deynost*, affirms that the Charter of Fundamental Rights applies to Member States only when implementing EU law.[24] In that case, Mr Vinkov collided with a car whilst reversing in a car park. A local official imposed a small fine on Mr Vinkov and deducted four penalty points from his licence. That deduction triggered automatic disqualification. He appealed the decision to the District Court of Sofia which decided that, as the fine was below a certain amount, the decision could not be challenged in court. He appealed to the Administrative Court in Sofia which made a reference for a preliminary ruling to the CJEU. The Administrative Court asked, amongst other questions, whether EU law precluded the Bulgarian law in that it involved an infringement of the right to an effective remedy enshrined in Article 6 ECHR and Articles 47 and 28 of the Charter.

---

[21] [2003] EWHC 167 (Admin), para. 73.
[22] The judgment helpfully cites references to the Charter in other UK domestic case law and in opinions provided by Advocates-General in cases in the EU Courts.
[23] See Case C-339/10 *Asparuhov Estov and Others* [2010]; Case C-457/09 *Chartry* [2011]; and order of 14 December 2011 in Joined Cases C-483/11 and C-484/11 *Boncea and Others* [2012].
[24] Case C-27/11 *Anton Vinkov v Nachalnik Administrativno-nakazatelna deynost* [2012] CJEU.

5.28 Perhaps unsurprisingly, the reference for a preliminary ruling was declared inadmissible. Although reference to the 1998 Convention on Driving Disqualifications[25] and the Framework Decision on the mutual recognition of financial penalties[26] were made, the CJEU decided that it was

> not apparent from the order for reference that the national legislation constitutes a measure implementing EU law or that it is connected in any other way with EU law. Accordingly, the jurisdiction of the Court to rule on the reference for a preliminary ruling in so far as it relates to the fundamental right to an effective remedy is not established.

5.29 In reaching that conclusion, the CJEU emphasised that the principle of mutual recognition is only relevant to cross-border proceedings. Mr Vinkov's dispute was an internal matter: he resided in Bulgaria, the accident occurred in Bulgaria, and the Bulgarian authorities imposed the penalty. This decision demonstrates that before an individual may rely on Charter rights, there must be a sufficient cross-border element to the case. It is conceivable, therefore, that had Mr Vinkov been disputing the imposition of a penalty imposed by another Member State, the outcome may have been different.

5.30 Article 52(3) provides that, as far as interpretation of the Charter is concerned, where it provides for rights which are also guaranteed by the ECHR, the rights contained in the Charter shall be taken to have at least the same meaning and scope as the ECHR rights. This provision poses some difficulties, not least because in none of the Articles in the Charter are rights expressed in the same terms as those under the ECHR. Moreover, Article 52(3) does not restrict the Charter rights from being interpreted more expansively than the equivalents contained in the ECHR. A further problem is presented by the scope of some Articles being expressed in wider terms than the equivalent rights in the ECHR. For example, see Article 47 (see **5.44**).

5.31 To some extent these interpretative difficulties as to the scope of the Charter rights are addressed in a second corresponding document entitled the Explanations. This useful interpretative tool references the source of the Charter rights and sets out other legal provisions relevant to their interpretation. The Explanations are not legally binding but 'due regard' should be had to their content.[27]

Application of the Charter to the UK, Poland, and the Czech Republic

5.32 During the negotiations on the Lisbon Treaty the UK, together with Poland, secured Protocol No. 30, which sought to vary the application of the Charter to those countries. The Czech Republic has subsequently followed suit.[28] The primary objection made on behalf of the UK arose from political concerns as to the impact of 'solidarity' rights in Chapter IV of

---

[25] 98/C 216/01, the Convention creates a binding legal framework among the Member States such that drivers disqualified from driving in a Member State other than that in which they are principally resident may not escape the effects of disqualification when they leave the Member State in which the offence was committed. The Convention is not widely in force throughout the EU, although the UK and Ireland have entered into a bilateral agreement; see Part 3 of the Crime (International Cooperation) Act 2003 and the Mutual Recognition of Driving Disqualifications (Great Britain and Ireland) Regulations 2008.

[26] 2005/214/JHA.

[27] Article 6(1) TEU and preamble and Art. 52(7) of the Charter.

[28] On 29–30 October 2009, at the European Council meetings in Brussels, the Czech Republic negotiated inclusion within Protocol No. 30, which will be implemented when the next EU Treaty comes into force.

the Charter, for example the right to collective bargaining and action, on British business interests.

Article 1(1) of Protocol No. 30 states that the Charter does not permit the CJEU or the courts **5.33** in the UK to find that domestic 'laws, regulations or administrative provisions, practices or actions' of those countries are inconsistent with the Charter. Article 1(2) further specifies that the 'solidarity' rights established in Chapter IV of the Charter are also not justiciable, except insofar as those rights are provided for under the laws of the UK. Accordingly, Article 1(2) may be considered simply illustrative of the general rule in Article 1(1).

Article 2 of Protocol No. 30 states that the provisions of the Charter which refer to national **5.34** laws and practices shall only apply to the UK to the extent that the rights or principles that the Charter contains are recognised in the law or practices of those countries. There is overlap between Article 2 and the similar provisions in Article 52 (see **5.30**) of the Charter itself.

The effect of Protocol No. 30 has recently been considered by the CJEU. Following prelimi- **5.35** nary references under Article 267 TFEU from the Court of Appeal in England and Wales (*R (on the application of NS) v Secretary of State for the Home Department (Reference to CJEU)*)[29] and the High Court in Ireland, the CJEU gave judgment on 21 December 2011 in Joined Cases C-411/10 *NS v Secretary of State for the Home Department* and C-493/10 *ME and Others v Refugee Applications Commissioner, Minister for Justice, Equality and Law Reform*.

The English case of *R (on the application of NS) v Secretary of State for the Home Department* **5.36** concerned an Afghan national (NS) who had entered the UK after travelling through Greece. In 2008, in Greece, he had been arrested and detained. On release from custody he was ordered to leave Greece within 30 days. In January 2009 he arrived in the UK and lodged an asylum application. In July of that year, he was informed by the UK Border Agency that he would be transferred to Greece the following month under the 'Dublin II' Regulation.[30] This conclusion followed from the fact that, in the view of the Home Secretary, under the Dublin II Regulation, Greece was the proper country to consider NS's asylum application.

In *R (on the application of S) v Secretary of State for the Home Department*,[31] NS challenged this **5.37** decision before the High Court on the basis that there was a risk that the applicant's fundamental rights under the Charter and the ECHR would be infringed should he be sent back to Greece. Specifically, it was contended that the Greek asylum procedures involved inaccessible judicial remedies and inadequate conditions for asylum seekers. The Secretary of State's position in the High Court was that the relevant provisions of the Charter did not apply to the UK. The High Court concluded that the removal of NS to Greece was not incompatible with his Article 3 ECHR rights. The issues raised by the Court of Appeal for consideration by the CJEU included the following:

(a) whether the authorities of Member State A, which should transfer an asylum applicant to Member State B (as the Member State responsible for the examination of the asylum application), should check whether Member State B observes fundamental rights; and

---

[29] [2010] EWCA Civ 990.
[30] Council Regulation (EC) No. 343/2003 of 18 February 2003 establishing the criteria and mechanisms for determining the Member State responsible for examining an asylum application lodged in one of the Member States by a third country national ([2003] OJ L 50, p 1).
[31] [2010] EWHC 705 (Admin).

(b) whether the answers to this question should be qualified in order to take account of Protocol No. 30.

5.38 In relation to the first question, the CJEU held that EU law precludes Member State A from making a conclusive presumption that Member State B responsibly observes fundamental rights. The presumption of compliance is rebuttable, in that case by 'regular and unanimous' reports from international non-governmental organisations.[32] It follows that Member State A may not transfer an asylum seeker to Member State B where Member Sate A is aware of systemic deficiencies in the asylum procedure, and the reception conditions of asylum seekers amount to substantial grounds for believing that the asylum seeker would face a real risk of being subjected to inhuman or degrading treatment within the meaning of Article 4 of the Charter.

5.39 In relation to the second question, the CJEU concluded that no qualification applied. It held that Article 1(1) of Protocol No. 30 did not exempt the UK from its obligation to comply with the provisions of the Charter or prevent a domestic court from ensuring compliance with the provisions of the Charter. The CJEU observed that the third recital in the preamble to Protocol No. 30 confirmed that Article 6 of the Lisbon Treaty requires the Charter to be applied and interpreted by the courts of the UK. The sixth recital makes plain that the Charter does not create new rights or principles. To that extent, the CJEU found that Protocol No. 30 merely explains the application provisions of Article 51 of the Charter and does not amount to an opt-out. Following the decision in *NS*, the UK courts have been called upon to determine whether an individual's Charter rights have been breached without reference to the 'opt-out'.[33]

5.40 In *Medhanye, R (on the application of) v Secretary of State for the Home Department*,[34] the Administrative Court proceeded on the basis of a restrictive interpretation of the decision in *NS*, that is, that the rebuttable presumption of compliance applied only to Article 4 of the Charter and did not extend to other fundamental rights, such as the right to dignity set out in Article 1.[35] The judgment in *NS* repeatedly referred to 'fundamental rights' without specific reference to Article 4, although the CJEU made plain that 'it cannot be concluded... that any infringement of a fundamental right by the Member State responsible will affect the obligations of the other Member States.'[36] It is expected that the extent of the 'rebuttable presumption' will be the subject of further litigation.

---

[32] The CJEU's decision in *NS* has recently been applied in the context of extradition proceedings in *Krolik et al. v Several Judicial Authorities of Poland* [2012] EWHC 2357 (Admin) where the issue was whether extradition would breach the requested persons Art. 3 ECHR rights by reason of prison conditions in Poland.

[33] See *Medhanye, R (on the application of) v Secretary of State for the Home Department* [2012] EWHC 1799 (Admin).

[34] *Medhanye, R (on the application of) v Secretary of State for the Home Department* [2012] EWHC 1799 (Admin).

[35] *Medhanye, R (on the application of) v Secretary of State for the Home Department* [2012] EWHC 1799 (Admin), see Kenneth Parker J at para. 24:

> Any affront to dignity, falling short of degrading treatment, that might arguably on a broad conception of that term violate Article 1 may be left to be addressed exclusively by the public authorities, including the judicial authorities, in the receiving State... On the other hand where there is proven systemic treatment in another State of asylum seekers that is truly inhuman or degrading, the transferring State may not exercise its EU discretionary power to transfer asylum seekers to such a State.

[36] See para. 82.

Chapter VI: Justice

The Charter consists of 54 Articles divided into seven Chapters or Titles. The first six each **5.41** cover an area in which protection of rights is asserted: Dignity (I), Freedoms (II), Equality (III), Solidarity (IV), Citizens' Rights (V), and Justice (VI). The seventh Chapter provides for its interpretation and application. Unlike the ECHR, the Charter does not provide for rights-specific limitations for interference with Charter rights. Instead, Article 52(1) in Chapter VII of the Charter provides a general limitation clause set out in the following terms:

> Any limitation on the exercise of the rights and freedoms recognised by this Charter must be provided for by law and respect the essence of those rights and freedoms. Subject to the principle of proportionality, limitations may be made only if they are necessary and genuinely meet objectives of general interest recognised by the Union or the need to protect the rights and freedoms of others.

In addition, Article 54 prohibits the abuse of rights and Article 52(6) provides that the inter- **5.42** pretation of Charter rights should take full account of national laws and practices.

The substantive rights in relation to Justice are set out in Articles 47–50 in Chapter VI of the **5.43** Charter. These are:

(a) the right to an effective remedy and to a fair trial (Art. 47);
(b) the presumption of innocence and rights of the defence (Art. 48);
(c) the principle of legality and proportionality of criminal offences and penalties (Art. 49); and
(d) double jeopardy.

Article 47: right to an effective remedy and to a fair trial
Article 47 is set out in the following terms: **5.44**

> Everyone whose rights and freedoms guaranteed by the law of the Union are violated has the right to an effective remedy before a tribunal in compliance with the conditions laid down in this Article.

> Everyone is entitled to a fair and public hearing within a reasonable time by an independent and impartial tribunal previously established by law. Everyone shall have the possibility of being advised, defended and represented.

> Legal aid shall be made available to those who lack sufficient resources in so far as such aid is necessary to ensure effective access to justice.

According to the explanation of the draft Charter issued on 11 October 2008 by the **5.45** Convention[37] (see **5.21**), the first paragraph of Article 47 is based on Article 13 of the ECHR, which states:

> Everyone whose rights and freedoms as set forth in this Convention are violated shall have an effective remedy before a national authority notwithstanding that the violation has been committed by persons acting in an official capacity.

The protection in EU law is more extensive than in Article 13 as it guarantees a right to an **5.46** effective remedy before a court as opposed to a remedy before a national authority. The right has long been enshrined in the CJEU's case law.[38] This principle also applies to Member States

---

[37] Charter 4473/00, Convent 49.
[38] See e.g. Case 222/84 *Johnston* [1986] ECR 1651; Case 222/86 *Heylens* [1987] ECR 4097 and see C-97/91 *Borelli* [1992] ECR I-6313.

when implementing EU law. The explanations make plain that Article 47 was intended to be given effect through existing channels (ie those laid down in the Treaties), as opposed to creating any new route of appeal.

5.47 The second paragraph of Article 47 is in identical terms to Article 6(1) of the ECHR.

> In the determination of his civil rights and obligations or of any criminal charge against him, everyone is entitled to a fair and public hearing within a reasonable time by an independent and impartial tribunal established by law. Judgment shall be pronounced publicly but the press and public may be excluded from all or part of the trial in the interests of morals, public order or national security in a democratic society, where the interests of juveniles or the protection of the private life of the parties so require, or to the extent strictly necessary in the opinion of the court in special circumstances where publicity would prejudice the interests of justice.

5.48 Like the first paragraph, the protection afforded by the second is more extensive than Article 6(1). Under EU law the right to a fair hearing is not confined to disputes relating to civil rights and obligations and criminal charges. For example, see Case 294/83 *'Les Verts' v European Parliament*.[39] As noted earlier, this could potentially be of relevance in the context of immigration and extradition proceedings where individuals have been held not to enjoy protection under Article 6(1) ECHR. The relationship of this right to the process of trial *in absentia* (see **5.188**) and to investigations undertaken by OLAF (see **5.198**) is considered in more detail later (in Section K).

5.49 The third paragraph of Article 47 reflects the principle established by the Strasbourg Court under Article 6(1) in the case of *Ireland v Airey*;[40] that is, that provision should be made for legal aid where the absence of such aid would preclude an effective remedy. The issue of funding in cross-border cases receives further consideration later (see **5.125**).

5.50 There is also a system of legal assistance for cases before the CJEU.

Article 48: presumption of innocence and rights of the defence

5.51 Article 48 is in the following terms:

1. Everyone who has been charged shall be presumed innocent until proved guilty according to law.
2. Respect for the rights of the defence of anyone who has been charged shall be guaranteed.

5.52 Article 48 has the same meaning and scope as Article 6(2) and (3) ECHR. The particular application of this Article to investigations undertaken by OLAF is considered in more detail later (see **5.208**).

Article 49: principles of legality and proportionality of criminal offences and penalties

5.53 Article 49 is set out in the following terms:

1. No one shall be held guilty of any criminal offence on account of any act or omission which did not constitute a criminal offence under national law or international law at the time when it was committed. Nor shall a heavier penalty be imposed than that which was applicable at the time the criminal offence was committed. If, subsequent to the commission of a criminal offence, the law provides for a lighter penalty, that penalty shall be applicable.

---

[39] Judgment of 23 April 1986, [1988] ECR 1339.
[40] (1979–80) 2 EHRR 305.

2. This Article shall not prejudice the trial and punishment of any person for any act or omission which, at the time when it was committed, was criminal according to the general principles recognised by the community of nations.
3. The severity of penalties must not be disproportionate to the criminal offence.

It may be contrasted with Article 7 ECHR, which is worded as follows: **5.54**

1. No one shall be held guilty of any criminal offence on account of any act or omission which did not constitute a criminal offence under national or international law at the time when it was committed. Nor shall a heavier penalty be imposed than the one that was applicable at the time the criminal offence was committed.
2. This Article shall not prejudice the trial and punishment of any person for any act or omission which, at the time when it was committed, was criminal according to the general principles of law recognised by civilised nations.

As is clear, paragraph 1 of Article 49 protects against retroactive laws and criminal sanctions, **5.55** including a prohibition on the imposition of heavier penalties than were in effect at the time the criminal offence was committed and follows Article 7(1) ECHR. Paragraph 2 reflects Article 7(2). Paragraph 3 of Article 49 sets out the principle of proportionality between penalties and criminal offences.

Article 50: right not to be tried or punished twice in criminal proceedings for the same criminal offence

Article 50 is set out in the following terms: **5.56**

No one shall be liable to be tried or punished again in criminal proceedings for an offence for which he or she has already been finally acquitted or convicted within the Union in accordance with the law.

The principle of *ne bis in idem* is examined in detail later (see Section G). **5.57**

Chapter V: Citizens' Rights

In addition to the provisions in Chapter VI of the Charter that expressly contemplate **5.58** procedural protections in criminal proceedings, there is an additional right set out in Chapter V, which may be considered relevant, namely Article 41: right to good administration.

Article 41 provides: **5.59**

1. Every person has the right to have his or her affairs handled impartially, fairly and within a reasonable time by the institutions and bodies of the Union.
2. This right includes:
   – the right of every person to be heard, before any individual measure which would affect him or her adversely is taken;
   – the right of every person to have access to his or her file, while respecting the legitimate interests of confidentiality and of professional and business secrecy;
   – the obligation of the administration to give reasons for its decisions.
3. Every person has the right to have the Community make good any damage caused by its institutions or by its servants in the performance of their duties, in accordance with the general principles common to the laws of the Member States.
4. Every person may write to the institutions of the Union in one of the languages of the Treaties and must have an answer in the same language.

5.60 This principle, of the right to good administration, is well established in CJEU jurisprudence and the language of paragraphs 2 and 3 derives from the case law.[41]

5.61 Paragraph 3 of Article 41 reproduces the right guaranteed by Article 340 TFEU and paragraph 4 and reproduces the right guaranteed by Article 24 TFEU.

D. The Roadmap for Strengthening Procedural Rights of Suspected or Accused Persons in Criminal Proceedings

Introduction

5.62 On 28 April 2004, a draft Framework Decision on certain procedural rights in criminal proceedings throughout the EU was issued[42] which aimed 'to set common minimum standards as regards certain procedural rights applying in criminal proceedings throughout the European Union'. It was the first attempt to codify comprehensively a set of shared minimum procedural safeguards and defence rights across Member States, although it followed a long-standing acknowledgement that these were required.[43]

5.63 Expressly included in the draft Framework Decision were the rights to legal advice; interpretation and translation; protection for vulnerable defendants; minimum protections on detention; communication with consular authorities; and to have family members and employers informed on arrest. Its progress was delayed, however, as Member States (including the UK) expressed concern as to the potential implications for their domestic systems of criminal justice.[44]

5.64 On 4 December 2009, the draft Framework Decision on procedural rights was replaced with a Resolution of the Council of 30 November 2009 on a 'Roadmap' for strengthening procedural rights of suspected or accused persons in criminal proceedings.[45] In December 2009, the Roadmap was adopted as part of the Stockholm Programme, a five-year plan for legislative reform in relation to EU justice matters.

5.65 While the Roadmap has maintained the commitment to the rights identified in the 2004 draft Framework Decision, the strategy for implementation has been altered. Rather than codifying rights in a single instrument, the Roadmap provides for a series of legislative instruments or measures addressing different rights that Member States can opt into on a case-by-case basis. The Roadmap envisages that all of the measures will be adopted by 2014, although given progress so far this looks increasingly unlikely.

---

[41] See e.g. Case T-167/94 *Nölle v Commission* [1995] ECR II-2589; Case 222/86 *Heylens* [1987] ECR 4097; Case 374/87 *Orkem* [1989] ECR 3283.

[42] COM(2004) 328 final.

[43] See e.g. the Commission Communication to the Council and the European Parliament on Mutual Recognition of Final Decisions in Criminal Matters (COM(2000) 495 final, 26 July 2000); the Programme of Measures to Implement the Principle of Mutual Recognition of Decisions in Criminal Matters, adopted by the Council and the Commission ([2001] OJ C 12, 15.1.2001) and the European Commission Green Paper on Minimum Standards in Procedural safeguards in Criminal Proceedings (COM(2003) 75 final, 19 February 2003).

[44] See 2008 Université Libre de Bruxelles report on the future of mutual recognition in criminal matters in the EU, and conclusions 33 and 37 of the Tampere Programme, 15–16 October 2009.

[45] [2009] OJ C 295/01.

The areas covered by the six measures, as originally envisaged, are considered in detail in the **5.66** following sections:

Measure A: Translation and Interpretation (see **5.67**).
Measure B: Information on Rights and Information about Charges (see **5.80**).
Measure C: Legal Advice and Legal Aid (see **5.90**).
Measure D: Communication with Relatives, Employers and Consular Authorities (see **5.90**).
Measure E: Special Safeguards for Suspected or Accused Persons who are Vulnerable (see **5.120**).
Measure F: A Green Paper on Pre-Trial Detention (see **5.112**).

Right to interpretation and translation

The right to interpretation and translation, while not specifically mentioned in the Charter, **5.67** was among the 'basic rights' identified in the 2003 Green Paper on Procedural Safeguards that formed the background to the 2004 draft Framework Decision. Having noted the relevant provisions of Articles 5 and 6 ECHR, Article 14(3) of the International Covenant on Civil and Political Rights, and Articles 55 and 67 of the Rome Statute, the authors of the Green Paper observed that 'The difficulty is not in establishing the existence of this right, but rather one of implementation.'

The Green Paper, drawing on research carried out by the Commission's Grotius Project in **5.68** four Member States (including the UK), set out a number of proposals focusing on training and resources for translators and interpreters.

The subsequent draft Framework Decision on procedural rights included access to free inter- **5.69** pretation and translation as one of the five areas where common minimum standards among Member States were proposed. This was unsurprising, given the Commission's long-standing stress on promoting the principle of mutual recognition, on rights with a 'transnational element'.

In May 2009, following the abandonment of the 2004 draft Framework Decision and **5.70** the adoption of the Roadmap, the Commission published a new proposal for a Council Framework Decision. This document dealt only with the right to interpretation and translation, on the basis that this had been the least controversial of the rights previously considered and a body of information and research was available in that respect.

The new proposed Framework Decision contained 6 Articles. It is interesting to note that **5.71** the right to interpretation (Art. 2, set out at **5.75**) and the right to translation (Art. 3, set out at **5.76**) were treated separately. This reflected the earlier Green Paper's emphasis on inter- preters and translators being two separate professional groups, with different roles to play in criminal proceedings. The explanatory memorandum to the Framework Decision described Article 2 as laying down a general provision, namely that interpretation should be provided free of charge during both investigative and judicial phases of criminal proceedings. Article 3, by contrast, related to the more specific right to the translation of the essential documents in criminal proceedings, such as the indictment and key witness statements.

As previously noted, the right to translation and interpretation, now again treated as a sin- **5.72** gle entity, was the first of five measures (A–E) set out in the November 2009 Roadmap Resolution. The short explanation to the Resolution, as well as mentioning the need for interpretation and the translation of essential documents, also referred to the need for attention to be paid to the position of those with hearing impediments.

5.73 Following the endorsement of the Roadmap by the Stockholm Programme, Measure A became the subject of the European Parliament and Council Directive on the right to interpretation and translation in criminal proceedings (2010/64/EU). The Directive contains 12 Articles. Article 2 relates to the right to interpretation, and Article 3 to the right to translation of essential documents. While the numbering of these Articles is the same as that adopted in the 2009 proposed Framework Decision, the Directive Articles are different from, and more detailed than, the 2009 versions.

5.74 The scope of the Directive is set out in Article 1. The rights referred to relate both to criminal proceedings and to those for the execution of a EAW. Those rights apply from the time a person is notified that he is suspected or accused of an offence, until the final disposal of the proceedings, including any appeal. Any existing national law in relation to legal representation at any stage of criminal proceedings, or the right of access to documents during criminal proceedings, is unaffected by the Directive.

5.75 Article 2 of the Directive provides:

Right to interpretation

1. Member States shall ensure that suspected or accused persons who do not speak or understand the language of the criminal proceedings concerned are provided, without delay, with interpretation during criminal proceedings before investigative and judicial authorities, including during police questioning, all court hearings and any necessary interim hearings.

2. Member States shall ensure that, where necessary for the purpose of safeguarding the fairness of the proceedings, interpretation is available for communication between suspected or accused persons and their legal counsel in direct connection with any questioning or hearing during the proceedings or with the lodging of an appeal or other procedural applications.

3. The right to interpretation under paragraphs 1 and 2 includes appropriate assistance for persons with hearing or speech impediments.

4. Member States shall ensure that a procedure or mechanism is in place to ascertain whether suspected or accused persons speak and understand the language of the criminal proceedings and whether they need the assistance of an interpreter.

5. Member States shall ensure that, in accordance with procedures in national law, suspected or accused persons have the right to challenge a decision finding that there is no need for interpretation and, when interpretation has been provided, the possibility to complain that the quality of the interpretation is not sufficient to safeguard the fairness of the proceedings.

6. Where appropriate, communication technology such as videoconferencing, telephone or the Internet may be used, unless the physical presence of the interpreter is required in order to safeguard the fairness of the proceedings.

7. In proceedings for the execution of a European arrest warrant, the executing Member State shall ensure that its competent authorities provide persons subject to such proceedings who do not speak or understand the language of the proceedings with interpretation in accordance with this Article.

8. Interpretation provided under this Article shall be of a quality sufficient to safeguard the fairness of the proceedings, in particular by ensuring that suspected or accused persons have knowledge of the case against them and are able to exercise their right of defence.

Article 3 provides: **5.76**

Right to translation of essential documents

1. Member States shall ensure that suspected or accused persons who do not understand the language of the criminal proceedings concerned are, within a reasonable period of time, provided with a written translation of all documents which are essential to ensure that they are able to exercise their right of defence and to safeguard the fairness of the proceedings.
2. Essential documents shall include any decision depriving a person of his liberty, any charge or indictment, and any judgment.
3. The competent authorities shall, in any given case, decide whether any other document is essential. Suspected or accused persons or their legal counsel may submit a reasoned request to that effect.
4. There shall be no requirement to translate passages of essential documents which are not relevant for the purposes of enabling suspected or accused persons to have knowledge of the case against them.
5. Member States shall ensure that, in accordance with procedures in national law, suspected or accused persons have the right to challenge a decision finding that there is no need for the translation of documents or passages thereof and, when a translation has been provided, the possibility to complain that the quality of the translation is not sufficient to safeguard the fairness of the proceedings.
6. In proceedings for the execution of a European arrest warrant, the executing Member State shall ensure that its competent authorities provide any person subject to such proceedings who does not understand the language in which the European arrest warrant is drawn up, or into which it has been translated by the issuing Member State, with a written translation of that document.
7. As an exception to the general rules established in paragraphs 1, 2, 3 and 6, an oral translation or oral summary of essential documents may be provided instead of a written translation on condition that such oral translation or oral summary does not prejudice the fairness of the proceedings.
8. Any waiver of the right to translation of documents referred to in this Article shall be subject to the requirements that suspected or accused persons have received prior legal advice or have otherwise obtained full knowledge of the consequences of such a waiver, and that the waiver was unequivocal and given voluntarily.
9. Translation provided under this Article shall be of a quality sufficient to safeguard the fairness of the proceedings, in particular by ensuring that suspected or accused persons have knowledge of the case against them and are able to exercise their right of defence.

Article 4 provides that all costs of interpretation and translation required as a result of the   **5.77**
application of Articles 2 and 3 are to be met by Member States, regardless of the outcome of proceedings. In this context, it is to be noted that the case law in relation to Article 6(3)(e) ECHR makes it clear that the right to be provided with a free interpreter is unqualified; see *Luedicke, Belkacem and Koc v Germany*;[46] *Cuscani v United Kingdom*.[47]

Articles 5–12 deal with ancillary matters, including quality assurance (Art. 5), and training   **5.78**
(Art. 6). Article 11 provides that the Directive will enter into force on the twentieth day following its publication in the Official Journal of the European Union.

The UK, together with Ireland, has notified its wish to take part in the adoption and appli-   **5.79**
cation of the Directive, pursuant to Article 3 of Protocol No. 21. This would seem to have

---

[46] (1978)2 EHRR 149.
[47] (2003) 36 EHRR 2.

few, if any, implications for domestic law.[48] The right to an interpreter, and to have the prosecution case translated, are well established in English law, and indeed long pre-date the incorporation of the ECHR.[49]

Right to information on arrest

5.80 A Directive of the European Parliament and Council on the right to information in criminal proceedings[50] was adopted in March 2012. This was the second of the Roadmap 'steps', following the adoption of the Directive on the right to interpretation and translation. Subsequently, in July 2010, the Commission issued a proposal for a Directive on the right to information in criminal proceedings, in similar terms to that ultimately adopted.[51]

5.81 The Directive is expressed to build upon the rights laid down in the Charter (in particular Arts 6, 47, and 48) and in Articles 5 and 6 ECHR. It lays down minimum rules without prejudice to the rights established by those provisions and other relevant national and EU law.

5.82 This Directive is evidently intended to have a close relationship to the ECHR jurisprudence in relation to the right to information about procedural rights. Where used in the Directive, the term 'accusation' is stated to have the same meaning as 'charge' in Article 6(1) ECHR.

5.83 Articles 1–7 of the Directive provide as follows:

Article 1 Subject matter

This Directive lays down rules concerning the right to information of suspects or accused persons, relating to their rights in criminal proceedings and to the accusation against them. It also lays down rules concerning the right to information of persons subject to a European Arrest Warrant relating to their rights.

Article 2 Scope

1. This Directive applies from the time persons are made aware by the competent authorities of a Member State that they are suspected or accused of having committed a criminal offence until the conclusion of the proceedings, which is understood to mean the final determination of the question whether the suspect or accused person has committed the criminal offence, including, where applicable, sentencing and the resolution of any appeal.
2. Where the law of a Member State provides for the imposition of a sanction regarding minor offences by an authority other than a court having jurisdiction in criminal matters, and the imposition of such a sanction may be appealed to such a court, this Directive shall apply only to the proceedings before that court, following such an appeal.

Article 3 Right to information about rights

1. Member States shall ensure that suspects or accused persons are provided promptly with information concerning at least the following procedural rights, as they apply under national law, in order to allow for those rights to be exercised effectively:
   (a) the right of access to a lawyer;
   (b) any entitlement to free legal advice and the conditions for obtaining such advice;

---

[48] However, there has been significant criticism of the quality of interpretation following the recent controversial privatisation of court interpreting services, see e.g. Owen Bowcott, 'Court Interpreting Criticised as "Wholly Inadequate" in Damning NAO Report', *The Guardian*, 12 September 2012.

[49] See e.g. *R v Iqbal Begum* 93 Cr App R 96, CA; *R v Lee Kun* [1916] 1 KB 337.

[50] Directive 2012/13/EU.

[51] The rights of suspects in the context of OLAF investigations are considered separately at **5.207**.

    (c) the right to be informed of the accusation, in accordance with Article 6;

    (d) the right to interpretation and translation;

    (e) the right to remain silent.

2. Member States shall ensure that the information provided for under paragraph 1 shall be given orally or in writing, in simple and accessible language, taking into account any particular needs of vulnerable suspects or vulnerable accused persons.

Article 4 Letter of Rights on arrest

1. Member States shall ensure that suspects or accused persons who are arrested or detained are provided promptly with a written Letter of Rights. They shall be given an opportunity to read the Letter of Rights and shall be allowed to keep it in their possession throughout the time that they are deprived of liberty.

2. In addition to the information set out in Article 3, the Letter of Rights referred to in paragraph 1 of this Article shall contain information about the following rights as they apply under national law:

    (a) the right of access to the materials of the case;

    (b) the right to have consular authorities and one person informed;

    (c) the right of access to urgent medical assistance; and

    (d) the maximum number of hours or days suspects or accused persons may be deprived of liberty before being brought before a judicial authority.

3. The Letter of Rights shall also contain basic information about any possibility, under national law, of challenging the lawfulness of the arrest; obtaining a review of the detention; or making a request for provisional release.

4. The Letter of Rights shall be drafted in simple and accessible language. An indicative model Letter of Rights is set out in Annex I.

5. Member States shall ensure that suspects or accused persons receive the Letter of Rights written in a language that they understand. Where a Letter of Rights is not available in the appropriate language, suspects or accused persons shall be informed of their rights orally in a language that they understand. A Letter of Rights in a language that they understand shall then be given to them without undue delay.

Article 5 Letter of Rights in European Arrest Warrant proceedings

1. Member States shall ensure that persons who are arrested for the purpose of the execution of a European Arrest Warrant are provided promptly with an appropriate Letter of Rights containing information on their rights according to the law implementing Framework Decision 2002/584/JHA in the executing Member State.

2. The Letter of Rights shall be drafted in simple and accessible language. An indicative model Letter of Rights is set out in Annex II.

Article 6 Right to information about the accusation

1. Member States shall ensure that suspects or accused persons are provided with information about the criminal act they are suspected or accused of having committed. That information shall be provided promptly and in such detail as is necessary to safeguard the fairness of the proceedings and the effective exercise of the rights of the defence.

2. Member States shall ensure that suspects or accused persons who are arrested or detained are informed of the reasons for their arrest or detention, including the criminal act they are suspected or accused of having committed.

3. Member States shall ensure that, at the latest on submission of the merits of the accusation to a court, detailed information is provided on the accusation, including the nature and legal classification of the criminal offence, as well as the nature of participation by the accused person.

4. Member States shall ensure that suspects or accused persons are informed promptly of any changes in the information given in accordance with this Article where this is necessary to safeguard the fairness of the proceedings.

Article 7 Right of access to the materials of the case

1. Where a person is arrested and detained at any stage of the criminal proceedings, Member States shall ensure that documents related to the specific case in the possession of the competent authorities which are essential to challenging effectively, in accordance with national law, the lawfulness of the arrest or detention, are made available to arrested persons or to their lawyers.
2. Member States shall ensure that access is granted at least to all material evidence in the possession of the competent authorities, whether for or against suspects or accused persons, to those persons or their lawyers in order to safeguard the fairness of the proceedings and to prepare the defence.
3. Without prejudice to paragraph 1, access to the materials referred to in paragraph 2 shall be granted in due time to allow the effective exercise of the rights of the defence and at the latest upon submission of the merits of the accusation to the judgement of a court. Where further material evidence comes into the possession of the competent authorities, access shall be granted to it in due time to allow for it to be considered.
4. By way of derogation from paragraphs 2 and 3, provided that this does not prejudice the right to a fair trial, access to certain materials may be refused if such access may lead to a serious threat to the life or the fundamental rights of another person or if such refusal is strictly necessary to safeguard an important public interest, such as in cases where access could prejudice an ongoing investigation or seriously harm the national security of the Member State in which the criminal proceedings are instituted. Member States shall ensure that, in accordance with procedures in national law, a decision to refuse access to certain materials in accordance with this paragraph is taken by a judicial authority or is at least subject to judicial review.
5. Access, as referred to in this Article, shall be provided free of charge.

5.84 It can be seen that the scope of the Directive embraces two essentially separate areas. As Article 2 makes clear, the Directive applies from the earliest point that a person is informed that he is suspected or accused of an offence until the final determination of the case, including any appeal. Therefore the Directive applies as much to the trial process as to what might loosely be described as the post-arrest phase.

5.85 Articles 3–6 apply essentially to the pre-trial phase, including the point where any challenge can be made to the fact of detention, or continuing detention. In the context of English domestic law, this clearly includes court proceedings such as bail applications and applications for/objections to warrants for continuing detention. While Article 7 clearly also has relevance at that stage, its provisions would, consistent with the stated scope of the Directive, appear to embrace the trial element of proceedings, including the determination of any appeal.

5.86 The content of Articles 3–7, insofar as they relate to the pre-trial phase of criminal proceedings, sets out minimum standards which are evidently already met in English domestic law. It is to be noted that the 'Letter of Rights', a very distinctive concrete product of the Directive, has an English counterpart in the Notice of Rights and Entitlements issued to detained persons pursuant to Code C (para. 3.2) of the Police and Criminal Evidence Act 1984.

5.87 As far as the impact of Article 7 on the trial process is concerned, English domestic law and procedure would appear to guarantee the minimum rights expounded. While 'material evidence...for or against the defence' is a broad category embracing what is referred to in English criminal procedure as 'unused material', the detailed disclosure regime provided by the Criminal Procedure and Investigations Act 1996 would seem to guarantee the minimum standards set out here. That disclosure regime requires the disclosure of material which might reasonably be considered capable of undermining the case for the prosecution against the accused, or of assisting the case for the accused (s. 3(1)). There is no requirement for the disclosure of unused material which is harmful to the defence case, or is neutral. If the reference in Article 7 to material 'for or against suspected or accused persons' is taken to refer, on the one hand, to prosecution evidence and, on the other, to material not relied on by the prosecution, then there is clear compliance in English domestic law.

The derogation permitted by paragraph 4 of Article 7 would appear comfortably to encompass the position in English domestic law in respect of unused material attracting public interest immunity, as provided for by section 3(6) of the Criminal Procedure and Investigations Act 1996 and expounded in *R v H and C*.[52] **5.88**

The UK has notified its wish to take part in the adoption and application of the Directive, pursuant to Article 3 of Protocol No. 21. The Directive was published in the Official Journal of the European Union on 22 May 2012 and pursuant to Article 13 of the Directive it will enter into force on the twentieth day following that publication. Member States have two years thereafter to transpose its provisions into their national laws. **5.89**

Right of access to a lawyer and to communicate on arrest

It is convenient to deal together with Measures C and D, which address different aspects of the right of a suspect to communicate with third parties. Measure C of the Roadmap provides for the rights of a suspected or accused person to legal advice and legal aid. The short explanation for this measure is stated to be: 'The right to legal advice (through a legal counsel) for the suspected or accused person in criminal proceedings at the earliest appropriate stage of such proceedings is fundamental in order to safeguard the fairness of the proceedings; the right to legal aid should ensure effective access to the aforementioned right to legal advice.' Measure D provides for the right to access third parties such as the suspect's family or, in recognition of the cross-border nature of the document, consular authorities. **5.90**

The European Commission adopted the proposal for a Directive of the European Parliament and of the Council on the right of access to a lawyer and on the right to communicate on arrest on 8 June 2011.[53] The purpose of the Directive is to facilitate the practical application of existing ECHR and other rights, with the aim of safeguarding the right to fair proceedings. **5.91**

The preamble notes that the right of access to a lawyer is enshrined in Article 6 ECHR and refers to the jurisprudence of the ECtHR, which has **5.92**

> consistently held that a suspect or accused person, at least when in police custody, has a general right of access to a lawyer from the first interrogation by the police in order to protect the right to a fair trial, and in particular the privilege against self-incrimination and to avoid ill treatment. The Court has also held that this right applies unless it is demonstrated

---

[52] [2004] 2 AC 134, HL.
[53] (COM) 2011/1054.

in the light of the particular circumstances of each case that there are compelling reasons to restrict this right.[54]

5.93 The proposed Directive further refers to Article 47 of the Charter, which guarantees 'the right to an effective remedy and to a fair trial' and the guarantee of respect for the rights of the defence enshrined in Article 14 of the International Covenant on Civil and Political Rights.[55] Article 47 of the Charter is set out at **5.43**.

5.94 The right to communicate with a third party constitutes one of the safeguards against the ill treatment prohibited by Article 3 ECHR. However, the statutory basis for the proposed right to communicate on arrest is less clearly defined than that relating to the right of access to a lawyer. Article 8 ECHR guarantees the right to respect for private and family life, which in the context of the proposed Directive is taken to include the right to contact a family member on arrest. The 1963 Vienna Convention on Consular Relations (VCCR), which provides that on arrest or detention a foreign national has the right to ask for his consulate to be informed of the detention and to receive visits from consular officials, also receives reference in the preamble.

5.95 The proposed Directive is not intended to apply to relatively minor offences, in certain circumstances. For example, a competent authority would not be expected to ensure all of the Directive rights in respect of traffic offences, minor prison offences, or military offences dealt with by a commanding officer. Further, the proposed Directive expressly excludes from its scope administrative proceedings leading to sanctions such as competition or tax proceedings.

5.96 Article 1 of the proposed Directive sets out its objectives, namely to establish rules relating to the rights of suspects and accused persons in criminal proceedings and in proceedings for the execution of a EAW (ie those subject to proceedings pursuant to Council Framework Decision 2002/584/JHA). Those rights concern access to a lawyer and the right to communicate upon arrest with a third party.

5.97 Article 2 provides that the proposed Directive applies from the time a person has been made aware by the competent authorities of a Member State that he is suspected or accused of having committed a criminal offence until the conclusion of the proceedings. Proceedings are taken to include sentencing and the resolution of any appeal.

5.98 Article 3 ensures access to a lawyer as soon as possible and in any event:

(a) before the start of questioning by the police or other law enforcement authorities;

(b) when any procedural or evidence-gathering act is carried out, at which the person's presence is either required or permitted, unless this would prejudice the acquisition of evidence; or

(c) once a person is deprived of his liberty.

5.99 The timing and manner of legal access must be such as to allow the suspect or accused person to exercise his rights of defence effectively.

5.100 Article 4 of the proposed Directive provides for the right of a suspect or an accused person to meet with the lawyer representing him and prohibits any limitation on the duration and

---

[54] See para. 11 of the preamble to the proposed Directive and *Salduz v Turkey* (App. No. 3639/02) [2008] ECHR 1542 (27 November 2008); *Dayanan v Turkey* (App. No. 7377/03) (13 January 2010); *Brusco v France* (App. No. 1466/07) (14 October 2010); and *Panovits v Cyprus* (App. No. 4268/04) (11 December 2008).

[55] 16 December 1966, United Nations, Treaty Series, vol. 999, p 171.

frequency of such meetings that might prejudice the rights of the defence. The Article gives the lawyer the right to be present at any questioning or hearing and also to check the conditions in which the suspect or accused person is being detained and have access to the place of detention in order to do so.

Article 5 provides a suspect or accused person in criminal proceedings or EAW proceedings, upon being deprived of their liberty, with the right to communicate with at least one person named by him as soon as possible (see also Art. 11 in relation to EAWs). **5.101**

Article 6 provides non-nationals who are deprived of their liberty with the right to have consular or diplomatic authorities of their national State informed of their detention as soon as possible. **5.102**

Article 7 ensures the confidentiality of all forms of communication between a lawyer and client. **5.103**

Articles 8 and 9 deal with derogation from and waiver of the rights protected by the measure. Article 8 provides that derogation by a Member State from the provisions of the proposed Directive shall be permitted only in exceptional circumstances, shall not go beyond what is necessary, and shall not prejudice the fairness of proceedings. Derogation must not be based exclusively on the type or seriousness of the alleged offence. Article 9 provides that the rights to a lawyer provided pursuant to the proposed Directive may be waived in circumstances where the suspect or accused person has received prior legal advice or is otherwise made aware of the consequences of waiver and gives the waiver voluntarily. **5.104**

Article 11 provides that any person subject to EAW proceedings shall have the right of access to a lawyer promptly upon arrest. The right to a lawyer extends to: **5.105**

(a) access to a lawyer in such time and manner as to allow him to exercise his rights effectively;
(b) the right to meet with the lawyer and for the duration and frequency of such meetings not to be limited in such a way as to prejudice his rights;
(c) the right to have a lawyer present any questioning and hearing; and,
(d) access by the lawyer to any place of detention in order to check the conditions of detention.

Article 12 states that the proposed Directive does not provide for legal aid, save to note that the domestic provisions on legal aid should not be applied less favourably by Member States to the rights of access provided pursuant to the Directive. This provision receives further analysis in the context of funding for cross-border cases at **5.123**. **5.106**

Article 13 provides that a person to whom the proposed Directive applies shall have an effective remedy in circumstances where his right of access to a lawyer has been breached. The remedy 'shall have the effect of placing the suspect or accused person in the same position in which he would have found himself had the breach not occurred.' Any statements made by a suspect or accused person, or other evidence obtained in breach of the right of access to a lawyer, may not be used in evidence against him, 'unless the use of such evidence would not prejudice the rights of the defence'. **5.107**

On 22 September 2011, the UK, together with Belgium, France, Ireland, and the Netherlands, submitted a Note on the proposed Directive.[56] The UK announced its decision not to opt into the Directive, pursuant to Article 3 of Protocol No. 21 to the Lisbon Treaty. **5.108**

---

[56] Council of the European Union, 14495/11.

5.109 The Note affirmed the commitment to the Roadmap and accepted that the right of access to a lawyer represented one of the key elements of a defendant's right to a fair trial. In the context of the importance of this right, the Note expressed and explained the serious reservations of the UK and the other contributing Member States to the proposed Directive, which 'as published would present substantial difficulties for the effective conduct of criminal proceedings by way of their investigating, prosecuting and judicial authorities.'[57] The Note identified three principal objections:

(a) *The proposed Directive would hamper the effective conduct of criminal investigations and proceedings* The first objection is based upon the perceived failure of the proposed Directive to balance the rights of the defendant against the resources and functioning of the criminal justice system. For example, it is contended that the mandatory presence of a lawyer at every investigative measure where the presence of the suspect is required or permitted (e.g. the taking of fingerprints) would lead to delay and expend considerable resources without achieving a commensurate improvement in the protections afforded to suspects.

(b) *The proposed Directive must establish minimum standards in a way which takes into account the different ways in which Member State systems secure the right to a fair trial* The second principal objection argues that the proposed Directive fails to take into account the considerable differences between national justice systems when setting minimum standards. It is suggested that the Directive fails to distinguish, for example, between the rights of access to a lawyer provided to someone accused of a minor traffic offence and someone detained on suspicion of a serious assault. The proposed Directive is also said to ignore the fact that different rights will be applicable at different stages of criminal proceedings.

(c) *The Directive's relationship with the requirements of the ECHR is unclear* The proposed Directive is criticised under this head for going beyond the current requirements of the ECHR, without a prior evaluation of the impact this will have on the rights of individuals and the wider needs of criminal justice systems. The proposed Directive is said not to reflect existing Article 5 ECHR case law; for example, there is no established right to have a lawyer inspect a place of detention or to communicate with a third party of one's choice upon detention. It is pointed out that neither has the ECHR envisaged circumstances in which the physical presence of a lawyer is required at every stage of the investigation.

5.110 In light of the Note, revision of the proposed Directive was undertaken. A 'State of Play' document was issued on 21 October 2011, following an ongoing process of revision and refinement and contributions by Member States. A revised draft was submitted by the Presidency of the Council of the EU on 9 March 2012, following a meeting on 8–9 February 2012 of the Working Party on Substantive Criminal Law. It included the following relevant changes:

(a) minor offences, defined as offences which may only be dealt with by way of a fine, are excluded from its application until such time as the offence reaches a court of criminal jurisdiction (Art. 2);

(b) the right of a suspect or an accused person to have a lawyer present at investigative or other evidence-gathering acts is to be determined by Member States. The suspect or

---

[57] Council of the European Union, 14495/11, p 2.

accused person shall have at least the right for his lawyer to attend identity parades, confrontations, and crime reconstructions (Art. 3);

(c) access to a lawyer is now required before interview, rather than before the start 'of any questioning' (Art. 3); and

(d) Member States are to have the ability to derogate from the right to confidentiality of communications between lawyer and client where this is justified by either an urgent need to prevent serious crime or sufficient reason to believe the lawyer and client are involved in a criminal offence (Art. 4—now 'Confidentiality').

Discussions on the proposed Directive are ongoing. On 4 October 2012, the latest draft of **5.111** the proposed Directive by the Council Presidency was published along with comments on the positions taken by the Commission and the Parliament and options for Member States to consider.[58]

Green Paper on pre-trial detention

Following an invitation by the Council, and pursuant to the Roadmap, on 14 June 2011 the **5.112** Commission published 'Strengthening mutual trust in the European union judicial area—A Green Paper on the application of EU criminal justice legislation in the field of detention' (Measure F).

The Green Paper addresses both the legal and physical aspects of pre-trial detention. As its **5.113** title suggests, it focuses on the potential effects of pre-trial detention issues on mutual trust, and hence judicial cooperation, among Member States. Therefore, while recognising that the terms of pre-trial detention and prison management are ultimately issues for Member States, the Green Paper seeks to explore, through ten questions for discussion, ways in which greater cooperation between Member States might nevertheless be achieved.

Specific consideration is given to the impact of pre-trial detention issues on the EAW, and **5.114** also on three 'mutual recognition instruments'. These are the Council Framework Decisions on the transfer of prisoners,[59] on probation and alternative sanctions,[60] and on European Supervision Orders.[61] In each case, issues which might hinder mutual trust and cooperation are identified.

The Green Paper points out that the length of pre-trial detention varies widely among **5.115** Member States. In some Member States, pre-trial detention may last as long as four years. Consideration is invited as to whether there should be EU minimum rules in respect of maximum pre-trial detention periods, and also mechanisms for regular review of pre-trial detention.

As far as the physical conditions of detention are concerned, the Green Paper acknowledges **5.116** that there is no need to create an EU network for monitoring prisons. This is because that task is undertaken already by the Council of Europe, which has drawn up the European Prison Rules. These, although non-binding, have been widely endorsed. However the Green Paper does invite views as to how the monitoring of prison conditions by Member States

---

[58] DS 1650/12. For a critique of the proposals see the Joint Statement on the Directive by Fair Trials International, the European Criminal Bar Association, Justice, the Helsinki Foundation et al., 7 May 2012.
[59] 2008/909/JHA of 27 November 2008.
[60] 2008/947/JHA of 27 November 2008.
[61] 2009/829/JHA of 23 November 2009.

might be better promoted. The Green Paper also invites consideration of the position of children, and whether there are any specific alternatives to detention which might be developed for them.

5.117 Clearly, wide variations in pre-trial detention periods are capable of undermining mutual trust between Member States, as are concerns about prison conditions in particular States. Indeed the Green Paper cites by way of example the decision of the Irish Supreme Court in *Minister for Justice Equality and Law Reform v Rettinger*[62] where the surrender of an accused person pursuant to an EAW was declined because of concerns about the adequacy of detention conditions in the issuing State.

5.118 There is nevertheless a tension, which the Green Paper reflects, between, on the one hand, the need to address such issues and, on the other, the fact that Member States are ultimately responsible for both their own domestic laws in relation to detention before trial and for the conditions in their penal establishments.

5.119 The statistical tables appended to the Green Paper highlight another difficulty. Prison populations and rates of imprisonment vary widely among Member States, as do the proportion of prisoners in pre-trial detention and the proportion of non-national prisoners detained. In those circumstances, establishing effective EU-wide measures, which will build trust and cooperation between Member States, is unlikely to be straightforward.

Special safeguards for suspected or accused persons who are vulnerable

5.120 The short explanation in the Roadmap for Measure E states that:

> In order to safeguard the fairness of the proceedings, it is important that special attention is shown to suspected or accused persons who cannot understand or follow the content or the meaning of the proceedings, owing, for example, to their age, mental or physical condition.

5.121 To date, Measure E has received the least attention of the Roadmap measures. At present, the Commission is working towards a 'Legislative proposal on special safeguards in criminal procedures for Suspected or accused Persons who are vulnerable'. The Commission's indicative plan for this proposal recognises that there is a disparity in protection for vulnerable individuals across Member States, with particular reference to vulnerable adults for which there is 'very little' legislation aimed at their protection. The Commission notes that protection is afforded to vulnerable individuals through measures to identify such individuals, access to a lawyer, and by special measures to ensure effective participation in criminal proceedings. When the legislative proposal is published, the measures are likely to be focused on those areas. The Commission's indicative roadmap also notes that an impact assessment will be carried out. As a result, it is likely to be several years before a draft Directive in this area is published.

E. Funding in Cross-Border Cases

5.122 Despite the obvious cost implications arising from the implementation of the proposed Directive on access to a lawyer in criminal proceedings and the right to communicate upon arrest, the practical issue of funding the rights of access to a lawyer which the Directive

---

[62] [2010] IESC 45.

provides for is not addressed. Article 12 provides that 'The Directive is without prejudice to domestic provisions on legal aid'. The intention is that an EU-wide consensus on criminal legal aid will be dealt with in a future Directive under the Roadmap. This Directive has not yet been drafted.

The legislative basis for a Directive on criminal legal aid is clear. Article 47(3)[63] of the Charter **5.123** provides; 'Legal aid shall be made available to those who lack sufficient resources in so far as such aid is necessary to ensure effective access to justice'. Article 6(3) of the ECHR provides that 'Everyone charged with a criminal offence is entitled to free legal assistance if he has not sufficient means to pay for [it] . . . when the interest of justice so requires it.' Currently, the only pan-European initiative engaging with the issue of EU-wide provisions on legal aid in criminal cases is the European Commission's 'Study on Cross Border Legal Aid Project', which is being conducted with the assistance of the Council of Bars and Law Societies of Europe (CCBE) and the European Criminal Bar Association (ECBA). Definitive provisions regarding the availability of legal aid across the EU have not resulted from this project.

The Note from five countries, including the UK, raising concerns about the proposed **5.124** Directive (see **5.108**) makes lengthy reference to the failure to address the issue of legal aid, describing this as the 'missing element' of the proposal. It is argued that 'the right of access of a lawyer is not effective unless it is supported by an appropriate system of legal aid'.[64] It goes on to argue that a Directive on legal aid must be drafted before the proposed Directive comes into force, otherwise an untenable situation would be created: rights enshrined in EU law would be unenforceable due to a lack of legislation providing for mandatory State funding of the legal representation guaranteed as of right.

In the absence of specific EU-wide legislation on legal aid, the issue of funding in cross-border **5.125** cases is dealt with under domestic legislation. Cross-border cases are defined as cases which involve EU nationals who do not hold a passport issued by a Member State, and cases involving the execution of an EAW.

Domestic legal aid provisions do not discriminate between nationals of the UK and **5.126** non-nationals. All arrested persons are entitled to free and independent legal advice. All subsequent applications for legal aid to cover representation in court are then assessed according to the same criteria, regardless of nationality. The case must first pass the 'merits' test, or the 'Widgery' criteria.[65] At certain stages of the case, eligibility for legal aid is also subject to a means test.

In EAW cases, legal aid is applied for in the same manner as other criminal cases. There is **5.127** no specific provision which allows for legal advice from a lawyer outside the UK (ie in the requesting State) to be obtained with State funding. If a lawyer in the UK believes that it is necessary to obtain such advice, an application must be made to the Legal Services Commission (the non-departmental public body which administers the legal aid fund) to

---

[63] Set out in full at **5.49**.
[64] Council of the European Union, 14495/11, p 6.
[65] Paragraph 5, Sch. 3 to the Access to Justice Act 1999 sets out the 'Widgery' criteria, so-called after Lord Widgery, Lord Chief Justice, who originally laid down the criteria. They include whether the defendant is likely to lose his liberty, livelihood, or suffer serious reputational damage; the complexity of the proceedings; the defendant's level of understanding; whether expert evidence will be required and whether it is in another's interests that the defendant is represented.

sanction the funding of this as a disbursement. State funding of advice from the requesting State is thus discretionary. This will remain the position unless a Directive is signed by the UK, which enshrines more extensive legal aid provisions.

F. Pre-Trial Supervision

5.128 The European Council Framework Decision on the application, between Member States of the EU, of the principle of mutual recognition to decisions on supervision measures as an alternative to provisional detention[66] lays down rules according to which one Member State recognises a decision on pre-trial supervision measures issued in another Member State.[67]

5.129 This Framework Decision was intended to provide for the transfer of a pre-trial non-custodial supervision measure (e.g. release from pre-trial detention on bail) from the Member State where a non-resident is suspected of having committed an offence, to the Member State where he is normally resident. A process is provided whereby Member States can be required to enforce the bail conditions of another Member State. This will allow a suspected person to be subject to a supervision measure in his home State until the trial takes place in the requesting Member State.

5.130 The Framework Decision seeks to enhance the right to liberty and the presumption of innocence in the EU and ensure cooperation between Member States when a person is subject to obligations or supervision pending a court decision.[68] The preamble also notes that in a common European area of justice without internal borders, it is necessary to take action to ensure that a person subject to criminal proceedings who is not resident in the trial State is not treated any differently from a person subject to criminal proceedings who is not so resident.[69] The Framework Decision entered into force on 1 December 2009 and has an implementation date of 1 December 2012.

5.131 It applies to the following supervision measures:[70]

(a) an obligation for the person to inform the competent authority in the executing State of any change of residence;
(b) an obligation not to enter certain localities, places, or defined areas;
(c) an obligation to remain at a specified place;
(d) an obligation containing limitations on leaving the territory of the executing State;
(e) an obligation to report at specified times to a specific authority; and
(f) an obligation to avoid contact with specific persons in relation to the offence(s) allegedly committed.

5.132 Each Member State may also indicate a preparedness to monitor other additional measures, including:[71]

---

[66] European Council Framework Decision 2009/829/JHA of 23 October 2009 on the application, between Member States of the European Union, of the principle of mutual recognition to decisions on supervision measures as an alternative to provisional detention.
[67] European Council Framework Decision 2009/829/JHA, Art. 1.
[68] European Council Framework Decision 2009/829/JHA, preamble, para. (4).
[69] European Council Framework Decision 2009/829/JHA, preamble, para. (5).
[70] European Council Framework Decision 2009/829/JHA, Art. 8(1).
[71] European Council Framework Decision 2009/829/JHA, Art. 8(2).

(a) an obligation not to engage in specified activities;
(b) an obligation not to drive a vehicle;
(c) an obligation to deposit a certain sum of money or to give another type of guarantee;
(d) an obligation to undergo therapeutic treatment or treatment for addiction; and
(e) an obligation to avoid contact with specified objects.

A decision on supervision measures may be forwarded to the competent authority of the Member State where the person is lawfully and ordinarily residing, in cases where the person, having been informed about the measures concerned, consents to return to that State.[72] **5.133**

The competent authority in the issuing State may, upon request of the person, forward the decision on supervision measures to the competent authority of a Member State other than the Member State in which the person is lawfully and ordinarily residing, on condition that the latter authority has consented to such forwarding.[73] **5.134**

The Framework Decision also provides for the procedure for forwarding a decision on supervision measures[74] and for competence over the monitoring of the supervision measures.[75] **5.135**

The decision of the executing State must be made as soon as possible and within 20 days of receipt of the decision on supervision measures and certificate.[76] In order to give rise to recognition of a decision on supervision measures, an offence must either fall within the list of Framework offences or satisfy the requirement of dual criminality.[77] **5.136**

The Framework Decision provides certain grounds for the non-recognition by the executing State of the decision on supervision measures:[78] **5.137**

(a) the certificate issued is incomplete or obviously does not correspond to the decision on supervision measures;
(b) the criteria laid down in Article 9(1), 9(2), or 10(4) are not met;
(c) recognition of the decision on supervision measures would contravene the *ne bis in idem* principle;
(d) where applicable, the decision on supervision relates to an act which would not constitute an offence under the law of the executing State;
(e) the criminal prosecution is statute-barred under the law of the executing State and relates to an act which falls within the competence of the executing State under its national law;
(f) there is immunity under the law of the executing State, which makes it impossible to monitor supervision measures;
(g) under the law of the executing State, the person cannot, because of his age, be held criminally responsible for the act on which the decision on supervision measures is based; and
(h) it would, in case of breach of the supervision measures, have to refuse to surrender the person concerned in accordance with the Framework Decision on the EAW.

---

[72] European Council Framework Decision 2009/829/JHA, Art. 9(1).
[73] European Council Framework Decision 2009/829/JHA, Art. 9(2).
[74] European Council Framework Decision 2009/829/JHA, Art. 10.
[75] European Council Framework Decision 2009/829/JHA, Art. 11.
[76] European Council Framework Decision 2009/829/JHA, Art. 12.
[77] European Council Framework Decision 2009/829/JHA, Arts 14(1) and 14(2).
[78] European Council Framework Decision 2009/829/JHA, Art. 15(1).

5.138 If the issuing State has issued an arrest warrant or any other enforceable judicial decision having the same effect, the person shall be surrendered in accordance with the Framework Decision on the EAW.

5.139 It is important to note that the Framework Decision does not confer any additional rights to the individual to be granted bail.

G. Jurisdiction and Forum

5.140 Article 82 TFEU[79] provides that the European Parliament and the Council shall adopt measures to prevent and settle conflicts of jurisdiction between Member States.

Eurojust

5.141 Of importance in this context is the European Judicial Cooperation Unit (Eurojust). Established in 2002, Eurojust's role is to coordinate national investigations and prosecutions; to improve cooperation between national authorities by facilitating judicial cooperation and mutual recognition; and to support the effectiveness of national investigations and prosecutions.[80] In practice, Eurojust deals primarily with large and complex cross-border cases, usually involving more than two EU Member States.

5.142 Article 83(1) TFEU gives the European Council and the Parliament power to determine Eurojust's structure, operation, field of action, and tasks. The tasks may include requesting Member State authorities to begin investigations or prosecutions, the coordination of investigations and prosecutions, and the strengthening of judicial cooperation including by resolution of conflicts of jurisdiction.

5.143 The published Eurojust guidelines *Which Jurisdiction Should Prosecute?* lay down a rebuttable presumption that a prosecution should take place in the jurisdiction where the majority of the criminality occurred or where the majority of the loss was sustained. The guidelines then set out a number of relevant factors for consideration in this context, including:

(a) the avoidance of delay;
(b) the interests of victims;
(c) the availability and protection of witnesses;
(d) the location of the accused;
(e) the availability of extradition surrender from one jurisdiction to another;
(f) the desirability of prosecuting multiple defendants in one jurisdiction;
(g) the availability of reliable, credible, and admissible evidence;
(h) whether sentencing powers are available in a given jurisdiction which reflect the seriousness of the alleged conduct;
(i) the powers available to restrain, recover, seize, and confiscate the proceeds of crime; and
(j) the costs of prosecuting a case or its impact on the resources of a prosecution office.

---

[79] Set out at Chapter **1.55**.
[80] The purposes of Eurojust are set out in Art. 85, see Chapter **2.36**.

The Framework Decision on conflicts of jurisdiction

The European Council Framework Decision on prevention and settlement of conflicts of **5.144** exercise of jurisdiction in criminal proceedings[81] (the Framework Decision on conflicts of jurisdiction) is intended to prevent a breach of the *ne bis in idem* principle and ensure that a person is not subjected to criminal proceedings in different Member States in respect of the same facts or conduct. It aims to promote closer cooperation between the competent authorities of two or more Member States conducting criminal proceedings in order to improve the efficient and proper administration of justice.[82] Member States are expected to consult and cooperate in order to avoid an infringement of the *ne bis in idem* principle.[83] Procedures are established for the exchange of information between the competent authorities of Member States with a view to reaching a solution by consensus.[84]

Where a competent authority of a Member State has reasonable grounds to believe that **5.145** parallel proceedings are being conducted in another Member State, it shall contact the competent authority of that other Member State, with a view to initiating consultation.[85] An obligation then arises upon the other Member State to reply to such contact within any reasonable deadline or without undue delay.[86]

A request must contain the minimum information specified in Article 8 of the Framework **5.146** Decision, including the contact details of the competent authority; a description of the facts and circumstances that are the subject of the criminal proceedings concerned; all relevant details about the identity of the suspected or accused person and about the victim, if applicable; the stage that has been reached in the criminal proceedings; and information about provisional detention or custody of the suspected or accused person, if applicable.[87]

A response to such a request must also contain minimum information, including whether **5.147** criminal proceedings are being or were conducted in respect of some or all of the same facts as those which are the subject of the criminal proceedings referred to in the request for information submitted by the contacting authority, and whether the same persons are involved. If so, the stage of those proceedings or, where there is a final decision in existence, the nature of that final decision must be outlined.[88]

Where such communication establishes that parallel proceedings exist, the competent **5.148** authorities of the Member States concerned are required to enter into direct consultations in order to reach consensus on any effective solution aimed at avoiding the consequences arising from such parallel proceedings, which may, where appropriate, lead to the concentration of the criminal proceedings in one Member State.[89]

---

[81] European Council Framework Decision 2009/948/JHA of 30 November 2009 on prevention and settlement of conflicts of exercise of jurisdiction in criminal proceedings.
[82] European Council Framework Decision 2009/948/JHA, Art. 1(1).
[83] European Council Framework Decision 2009/948/JHA, Art. 1(2).
[84] European Council Framework Decision 2009/948/JHA, Art. 2(1). *Ne bis in idem* is examined at **5.158**.
[85] European Council Framework Decision 2009/948/JHA, Art. 5(1).
[86] European Council Framework Decision 2009/948/JHA, Art. 6(1).
[87] European Council Framework Decision 2009/948/JHA, Art. 8(1).
[88] European Council Framework Decision 2009/948/JHA, Art. 9(1).
[89] European Council Framework Decision 2009/948/JHA, Art. 10(1).

5.149 This Framework Decision entered into force on 15 December 2009. It had an implementation date of 15 June 2012.

5.150 It is important to note that this Framework Decision is complementary to and without prejudice to the power to refer the decision to Eurojust where it has not been possible to reach a consensus.[90]

Forum

5.151 The question of forum in criminal proceedings is becoming increasingly significant and controversial. This is notably the case in extradition proceedings for criminal offences that can properly be said to have been committed across more than one national jurisdiction. The Extradition Act 2003 was amended in 2006 to include 'forum' as a bar to extradition.[91] This provision has to date not been brought into force; however, on 16 October 2012, the Home Secretary announced that as soon as parliamentary time allows a new forum bar will be introduced that 'will be carefully designed to minimise delays'.[92] On 25 October 2012, the Crown Prosecution Service published interim prosecutor's guidance for cases of concurrent jurisdiction. The guidelines have immediate effect subject to a public consultation period which concludes on 31 January 2013.[93]

5.152 The UK courts have been reluctant to consider the question of forum in extradition proceedings. In *R (Williams) v Public Prosecutor of Lille & Court of First Instance, France*[94] the requested persons were sought by France pursuant to an EAW for drug trafficking offences that had been committed across Belgium, the UK, and France. The High Court considered the Framework Decision on conflicts of jurisdiction and reiterated that its purpose was to enhance cooperation between EU countries, in order to prevent unnecessary parallel criminal proceedings and to deal with cross-border criminality. The court would not be drawn into an analysis of the more convenient forum.

5.153 It would seem that the UK courts will continue to be anxious to ensure that the question of forum is one reserved for the relevant prosecuting authorities and Eurojust. As the court noted in *Williams*:

> the intention is to direct prosecuting authorities towards consensus and provide the means by which agreement may be achieved. They are not intended to form the subject of a debate in which potential defendants are involved.[95]

5.154 The court identified two reasons why it would not readily engage in a detailed analysis of forum. First, the Framework Decision on the EAW and Part 1 of the 2003 Act require the speedy resolution of an extradition request. This would be undermined if the court were to engage in an investigation into the question of forum. Secondly, the court considered it would usually be 'ill-equipped' to decide such a question.[96]

---

[90] European Council Framework Decision 2009/948/JHA, Art. 12.

[91] The Extradition Act 2003, s. 19B was added by the Police and Justice Act 2006.

[92] Hansard HC Deb, 16 October 2012, cols 164–6.

[93] See <http://www.cps.gov.uk/consultations/concurrent_jurisdiction_consultation.html>.

[94] *R (Williams) v Public Prosecutor of Lille & Court of First Instance, France* [2012] EWHC 2128 (Admin).

[95] *R (Williams) v Public Prosecutor of Lille & Court of First Instance, France* [2012] EWHC 2128 (Admin), para. 48.

[96] *R (Williams) v Public Prosecutor of Lille & Court of First Instance, France* [2012] EWHC 2128 (Admin), para. 48.

H. *Ne Bis in Idem*

Sources

The resolution of conflicts of jurisdiction between Member States in which criminal pro- **5.155** ceedings are coexistent, discussed earlier, is an application of the principle of *ne bis in idem*. Article 54 of the Convention Implementing the Schengen Agreement (CISA) articulates the *ne bis in idem* principle as follows: 'A person whose trial has been finally disposed of in one Contracting Party may not be prosecuted in another Contracting Party for the same acts provided that, if a penalty has been imposed, it has been enforced, is actually in the process of being enforced or can no longer be enforced under the laws of the sentencing Contracting Party.' The meaning that the CJEU has attributed to the phrases 'finally disposed of' and 'the same acts' in this Article are considered later (at **5.172** and **5.177** respectively).

Article 50 of the Charter of Fundamental Rights provides: 'No one shall be liable to be tried **5.156** or punished again in criminal proceedings for an offence for which he or she has already been finally acquitted or convicted within the Union in accordance with the law.'

This principle, otherwise known as the rule against double jeopardy, is reflected in UK law **5.157** through the plea of *autrefois acquit/convict* and the broader doctrine of abuse of process rec-ognised in this context in *Connelly v DPP*.[97] That said, the first question for consideration is the extent to which the UK court's approach to the principle of double jeopardy is, or ought to be, informed by CISA.

Are UK courts bound by the principle of *ne bis in idem*?

The UK is not a signatory to CISA and therefore is not a part of the Schengen area. The **5.158** Schengen Agreement and related provisions (the Schengen Acquis) were incorporated into EU law by the Treaty of Amsterdam under Protocol No. 2 to the EC Treaty and TEU. Its ele-ments were split across first-pillar and third-pillar law by Council Decision 1999/436/EC.[98]

The UK did not participate in Schengen generally but had the right to 'opt in' to certain pro- **5.159** visions. Council Decisions 2000/365/EC, 2004/926/EC, and 2010/779/EU identified the Schengen provisions which the UK would adopt, which included Article 54. The second of these Decisions (2004/926/EC) stipulated the date on which it was to be given effect, namely 1 January 2005. As a matter of EU law, CISA takes effect under the general obligations under Article 4(3) TEU (ex Art. 10 EC). As a matter of English law, its binding force derives from the European Communities Act 1972 as amended, in this case by the European Communities (Amendment) Act 1998 which expressly incorporates the Protocols to the Amsterdam Treaty into the body of binding European Treaty law. Certain primary UK legislation also expressly identifies Article 54: see, for example, section 76(4)(c) of the Criminal Justice Act 2003, which permits the quashing of an acquittal and the retrial of the acquitted person in certain circumstances,[99] and section 10 of the Double Jeopardy (Scotland) Act 2011.

As third-pillar law, Article 54 would not enjoy supremacy over domestic law. However, **5.160** following the principles set down by the CJEU in *Pupino*,[100] the domestic courts should

---

[97] [1964] AC 1254.
[98] For an explanation of the three pillars, see Chapter 1.
[99] The provisions of the Criminal Justice Act 2003 are further addressed at **5.181**.
[100] Case C-105/03.

interpret domestic law in light of third-pillar law as far as it is possible to do so consistently with Article 7 ECHR (no punishment without law). There would be a strong case that this rule applied in relation to Article 54 CISA, as the principle of *ne bis in idem* operates to an accused person's benefit.[101]

5.161 As far as enforcement is concerned, it is not clear whether the principle of *ne bis in idem* has direct effect, nor whether State liability in damages would be available for breach of a third-pillar obligation. This is likely to remain unclear, at least for the immediate future. These matters cannot be referred to the CJEU in the domestic context as the UK has not opted in to the preliminary reference jurisdiction of the CJEU as regards Framework Decisions (the main form of legal instrument under the old third pillar).

5.162 This position is likely to change and become clearer as the UK progresses through the transitional phase following the Treaty of Lisbon.

5.163 If the UK decides not to exercise the opt-out from existing EU criminal justice measures (see 1.42), then it will continue to be bound by third-pillar law, and any question over the force of that body of law should be removed, as the CJEU will gain full jurisdiction over it.

5.164 If the UK decides to exercise the opt-out, then third-pillar law will cease to apply to the UK. However, even in those circumstances, the principle of *ne bis in idem* remains part of the Charter of Fundamental Rights, which after the Lisbon Treaty has the force of the Treaties as a matter of EU law. The principle is also recognised in Article 4 of Protocol No. 7 to the ECHR which, although not ratified by the UK, will now form a fundamental principle of EU law after the Lisbon Treaty accession of the EU to the Convention.

5.165 The position with regard to the binding force of the *ne bis in idem* principle is therefore complex and to a large extent untested, although it should become simpler one way or another at the end of the post-Lisbon transition period. It is at least arguable that, as the law presently stands, the principle as articulated by the CJEU is already relevant to the determination of a UK court in a situation where the rule against double jeopardy is engaged. It is clear that the principle has application in cross-border cases, and in cases where the UK court is interpreting national legislation which was enacted to implement EU law, as in the case of the Extradition Act 2003. However, using the mechanisms outlined in this section, it may also be arguable that the European Court's jurisprudence on the principle, summarised later, is of some force even in a 'purely domestic' situation, with no cross-border element.[102]

Extradition

5.166 Article 3(2) of Framework Decision 2002/584/JHA on the EAW and the surrender procedures between Member States provides for mandatory non-execution of an EAW 'if the

---

[101]   The effect of the *Pupino* decision as a matter of UK law has been questioned following the recent decision of the Supreme Court in *Assange v The Swedish Prosecution Authority* [2012] UKSC 22 (per Lord Mance at paras 207–17). However, this ruling was in the context of an EU Framework Decision adopted under Title VI TEU which falls without the scope of Treaty law for the purposes of the 1972 legislation, whereas, as noted at **5.159**, CISA appears also to derive force directly under the 1972 Act.

[102]   On this issue see the argument of David Anderson QC and Cian Murphy that all UK domestic legislation on justice and home affairs might henceforth be considered to be within the scope of EU law and hence fall to be interpreted in light of the Charter of Fundamental Rights, even where the UK has specifically opted out of an EU measure on the area under consideration: 'The Charter of Fundamental Rights: History and Prospects in a Post-Lisbon Europe', European University Institute, Working Paper Law/2001/08.

executing judicial authority is informed that the requested person has been finally judged by a Member State in respect of the same acts provided that, where there has been a sentence, the sentence has been served or is currently being served or may no longer be executed under the law of the sentencing Member State.'

Article 4(3) of that Framework Decision further provides for optional non-execution 'where **5.167** the judicial authorities of the executing Member State have decided either not to prosecute for the offence on which the European Arrest Warrant is based or to halt proceedings, or where a final judgment has been passed upon the requested person in a Member State, in respect of the same acts, which prevents further proceedings.'

These Articles are implemented in part into UK law by section 12 of the Extradition Act **5.168** 2003 which states:

> A person's extradition to a category 1 territory is barred by reason of the rule against double jeopardy if (and only if) it appears that he would be entitled to be discharged under any rule of law relating to previous acquittal or conviction on the assumption
> (a) that the conduct constituting the extradition offence constituted an offence in the part of the United Kingdom where the judge exercises jurisdiction;
> (b) that the person were charged with the extradition offence in that part of the United Kingdom.

In their recent review of the UK's extradition arrangements Sir Scott Baker, David Perry QC, **5.169** and Anand Doobay considered whether the optional non-execution condition in Article 4(3) of the Framework Decision required further implementation into UK law.[103] The review concluded that:

> we see no need to legislate so as to provide a statutory bar to surrender in circumstances where the UK has decided not to prosecute for the offence on which the European Arrest Warrant is based or to halt proceedings. We have reached this conclusion for three principal reasons. First, the situation envisaged by Article 4(3) can be dealt with by the human rights bar and no further protection is necessary. Secondly, Article 54 of the Schengen Convention would oper-ate to prevent prosecution in the issuing Member State that is if a decision not to prosecute had been taken on the merits in any other Member State, including the UK. Thirdly, we would not expect the UK courts to surrender a requested person who had been provided with an assur-ance that he would not be prosecuted domestically for the offence on which the European Arrest Warrant is based, and the courts' abuse of process jurisdiction is broad enough in scope to provide the necessary protection against oppression.

In the case of *Mantello*[104] the CJEU provided its interpretation of Article 3(2) of the 2002 **5.170** Framework Decision and declared that:

> In view of the shared objective of Article 54 of the CISA and Article 3(2) of the Framework Decision, which is to ensure that a person is not prosecuted or tried more than once in respect of the same acts, it must be accepted that an interpretation of that concept given in the context of the CISA is equally valid for the purposes of the Framework Decision.

The meaning of *ne bis in idem* in Article 54

The concept of *ne bis in idem* therefore has a single autonomous interpretation, which applies **5.171** equally whether the issue falls to be considered in the extradition context under Article 3(2)

---

[103] 'A Review of the United Kingdom's Extradition Arrangements', Presented to the Home Secretary on 30 September 2011, at <http://www.homeoffice.gov.uk>.
[104] C-261/09.

of the Framework Decision, or more generally under Article 54 CISA. As to how the principle is to be interpreted, the CJEU has had significant opportunity to consider the issue in a string of cases which have considered the meaning of the terms 'finally disposed of' and 'same acts' that appear in Article 54 CISA.

'Finally disposed of'

5.172   In the case of *Gözütok and Brügge*,[105] the CJEU found that an out of court disposal which barred further prosecution in the State in which it was issued finally disposed of the matter for the purposes of Article 54, and hence barred any future prosecution in respect of the same acts in another Member State. The Court emphasised the need for mutual recognition of the criminal law of other Member States in this context, even where the domestic legal system in the Member State where the fresh proceedings are being contemplated might not recognise such non-judicial disposals, or would treat them differently. Furthermore, the Court emphasised more generally that the application of the principle could not be tied to procedural or merely formal matters such as the legal classification and formulation of a criminal offence. These are bound to differ from one Member State to another and such an approach would therefore undermine the intended effect of Article 54.

5.173   In *Van Straaten*,[106] the Court stated that 'In the event of an acquittal, any subsequent step is prohibited, provided the State monopoly on punishing crime has come into operation, in the form of an analysis of "the merits".' The Court went on to examine the different types of 'acquittal' which would be classified as involving an analysis of the merits, which included those based on grounds intrinsic to the defendant (e.g. age or mental disorder), those based on extrinsic factual circumstances (e.g. self-protection or necessity), those relating to the passage of time and those that go to the substantive truth of the facts under analysis. In the case of the latter category, it is perhaps unsurprising that the Court in *Van Straaten* concluded (contrary to submissions on behalf of Italy) that the *ne bis in idem* principle extends to an acquittal due to a 'lack of evidence'. Indeed, it is submitted that it is difficult to classify an acquittal by a jury after trial in the UK in any other way.

5.174   The somewhat surprising conclusion that the principle extends to cover a situation in which prosecution has become time-barred in another Member State was confirmed in *Gasparini*.[107] It is submitted that this decision was wrong, and that the contrary view articulated by academic commentators[108] and the Court's own Advocate-General in that case is to be preferred, namely that such a time-barred prosecution will not normally involve the examination of the merits in any real sense, and that the principle is therefore not typically engaged. However, at present the CJEU's case law is clear, to the benefit of a potential defendant whose prosecution is declared time-barred in one Member State and who subsequently finds himself in another Member State with jurisdiction to bring the prosecution where proceedings are not time-barred.

5.175   In *Bourquain*,[109] the CJEU confirmed that the principle could apply to judgments properly returned in the absence of the accused, and that the matter was to be considered finally

---

[105]   C-385/01.
[106]   C-150/05.
[107]   C-467-04.
[108]   See e.g. Andre Klip, *European Criminal Law: An Integrative Approach*, 2nd edn (Antwerp: Intersentia, 2009), 256.
[109]   C-297/07.

disposed of where it was no longer possible lawfully to enforce the sentence which followed a conviction in such circumstances (because the sentence of the court at that time, in this case the death penalty, was no longer in force).

In *Turansky*,[110] a decision by Slovakian police officers to suspend an investigation did not **5.176** constitute a final disposal of the case for the purposes of the *ne bis in idem* principle (and therefore did not bar a prosecution in Austria) because such a suspension did not definitively bar further prosecution in Slovakia itself.

'Same acts'

In *Van Esbroek*,[111] the CJEU had to consider whether a conviction for importing drugs **5.177** into Norway from Belgium barred a subsequent prosecution in Belgium in respect of the exportation of the same drugs. The Court concluded that the principle applies to the 'same acts' understood in the sense of the existence of a set of concrete circumstances, which are inextricably linked together. Interestingly, the primary justification given by the Court for this broad substantive approach was couched in terms of the free movement of persons, which it held was:

> effectively guaranteed only if the perpetrator of an act knows that, once he has been found guilty and served his sentence, or, where applicable, been acquitted by a final judgment in a Member State, he may travel within the Schengen territory without fear of prosecution in another Member State on the basis that the legal system of that Member State treats the act concerned as a separate offence.

Comparisons with the UK approach to the rule against double jeopardy

The breadth of the substantive approach of the CJEU ('concrete set of circumstances inextri- **5.178** cably linked together', as was expressed in *Van Esbroek*[112]) can be contrasted with the traditionally narrow approach of the UK courts towards the application of the special plea in bar of *autrefois acquit/convict.* Such a plea is only considered to be available where 'the crime or offence charged in the later indictment is the same or is in effect or is substantially the same as the crime charged (or in respect of which there could have been a conviction) in a former indictment and that it is immaterial that the facts under examination or the witnesses being called in the later proceedings are the same as those in some earlier proceedings.'[113] Although this narrow approach is ameliorated by the discretionary power of the courts to stay unfair or oppressive prosecutions as an abuse of process, there seems to be a strong argument that the current European approach to the principle of *ne bis in idem* is broader and more generous in its scope than the corresponding principles in UK law.

Subject to the earlier analysis (at **5.158**) on the current applicability of the EU principle in **5.179** the UK courts (and to the way this might change in 2014 at the end of the post-Lisbon transition period), this raises a number of interesting possibilities in terms of the interaction of UK and EU law in this area. For instance, it seems fairly clear that a District Judge considering an extradition request in the UK courts would be bound by the EU jurisprudence in this area through his obligation to interpret the Extradition Act 2003 in light of the Framework Decision which it implements, which we have seen contains provisions on the *ne bis in idem*

---

[110]   C-491/07.
[111]   C-436/04.
[112]   C-436/04.
[113]   *Connelly v DPP* [1964] AC 1254, per Lord Morris at 1306.

principle (which, in turn, the CJEU has stated must be interpreted in the same way as Art. 54 CISA). This would appear to mean that a UK judge would be obliged to refuse to execute an arrest warrant for the extradition of an individual where to do so would offend against the broad principle as articulated by the CJEU, even in circumstances where the requested person might be unable to avail himself of the domestic *autrefois* doctrine were he charged with the same offence in the UK.

5.180 More generally, a defendant concerned about the likely success of a plea of *autrefois* under the narrow UK doctrine, or his prospects of success under the discretionary abuse of process jurisdiction, might seek to rely upon the European jurisprudence summarised earlier in order to argue for a broader, more substantive interpretation of the question of whether a 'crime or offence charged in the later indictment is the same or is in effect or is substantially the same as the crime charged (or in respect of which there could have been a conviction) in a former indictment.'[114]

New and compelling evidence cases

5.181 A particular area of potential interest in this connection is contained within the provisions of Part 10 of the Criminal Justice Act 2003 (CJA 2003), which allow for the quashing of an acquittal and the retrial of the acquitted person in cases where new and compelling evidence comes to light. Whereas Article 4 of Protocol No. 7 to the ECHR (which has not been ratified by the UK) contains an explicit exception to the double jeopardy principle, in such circumstances[115] the EU jurisprudence on *ne bis in idem* at present appears silent on this issue. To the extent that an individual can currently rely on the EU *ne bis in idem* principle in purely domestic criminal proceedings by invoking the indirect effect of old third-pillar law (under *Pupino*), it is clear that this could not prevent a fresh prosecution under Part 10 of the CJA 2003, since its provisions are clear, and the *Pupino* principle does not extend to permitting a *contra legem* interpretation.

5.182 Nonetheless, the lack of any guidance on the relationship between fresh evidence cases and the *ne bis in idem* principle could create problems in the context of other Member States considering extradition requests for individuals previously acquitted in the UK. After *Mantello*[116] and *Turansky*,[117] a national court considering whether the *ne bis in idem* principle should bar execution of a warrant are required to answer the question of whether there has been a decision which definitively bars further prosecution in another Member State. To what extent might the existence of the provisions of Part 10 of the CJA 2003 provide a barrier to such a conclusion where another Member State considers the status of an acquittal in a UK court? And how would another Member State approach the question of an extradition request from the UK in respect of a person previously acquitted in the EU, in respect of whom new and compelling evidence has come to light and whose extradition the UK prosecuting authorities are requesting with a view to a fresh proceedings under Part 10 of the CJA 2003? There is an express obligation placed upon the DPP by section 76(4)(c) of the CJA 2003 not to authorise an application to the Court of Appeal to re-open an acquittal unless satisfied that 'any trial

---

[114] *Connelly v DPP* [1964] AC 1254, per Lord Morris at 1306.
[115] '[The principle] shall not prevent the reopening of the case in accordance with the law and penal procedure of the State concerned, if there is evidence of new or newly discovered facts, or if there has been a fundamental defect in the previous proceedings, which could affect the outcome of the case.'
[116] C-261/09, see **5.170**.
[117] C-491/07, see **5.176**.

pursuant to an order on the application would not be inconsistent with obligations of the UK under Article 31 or 34 of the Treaty on European Union relating to the principle of *ne bis in idem.*' This provision is interesting in that it appears to recognise the binding force of the principle in domestic UK law, but no further guidance is provided on when a re-trial under this Part might be reconcilable with the broad principles articulated by the CJEU in this area, nor indeed when, if ever, the application of the principle might prevent a fresh prosecution that would otherwise satisfy the statutory requirements under the CJA 2003.

I. Trial in Absence

Sources

Article 47 of the Charter of Fundamental Rights provides in part that: **5.183**

Everyone is entitled to a fair and public hearing within a reasonable time by an independent and impartial tribunal previously established by law. Everyone shall have the possibility of being advised, defended and represented.

In *Krombach v Bamberski*,[118] the Luxembourg Court stated that 'the right to be   **5.184** defended...occupies a prominent position in the organisation and conduct of a fair trial and is one of the fundamental rights deriving from the constitutional traditions common to the Member States.'

These general principles of EU law clearly reflect settled jurisprudence under Article 6   **5.185** ECHR. In particular, Article 6(3)(c) provides that a person has the right 'to defend himself in person or through legal assistance of his own choosing' and the Strasbourg case law clearly treats the attendance of a criminal defendant at his trial as a matter of central importance,[119] albeit a right which can in certain circumstances be waived.[120] The settled position in domestic law with respect to the trial on indictment of a criminal defendant in his absence is set out in *Jones*,[121] in which the House of Lords endorsed (with one exception) the list of relevant factors set out by the Court of Appeal in that case. When deciding whether to exercise the exceptional judicial discretion to proceed in a defendant's absence those factors are:

(i) the nature and circumstances of the defendant's behaviour in absenting himself from the trial or disrupting it, as the case may be and, in particular, whether his behaviour was deliberate, voluntary and such as plainly waived his right to appear;
(ii) whether an adjournment might result in the defendant being caught or attending voluntarily and/or not disrupting the proceedings;
(iii) the likely length of such an adjournment;
(iv) whether the defendant, though absent, is, or wishes to be, legally represented at the trial or has, by his conduct, waived his right to representation;
(v) whether an absent defendant's legal representatives are able to receive instructions from him during the trial and the extent to which they are able to present his defence;
(vi) the extent of the disadvantage to the defendant in not being able to give his account of events, having regard to the nature of the evidence against him;

---

[118] C-7/98.
[119] *Poitrimol v France* (1993) 18 EHRR 130, 146, para. 35; *Pelladoah v The Netherlands* (1994) 19 EHRR 81, 94, para. 40; *Lala v The Netherlands* (1994) 18 EHRR 586, 597, para. 33.
[120] *Poitrimol v France* (1993) 18 EHRR 130, para. 31.
[121] [2003] 1 AC 1.

(vii) the risk of the jury reaching an improper conclusion about the absence of the defendant;

(viii) [expressly disapproved by the House of Lords]

(ix) the general public interest and the particular interest of victims and witnesses that a trial should take place within a reasonable time of the events to which it relates;

(x) the effect of delay on the memories of witnesses;

(xi) where there is more than one defendant and not all have absconded, the undesirability of separate trials, and the prospects of a fair trial for the defendants who are present.

5.186 The court concluded that this approach was consistent with the ECHR case law, which set down neither an absolute prohibition on criminal trials in a defendant's absence, nor an absolute rule that such a defendant was entitled as of right to a complete re-trial if and when apprehended.

5.187 In addition to the influence of those general principles of EU law set out earlier, the primary impact of EU law on domestic law in this area is likely to be in the context of extradition proceedings.

The extradition of persons convicted *in absentia*

5.188 The European Council recognises that Article 6 ECHR provides an accused person the right to appear in person at trial. It is also acknowledged that the right to appear is not absolute and that an accused person may waive that right. This was reflected in Article 5 of the Framework Decision on the EAW, which provides that a Member State may surrender a person who has been convicted *in absentia* and had not been summoned in person or otherwise informed of the date and place of the hearing which led to the decision, subject to the condition that the person will have an opportunity to apply for a retrial.

5.189 The European Council Framework Decision on Trials in Absentia[122] has inserted Article 4(a) into the Framework Decision on the EAW. The intention was to enhance the rights of requested persons convicted in their absence. The *pro forma* EAW was also amended in relation to the information that ought to be provided in relation to the presence or otherwise of the requested person at trial.

5.190 In essence, the Framework Decision now provides that a conviction rendered *in absentia* should be recognised and executed where:

(a) the accused was summoned in person and informed of the date and place of trial, or received official information of the scheduled date and place of trial, in such a manner that it was unequivocally established that he or she was aware of the scheduled trial; or

(b) the accused, being aware of the scheduled trial, was represented at the trial by a lawyer whom he had instructed and who was entitled to defend him; or

(c) the person was served with a decision and expressly informed about the right to appeal or re-trial and expressly stated that he did not contest the original decision.

5.191 The Framework Decision on trials *in absentia* entered into force on 28 March 2009. It had an implementation date of 28 March 2011, however, no amendment has been made to the

---

[122] European Council Framework Decision 2009/299/JHA of 26 February 2009 amending Framework Decisions 2002/584/JHA, 2005/214/JHA, 2006/783/JHA, 2008/909/JHA and 2008/947/JHA, thereby enhancing the procedural rights of persons and fostering the application of the principle of mutual recognition to decisions rendered in the absence of the person concerned at the trial.

Extradition Act 2003 in relation to trials in absence as section 20, as enacted originally, contained sufficient safeguards to protect persons convicted in their absence in the requesting territory.

In *Rexha v Office of the Prosecutor attached to the Court in Rome*,[123] the High Court held **5.192** that Article 4a(1) of the Framework Decision on the EAW, as amended by the Framework Decision on trials *in absentia*, was discretionary and not obligatory. In essence, an executing judicial authority 'may' refuse to execute an EAW. The court also noted that the provisions of section 20 of the 2003 Act were more stringent. The absence of an assurance in an EAW that the requested person had the right to a retrial did not compel the District Judge to refuse to execute the warrant.

J. Data Protection

Article 8 of the Charter recognises the right to protection of personal data as a fundamental **5.193** right. The Council Framework Decision on the protection of personal data processed in the framework of police and judicial cooperation in criminal matters[124] addresses the issue of data protection in considerable detail.

The Framework Decision on the protection of personal data is considered in more detail in **5.194** Chapter 6.[125] Its relevance to the topic of procedural safeguards would seem to be limited, not least because the scope of the Framework Decision extends only to the processing of personal data transmitted or made available *between* Member States. It therefore has no application to suspected or accused persons in criminal proceedings which have no transnational element.

Certain aspects of the Framework Decision are, however, worthy of note in the context of **5.195** procedural safeguards for suspected or accused persons. First, it does not apply to the transmission of personal data to private parties, such as defence lawyers, in the course of criminal proceedings. It does not, therefore, impinge upon, or derogate from, the fundamental right to information in criminal proceedings.

Secondly, Article 7 of the Framework Decision on the protection of personal data provides **5.196** that:

> A decision which produces an adverse legal effect for the data subject or significantly affects him and which is based solely on automated processing of data intended to evaluate personal aspects relating to the data subject shall be permitted only if authorised by a law which also lays down measures as to safeguard the data subject's legitimate rights.

Subject to the requirement for a transnational aspect, this provision may affect the extent to which prosecutions could be brought in circumstances where the sole or decisive evidence relied upon was obtained from previously gathered data, for example where such data was used to identify the defendant as the alleged offender.

Thirdly, Article 19 (right to compensation) and Article 20 (judicial remedies) of the **5.197** Framework Decision on the protection of personal data provide remedies to persons who suffer damage or otherwise have their rights infringed by unlawful data processing activities.

---

[123] *Rexha v Office of the Prosecutor attached to the Court in Rome* [2012] EWHC 1274 (Admin).
[124] 2008/977/JHA.
[125] It is also considered in the context of OLAF investigations, see **5.206**.

While these provisions are of general application, they would clearly be available to suspected or accused persons, where the unlawful data processing occurred in connection with criminal proceedings against them.

K. OLAF Investigations

Background

5.198 The European Anti-Fraud Office (l'Office européen de lutte antifraude) was established pursuant to a Commission Decision in 1999.[126] As the successor to the European Commission's Task Force for Co-ordination of Fraud Prevention, the primary function of OLAF is to protect the 'financial interests of the European Union' through 'the fight against fraud, corruption and any other illegal activity affecting the financial interests' of the EU.[127]

5.199 To achieve this aim, OLAF is empowered to conduct administrative external investigations into individuals and legal entities. External investigations are conducted in Member States and third party countries and consist of 'on-the-spot inspections and checks, examination of financial transactions and business records, access to [and copying of] relevant documents, interviews, etc.' OLAF is required to inform Member States of investigations conducted within their territory and, in turn, Member States are obliged to provide assistance to OLAF (Arts 3 and 6(6)[128]). OLAF's other responsibilities include cooperating with, and providing assistance to, Member States (Art. 1(2)) and internal investigations into EU institutions, bodies, offices, and agencies (Art. 4).[129]

5.200 EC Regulation No. 1073/1999 sets out rules on the opening of OLAF investigations and the procedure for those investigations (Arts 5 and 6). However, the ambiguity of these brief Articles and the breadth of OLAF's investigatory powers have led to concern regarding the impact of OLAF investigations on fundamental rights.[130]

5.201 Following an investigation, OLAF may provide a report on its conclusions to the Member State concerned (Art. 9). OLAF is not vested with powers of prosecution and as a result Member States retain discretion as to whether to take any action on receipt of the report. To assist Member States, reports address the facts established, details of any financial loss, the findings of the investigation, and any recommendations on future action. Significantly, Article 9(2) and (3) provides that reports of external investigations shall constitute admissible evidence in national administrative or judicial proceedings, taking into account the domestic procedural requirements.

5.202 Subjects of OLAF reports have initiated proceedings in the Court of First Instance (CFI, now the General Court) and CJEU on the basis that their rights have been breached and that the report should be annulled pursuant to what is now Article 263 TFEU, which provides that the EU Courts may review the legality of acts of EU institutions. The rights alleged to

---

[126] [1999] OJ L 316, 31.05.1999.
[127] Article 280 EC and Art. 1(1) Council Regulation No. 1073/1999 ([1999] OJ L 136, 31.05.1999). See also Chapter **2.42**.
[128] EC Regulation No. 1073/1999.
[129] See further Constantin Stefanou, Simone White, and Helen Xanthaki, *OLAF at the Crossroads: Action Against EU Fraud* (Oxford: Hart Publishing, 2011).
[130] See e.g. [2011] OJ C 124/05, 27.04.2011.

have been infringed include the presumption of innocence, data protection, confidentiality, and access to information. The CJEU has declared these applications inadmissible on the basis that the report is a preparatory measure without legal effect. Individuals can nonetheless seek damages as a result of the effect of the report pursuant to Article 340 TFEU, which provides that the EU shall make good any damage caused by its institutions in the performance of their duties.

The Director of OLAF is obliged to be independent of the Member States and EU institutions. Article 11 of EC Regulation No. 1073/1999 provides for an independent Supervisory Committee to monitor the implementation of OLAF's investigative functions. The Parliament, the Council, and the Commission appoint five members to the Committee, including a Chairman. The Committee is empowered to oversee the activities of OLAF including the length of investigations and cases requiring information to be forwarded to a national judicial authority. The Committee is also required to produce at least one report a year on OLAF's activities and can make recommendations as to its operations. These arrangements raise concern about the independence of OLAF, particularly where it is called upon to investigate the Commission to which it was previously attached. **5.203**

Procedural rights

The particular rights of those under investigation by OLAF, which have been developed in the jurisprudence of the CJEU, are examined later (Section K).[131] **5.204**

Presumption of innocence

Article 48(1) of the Charter provides that anyone charged with an offence shall have the right to be presumed innocent until proven guilty according to law. In the context of OLAF, in the case of *Yves Franchet and Daniel Byk v Commission*,[132] the CFI found that the presumption of innocence had been breached where OLAF had issued a press release that suggested that the individuals concerned in its investigation were guilty of criminal offences. **5.205**

OLAF has also been criticised by the Courts for failing to respect individuals' data protection rights and Article 8 of Regulation 1073/1999 (information forwarded or obtained in the course of internal investigations shall be subject to professional secrecy and the provisions of EU legislation). In the *Franchet and Byk* case, the CJEU found that OLAF disclosed information to the media in breach of its obligation to communicate information only to those within the EU or Member States whose functions require them to have it. The CJEU awarded damages against OLAF as a result of the breach.[133] **5.206**

Right to be notified and to be heard

Article 4 of Decision 1999/396 (relating to internal investigations) obliges OLAF to notify individuals subject to an investigation of the fact of the investigation for the purposes of an interview. This notification can be postponed if the investigation requires secrecy. In addition, Article 41(2) of the Charter provides for a general right to be heard 'before any individual measure which would affect him or her adversely is taken'. In *Franchet and Byk*,[134] OLAF **5.207**

---

[131] For an overview see OLAF's Operation Manual, pp 119–30. Also, see OLAF Instructions to Staff on Investigative Procedures.
[132] Case T-48/05, 8 July 2008.
[133] See also Case T-259/03 *Nikolaou v Commission*, 9 December 2003.
[134] Case T-48/05, 8 July 2008.

disclosed its report to the French and Luxembourg judicial authorities without informing and hearing from the individuals subject to the investigation. As a result, the CFI found a series of breaches of individual rights and Decision 1999/396 and awarded damages.

5.208 No right exists in either Decision 1999/396 or Regulation 1073/1999 to be informed of an external OLAF investigation. However, according to its Operation Manual, OLAF will inform the subject of an external investigation of the fact of the investigation and 'enable the person concerned to express his views on all the facts that concern him before drawing any final conclusions' subject to the need for secrecy. In addition, the jurisprudence of the CJEU establishes a right to be heard where there is no specific legislative provision for such a right.[135]

5.209 It is important to note that those subject to an OLAF investigation have no right of access to the information held by OLAF. This flows from the fact that an OLAF report does not amount to a criminal charge and therefore withholding such information does not offend Article 48(2) of the Charter (which provides for the rights of the defence 'of anyone charged' to be guaranteed). See *Nikolaou v Commission*.[136] Access to an OLAF report may be secured from a national judicial authority if OLAF has communicated it to them. The independent Supervisory Committee on OLAF has also recommended that OLAF provide subjects of an investigation with the full report.[137]

Right to silence

5.210 According to the OLAF Operations Manual, 'Not only natural persons but also economic operators have the right not to make any statements which might be self-incriminating.' In this way, protection is given to the principle against self-incrimination. The CJEU has affirmed the principle in relation to competition cases.[138]

Right to representation

5.211 Article 47 of the Charter provides that everyone shall have the possibility of being advised, defended, and represented. The CJEU jurisprudence is clear that respect must be given to the right to legal representation from the outset of an OLAF inquiry.[139]

Length of investigations

5.212 Article 6(5) of Regulation 1073/1999 requires OLAF investigations to be conducted continuously over a period proportionate to the circumstances and complexity of the case. Article 11(7) provides that where an investigation has been in progress for more than nine months, the Director is required to inform the Supervisory Committee of the reasons for the delay and the expected time of completion. OLAF is required to act with diligence but there is no time limit for the conclusion of an investigation. As a guide to an inappropriate length of investigation, in *Jean Paul François v Commission*,[140] the Commission awarded damages in circumstances where disciplinary measures had been imposed eight years after the alleged events occurred. According to OLAF's Annual Plan 2012, the average length of an investigation in 2011 was 22.8 months. In 2012, OLAF aims to complete its investigation within 22 months. In 2013 and 2014, the target is 21 and 20 months respectively.

---

[135] See e.g. Case T-260/94 *Air Inter SA v Commission* [1991] ECR II-997, para. 60.
[136] Case T-259/03, 9 December 2003.
[137] See its Opinion 2/206 concerning the reform of Regulation 1073/99.
[138] See e.g. Case 374/87 *Orkem v Commission*, 18 October 1989.
[139] See e.g. Case 374/87 *Orkem v Commission*.
[140] Case T-307/01, 10 June 2004.

Conclusion

In March 2011, the Commission recognised concerns about the adequacy of existing proce-   **5.213**
dural protections in the context of OLAF investigations in its proposal for the amendment
of Regulation 1073/99. The proposal accordingly aims to strengthen the procedural rights
of persons concerned by investigations and sets out suggested procedural guarantees for both
internal and external investigations. Article 7a is entitled 'Procedural Guarantees' and sets
out specific provisions for the conduct of interviews and states that OLAF will be obliged to
seek evidence for and against persons concerned during the course of its investigation. Article
7b proposes a review procedure whereby those subject to an OLAF investigation may ask the
'Review Adviser' to provide an independent opinion regarding OLAF's regard for procedural
guarantees, both during the investigation and for one month after its completion.

L. Victim Protection

Background

The EU has a long-held concern for the protection of the rights of the victims of crime. Article   **5.214**
82 TFEU[141] provides for the Parliament and Council to establish, through Directives, minimum rules, to include the rights of the victims of crime.[142] The Tampere European Council
of 15 and 16 October 1999 on the creation of an area of freedom, security, and justice recognised the need for a 'genuine area of justice, where people can approach courts and authorities in any Member State as easily as their own.'[143] One of the requirements of this milestone
was a focus upon the protection of the victims of crime. The Presidency concluded that:

> minimum standards should be drawn up on the protection of victims of crime, in particular
> on crime victim's access to justice and on their rights to compensation for damages, including
> legal costs. In addition, national programmes should be set up to finance measures, public and
> non-governmental, for assistance to and protection of victims.[144]

The conclusion reflected the belief that free movement within the EU is strengthened when   **5.215**
EU citizens are protected throughout the Union, should they become the victims of crime.
This was emphasised in a Commission Communication on the issue[145] and a subsequent
Resolution adopted by the European Parliament.[146]

The 2001 Framework Decision on the standing of victims in criminal proceedings[147]

Following the conclusions of the Council meeting in Tampere, on 15 March 2001, the   **5.216**
Council adopted Framework Decision 2001/220/JHA on the standing of victims in criminal proceedings.

Article 1 of the Decision provides the definition of a 'victim':   **5.217**

> 'victim' shall mean a natural person who has suffered harm, including physical or mental
> injury, emotional suffering or economic loss, directly caused by acts or omissions that are in
> violation of the criminal law of a Member State.

---

[141] Set out at Chapter **1.55**.
[142] Article 2(2) TFEU.
[143] Tampere European Council, 15–16.10.99, Conclusions of the Presidency, para. 5.
[144] Tampere European Council, 15–16.10.99, Conclusions of the Presidency, para. 32.
[145] 'Crime Victims in the European Union: Reflections on Standards and Action', European Commission,
14 July 1999.
[146] 15 June 2000.
[147] 2001/220/JHA.

5.218 This definition has provided a basis for all subsequent EU legislation on the issue. The meaning of 'victim' has subsequently been considered by the CJEU. In *Dell'Orto*,[148] in which the victims were companies, the question arose as to whether the Framework Decision was applicable where the victim was not a natural person but a legal person. In the judgment of the Court, the Decision was applicable only to 'natural persons who have suffered harm directly caused by conduct which infringes the criminal law of a Member State' and the definition excluded legal persons, even where such entities had suffered harm directly caused by criminal offences.[149] In *Eredics and Sapi*[150] it was again concluded that the definition excluded legal persons.

5.219 Article 2(1) provides that all Member States are to ensure that victims have a 'real and appropriate role in its criminal legal system'. They are to be treated with 'due respect for the dignity of the individual'.

5.220 Article 3 requires Member States to allow victims to be heard during proceedings and to supply evidence.

5.221 Victims are to have access to information on the support and protection available to them (Art. 4(1)). They are to be kept up to date on the outcome of criminal proceedings and of any sentence passed, if they 'have expressed a wish to this effect' (Art. 4(2)). Upon release of an offender, a decision may be taken to notify the victim in cases where they might be exposed to the risk of danger (Art. 4(4)).

5.222 Member States are to ensure a 'suitable level of protection for victims and, where appropriate, their families' (Art. 8(1)). This extends to appropriate measures to protect the privacy and photographic images of victims and their families in court proceedings. Contact between victims and offenders in court premises is to be avoided (Art. 8(3)) and victims are to be protected from the effects of giving evidence in open court, where necessary (Art. 8(4)).

5.223 Article 9 provides for a right to compensation and for the return of recoverable property to victims without delay, unless it is urgently required for criminal proceedings.

5.224 Article 11 provides that efforts are to be made by Member States to overcome difficulties faced by victims of criminal offences which are committed other than in their country of residence; for example a victim should be able to make his complaint in his Member State of residence even if the crime was not committed there.

5.225 Member States are to encourage action by specialist services and victim support organisations, which assist victims before, during, and after proceedings (Art. 13(2)).

5.226 Training is to be provided for personnel who come into contact with victims, in particular police officers and legal practitioners (Art. 15).

5.227 Measures available for the support and assistance of victims of crime in the UK broadly reflect the obligations outlined in the Framework Decision. In England and Wales, a Code of Practice for Victims of Crime[151] governs the services which are to be provided to the victims

---

[148] Case C-467/05 *Dell'Orto*.
[149] Case C-467/05 *Dell'Orto*, paras 53 and 54.
[150] Case C-205/09 *Eredics*.
[151] Issued by the Home Secretary under the Domestic Violence, Crime and Victims Act 2004, s. 32, introduced on 3 April 2006.

of criminal conduct occurring within the jurisdiction by various bodies, including the CPS, the Prison Service, and Her Majesty's Court Service. The Code requires that services be given to any person 'who has made an allegation to the police, or had an allegation made on his or her behalf, that they have been directly subjected to criminal conduct.'[152] The services are limited to direct victims of crime; third parties or indirect victims are ineligible.[153]

The rights available to victims under the Code reflect some of the measure included within the 2001 Framework. An enhanced level of service is provided for vulnerable or intimidated victims. The duties imposed by the Code include the following: **5.228**

(a) the police are required to update victims as to key stages in the investigations and bringing of criminal proceedings, such as a decision not to investigate a crime, the arrest of a suspect, and the interviewing and/or reporting of a suspect for relevant criminal offences;

(b) the CPS must ensure that victims are informed of charging decisions taken by the CPS, or decisions resulting in criminal proceedings either not being brought or being discontinued at a later stage. Stringent timetables are set down for the provision of this information to the victims of crime. Prosecutors have a discretion not to provide such notification if it is decided, in accordance with CPS guidance, that it is not appropriate or necessary to do so in the circumstances;

(c) meetings should take place, where possible, between prosecutors and victims at court, during which an indication as to the length of any delay before they give evidence should be given;

(d) consideration must be given by prosecutors to the making of an application to the court for a special measure direction under Chapter 1 of Part II of the Youth Justice and Criminal Evidence Act 1999;

(e) the CPS must pay expenses due to a victim within a ten-day time frame following receipt of the correct form;[154] and

(f) the CPS must answer any questions a witness has about the sentence in their case.

Since 2001, the role of the victim in criminal proceedings in England and Wales has been further enhanced by the Victim Personal Statement scheme.[155] Under the scheme, a victim or the relative of a victim can, should they wish to do so, say in statement form how a crime has affected them. The court must consider and take into account the content of any such statement prior to passing sentence. **5.229**

The principal route to compensation for a victim of crime in England and Wales is through the Criminal Injuries Compensation Scheme (2008), which provides for compensation to an applicant who has suffered criminal injury. 'Criminal injury' is relatively narrowly defined and requires that the injury be sustained as a direct result of a crime of violence, trespass on the railways, or during the apprehension or attempted apprehension of an offender. The courts also have power to make compensation orders against convicted offenders, requiring the payment of compensation for personal injury, loss, or damage resulting from their offending.[156] **5.230**

---

[152] The Code of Practice for Victims of Crime, para. 3.1.
[153] The Code of Practice for Victims of Crime, para. 3.2.
[154] Crown Prosecution Service (Witnesses' etc Allowances) Regulations 1988.
[155] Practice Direction (Criminal Proceedings: Consolidation) para. III.28 [2002] 1 WLR 2870 as substituted by Practice Direction (Criminal Proceedings: substituted and additional provisions) [2009] 1 WLR 1396.
[156] Powers of Criminal Courts (Sentencing) Act 2000, s. 130.

Recommendations on assistance to crime victims

5.231   In 2006, the Committee of Ministers of the Council of Europe issued Recommendations on Assistance to Crime Victims, which were adopted by the Council of Ministers under Article 15(b) of the Statute of the Council of Europe.[157] The Recommendations required States to ensure the effective recognition of, and respect for, the rights of victims with regard to their human rights and set out the assistance to be provided. The definition of 'victim' was extended from that used in the 2001 Framework decision to include 'where appropriate, the immediate family or dependants of the direct victim'.[158]

5.232   The Recommendations marked a development in the assistance to victims of crime which is likely to impact on the EU's approach. Emphasis was placed on the following factors, which were not addressed in the 2001 Framework Decision:

(a)   the need for specific and targeted assistance for crimes of mass victimisation, including terrorism;[159]

(b)   the need to protect against repeat victimisation by addressing the risks posed to individual victims;[160] and

(c)   the need to raise public awareness of the effects of crime through 'government funding and publicity campaigns'.[161]

5.233   The role of mediation in victim assistance was approached with a greater element of caution in the Recommendations. Whilst it was recognised this may be an appropriate course where available, particular care was required:

13(2)   The interests of victims should be fully and carefully considered when deciding upon and during a mediation process. Due consideration should be given not only to the potential benefits but also to the potential risks for the victim.

13(3)   Where mediation is envisaged, states should support the adoption of clear standards to protect the interests of victims. These should include the ability of the parties to give free consent, issues of confidentiality, access to independent advice, the possibility to withdraw from the process at any stage and the competence of mediators.

The EU commitment to victim protection: an ongoing process

5.234   The commitment by the EU to victim protection, as a corollary to the commitment to the creation of an area of freedom, security, and justice, is reflected in the legislation post-dating the 2001 Framework Decision. One of the aims of the EU is the abolition of obstacles to the free movement of people between Member States and the fulfilment of this aim includes the implementation of measures to ensure the protection of the rights of those who become victims in Member States other than their own.

5.235   The rights of those who become the victims of crime while exercising their freedom to travel between different Member States was considered by the CJEU in *Cowan v Trésor Public*.[162] A citizen of the UK, Cowan, sought compensation for an injury he had sustained following

---

[157]   Recommendation Rec (2006)8 of the Committee of Ministers to Member States on assistance to crime victims.

[158]   Recommendation Rec (2006)8, Art. 1(1).

[159]   Recommendation Rec (2006)8, Art. 5(3).

[160]   Recommendation Rec (2006)8, Art. 10(5).

[161]   Recommendation Rec (2006)8, Art. 16.

[162]   [1989] ECR 195.

a violent assault on the Paris Metro, but was denied compensation otherwise available to French citizens or to nationals of a State which had reciprocal arrangements with France. The CJEU considered the application of Article 7 of the EEC Treaty, which prohibits any discrimination on the grounds of nationality. In the judgment of the Court, the prohibition of discrimination laid down in Article 7 must be interpreted as meaning that compensation to a person whose freedom to travel to Member States is guaranteed by EU law, could not be restricted on the grounds of nationality or residence.[163]

Directive on Cross-Border Compensation

The decision in *Cowan* was referred to in the preamble to the Directive on Cross-Border Compensation and Violent Crime,[164] which was approved by the Council on 29 April 2009. The Directive addressed the requirement for a system to facilitate access to compensation in cases where the crime was committed in a Member State other than that of the victim. The ratio in *Cowan*[165] is upheld in the Directive; a non-resident victim has a right to obtain compensation in the Member State in which the crime was committed.[166]   **5.236**

Article 1 of the Directive on Cross-Border Compensation provides that where a violent international crime has been committed in a Member State other than that where the applicant for compensation normally resides, the applicant may submit a compensation application to any relevant authority or body within the State where the crime occurred. Compensation is to be paid by the State on whose territory the crime was committed (Art. 2).   **5.237**

The Directive places considerable emphasis on the convenience of the victim. Applications are to be transmitted[167] and considered[168] expediently. The intrusion into the sovereignty of Member States is, however, restricted; the development of national systems of victim compensation remains the responsibility of individual Member States: **5.238**

(1) The rules on access to compensation in cross-border situations drawn up by this Directive shall operate on the basis of Member States' schemes on compensation to victims of violent intentional crimes committed in their respective territories.
(2) All Member States shall ensure their national rules provide for a scheme on compensation to victims of violent intentional crimes committed in their respective territories, which guarantees fair and appropriate compensation to victims.

Directive on Preventing and Combating Trafficking in Human Beings and Protecting its Victims[169]

On 5 April 2011, Directive 201136/EU came into force. It dealt with the needs of the victims of human trafficking, with the express aim of safeguarding the human rights of victims and avoiding further victimisation.[170]   **5.239**

The Directive recognises that men and women are often trafficked for different purposes and that assistance and support measures should therefore be gender-specific, where appropriate.   **5.240**

---

[163] *Cowan v Trésor* [1989] ECR 195, para. 20.
[164] 2004/80/EC.
[165] [1989] ECR 195.
[166] 2004/80/EC, Art. 12(1).
[167] 2004/80/EC, Art. 7.
[168] 2004/80/EC, Art. 9.
[169] Directive 2011/36/EU.
[170] Directive 2011/36/EU, preamble at 14.

It acknowledges that a broader concept of human trafficking is required to meet recent developments and includes additional forms of exploitation, such as forced begging and the exploitation of a person to commit criminal offences. The particular vulnerability of children is asserted. The protection of victims from prosecution for offences arising as a direct result of the trafficking of the victim, such as the use of false documents, or offences contrary to the laws on prostitution or immigration, is one of the aims of the Directive and the subject of its Article 8.

5.241   The key provisions of the Directive are as follows:

(a) once the authorities have an indication on reasonable grounds that a person may be the victim of human trafficking, measures necessary to ensure assistance or support are to be taken by Member States, regardless of the willingness of the victim to cooperate in criminal proceedings. The individualised needs of the victim are to be taken into account when assistance is provided (Art. 11);

(b) 'secondary victimisation' (the victimisation of the victim by the authorities investigating the original crime by, for example unnecessary questioning about their private life), is to be prevented. A margin of appreciation is granted to Member States in terms of the specific measures to be used to prevent this (Art. 12); and

(c) special measures are to be taken by Member States to ensure the protection of the best interests[171] of child victims of human trafficking. Such measures include the appointment of a guardian or other representative for child victims and for appropriate measures to be adopted during the interviewing of child victims (Arts 13–16).

5.242   The protection of victims of human trafficking from prosecution for criminal offences resulting directly from the trafficking of the victim also received recognition in Article 26 of the Council of Europe Convention on Action against Trafficking in Human Beings. Article 26 requires each party 'to provide for the possibility of not imposing penalties on victims for their involvement in unlawful activities, to the extent that they have been compelled to do so.'

5.243   The Convention was ratified by the UK in December 2008. Article 26 has been considered by the Court of Appeal in the context of a number of appeals against conviction by defendants who themselves may have been victims of trafficking and consequent exploitation.

5.244   In *R v N, R, LE*,[172] the Court of Appeal concluded that Article 26 was directed at the sentencing hearing, rather than the decision to prosecute. It introduced the possibility of not imposing penalties relating to criminal activities in which the victims of trafficking had been compelled to participate and for which the defence of duress was unavailable; what the Article did not provide for was a general prohibition on imposing penalties relating to criminal activities.[173]

5.245   The court considered that the implementation of the UK's Convention obligations could normally be achieved by a proper exercise of the prosecutorial discretion of the CPS, which could determine that the prosecution of an individual falling within the protective ambit of Article 26 should not take place, despite the strength of the evidence against such an individual. If the CPS fails to exercise its discretion in such circumstances, the remedy for the

---

[171]   Directive 2011/36/EU, Art. 13(1).
[172]   [2012] EWCA Crim 189.
[173]   [2012] EWCA Crim 189, para. 13.

individual is to seek a stay of the proceedings or invite the court to deal with the matter, upon conviction, by way of an absolute or conditional discharge.

Directive establishing minimum standards on the rights, support, and protection of victims of crime[174]

On 18 May 2011, the Commission submitted a proposal for a Directive of the Parliament and **5.246** of the Council. In the Explanatory Memorandum accompanying the proposed Directive it was stated that the 'objectives of the Council Framework Decision have not been fully realized'; it is the aim of the proposed Directive, which will replace the 2001 Framework Decision,[175] to achieve these objectives and to extend protection of victims of crime throughout the EU. On September 2012, the European Parliament approved the proposed Directive and Member States will have three years to implement the provisions into national legislation.

Article 2 of the Directive defines 'victim' in more closely regulated terms that the 2006 **5.247** Recommendation:

> For the purposes of this Directive:
>
> (a) 'victim' means:
>   i. A natural person who has suffered harm, including physical or mental injury, emotional suffering or economic loss directly caused by a criminal offence;
>   ii. The family members of a person whose death has been caused by a criminal offence;
> (b) 'family members' means the spouse, non-marital cohabitee, registered partner, the relatives in direct line, the brothers and sisters, and the dependants of the victim;
> (c) 'non-natural cohabitee' means a person who is living with the victim on a stable and continuous basis without that relationship being registered with an authority.

The Directive on the protection of victims extends the protection offered under the 2001 **5.248** Framework Decision in the following ways:

(a) Article 3 provides the right of a victim to receive information from first contact with a competent authority. The information includes details on how and where to make a complaint, support organisations, and their entitlement to compensation.
(b) The victim's entitlement to information (translated if required) about their case is put into clear language; this includes the right to any decision, accompanied by reasons, if no further action is taken in relation to a complaint (Art. 4). This is linked to the right to have any decision not to prosecute reviewed (Art. 10).

> In July 2012, following the decision of the Court of Appeal in *R v Killick*,[176] the Director of Public Prosecutions announced that guidance will be issued on the right of victims to have a decision not to prosecute reviewed.[177] In *Killick*, Lord Justice Thomas referenced the then proposed Article 10 and concluded, 'as a decision not to prosecute is in reality a final decision for a victim, there must be a right to seek a review of such a decision'.

(c) A minimum right of access to support services is specified in the following terms:
  (A) Provision of information, advice and support on accessing state compensation schemes and on the role of the victim in criminal proceedings;
  (B) Information regarding referral services;
  (C) Emotional and psychological support;
  (D) Advice relating to any financial and practical issues arising from the situation (Article 7).

---

[174] 2011/0129 (COD).
[175] 2011/0129 (COD), Art. 28.
[176] [2011] EWCA Crim 1608.
[177] 'Finality in Criminal Justice: When Should the CPS Reopen a Case?' [2012] Crim LR 7, 526–34.

(d) A more nuanced approach, mirroring that taken in the 2006 Recommendations, is taken in relation to mediation. Safeguards are to be put in place to protect the victim from intimidation or further victimisation (Art. 11).

(e) Victims are to have access to legal aid, in accordance with procedures in national law, where they have the status of parties to criminal proceedings (Art. 12).

(f) A right to a decision, within a reasonable period of time, on whether compensation can be obtained from the offender is established (Art. 15).

(g) Where the victim of a criminal offence resides in another Member State to that in which the criminal offence occurred, they may make a complaint to the authorities of their State of residence (Art. 16).

(h) Vulnerable victims are to be identified and given an individual assessment in a timely manner. Children, persons with disabilities, victims of sexual violence, and victims of human trafficking are all to be considered vulnerable (Art. 20).

(i) Vulnerable victims and children are entitled to special treatment during the preparation of the case and at court. Measures which closely approximate to the special measures provisions under English law[178] are to be offered to vulnerable victims during court proceedings (Arts 21 and 22).

(j) Practitioners who come into contact with victims, such as police, prosecutors, and members of the judiciary, are to receive appropriate training (Art. 24).

5.249 The UK opted into the proposed Directive on 26 August 2011 and thus it will apply domestically when it comes into force.

The European Protection Order for crime victims

5.250 On 13 December 2011 the Parliament endorsed a European Protection Order (EPO) for crime victims. The UK had already opted into this measure. The Directive is stated to apply to:

> protection measures which aim *specifically* at protecting a person against a criminal act of another person which may, in any way, endanger his life, physical, psychological and sexual integrity, e.g. by preventing any form of harassment, as well as his dignity or personal liberty, e.g. by preventing abductions, stalking and other forms of indirect coercion, and aiming at avoiding new acts of crime or at reducing the consequences of previous acts of crime.[179]

5.251 The EPO extends protection for victims of crime under Article 82(1) TFEU (judicial cooperation in criminal matters to be based on mutual recognition of judgments and judicial decisions). An EPO enables a Member State to take appropriate measures under its own national law to enforce a judgment passed in another Member State aimed at protecting a victim.[180]

5.252 Article 5 provides that an EPO may only be issued when a protection measure has been previously ordered in the issuing State, imposing on the person causing danger, one or more of the following obligations or prohibitions:

(a) a prohibition from entering certain localities or places where the protected person resides or that he visits;

(b) a prohibition or regulation of contact in any form with the protected person; and

(c) a prohibition or regulation on approaching the protected person closer than a prescribed distance.

---

[178] See *Blackstone's Criminal Practice 2012*, D14.2.
[179] Directive 14471/11.
[180] Directive 14471/11, Art. 2.

An EPO may be issued when the protected person decides either to stay or reside in another **5.253**
Member State. In deciding whether to issue an EPO, the length of the stay envisaged and
the seriousness of the need for protection are to be taken into account (Art. 6(1)). Before the
EPO is issued, the person causing the danger shall be given the right to be heard and to challenge the protection measure, if he had not previously exercised such a right.

The form and content of an EPO is set out in prescribed form in the Annex to the Directive **5.254**
and must contain the information set out in Article 7, including the identity and nationality
of both the protected person and the person causing the danger, together with a summary
of the facts and circumstances leading to the imposition of the protection measure in the
issuing State.

Article 10 sets out the grounds under which an executing State may refuse to recognise an **5.255**
EPO.

Where an EPO is in force and a breach occurs, the Member State which granted the EPO can **5.256**
impose criminal sanctions or take any non-criminal decisions related to the breach provided
the breach amounts to a criminal offence under the law of the executing State (Art. 11(2)(a)).

An EPO is to be given the same priority as a national case with similar facts.[181] **5.257**

---

[181] Directive 14471/11, Art. 15.

6

SUBSTANTIVE LAW AND SANCTIONS

A. Overview

6.01 The creation and administration of substantive criminal law is a defining characteristic of national sovereignty. Any encroachment into this arena by EU law has, as a result, been politically sensitive and correspondingly cautious.[1] The EU has recognised this issue and, until relatively recently, has been at pains to reassure Member States as to its respect for the sovereignty of Member States over the administration of justice and particularly criminal justice within their borders. Articles 135 and 280 TFEU reserved expressly to the Member States the application of national criminal law and the administration of justice. Article 135 states that the Council shall take measures in order to strengthen customs cooperation between Member States, whereas Article 280 encourages cooperation to counter fraud and other illegal activities affecting the financial interest of the Union. However, both articles include the provision that 'These measures shall not concern the application of national criminal law or the national administration of justice.'

---

[1] See G. Dannecker in A. Eser and E. Huber (eds), *Strafrechtsentwicklung in Europa*, vol. 4.3 (Freiburg im Breisgau: Iuskrim, 1995).

Prior to the TFEU, the TEU increased momentum towards the creation of 'European crimi- **6.02**
nal law' by establishing the third pillar. The pillar did not create supranational law, but
it made clear that cooperation in criminal cases was a matter of common importance to
all Member States. This recognised the obvious: that crime was not restricted to national
boundaries but often, and increasingly, had a pan-European dimension. In order to prevent
the creation of 'safe havens' minimum standards for criminal proceedings and rights had to
be imposed.

This included an aspiration to ensure the imposition of common sanctions for criminal **6.03**
conduct. It has long been recognised that the EU is competent to require Member States to
impose penalties for breaches of EU law. In *Commission v Greece: re Greek maize*, the Court
held:

> where Community legislation does not specifically provide any penalty for an infringement or
> refers for that purpose to national laws, regulations and administrative provision, Article 5 of
> the Treaty requires the Member States to take all measures necessary to guarantee the applica-
> tion and effectiveness of Community law.
>
> For that purpose, whilst the choice of penalties remains within their discretion, they must
> ensure in particular that infringements of Community law are penalised under conditions,
> both procedural and substantive, which are analogous to those applicable to infringements
> of national law of a similar nature and importance and which, in any event, make the penalty
> effective, proportionate and dissuasive.
>
> Moreover, the national authorities must proceed, with respect to infringements of Community
> law, with the same diligence as that which they bring to bear in implementing corresponding
> national laws.[2]

The TFEU provides a new legal framework for criminal legislation. It gives the EU three **6.04**
specific competencies with respect to criminal law:

(a) establishing minimum rules on European crimes (Art. 83(1) TFEU);
(b) establishing criminal law for the enforcement of EU policies (Art. 83(2) TFEU); and
(c) protection of EU public money (Arts 310(6), 325, 85, and 86 TFEU).

The EU's objective is laid out in Article 67(3):

> The Union shall endeavour to ensure a high level of security through measures to prevent and
> combat crime, racism and xenophobia, and through measures for coordination and coop-
> eration between police and judicial authorities and other competent authorities, as well as
> through the mutual recognition of judgments in criminal matters and, if necessary, through
> the approximation of criminal laws.

Article 83(2)[3] creates a general power to create criminal legislation if it is 'essential to ensure **6.05**
the effective implementation of Union policy in an area which has been subject to harmonisation measures'. The mechanism is thus not, as with Article 83(1), a free-standing one. It
requires a pre-existing area of Union harmonisation for which criminal legislation is essential
to implement effectively. For example, Article 82(2) states:

> If the approximation of criminal laws and regulations of the Member States proves essential
> to ensure the effective implementation of a Union policy in an area which has been sub-
> ject to harmonisation measures, directives may establish minimum rules with regard to the

---

[2] At paras 23–5.
[3] Set out and further discussed at Chapter **1.60**.

definition of criminal offences and sanctions in the area concerned. Such directives shall be adopted by the same ordinary or special legislative procedure as was followed for the adoption of the harmonisation measures in question, without prejudice to Article 76.

6.06 Examples of areas which may now be the subject of legislation under Article 83(2) include:

- road transport, concerning, for example, serious infringements of EU social, technical, safety, and market rules for professional transports;
- data protection, for cases of serious breaches of existing EU rules;
- customs rules concerning the approximation of customs offences and penalties;
- environmental protection, if the existing criminal law legislation in this area requires further strengthening in the future in order to prevent and sanction environmental damage;
- fisheries policy, where the EU has adopted a 'zero tolerance' campaign against illegal, unreported, and unregulated fishing; and
- internal market policies to fight serious illegal practices, such as counterfeiting and corruption or undeclared conflict of interests in the context of public procurement.[4]

6.07 The TFEU seeks to develop the concept of 'European criminal law' through legislation relating to four interrelated areas:

- harmonisation of the definitions of criminal conduct;
- harmonisation of the criminal sanctions imposed in relation to that criminal conduct;
- mutual recognition of judgments and custodial sanctions in criminal matters between Member States; and
- mutual recognition and administration of non-custodial sanctions between Member States.

6.08 The form of legislation by which these harmonisation measures have been pronounced and, if necessary, enforced, is the Framework Decision. In this chapter the Framework Decisions which are likely to be of most relevance to the criminal practitioner will be discussed, together with an analysis of the extent to which the criminal law of England and Wales meets the requirements of the relevant Framework Decision.

6.09 This analysis is divided into two sections: existing obligations to which the UK has sought, at least to some extent, to give effect. These are dealt with as follows:

(a) terrorism (see **6.12**);
(b) corruption (see **6.16**);
(c) counterfeiting (see **6.19**);
(d) fraud and counterfeiting of non-cash means of payment (see **6.26**);
(e) money laundering (see **6.29**);
(f) attacks against information systems (see **6.30**);
(g) 'criminal organisations' (see **6.33**);
(h) illicit drug trafficking (see **6.38**);
(i) sexual exploitation of children and child pornography (see **6.46**);
(j) trafficking for exploitation (see **6.56**);
(k) racism and xenophobia (see **6.60**); and
(l) ship-source pollution (see **6.66**).

---

[4] See Communication from the Commission to the European Parliament, the Council, the European Economic and Social Committee and the Committee of the Regions: Towards an EU Criminal Policy: Ensuring the effective implementation of EU policies through criminal law.

Secondly, it is appropriate to have a short look into the future as to the areas into which the   **6.10**
EU may encroach. In each area, this analysis involves consideration of the conduct the EU
has sought to criminalise, and the penalties it has identified for that conduct. In the latter
regard, consideration is also given to the upper limits on sentencing the EU has identified (see
6.71), the recognition of judgments (Section D) and mutual recognition of non-custodial
sanctions in criminal cases (Section E).

It is necessary in reading this chapter to have in mind the potential effect of the UK's opting   **6.11**
out of the police and criminal justice measures under Protocol No. 36 of the Lisbon Treaty.
Were the UK to opt out as the Home Secretary has indicated that the Government at present
is minded to do, it would in fact have a limited effect on the offences which are specified
under the Framework Decisions that would fall within the 'opt-out'. As will be seen, the
conduct specified has already been criminalised within the UK with maximum sentences
which exceed those prescribed by the Framework Decisions. Additionally, the UK is bound
by other treaties made with the Council of Europe, the United Nations, and the OECD.
Nevertheless, any opt-out would allow for more freedom to change maximum sentences and
limit European influence in the criminal law of the UK.

B. Existing Obligations

Terrorism

In the field of terrorism, Council Framework Decision 2002/475/JHA of 13 June 2002 on   **6.12**
combating terrorism[5] imposes a number of requirements. The first requirement is a general
one: Member States must ensure that the offences contained in Articles 1–4[6] are punishable
by 'effective, proportionate and dissuasive' criminal penalties. The second requirement is
more precise: essentially Member States must ensure that the custodial sentence available
for the conduct specified in Article 1 must be 'heavier' than would be the case where the
relevant conduct lacks the 'terrorist' intent. The exception to this rule is where the maximum
sentence is already the maximum available under national law, and this exception applies to
England and Wales: the conduct mentioned in Article 1 (life threatening attacks, etc) would
involve the commission of any number of offences for which the available sentence would be
the maximum sentence available under national law, namely a 'life' sentence.[7] It follows that
both the first and second requirements are met.

The third requirement concerns the offences relating to a terrorist group mentioned in Article   **6.13**
2. The offence of 'directing' a terrorist group must be punishable by a sentence of not less
than 15 years' imprisonment.[8] In England and Wales this requirement is met. By reason of

---

[5] As amended by the Council Framework Decision 2008/919/JHA of 28 November 2008.
[6] These offences are the particularly grave 'terrorist' offences listed in Art. 1 (e.g. committing or threatening
to commit: life-threatening attacks, attacks on public utilities, and offences involving weaponry, where carried
out with the relevant terrorist intention); those offences listed in Art. 2 relating to a 'terrorist' group (e.g. directing
or participating in an established 'terrorist group'), the offences listed in Art. 3 which are 'linked to terrorist
activities' (e.g. in relation to terrorist acts: incitement thereof, training and recruitment for, and certain preparatory
acts) and the offences listed in Art. 4 (the aiding, abetting, inciting, and attempting to commit certain of the
offences mentioned in Arts 1–3).
[7] e.g. criminal damage with intent to endanger life, contrary to the Criminal Damage Act 1971, s. 1(2).
[8] The Framework Decision provides for an exception, namely where the terrorist group is established to
'threaten' to commit terrorist offences as opposed to actually committing those offences, the requirement is that
the sentence should be not less than eight years' imprisonment.

section 56 of the Terrorism Act 2000 'directing a terrorist organisation' is an indictable only offence, carrying a maximum sentence of 'life' imprisonment. Furthermore, the Framework Decision requires that 'participating' in the activities of a terrorist group must be punishable by a maximum sentence of not less than eight years' imprisonment. In England and Wales there is no offence of 'participating' in terrorism, but the relevant conduct mentioned in Article 2 (supplying information or resources, or funding the terrorist group) would be caught by various offences under the Terrorism Act 2000, including possession of articles for terrorist purposes (s. 57, for which a maximum sentence of 15 years' imprisonment is available), the collection or possession of information of a type likely to be useful to a person committing or preparing an act of terrorism (s. 58, for which the maximum sentence available is ten years' imprisonment), and fundraising for the purposes of terrorism (s. 15, for which the maximum sentence available is 14 years' imprisonment).

6.14 Article 8 requires Member States to ensure penalties are available against 'legal persons' (e.g. companies) where a 'leading person' (e.g. director) within the company commits one of the terrorist offences mentioned in Articles 1–4 for the company's benefit. The available penalty must be 'effective, proportionate and dissuasive' and 'shall include criminal or non-criminal fines'. Thus, the Framework Decision does not necessarily require that that companies should be held *criminally* liable, although in England and Wales they may be, following ordinary principles of corporate liability where an offence is committed by a person who represents the directing mind and will of the company.

6.15 More generally the Framework Decision envisages penalties against companies where a lack of supervision or control by a legal person holding a leading position in the company 'makes possible' the commission of one of the terrorist offences listed in Articles 1 and 4. This implies a form of liability based on mere negligence but, as noted earlier, there is no requirement that any penalty be 'criminal'. There is no comparable criminal offence in England and Wales, although in practice a company that had been used for a terrorist purpose would be liable to be wound up by the Companies Court.

Corruption

6.16 Article 2 of Council Framework Decision 2003/568/JHA of 22 July 2003 on combating corruption in the private sector requires Member States to criminalise 'active and passive corruption' in the private sector, subject to exceptions,[9] and to make such conduct punishable by 'effective, proportionate and dissuasive criminal penalties'. Article 3 requires Member States to criminalise the instigation, aiding, and abetting of Article 2 offences.

6.17 Article 4 requires Article 2 offences to be punishable by a penalty of 'a maximum of at least one to three years of imprisonment'. This requirement was met in England and Wales by sections 1, 2, and 6 of the Bribery Act 2010, each punishable by a maximum sentence of ten years' imprisonment. As well as requiring strong punitive sentences, the Framework Decision also directs the availability of preventive measures. Article 4(3) requires Member States to take the necessary measures to ensure that, where a person who had a leading position in a company is convicted of 'corruption', he 'may be temporarily prohibited from

---

[9] By Art. 2(3) a Member State may declare that it will limit the scope of the offence referred to in Art. 2 to such conduct which involves, or could involve, a distortion of competition in relation to the purchase of goods or commercial services.

carrying on this particular or comparable business activity in a similar position or capacity'. In England and Wales, following a conviction, a court would have power to disqualify a person from holding the position of director.[10]

Article 5 requires Member States to ensure legal persons can be held liable (though not necessarily criminally liable) for Article 2 and Article 3 offences and that such persons are punishable by effective, proportionate, and dissuasive penalties, including financial penalties. As discussed at **6.14**, a company may be held criminally liable in certain circumstances. Moreover, section 7 of the Bribery Act 2010 creates the offence of 'failure of a commercial organisation to prevent bribery' in certain limited circumstances.[11]   **6.18**

Criminalisation of counterfeiting

The Framework Decision 2000/383/JHA of 29 May 2000 on increasing protection by criminal penalties and other sanctions against counterfeiting in connection with the introduction of the Euro, legislated in respect of minimum standards for conduct which may loosely be described as 'counterfeiting'. This is not limited to the Euro. Articles 3–5 require Member States to take the necessary measures to ensure that certain types of conduct in connection with counterfeiting are 'punishable by effective, proportionate and dissuasive criminal penalties, including penalties involving deprivation of liberty which can give rise to extradition'.   **6.19**

The requirements as to criminality and punishment in respect of Article 3 are met in England and Wales, as follows: **6.20**

(a) Article 3 requires the prohibition of the fraudulent making or altering of currency, whatever means are employed. Such conduct is criminalised in England and Wales by the offence of 'making' counterfeit[12] currency,[13] contrary to section 14 of the Forgery and Counterfeiting Act 1981. This offence carries a maximum sentence of two years' imprisonment or, where the maker of the counterfeit currency intends that it shall be passed or tendered as genuine, ten years' imprisonment.

(b) The fraudulent 'uttering' of currency. This conduct is criminalised by the law of England and Wales by the offence of 'passing' or 'tendering' or 'delivery' of counterfeit currency, contrary to section 15(1) of the Forgery and Counterfeiting Act 1981. This offence carries a maximum sentence of ten years' imprisonment.

(c) The import, export, transport, receiving, or obtaining of counterfeit currency with a view to uttering the same and with knowledge that it is counterfeit. This conduct is criminalised by the law of England and Wales by a variety of offences, in particular: the offence of 'passing', 'tendering', or 'delivering' counterfeit currency (which, as noted earlier, is an offence contrary to s. 15(1)) and carries a maximum of ten years' imprisonment;

---

[10] The Company Directors Disqualification Act 1986, s. 1, empowers the court to make an order disqualifying a convicted person from holding the office of 'director' or 'receiver' or to 'be concerned in or take part in the promotion, formation or management of a company unless he has the leave of the court'.

[11] The circumstances are where a person associated with the commercial organisation bribes another intending to obtain or retain business for the commercial organisation or to obtain or retain an advantage in the conduct of business for the commercial organisation.

[12] The definition of 'counterfeit' is wide enough to encompass a currency note or protected coin which has been so altered that it is reasonably capable of passing for a currency note or protected coin of some other description. On this basis a person who 'altered' a currency note (as envisaged by the Framework Decision) would have 'made' it within the meaning of the Forgery and Counterfeiting Act 1981.

[13] The definition of 'currency' is wide and includes, e.g., any note lawfully issued in any overseas country which is or has been customarily used in the country where it was issued. Plainly, this would include the Euro.

the offence of having custody or control of counterfeit currency, contrary to section 16 of the Forgery and Counterfeiting Act 1981 which carries a maximum of two years' imprisonment or, where there is an intention that the currency be passed or tendered as genuine, ten years' imprisonment; the offences of importing and exporting counterfeit currency, contrary to sections 20 and 21 of the Forgery and Counterfeiting Act 1981 and section 50 of the Customs and Excise Management Act 1979 which are each punishable by a maximum of ten years' imprisonment.[14]

(d) The fraudulent making, receiving, or obtaining of instruments, articles, computer programs, and any other means peculiarly adapted for the counterfeiting or altering of currency, or holograms or other components of currency which serve to protect against counterfeiting. This conduct is caught by the law of England and Wales by section 17 of the Forgery and Counterfeiting Act 1981, which criminalises (under s. 17(2)) the making or having custody or control of anything specially designed or adapted for the making of counterfeit currency, for which the maximum penalty is two years' imprisonment and (under s. 17(1)) the making of or having custody or control of any thing which a person intends for use in making counterfeit currency intending that it be passed or tendered as genuine.

6.21 Article 4 is aimed at combating the circulation of genuine currency manufactured without the competent authorities' agreement (as distinct from counterfeit currency per se). In this way, Article 4 appears to have been designed to ensure the integrity of the Euro in advance of its introduction. It requires that the conduct referred to in Article 3 is punishable also with respect to the manufacture of bank notes or coins by use of legal facilities or materials in violation of the rights or the conditions under which the competent authorities may issue currency, without those authorities' agreement. It appears that the offence proposed by the Framework Decision could not be committed in the UK as there are no facilities to mint the Euro.

6.22 Article 5 requires Member States to take the necessary measures to ensure that the conduct referred to in Articles 3 and 4 is punishable if it relates to banknotes and coins which are not yet issued but are designated for circulation, and are of currency which is legal tender.[15] There does not appear to be any offence contrary to the law of England and Wales which specifically addresses this conduct.

6.23 Article 6 concerns specific requirements as to the available sanctions. The first requirement is that the conduct referred to in Articles 3–5 must be 'punishable by effective, proportionate and dissuasive criminal penalties, including penalties involving deprivation of liberty which can give rise to extradition.' As far as Article 3 is concerned, as noted earlier, the available penalties under the law of England and Wales range from two to ten years. As to Article 4, as noted earlier, the conduct there specified is not fully reflected in the law of England and Wales. Insofar as the offence contrary to section 18 of the Forgery and Counterfeiting Act 1981 does address this conduct, the maximum available sentence is a financial penalty, whereas Article 6 envisages that the conduct set out in Article 3, but committed with respect

---

[14] See the Customs and Excise Management Act 1979, s. 50(5A).

[15] A further requirement was for Member States to ensure that the conduct referred to in Arts 3 and 4 is punishable if it relates to the future banknotes and coins of the Euro and is committed before 1 January 2002. Plainly this requirement pre-empted the introduction of the Euro; with the passing of 1 January 2002 it no longer has effect.

to genuine notes and coins manufactured without consent, should be punishable by penalties involving deprivation of liberty. In relation to Article 5, since the law of England and Wales does not criminalise the conduct specified it follows that the requirements as to the available penalties are not met either.

The second requirement as to available penalties is that the offence of fraudulent making **6.24** or altering of currency must be punishable by terms of imprisonment, the maximum being not less than eight years. As noted earlier, the relevant offence under the law of England and Wales is section 14 of the Forgery and Counterfeiting Act 1981, for which the maximum sentence is ten years' imprisonment (at least where a specific intent is present).

Articles 8 and 9 contain the usual requirements as to the liability and punishment of **6.25** 'legal persons'. As discussed at **6.14**, a company may be held criminally liable in certain circumstances.

Fraud and counterfeiting of non-cash means of payment

Council Framework Decision 2001/413/JHA of 28 May 2001 on combating fraud and **6.26** counterfeiting of non-cash means of payment requires Member States to criminalise certain conduct, specified in Articles 2–5, which is to be 'punishable by effective, proportionate and dissuasive criminal penalties including, at least in serious cases, penalties involving deprivation of liberty which can give rise to extradition.' The relevant conduct in Article 2 concerns, in summary, the misappropriation, falsification, or misuse of a payment instrument or fraudulent payment instrument (ie a corporeal instrument other than legal tender). Article 3 concerns money transfers effected by means of an interference with identification data or a computer program. Article 4 concerns the making, receiving, obtaining, sale or transfer, or possession of certain instruments, articles, and computer programs for the purpose of one of the offences there specified. All of this conduct must be criminalised and, by reason of Article 5, those who participate in, instigate, and attempt a limited class of the conduct set out earlier should also be punished as criminals.

The requirement that imprisonment for certain conduct should be available in 'serious cases' **6.27** is rather nebulous but because, in England and Wales, the maximum sentence available is fixed by reference to the type of offence committed, and not by the way in which the offence was committed, this requirement is met. The offences enacted into the law of England and Wales which meet the requirements of the Framework Decision[16] carry sentences of at least ten years' imprisonment, and this would be the case whether the offender was a principal, secondary party, or had merely attempted the commission of an offence.

The Framework Decision also makes a (by now familiar)[17] requirement that legal persons **6.28** should also be liable (although not necessarily by criminal sanctions). As discussed at **6.14**, a company may be held criminally liable in certain circumstances.

---

[16] By way of example, 'theft' contrary to the Theft Act 1968, s. 1, carries a maximum seven year sentence; fraud by false representation, contrary to the Fraud Act 2006, s. 2, carries a maximum sentence of 10 years' imprisonment; possession of articles for use in fraud, contrary to the Fraud Act 2006, s. 6, carries a maximum sentence of six years' imprisonment; 'converting' criminal property, contrary to the Proceeds of Crime Act 2002, s. 327, which carries a maximum of 14 years' imprisonment. This conduct is also covered by an offence in the Computer Misuse Act 1990 for which a maximum sentence of ten years' imprisonment can be imposed.
[17] See **6.12**.

Money laundering

6.29 Council Framework Decision 2001/500/JHA of 26 June 2001 on money laundering, the identification, tracing, freezing, seizing and confiscation of instrumentalities and the proceeds of crime, requires Member States to ensure that certain money laundering offences are punishable by deprivation of liberty for a maximum of not less than four years. The offences to which this rule applies are the money laundering offences referred to in Article 6(1)(a) and (b) of the Strasbourg Convention.[18] In summary, these are: 'converting', 'transferring', 'concealing', or 'disguising' the proceeds of crime. The law of England and Wales meets this requirement: section 327 of POCA (the offence of concealing, disguising, converting, transferring, and removing criminal property) carries a maximum sentence of 14 years' imprisonment.

Attacks against information systems

6.30 Council Framework Decision 2005/222/JHA of 24 February 2005 on attacks against information systems requires Member States to ensure that certain conduct concerning 'information systems' is 'punishable' as a criminal offence. The relevant conduct is: access to information systems (Art. 2); or interference with them (Art. 3); or interference with computer data on an information system (Art. 4). If the relevant act in any of these cases is done 'without right', the conduct is to be punishable (at least in cases which are not minor). Moreover, the instigation, aiding, and abetting of such offences, and attempts to commit such offences, are to be punishable (subject to exceptions).

6.31 As well as the general requirement that penalties for these offences should be 'effective, proportional and dissuasive', the offences referred to in Article 3 (illegal system interference) and Article 4 (illegal data interference) must, by reason of Article 6, be punishable by criminal penalties of a maximum of at least between one and three years' imprisonment.[19] The law of England and Wales meets this requirement,[20] because the offence which fulfils the requirements of Articles 3 and 4[21] is punishable by a maximum of ten years' imprisonment.

6.32 Article 8 requires Member States to ensure that 'legal persons' held liable for any of the offences mentioned in Articles 2–5 are subject to sanctions, though not necessarily criminal fines. As discussed at **6.14**, a company may be held criminally liable in certain circumstances. Moreover, a company which had been used to commit a human trafficking offence[22] would be liable to be wound up in the Companies Court.

Criminalisation of 'criminal organisations'

6.33 Framework Decision 2008/841/JHA of 24 October 2008 on the fight against organised crime is designed to secure cooperation between Member States in order to counter the dangers and proliferation of criminal organisations. Article 2 requires Member States to take

---

[18] The Convention on Laundering, Search, Seizure and Confiscation of the Proceeds of Crime, Strasbourg, 8 September 1990.

[19] Or, where the offence is committed within the framework of a criminal organisation, as defined, a higher maximum of at least between two and five years' imprisonment.

[20] e.g. Computer Misuse Act 1990.

[21] Unauthorised acts with intent to impair, or with recklessness as to impairing, operation of computer etc, contrary to the Computer Misuse Act 1990, s. 3.

[22] See **6.56**.

necessary measures to ensure that one or both of the following types of conduct are regarded as offences:

(a) conduct by any person who, with intent and with knowledge of either the aim and general activity of the criminal organisation or its intention to commit the offences in question, actively takes part in the organisation's criminal activities, including the provision of information or material means, the recruitment of new members, and all forms of financing of its activities, knowing that such participation will contribute to the achievement of the organisation's criminal activities; or

(b) conduct by any person consisting in an agreement with one or more persons that an activity should be pursued which, if carried out, would amount to the commission of offences referred to in Article 1,[23] even if that person does not take part in the actual execution of the activity.

In England and Wales requirement (a) is not met by one offence although specific conduct **6.34** that might fall within this definition might equate to the commission of specific criminal offences, but requirement (b) is met, on the basis that an agreement to commit an offence referred to in Article 1 would involve the commission of a statutory conspiracy, contrary to section 1 of the Criminal Law Act 1977.

Article 3 concerns penalties and requires that the offence referred to in Article 2(a) should **6.35** be punishable by a maximum term of imprisonment of at least between two and five years. As to the offence referred to in Article 2(b), which is the conduct applicable to England and Wales, the Framework Decision requires Member States to ensure the offence is punishable by the same maximum term of imprisonment as the offence at which the agreement is aimed, or by a maximum term of imprisonment of at least between two and five years. The criminal law of England and Wales complies with the sentencing requirements of the Framework Decision in that, by reason of section 3 of the Criminal Law Act 1977, the maximum term of imprisonment available for a conspiracy to commit an imprisonable offence is the same as the maximum term for the substantive offence.

Article 4 permits Member States to reduce penalties, or to exempt the offender from penalties, **6.36** where the offender provides assistance to the administrative or judicial authorities. This requirement is met by the availability of immunity or alternatively a reduction in sentence to reflect assistance provided in accordance with the Serious Organised Crime and Police Act 2005.

Articles 5 and 6 contain requirements as to the liability of legal persons. As discussed at **6.14**, **6.37** a company may be held criminally liable in certain circumstances.

Criminalisation of illicit drug trafficking

Framework Decision 2004/757/JHA of 25 October 2004 on laying down minimum provi- **6.38** sions on the constituent elements of criminal acts and penalties in the field of illicit drug trafficking is designed to achieve a common approach at EU level in the fight against trafficking in illicit drugs.[24] Consistent with this aim, Article 2 requires Member States to ensure

---

[23] That is, offences which are punishable by deprivation of liberty or detention order of a maximum of at least four years.

[24] Drugs being defined as any of the substances covered by the 1961 Single Convention on Narcotic Drugs (as amended), the 1971 Vienna Convention on Psychotropic Substances, and the substances subject to controls under Joint Action 97/396/JHA of 16 June 1997.

certain conduct is punishable by 'effective, proportionate and dissuasive criminal penalties'. Excepting conduct committed by persons exclusively for their own personal use, the conduct which must be criminalised is as follows:

(a) the production, manufacture, extraction, and preparation of drugs (which conduct is criminalised in England and Wales by reason of the offence of 'producing'[25] a controlled drug, contrary to the Misuse of Drugs Act 1971, s. 4(2)(a));

(b) offering for sale, distribution, or delivery on any terms whatsoever (which conduct would be caught by the offences of 'supplying'[26] or 'offering to supply' a drug, contrary to the Misuse of Drugs Act, s. 4(3)(a));

(c) brokerage, dispatch in transit, or transport of drugs (which conduct would, depending on the circumstances, be caught by the offence of 'being concerned in the supply of controlled drugs' contrary to the Misuse of Drugs Act, s. 4(3)(b));

(d) importation or exportation of drugs (which conduct is criminalised in England and Wales by reason of the restrictions on imports and exports as contained in the Misuse of Drugs Act 1971, s. 3 and the Customs and Excise Management Act 1979, s. 170);

(e) the cultivation of opium poppy, coca bush, and cannabis plants. In respect of the cultivation of the cannabis plant, this conduct is criminalised by the offence of 'cultivation of a cannabis plant' contrary to the Misuse of Drugs Act 1971, s. 6(2). However, there is no offence of cultivating either opium poppy or the coca bush, albeit where the evidence showed that the cultivating of these plants involved the 'production' of a controlled drug (e.g. heroin or cocaine) the conduct would fall within the offence of 'producing' a controlled drug, contrary to the Misuse of Drugs Act 1971, s. 4(2)(a);

(f) the possession or purchase of drugs with a view to conducting one of the activities listed in point (a). Such conduct would ordinarily be caught by the offence of 'possession of a controlled drug with intent to supply it to another' contrary to the Misuse of Drugs Act 1971, s. 5(3);

(g) the manufacture, transport, or distribution of 'precursors',[27] knowing that they are to be used in or for the illicit production or manufacture of drugs. Such conduct would be caught by the offence of 'being concerned in the production of controlled drugs' contrary to the Misuse of Drugs Act 1971, s. 4(2)(b) or encouraging or assisting a relevant offence, contrary to the Serious Crime Act 2007.

6.39 By reason of Article 3, Member States must make it a criminal offence to incite, aid, abet, or attempt any of the offences referred to in Article 2 (albeit Member States may exempt from criminal liability an attempt to offer or prepare drugs, or an attempt to possess drugs). To the extent that the criminal law of England and Wales meets the requirements of Article 2 (as discussed earlier), it also meets the requirements of Article 3, having regard to general common law principles of secondary liability which would be apt to capture the aiding and abetting of offences, while the Serious Crime Act 2007 would capture incitement and the Criminal Attempts Act 1981 would capture attempts.

---

[25] Which is defined widely as the production of the controlled drug by manufacture, cultivation, or any other method: Misuse of Drugs Act 1971, s. 37(1).
[26] 'Supplying' includes 'distributing': Misuse of Drugs Act 1971, s. 37.
[27] 'Precursors' are defined as any substance scheduled in EU legislation giving effect to the obligations deriving from Art. 12 of the UN Convention against Illicit Traffic in Narcotic Drugs and Psychotropic Substances of 20 December 1988.

Article 4 makes four specific requirements of Member States in respect of penalties. The **6.40** first requirement is general: that Member States shall take the measures necessary to ensure that the offences mentioned in Articles 2 and 3 are punishable by 'effective, proportionate and dissuasive criminal penalties'. The second requirement is more specific, that each of the offences referred to in Article 2 shall be punishable by criminal penalties of a maximum of at least between one and three years' imprisonment. Each of these requirements are easily met by the applicable law in England and Wales, on the basis that the maximum sentences for these offences are well in excess of one year. For example, each of the offences of importing controlled drugs, supplying or offering to supply controlled drugs, possessing a controlled drug with intent to supply it to another, and the production of controlled drugs are punishable with life imprisonment (in respect of Class A drugs) and 14 years' imprisonment (Classes B and C). Moreover, cultivation of cannabis carries a maximum of 14 years' imprisonment. The third requirement is that the offences mentioned in points (a), (b), and (c) in **6.38** should be punishable by a maximum of at least between five and ten years' imprisonment where there are particular aggravating factors.[28]

As already noted, the maximum sentences available in England and Wales easily meet this **6.41** requirement and, moreover, the Sentencing Council's Definitive Guideline on drug offences recognises that these aggravating factors would justify greater sentences. In addition, the Framework Decision requires that these same offences (the offences mentioned in points (a), (b), and (c) in **6.38**), where the aggravating features are present, should be punishable by a maximum of at least ten years of deprivation of liberty where the offence was committed within the framework of a criminal organisation.[29] In this regard, it is right to note that the maximum sentences described earlier exceed the minimum requirements of the Framework Decision. In addition, sentencing practice in England and Wales matches the expectations of the Framework Decision: the Sentencing Council's Definitive Guideline[30] contemplates that offending which involves a large-scale or commercial operation will ordinarily attract a greater sentence. The fourth requirement is that the offences mentioned in point (d), where they are committed within the framework of a criminal organisation, as defined, should be punishable by a maximum of at least between five and ten years. As to this requirement, it is sufficient to note that a secondary participant in the offending would be liable to the same maximum sentence as a principal, and where the offence is an offence of 'encouraging or assisting crime' contrary to the Serious Crime Act 2007, the offender is liable to the penalty for which he would be liable for the offence he encourages.

Furthermore, the Framework Decision requires each Member State to take necessary meas- **6.42** ures to enable the confiscation of substances and instrumentalities used or intended to be used for these offences. The requirement for this sanction to be available is readily met by the availability of deprivation orders, under section 143 of the Powers of Criminal Courts (Sentencing) Act 2000 and forfeiture orders, under section 27 of the Misuse of Drugs Act 1971.

---

[28] 'Aggravating factors' are: where the offence involves 'large quantities' of drugs; or where the offence either involves drugs which cause the most harm to health or has resulted in significant damage to the health of a number of persons.
[29] As defined in Joint Action 98/733/JHA of 21 December 1998 on making it a criminal offence to participate in a criminal organisation in the Member States of the EU.
[30] Issued on 24 January 2012.

6.43   As to a requirement for the availability of confiscation of the proceeds of offences (without prejudice to the rights of victims and of other bona fide third parties), or the confiscation of property the value of which corresponds to that of such proceeds, substances, or instrumentalities, this is met by the various means of asset forfeiture available under the Proceeds of Crime Act 2002.

6.44   It is of interest that the Framework Decision permits (but does not require) Member States to take necessary measures to ensure that penalties imposed for drug trafficking offences may be reduced if the offender provides relevant assistance to the administrative or judicial authorities. In England and Wales, such assistance would ordinarily be taken into account as part of an offender's mitigation. In addition, a reduction of sentence for assistance of this type is now contemplated by the statutory regime contained in the Serious Organised Crime and Police Act 2005.

6.45   Article 6 contains the usual requirement that legal persons can be held liable and punished by criminal or non-criminal fines for any of the criminal offences referred to in Articles 2 and 3. As discussed at **6.14**, a company may be held criminally liable in certain circumstances. As well as the common law basis for corporate liability under the law of England and Wales, section 21 of the Misuse of Drugs Act 1971 widens the net of liability by ensuring that certain company officers may be held liable where an offence is committed with the consent or connivance or attributable to the neglect of the officer in question.

Criminalisation of the sexual exploitation of children and child pornography

6.46   Council Framework Decision 2004/68/JHA of 22 December 2003 on combating the sexual exploitation of children and child pornography was designed to contribute to the fight against the sexual exploitation of children (ie any person below the age of 18 years) and child pornography.

6.47   Article 2 requires Member States to take the necessary measures to ensure that certain conduct is punishable:

(a)   Coercing a child into prostitution or into participating in pornographic performances, or profiting from or otherwise exploiting a child for such purposes. Such conduct is reflected in the offences of causing or inciting child prostitution or pornography, contrary to section 48 of the Sexual Offences Act 2003 and 'controlling a child prostitute or a child involved in pornography' contrary to section 49 of the same Act. For these purposes 'child' means a person under the age of 18 and so conforms with the requirement of the Framework Decision.

(b)   Recruiting a child into prostitution or into participating in pornographic performances. This conduct would usually be caught by the two offences mentioned in point (a)[31] but it could also be charged as an offence of 'arranging or facilitating child prostitution or pornography', contrary to section 50 of the Sexual Offences Act 2003 (which also relates to persons under 18 years of age).

(c)   Engaging in sexual activities with a child, where:
   (i)   use is made of coercion, force or threats;
   (ii)   money or other forms of remuneration or consideration is given as payment in exchange for the child engaging in sexual activities; or
   (iii)   abuse is made of a recognised position of trust, authority, or influence over the child.

---

[31]   Sexual Offences Act 2003, ss. 48 and 49.

As to point (i), this conduct would ordinarily be caught by the offence of 'sexual activity with a child' contrary to section 9 of the Sexual Offences Act 2003. This offence does not require there to have been coercion, force, or threats but it applies only where the child is under 16. Presumably where the victim was over 16 but under 18 and subjected to coercion, force, or threats the offender could be charged with the general offences applicable to victims of all ages, where the relevant activity is non-consensual (e.g. rape and sexual assault).

As to point (ii), this conduct would be caught by the offence of 'paying for sexual services of a child' contrary to section 47 of the Sexual Offences Act 2003. This offence applies where the victim is under the age of 18; 'payment' is defined as any financial advantage and is therefore wide enough to meet the requirements of the Framework Decision.

As to point (iii), this conduct is reflected in the offence of 'sexual activity with a child where there exists a position of trust', contrary to section 16 of the Sexual Offences Act 2003.

Article 3 requires Member States to take necessary measures to ensure that certain conduct relating to child pornography is punishable. 'Child pornography' is defined in Article 1 as pornographic material that visually depicts or represents: (a) a real child involved or engaged in sexually explicit conduct; or (b) a real person appearing to be a child involved or engaged in sexually explicit conduct, or (c) realistic images of a non-existent child involved or engaged in sexually explicit conduct. The relevant conduct which must be criminalised is: **6.48**

(a) production of child pornography;
(b) distribution, dissemination, or transmission of child pornography;
(c) supplying or making available child pornography; and
(d) acquisition or possession of child pornography.

The conduct described in the previous paragraph could be charged under a number of statutes, depending on the circumstances, such as the taking, making, distribution, possession with intent to distribute, or the publishing of indecent photographs or pseudo-photographs[32] of a child contrary to section 1 of the Protection of Children Act 1978. Further, the simple possession of indecent photographs or pseudo-photographs is criminalised by section 160 of the Criminal Justice Act 1988. **6.49**

The Framework Decision permits Member States to exclude from criminal liability certain types of conduct falling into three categories. First, there is no requirement to criminalise pornography which depicts a real person who appears to be a child, where the person is in fact an adult.[33] Secondly, there is no requirement to criminalise the production and possession of what would otherwise be pornography, where the child depicted has reached the age of consent and the child has given his or her consent.[34] Thirdly, there is no requirement to criminalise the production and possession of 'realistic images' where the material is produced **6.50**

---

[32] A 'pseudo-photograph' means an image whether made by computer graphics or otherwise, which appears to be a photograph. This definition would appear to be approximate to the term used in the Framework Decision, 'realistic images'.

[33] The criminal law of England and Wales concerning child pornography would not recognise such conduct as criminal, save for possible exceptions on particular facts where pseudo-photographs were involved: Protection of Children Act 1978, s. 7(8).

[34] This exception is recognised by the Protection of Children Act 1978, s. 1A, and the Criminal Justice Act 1988, s. 160A, which exclude liability for certain conduct in respect of photographs and pseudo-photographs where the images were created in the context of marriage, civil partnership, or enduring partnership.

and possessed by the producer solely for his or her own private use (and subject to a number of other exceptions).[35]

6.51 Article 4 requires Member States to ensure that secondary parties in respect of certain types of conduct, and those who attempt certain conduct, are liable to punishment. This requirement is met in England and Wales under ordinary principles of secondary participation and 'attempt'.

6.52 Article 5 sets out certain minimum requirements in respect of penalties. The first is that the offences referred to in Articles 2, 3, and 4 are punishable by criminal penalties of at least between one and three years' imprisonment. This requirement is met in England and Wales: the offences established by the Protection of Children 1978 are punishable by way of a maximum penalty of ten years' imprisonment and the offence of simple possession under the Criminal Justice Act 1988 carries a maximum of five years' imprisonment. Moreover, the offences contrary to the Sexual Offences Act 2003 are punishable by maximum sentences as follows: sexual activity with a child (14 years' imprisonment); sexual activity with an abuse of trust (5 years' imprisonment); paying for the sexual services of a child (life imprisonment where the activity involves penetration); causing or inciting a child to become a prostitute, or controlling child prostitution or a child involved in child prostitution, or arranging or facilitating child prostitution or pornography (each carries a maximum of 14 years' imprisonment).

6.53 The second requirement, in summary, is that certain particularly grave offences, including those involving coercion or profit from the relevant conduct, should be punishable by criminal penalties of a maximum of at least between five and ten years' imprisonment. As described earlier, the sentences available in England and Wales are relatively severe, and this requirement relating to 'grave' offences is also met.

6.54 Aside from the availability of imprisonment, the Framework Decision envisages certain ancillary measures, namely that persons convicted of an offence mentioned in Articles 2, 3, and 4 may be temporarily or permanently prevented from exercising professional activities related to the supervision of children. Such measures are available to the courts in various forms, including Sexual Offences Prevention Orders under section 104 of the Sexual Offences Act 2003 and orders disqualifying a person from working with children under sections 28 and 29 of the Criminal Justice and Courts Services Act 2000. Moreover, the general requirement that an offender be added to the sexual offenders register and to comply with notification requirements serves to protect children following a conviction.

6.55 The Framework Decision requires liability of legal persons for the offences contained in Articles 2, 3, and 4. As discussed at **6.14**, a company may be held criminally liable in certain circumstances.

Trafficking for exploitation

6.56 The EU has recently legislated with respect to human trafficking. Directive 2011/36/EU of 5 April 2011 on preventing and combating trafficking in human beings and protecting its victims replaced the earlier Framework Decision 2002/629/JHA. This would not be

---

[35] In England and Wales this category of conduct remains subject to criminal liability under the relevant legislation already identified.

included in any opt out of the police and criminal justice measures. By reason of Article 4 of this Directive, Member States are required to ensure that the offences mentioned in Article 2 'concerning trafficking in human beings' are punishable by at least five years' imprisonment or, where the relevant conduct has certain specified features,[36] by at least ten years' imprisonment. The offences mentioned there are wide-ranging. They include, for example, the recruitment, transportation and harbouring, or reception of persons by fraud or coercion (whether financial or physical) for the purpose of 'exploitation'. An offence will be committed for the purpose of exploitation where it is for the purpose of sexual exploitation, forced labour, or services, including begging, slavery, or practices similar to slavery, servitude, or the exploitation of criminal activities, or the removal of organs. The conduct specified in Article 2 is criminalised in England and Wales and the available punishment meets the requirements of Article 4.[37] Moreover, the requirement, contained in Article 7, that the proceeds or instrumentalities should be liable for confiscation is amply met, having regard to the availability of orders for 'deprivation' and 'confiscation'.

Article 4(3) of the Directive requires Member States to take the necessary measures to ensure **6.57** that the fact that an offence mentioned in Article 2 was committed by a public official in the performance of his duties is to be regarded as an 'aggravating circumstance'. This aspect of the Directive is not specifically reflected in the law of England and Wales. There is, for example, no statutory provision requiring the court to increase the sentence to reflect this aggravating factor. However, it seems likely that, in practice, a sentencing court would treat the fact that a trafficking offence was committed by a public official as an aggravating feature, particularly having regard to the guidance issued by the Sentencing Council which stipulates that factors which indicate higher culpability include an 'abuse of power' or an 'abuse of position of trust'.[38]

Article 3 of the Directive requires Member States to ensure that the incitement, aiding **6.58** and abetting, and attempt of offences mentioned in Article 2 are also 'punishable'. No minimum sentences are prescribed: Article 4(4) only requires that the offence should be punishable by effective, proportionate, and dissuasive penalties, which may entail surrender. This requirement is met in England and Wales on the basis that persons who incite, aid, abet, or attempt such offences would be guilty under ordinary principles of secondary participation and the law of 'attempt'.[39] Moreover, a person guilty in this way would be liable to be punished as if he were the principal of the offence, or if the attempt had been completed.

---

[36] The features specified by Art. 4(2)(a) are: where the offence was committed against a 'particularly vulnerable' victim; or within the framework of a criminal organisation, as defined; or where the life of the victim was endangered either deliberately or by gross negligence; or where the offence was committed by use of serious violence or has caused particularly serious harm to the victim.

[37] The relevant offences under the law of England and Wales are the offence of holding a person in slavery or servitude etc, contrary to the Coroners and Justice Act 2009, s. 71, which carries a maximum sentence of 14 years' imprisonment; trafficking people for exploitation, contrary to the Asylum and Immigration (Treatment of Claimants) Act 2004, s. 4, which is punishable by 14 years' imprisonment; and various offences of trafficking for sexual exploitation, found in the Sexual Offences Act 2003, ss. 57–9, each of which is punishable by a maximum sentence of 14 years' imprisonment.

[38] Sentencing Council, Definitive Guideline, 'Overarching Principles: Seriousness', December 2004.

[39] A person might also be guilty of an offence contrary to the Serious Crime Act 2007 (encouraging or assisting crime).

6.59 Article 6 requires Member States to ensure that 'legal persons' liable for any of the offences mentioned in Articles 2 and 3 should be subject to sanctions, though not necessarily criminal fines. As discussed at **6.14**, a company may be held criminally liable in certain circumstances. Moreover, a company which had been used to commit a human trafficking offence would be liable to be wound up in the Companies Court.

Criminalisation of racism and xenophobia

6.60 Council Framework Decision 2008/913/JHA of 28 November 2008 on combating certain forms and expressions of racism and xenophobia by means of criminal law is designed to achieve approximation of Member States' criminal laws in order to tackle this form of social ill.

6.61 Article 1 requires each Member State to take the measures necessary to ensure that certain types of intentional conduct are punishable:

(a) Publicly inciting to violence or hatred directed against a group of persons or a member of such a group defined by reference to race, colour, religion, descent, or national or ethnic origin.

In England and Wales the offences which address this form of conduct include the use of words or behaviour intending thereby to stir up racial hatred, contrary to section 18(1)(a) of the Public Order Act 1986, and the equivalent offence for conducted concerning religious hatred, contrary to section 29B of the same Act. It is an ingredient of the offence that the words or behaviour must be 'threatening, abusive or insulting'. This limitation is, however, consistent with Article 1(2) of the Framework Decision which permits Member States to punish only conduct which is threatening, abusive, or insulting.

(b) The commission of an act referred to in point (a) by public dissemination or distribution of tracts, pictures, or other material.

Such conduct would be covered by the offences of publishing or distributing written material intending thereby to stir up racial hatred, contrary to section 19 of the Public Order Act 1986, and the equivalent offence involving religious hatred, section 29C of the same Act. In addition, there are similar offences contrary to the same Act, concerning both racial and religious hatred, which address the public performance of plays and the distribution, showing, or playing of a recording or the broadcasting of a programme.

(c) Publicly condoning, denying, or grossly trivialising crimes of genocide, crimes against humanity and war crimes as defined in Articles 6, 7, and 8 of the Statute of the International Criminal Court, directed against a group of persons or a member of such a group defined by reference to race, colour, religion, descent, or national or ethnic origin when the conduct is carried out in a manner likely to incite violence or hatred against such a group or a member of such a group.

There is no specific offence in the criminal law of England and Wales which precisely matches the conduct specified in the Framework Decision. However, such conduct would inevitably be caught by one of the offences contrary to the Public Order Act 1986 mentioned in point (b).

(d) Publicly condoning, denying, or grossly trivialising the crimes defined in Article 6 of the Charter of the International Military Tribunal appended to the London Agreement of 8 August 1945, directed against a group of persons or a member of such a group defined by reference to race, colour, religion, descent, or national or ethnic origin when the conduct is carried out in a manner likely to incite violence or hatred against such a group or a member of such a group.

There is no specific offence in the criminal law of England and Wales which precisely matches the conduct specified in the Framework Decision. However, such conduct would usually be caught, depending on the precise circumstances, by one of the offences contrary to the Public Order Act 1986 mentioned in point (b).

Article 2 requires Member States to ensure that the instigation of the conduct referred to in Article 1(1)(c) and (d) is punishable. Moreover, Member States must ensure that the aiding and abetting of any conduct referred to in Article 1 is also punishable. Both of these requirements are met under the law of England and Wales, having regard to ordinary principles of secondary liability. **6.62**

Article 3 concerns the available penalties, and requires Member States to ensure that the conduct referred to in Articles 1 and 2 is punishable by effective, proportionate, and dissuasive penalties. Moreover, the conduct referred to in Article 1 must be punishable by criminal penalties of a maximum of at least between one and three years' imprisonment. This requirement is met in England and Wales because each of the offences contrary to the Public Order Act 1986 mentioned earlier carries a maximum sentence of seven years' imprisonment. **6.63**

Article 4 requires Member States to ensure that racist and xenophobic motivation is considered an aggravating circumstance or, alternatively, that such motivation may be taken into consideration by the courts in the determination of penalties. This requirement is met in England and Wales: section 145 of the Criminal Justice Act 2003 requires the court to treat as an aggravating factor the fact that an offence was racially or religiously aggravated and to declare this in open court. **6.64**

The Framework Decision requires liability and penalties for 'legal persons'. As discussed at 6.14, a company may be held criminally liable in certain circumstances. **6.65**

Criminalisation of ship-source pollution

Framework Decision 2005/667/JHA of 12 July 2005 to strengthen the criminal law framework for the enforcement of the law against ship source pollution is designed to ensure cooperation of Member States in the fight against intentional or seriously negligent ship-source pollution. Article 2 requires each Member State to ensure that an infringement within the meaning of Articles 4 and 5 of Directive 2005/35/EC[40] shall be regarded as a criminal offence. In short, Article 4 of Directive 2005/35/EC defines infringements as intentional, reckless, or seriously negligent ship-source discharges of polluting substances[41] where the discharge occurs into: the internal waters of a Member State; the territorial sea of a Member State; the straits used for international navigation; or the exclusive economic zone of a Member State or the high seas. This requirement is subject to certain exceptions specified in Article 5 of Directive 2005/35/EC. Moreover, by reason of Article 3 of the Framework Decision, Member States must ensure that the aiding, abetting, and inciting of criminal infringements is also punishable. **6.66**

The law of England and Wales recognises an array of offences relating to the discharge of pollutants from ships. Of most significance is the Merchant Shipping (Implementation of **6.67**

---

[40] Directive 2005/35/EC of 7 September 2005 on ship-source pollution and on the introduction of penalties for infringements.
[41] Viz oil and noxious liquid substances in bulk: Art. 2 of Directive 2005/35/EC.

Ship-Source Pollution Directive) Regulations 2009 (SI 2009/1210) which amended the law in order to implement Directive 2005/35/EC. Consequently, the relevant offences are now to be found in the Merchant Shipping (Prevention of Oil Pollution) Regulations 1996 (SI 1996/2154), sections 128–136A of the Merchant Shipping Act 1995, and the Merchant Shipping (Dangerous or Noxious Liquid Substances in Bulk) Regulations 1996 (SI 1996/3010). This legislation contains a large number of offences for different types of conduct committed in different ways which are subject to defences. It would perhaps not be of great assistance to set out these offences exhaustively here. Suffice it to say that, as far as the author has been able to ascertain, the offences enacted into the law of England and Wales properly reflect those envisaged by the Framework Decision.

6.68 Article 4 concerns penalties. The first requirement is that each Member State must take the measures necessary to ensure that the offences referred to in Articles 2 and 3 are punishable by effective, proportionate, and dissuasive criminal penalties which shall include, at least for 'serious' cases, criminal penalties of at least between one and three years' imprisonment. Further requirements stipulate that greater custodial penalties should be available where the offence is committed either intentionally or recklessly, or where serious harm or damage is caused to animal or plant life, or where persons are killed or seriously injured. For example, one requirement is that each Member State shall take the measures necessary to ensure that where an Article 2 offence is committed intentionally, and caused significant and widespread damage to water quality, to animal or vegetable species or to parts of them, or the death or serious injury of persons, the available punishment is a maximum of at least between five and ten years' imprisonment.

6.69 Relevant conduct in England and Wales are offences for which the maximum available penalty is a financial penalty. This might appear to be inconsistent with the requirements of the Framework Decision but it is of interest to note that the requirements of the Framework Decision, insofar as they concern custodial penalties, are subject to Article 4.8, which states that, regarding custodial penalties, this Article shall apply without prejudice to international law and in particular Article 230 of the 1982 United Nations Convention on the Law of the Sea. Article 230 states:

1. Monetary penalties only may be imposed with respect to violations of national laws and regulations or applicable international rules and standards for the prevention, reduction and control of pollution of the marine environment, committed by foreign vessels beyond the territorial sea.
2. Monetary penalties only may be imposed with respect to violations of national laws and regulations or applicable international rules and standards for the prevention, reduction and control of pollution of the marine environment, committed by foreign vessels in the territorial sea, except in the case of a wilful and serious act of pollution in the territorial sea.

6.70 The Framework Decision requires the liability of legal persons. As discussed at **6.14**, a company may be held criminally liable in certain circumstances.

Upper limits on sentencing

6.71 While the EU imposes requirements as to 'minimum maximum' sentences, at the other end of the scale, the coming into force of the Charter of Fundamental Rights of the European Union places limits on the penalties available where Member States implement EU law. Article 2 of the Charter, concerning the right to life, provides:

1. Everyone has the right to life.
2. No one shall be condemned to the death penalty, or executed.

Article 49(3) of the Charter provides: **6.72**

The severity of penalties must not be disproportionate to the criminal offence.

C. Future Obligations

This process of harmonising the criminal law, and in particular the appropriate sanctions, is   **6.73**
an on-going one, as made clear by Article 83 TFEU. Article 83 gives power to the European
Parliament and Council to establish, by means of Directives, minimum rules concerning the
definition of criminal offences and sanctions. These Directives will legislate in the areas of
particularly serious crime with a cross-border dimension resulting from the nature or impact
of such offences or from a special need to combat them on a common basis. The areas of
crime are listed as:

- terrorism;
- trafficking in human beings;
- sexual exploitation of women and children. On 27 October 2011, the European Parliament
  approved a proposed Directive which will replace Framework Decision 2004/68/JHA.
  The proposed Directive is more prescriptive, both in terms of the types of conduct which
  must be criminalised and the maximum penalty which must be available where relevant
  conduct is committed;
- drug trafficking;
- arms trafficking;
- money laundering;
- corruption;
- counterfeiting;
- computer crime; and
- organised crime. In a Resolution dated 25 October 2011 the European Parliament declared
  that Framework Decision 2008/841/JHA had had an 'extremely limited impact' on
  the legislative systems of the Members States. The European Parliament called on the
  Commission to submit, by the end of 2013, a proposal for a Directive which should
  contain a more concrete definition of organised crime and contain further measures to
  combat it.

D. Mutual Recognition of Custodial Sentences

Introduction

Vital to any coherent system of European criminal justice is the need for mutual recogni-   **6.74**
tion of judgments and sentences. Not yet implemented into UK law is Framework Decision
2008/909/JHA of 27 November 2008 on the application of the principle of mutual recognition to judgments in criminal matters imposing custodial sentences or measures involving
deprivation of liberty for the purpose of their enforcement in the European Union. It is
designed to give effect to the Council's desire to establish mechanisms for mutual recognition of sentences. It replaces the existing conventions which govern such matters, in particular the European Convention on the transfer of sentenced persons of 21 March 1983 and the
Additional Protocol of 18 December 1997; the European Convention on the International
Validity of Criminal Judgments of 28 May 1970 (which the UK has not signed); Title III,

Chapter 5 of the Convention of 19 June 1990 implementing the Schengen Convention of 14 June 1985 on the gradual abolition of checks at common borders (which does not apply to the UK), and the Convention between Member States of the European Communities on the Enforcement of Foreign Criminal Sentences of 13 November 1991.

6.75 When implemented, the procedure envisaged by the Framework Decision will entail the rapid recognition of judgments, enabling sentences to be executed and convicted persons to serve their sentences in the appropriate Member State. It can be anticipated that it will operate in a manner bearing a resemblance to the European Arrest Warrant. Moreover, it seems likely that it will throw up the types of legal problem with which extradition practitioners will be familiar.

Initiating procedure

6.76 The Framework Decision lays down a system of rules and procedures by which persons sentenced by the 'issuing State' may be transferred to the 'executing State'. The executing State (ie the State which recognises the judgment and enforces the sentence) may be any Member State within the EU, falling into one of three categories:[42]

(a) the Member State of nationality of the sentenced person in which he lives;

(b) the Member State of nationality, to which, while not being the Member State where he lives, the sentenced person will be deported, once he is released from the enforcement of the sentence, on the basis of an expulsion or deportation order consequential to the sentencing judgment; or

(c) any other Member State, the competent authority of which consents to the forwarding of the judgment and the certificate to that Member State.[43]

6.77 The procedure for transfer of a sentenced person is ordinarily commenced by the issuing State.[44] Alternatively, either the executing State or the sentenced person himself may request the issuing State to commence the procedure.[45] Before the issuing State commences the procedure for transfer of a prisoner, it must first be satisfied that the enforcement of the sentence by the executing State would 'serve the purpose of facilitating the social rehabilitation of the sentenced person'. To this end, where appropriate in relation to Member States falling into categories (a) and (b) in the previous paragraph, the issuing State may consult with the executing State before commencing the transfer procedure. Where the executing State falls into category (c), the consultation procedure is mandatory.[46] Where the consultation procedure does take place, the executing State may issue a reasoned opinion to the effect that transfer would not serve the purpose of facilitating the social rehabilitation of the sentenced person.[47] Where the issuing State *is* satisfied that transfer would facilitate social rehabilitation even, perhaps, where the executing State

---

[42] Article 4.1.

[43] The requirement for consent may be waived by Member States where the sentenced person lives in and has been residing continuously for at least five years in the executing State and will retain a permanent right of residence in that State, or where the sentenced person is a national of the executing State in cases other than those provided for in points (a) and (b).

[44] Article 4.2.

[45] Article 4.5.

[46] Article 4.2.

[47] Article 4.4.

disagrees with this assessment, the issuing State may forward the judgment together with a certificate to the executing State.[48]

Save in certain circumstances, before the issuing State may forward the judgment and certificate, it is necessary to obtain the consent of the sentenced person.[49] The exception is where the judgment and certificate are to be forwarded to an executing State falling into categories (a) and (b), or to a Member State to which the sentenced person has fled in view of the criminal proceedings in the issuing State.[50]   **6.78**

Where the sentenced person is still in the issuing State, the sentenced person, or his legal representative, must be given an opportunity to make representations about the proposed action by the issuing State. Any such representations must be forwarded to the executing State and must be taken into account by the issuing State in deciding whether or not to forward the judgment.[51]   **6.79**

Where the issuing State decides to invoke the transfer procedure, the competent authority of the issuing State must inform the sentenced person of the decision and forward the judgment (or a certified copy) to the competent authority of the executing State. A certificate must also be forwarded, signed, and certified as accurate by the competent authority.[52]   **6.80**

Recognition and exceptions to recognition

The competent authority which receives a judgment and certificate which has complied with the procedure must decide, ordinarily within a period of 90 days of receipt of the judgment,[53] whether to recognise the judgment and enforce the sentence imposed.[54]   **6.81**

The default position is that the judgment 'shall' be recognised, subject to a number of matters. The first concerns the question of double criminality. Where the criminal offence which led to the imposition of the sentence is one listed in Article 7[55] the default position is there is no 'double criminality' requirement.[56]   **6.82**

---

[48] The Framework Decision appears to envisage that the issuing State may, notwithstanding a reasoned opinion from the executing State to contrary effect, conclude that the transfer would be in the interests of the sentenced person. It is not difficult to see that a conflict of views between Member States about what is in the best interests of the sentenced person may give rise to a 'tug of war' to determine where the sentenced person should lawfully serve his sentence.

[49] Article 6.1.

[50] Article 6.2.

[51] Article 6.3.

[52] Article 6.4. The Framework Decision itself contains a standard form of the certificate to be used.

[53] See Art. 12.

[54] Article 8.

[55] Participation in a criminal organisation; terrorism; trafficking in human beings; sexual exploitation of children and child pornography; illicit trafficking in narcotic drugs and psychotropic drugs; illicit trafficking in weapons, munitions, and explosives; corruption; fraud; laundering of the proceeds of crime; counterfeiting currency; computer-related crime; environmental crime; facilitation of unauthorised entry and residence; murder, grievous bodily injury; illicit trade in human organs and tissue; kidnapping, illegal restraint, and hostage taking; racism and xenophobia; organised or armed robbery; illicit trafficking in cultural goods; swindling; racketeering and extortion; counterfeiting and piracy of products; forgery of administrative documents and trafficking therein; forgery of means of payment; illicit trafficking in hormonal substances and other growth promoters; illicit trafficking in nuclear or radioactive materials; trafficking in stolen vehicles; rape; arson; crimes within the jurisdiction of the International Criminal Court; unlawful seizure of aircraft/ships; sabotage.

[56] A Member State may, however, declare itself not to be bound by the effect of the list, in which case all offences will need to satisfy the double criminality requirement.

6.83 However, where the offence is not listed in Article 7 (or the executing State has declared that double criminality is to be a requirement in all cases[57]) it may invoke the double criminality requirement, that is make the recognition of the judgment and the enforcement of the sentence subject to double criminality, viz a requirement that the offence relates to acts which also constitute an offence under its own laws.[58]

6.84 Further grounds for refusing to recognise the judgment are found in Article 9. These are, in summary: where the procedural requirements are not met (e.g. because the certificate is incomplete or does not correspond to the judgment[59] or the criteria in Article 4 are not met); where enforcement of the sentence would be contrary to the principle of *ne bis in idem*;[60] where it is impossible for the sentence to be enforced (because the sentenced person has immunity in the executing State, or the sentence has been imposed on a person who, under the law of the executing State, owing to his or her age, could not have been criminally liable for the acts in respect of which the judgment was issued); where the sentence includes a measure of psychiatric care which the executing State cannot execute; where at the time the judgment was received less than six months of the sentence remained to be served; the judgment was rendered *in absentia* (unless, in summary, the certificate states that the sentenced person was notified of the proceedings or the sentenced person has indicated that he does not contest the case); or, where the judgment relates to criminal offences which under the law of the executing State are regarded as having been committed wholly or for a major or essential part within its territory, or in a place equivalent to its territory.[61]

Adaptation of sentences and partial recognition of sentences

6.85 Where the form of sentence is incompatible with the law of the executing State, the competent authority of that State may by Article 8, 'adapt' the sentence, provided the adapted sentence does not 'aggravate' the sentence imposed in the issuing State in terms of its nature and duration.[62] So, where the sentence to be enforced is greater than the maximum sentence for similar offences under national law in the executing State, the sentence may be reduced to a level not below the maximum sentence available under national law.[63] Where the nature of the sentence to be enforced is incompatible with the available sentences in the executing State, the sentence may be adapted so that it corresponds as closely as possible to the sentence imposed by the issuing State. The sentence must not be converted into a pecuniary punishment.[64]

6.86 The Framework Decision contemplates 'partial recognition' by the executing State—that is, where, by reason of one of the exceptions set out earlier, the executing State is able only

---

[57] Article 7.4: any such declaration shall be published in the Official Journal of the European Union.
[58] Article 7.3.
[59] Where this occurs, Art. 11 provides for postponed recognition of the judgment while the issuing State corrects the error.
[60] This principle is considered in detail in Chapter 5.
[61] It is not entirely clear what the rationale for this rule is: why should a refusal to enforce a judgment be justified by the fact that the criminal offences took place in the executing State's territory? The authors suggest that this exception may envisage a situation where two Member States hold competing claims to prosecute a particular individual. The executing State may not accept the legitimacy of the prosecution in the issuing State and therefore may wish to refuse to recognise the penalty imposed.
[62] Article 8.4. The adaptation of the sentence would, presumably, have to be carried out by a court.
[63] Article 8.2.
[64] Article 8.3.

to recognise part of the sentence.[65] Before partial recognition may occur, the competent authorities of the issuing State and those of the executing State must, on a case-by-case basis, reach agreement as to the appropriate terms.[66] The agreement must not result in the aggravation of the duration of the sentence.[67] In the absence of such agreement, the certificate is to be withdrawn.

Transfer and transit

Articles 15 and 16 deal with the transfer and transit of sentenced persons. If the person sentenced is in the issuing State, he shall be transferred to the executing State no later than 30 days after the final decision on the recognition of the judgment and enforcement of the sentence. By Article 16, Member States are required to make arrangements to permit the transit of a sentenced person through their territory. **6.87**

Specialty

Article 18 concerns 'specialty'. It provides that a person transferred to the executing State shall not be prosecuted, sentenced, or otherwise deprived of his liberty for an offence committed before his transfer, other than that for which he was transferred. This rule is subject to exceptions, including cases where the sentenced person consented to the transfer.[68] Similarly, specialty would not apply where the issuing State consents to the sentenced person being prosecuted in the executing State. A request for consent must be acceded to where it is accompanied by the information which would ordinarily be contained in a European Arrest Warrant such that the issuing State would be under an obligation to surrender the sentenced person.[69] **6.88**

Implementation

Implementation of these provisions by Member States has been poor. By Article 29, Member States were supposed to implement the Framework Decision by 5 December 2011. As of 21 March 2012, the following countries had implemented the Framework Decision: Denmark, Italy, Malta, Austria, Poland, Finland, Ireland (subject to reservations), Bulgaria, and the Czech Republic (although in respect of Bulgaria and the Czech Republic the implementation was not yet in force). **6.89**

E. Mutual Recognition of Non-Custodial Criminal Sanctions

Introduction

The imposition of a non-custodial criminal sanction by a court in a Member State raises a number of issues, the most important of which is the mechanism by which that sanction can be enforced across the territory of the EU. This is a natural adjunct to the fundamental **6.90**

---

[65] Article 10.

[66] Since this function would involve the 'fixing' of a sentence it would have to be performed by a court.

[67] Article 10.2. Contrast this with the requirement in Art. 8.4 whereby an 'adapted' sentence must not be aggravated in terms of its duration *and* nature.

[68] The other exceptions, set out in Art. 18.2, are: where the person was transferred to the executing State but did not leave within 45 days of his final discharge or did leave, but later returned; where the offence is not punishable by a custodial sentence; when the criminal proceedings do not give rise to the application of a measure restricting personal liberty; when the sentenced person could be liable to a penalty not involving the deprivation of liberty; the sentenced person renounces his entitlement to rely on the specialty rule.

[69] See also Chapter 4 in relation to EAWs.

right of EU citizens to move themselves and their property freely across Member States. Early attempts at enforcing criminal sanctions failed to attract sufficient ratifications from Member States. However, in recent years a number of Framework Decisions have been implemented relating to the mutual recognition of:

(a) financial penalties (see **6.91**);
(b) non-custodial disposals (see **6.101**); and
(c) confiscation (see **6.108**).

Financial penalties

6.91 A Framework Decision on the mutual recognition of financial penalties was adopted in 2005.[70] This was the result of an initiative by the UK, France, and Sweden. Member States were required to apply the Framework Decision by 22 March 2007. The format of the Framework Decision is similar to that relating to European Arrest Warrants, in that a Member State is required to recognise the judgment of another Member State unless a ground for non-recognition exists. The requirement for dual criminality is abolished for a range of offences likely to be punishable with a financial penalty. The 39 relevant types of offence are set out at Article 5 of the Framework Decision:

- participation in a criminal organisation;
- terrorism;
- trafficking in human beings;
- sexual exploitation of children and child pornography;
- illicit trafficking in narcotic drugs and psychotropic substances;
- illicit trafficking in weapons, munitions, and explosives;
- corruption;
- fraud;
- laundering of the proceeds of crime;
- counterfeiting currency;
- computer-related crime;
- environmental crime;
- facilitation of unauthorised entry and residence;
- murder, grievous bodily injury;
- illicit trade in human organs and tissue;
- kidnapping, illegal restraint, and hostage taking;
- racism and xenophobia;
- organised or armed robbery;
- illicit trafficking in cultural goods;
- swindling;
- racketeering and extortion;
- counterfeiting and piracy of products;
- forgery of administrative documents and trafficking therein;
- forgery of means of payment;
- illicit trafficking in hormonal substances and other growth promoters;
- illicit trafficking in nuclear or radioactive materials;
- trafficking in stolen vehicles;

---

[70] FD 2005/214/JHA.

- rape;
- arson;
- crimes within the jurisdiction of the International Criminal Court;
- unlawful seizure of aircraft/ships;
- sabotage;
- conduct which infringes road traffic regulations;
- smuggling goods;
- infringements of intellectual property rights;
- threats and acts of violence against persons, including violence during sport events;
- criminal damage;
- theft; and
- offences established by the issuing State and serving the purpose of implementing obligations arising from instruments adopted under the EC Treaty or under Title VI of the EU Treaty.

The eight grounds for optional non-recognition and non-execution are set out at Article 7 of the Framework Decision. In summary they are: **6.92**

- double jeopardy;
- absence of dual criminality (for an offence not covered by Art. 5);
- statute bar in the executing State;
- extraterritoriality;
- immunity;
- age of the offender (below that of criminal liability in the executing State);
- *in absentia* proceedings; and
- fine below the financial threshold (currently €70).

Member States are given a broader, discretionary option to oppose the recognition and execution of the relevant penalties (Art. 20(3)). This may occur where the information provided gives rise to an issue that fundamental rights or legal principles, as enshrined in Article 6 of the EU Treaty, may have been infringed. This 'information' is, however, explicitly limited to that found within the certificate sent by the issuing State. The anodyne nature of the information contained within such a certificate is unlikely, on the face of it, to disclose a human rights issue pertaining to the original judgment. **6.93**

The Framework Decision was incorporated into domestic law by sections 80–92 of the Criminal Justice and Immigration Act 2008. The Act provides a mechanism for both the making of requests to other Member States and receipt of requests from them. **6.94**

The Act defines a financial penalty as a fine, compensation order, surcharge, costs order, or other such order as set out in section 80(5). It empowers a designated officer (s. 80(1) and (2)) to issue a certificate requesting the enforcement of a financial penalty in another Member State where is appears to the designated officer that the offender is normally resident in, or has property or income in, a Member State other than the UK (s. 80(2)(e)). The Lord Chancellor must then forward the certificate to the relevant Member State (s. 81(3)). **6.95**

If another Member State requests the enforcement of a financial penalty within England and Wales the certificate is forwarded by the Lord Chancellor to the relevant local justice area. The Lord Chancellor must also specify whether he thinks there are any grounds for **6.96** non-recognition or non-execution (s. 84(4)). The matter is then placed before the relevant magistrates' court, which must determine whether the enforcement of a penalty is suitable, having regard to Schedule 18 to the Act. In short, this requires that the offender is a person normally resident in England or Wales or, if not normally resident, had property or a source of income in the jurisdiction.

6.97 If the magistrates' court considers the enforcement of a penalty to be suitable it must then consider whether any grounds for non-recognition or non-execution exist. These are set out at Schedule 19 to the Act. Part 1 of Schedule 19 reiterates the grounds as set out in the Framework Decision and Part 2 of the Schedule sets out, verbatim, the 39 offence types identified at Article 5 of the Framework Decision. If the court decides to enforce the penalty, domestic legislation will apply as appropriate. In effect, the sum will be payable to the relevant magistrates' court.

6.98 Once the domestic court is satisfied that the enforcement of the penalty is suitable and that there are no grounds for refusal, it cannot reconsider the merits of the original judgment. It should be noted that any challenge to the imposition of the financial penalty must be conducted before the original court which imposed the penalty in the requesting Member State.

6.99 The Framework Decision was in force in 23 Member States as of 21 January 2011.[71] It is not yet clear how regularly it has been used or whether it has supplanted the use of European Arrest Warrants where fines have remained unpaid.

6.100 For the future, the Commission, through the aegis of the Stockholm Programme, has proposed an EU-wide mechanism for enforcing fines imposed for road traffic offences, based upon cross-border information exchange and enforcement of sanctions. The relevant offences are speeding, drink driving, failure to stop at a red light, and failure to use a seat belt and will apply to vehicles registered in a Member State other than that in which the offence takes place.

Non-custodial disposals

6.101 There has been provision for the EU-wide monitoring of offenders who have been released on parole or who have received probation or suspended sentences since 1964. In that year, a Council of Europe Convention established mechanisms for the supervision of conditionally sentenced or conditionally released prisoners if they relocated to a Member State other than that in which they had committed the relevant offence. Only 12 Member States ratified the Convention, some with significant reservations. On 27 November 2008 this Convention was superseded by a Framework Decision[72] on the application of mutual recognition of judgments and probation decisions. The deadline for the implementation of the Framework Decision expired on 6 December 2011, although the Commission report detailing the scale of adoption by Member States is not due until 6 December 2014.

6.102 The Framework Decision is limited in application to 11 categories of probation requirements, parole measures, or alternative sentences, although Member States may elect to

---

[71] Council General Secretariat: Implementation of the Framework Decision of the Council of the European Union of 24 February 2005 of the application of the principle of mutual recognition of financial penalties, 16924/2/10 (Brussels, 21 January 2011).
[72] FD 2008/947/JHA.

supervise other types of non-custodial sentences (Art. 4(2)). The categories of sentence identified are obligations for an offender to:

- inform a specific authority of any change of residence or working place;
- refrain from entering certain localities, places, or defined areas in the issuing or executing State;
- limit any departures from the territory of the executing State;
- observe instructions relating to behaviour, residence, education and training, leisure activities, or manner of carrying out a professional activity;
- report at specified times to a specified authority;
- avoid contact with specific persons;
- avoid contact with specific objects, which have been used or are likely to be used by the offender with a view to committing a criminal offence;
- compensate, and provide proof of such compensation, for prejudice caused by the offence;
- carry out community service;
- cooperate with a probation officer or other representative; and
- undergo therapeutic treatment or treatment for addiction (Art. 4(1)).

The obligation of mutual recognition only applies to the Member State in which the offender **6.103** is lawfully and ordinarily residing and only in cases where the offender has returned or wants to return to that Member State (Art. 5(1)). However, a Member State other than that described in Article 5(1) may consent to recognise the relevant judgment and supervise the offender during the currency of the sentence (Art. 5(2)). It is notable that the nationality of the offender would not seem to be determinative but that his consent to a transfer of the supervision of the sentence is. It is questionable whether, given the offender's right to free movement within the EU, there would be a sound legal basis for any Member State's refusal to supervise a sentence in the scenario envisaged by Article 5(2).

The executing State is entitled to adapt the nature or duration of the relevant sentence in **6.104** order to ensure its compatibility with domestic law. Any reduction in the duration of the sentence must not be below the maximum duration provided for equivalent offences under the law of the executing State (Art. 9(2)). Conversely, the executing State may not increase the length of the sentence beyond that which was originally imposed (Art. 9(3)).

The requirement for dual criminality in this context is abolished for 32 relevant types of **6.105** offence as set out at Article 10 of the Framework Decision:

- participation in a criminal organisation;
- terrorism;
- trafficking in human beings;
- sexual exploitation of children and child pornography;
- illicit trafficking in narcotic drugs and psychotropic substances;
- illicit trafficking in weapons, munitions, and explosives;
- corruption;
- fraud;
- laundering of the proceeds of crime;
- counterfeiting currency;
- computer-related crime;

- environmental crime;
- facilitation of unauthorised entry and residence;
- murder, grievous bodily injury;
- illicit trade in human organs and tissue;
- kidnapping, illegal restraint, and hostage taking;
- racism and xenophobia;
- organised or armed robbery;
- illicit trafficking in cultural goods;
- swindling;
- racketeering and extortion;
- counterfeiting and piracy of products;
- forgery of administrative document and trafficking therein;
- forgery of means of payment;
- illicit trafficking in hormonal substances and other growth promoters;
- illicit trafficking in nuclear or radioactive materials;
- trafficking in stolen vehicles;
- rape;
- arson;
- crimes within the jurisdiction of the International Criminal Court;
- unlawful seizure of aircraft/ships; and
- sabotage.

6.106 Article 10 is subject to the stipulation that the relevant offence must be *punishable* (as distinct from *punished*) by a custodial sentence or measure involving deprivation of liberty for a maximum period of at least three years. It will be apparent that suspended or non-custodial sentences will, in some cases, meet this threshold.

6.107 There are 11 grounds for the optional refusing of recognition and supervision which are set out at Article 11 of the Framework Decision. In summary they are:

- the certificate sent by the issuing State is in some way deficient;
- the relevant sanction is not identified in Article 4(1) and the executing State has not consented to supervise the sanction;
- double jeopardy;
- absence of dual criminality (for an offence not covered by Art. 10);
- statute bar in the executing State;
- immunity;
- age of the offender (below that of criminal liability in the executing State);
- *in absentia* proceedings;
- inability to provide or supervise the required medical/therapeutic treatment;
- duration of the relevant sanction less than six months' duration; and
- extraterritoriality.

Confiscation

6.108 The Proceeds of Crime Act (POCA) 2002, as amended, purported to conform to the UK's obligations to harmonise its domestic law in relation to the seizure of criminal assets through confiscation and civil recovery. A detailed analysis of this legislation is beyond the scope of this work, but it has been accepted that the POCA regime meets the requirements laid down in the Framework Decision of 24 February 2005 on confiscation of crime-related proceeds, instrumentalities, and property.[73]

The specific issue of the mutual recognition of confiscation orders made by Member States **6.109** was addressed in the Framework Decision of 6 October 2006.[74] This was to be implemented by Member States by 24 November 2008, with a Commission report on progress due by 24 November 2013.

The Framework Decision abolishes the necessity for dual criminality in this context for to **6.110** the same 32 offence categories as established in FD 2008/947/JHA (Art. 6) and the need for a possible maximum sentence of at least three years is repeated. Dual criminality does, therefore, continue to exist for all other offence categories and the relevant offences must be recognised in the executing State as permitting confiscation (Art. 6(3)). The executing State must enforce the confiscation order unless one of the reasons for non-recognition or non-execution exists. These are set out at Article 8:

- double jeopardy;
- absence of dual criminality (for an offence not covered by Art. 6);
- immunity;
- rights of third parties making it impossible for the executing State to enforce the order;
- *in absentia* proceedings;
- extraterritoriality;
- confiscation relates to an extended power of confiscation within the issuing State which is beyond the framework established in Framework Decision 2005/212/JHA; and
- statute bar in the executing State.

If one of these bars exists, the executing State may choose whether or not to enforce **6.111** the confiscation order. The executing State is required to put into place legal remedies to ensure that any interested party can challenge the recognition and execution of the confiscation order. Any such challenge must be brought in the executing State and, if successful, execution of the order will be suspended. It should be noted that any substantive challenge to the reasons for issuing the confiscation order must be mounted in the issuing State only (Art. 9).

The executing State may postpone the execution of the confiscation order for other reasons **6.112** (Art. 10):

- if there is a risk that the total amount of money derived from the execution of the confiscation order will exceed the amount specified in the order due to simultaneous execution in more than one Member State;
- where execution of the order may damage an ongoing criminal investigation or proceedings;
- where further time is required for the translation of the order; or
- where the relevant property is already the subject of confiscation proceedings in the executing State.

---

[73] FD 2005/212/JHA.
[74] FD 2006/783/JHA.

6.113 The Framework Decision had been largely anticipated by the provisions of the Proceeds of Crime Act 2002, as supplemented by the Proceeds of Crime Act 2002 (External Requests and Orders) Order 2005 (SI 2005/3181) and the Proceeds of Crime Act 2002 (External Requests and Orders) (Amendment) Order 2008 (SI 2008/302). The receipt and enforcement of requests for restraint and confiscation orders made in other jurisdictions are governed by sections 443–7 of POCA. This includes provision for appeals by affected parties. The procedure for making requests to foreign jurisdictions is outlined at section 74 of POCA, as amended by paragraph 35 of Schedule 8 to the Serious Crime Act 2007.

7

PRELIMINARY RULINGS AND DIRECT ACTIONS

A. Overview

Recourse can be had to the Courts of the EU, as described in Chapter 2, in two ways: by means **7.01** of direct actions and references for preliminary rulings. An individual, as opposed to a Member State or institution, may commence both types of action. The former are commenced in the Courts of the EU itself, whereas the latter, as the name suggests, uses the Courts of the EU as a court of reference from a matter commenced in the domestic courts.

Direct actions are those actions commenced and finally determined through the legislative **7.02** functions of the EU. The particular court in which such actions are issued will depend upon the nature of the action. Direct actions include actions to annul an EU measure which it is alleged to have been adopted contrary to a EU legal order, or against an EU institution for failing to act when it has a duty to act, or for damages against an EU institution. Often such actions are taken by an institution of the EU, or a Member State. However, in certain circumstances a private individual will have *locus standi* to bring an action as long as it directly and individually concerns him. This is governed by Article 263 TFEU (see 7.73).

Preliminary rulings and the ability to review and determine the proper interpretation of **7.03** EU law may be the most significant and commonly used aspect of the jurisdiction of the EU Courts. It is designed to ensure that domestic courts uphold and protect EU law which confers rights on individuals. This jurisdiction was originally to be found in the international Conventions, such as the Luxembourg Protocol to the 1968 Brussels Convention on Jurisdiction (Art. 3) or the 1998 Protocol on the interpretation of the Convention on Matrimonial Matters. These have now been replaced, however, by directly applicable regulations in relation to which the CJEU has full interpretative jurisdiction under the TFEU.

7.04 Preliminary rulings are those sought by national courts which seek a ruling from the CJEU to resolve domestic cases which involve the interpretation, application, or validity of EU law. These cases start and end in the national courts. At present it is the CJEU which has jurisdiction to hear and make preliminary rulings, but the TFEU provides for that jurisdiction to extend to the General Court in specific areas (see 7.07). These are considered first in this chapter as they are likely to be the most widely used by criminal practitioners facing an interpretive query before the domestic courts.

B. Preliminary Rulings under Article 267

The purpose of a preliminary ruling

7.05 Under the preliminary rulings procedure, the CJEU's role is to give an interpretation of EU law or to rule on its validity, not to apply that law to the factual situation underlying the main proceedings, which is the task of the national court.

7.06 Article 267 provides:

> The Court of Justice of the European Union shall have jurisdiction to give preliminary rulings concerning:
>
> (a) the interpretation of the Treaties;
> (b) the validity and interpretation of acts of the institutions, bodies, offices or agencies of the Union;
>
> Where such a question is raised before any court or tribunal of a Member State, that court or tribunal may, if it considers that a decision on the question is necessary to enable it to give judgment, request the Court to give a ruling thereon.
>
> Where any such question is raised in a case pending before a court or tribunal of a Member State against whose decisions there is no judicial remedy under national law, that court or tribunal shall bring the matter before the Court.
>
> If such a question is raised in a case pending before a court or tribunal of a Member State with regard to a person in custody, the Court of Justice of the European Union shall act with the minimum of delay.

The appropriate court

7.07 References for a preliminary ruling currently go exclusively to the CJEU. By virtue of Article 256(3), the General Court has 'jurisdiction to hear and determine questions referred for a preliminary ruling under Article 267, in specific areas laid down by the Statute.' However, the opportunity to amend the Statute and assign these specific areas has not yet been taken.

7.08 In 2011 there were 423 new cases of references for a preliminary ruling before the CJEU. This compares to just 81 new cases of direct actions. However, the number of references concerning the area of freedom, justice, and security remains relatively small as a proportion of overall references, with 44 new cases in 2011.[1]

---

[1] See Annual Report 2011, Court of Justice of the European Union at <http://www.curia.europa.eu>.

The stage and format of the reference

The stage and form of notice are set out in the 'Information Notice on references from national courts for a preliminary ruling'.[2] Between 1952 and 2011 there were 531 new references for a preliminary ruling from the UK. This was composed of 43 references from the House of Lords/Supreme Court, 69 references from the Court of Appeal, and 419 references from other courts and tribunals.[3] **7.09**

A national court or tribunal may refer a question to the CJEU for a preliminary ruling as soon as it finds that a ruling on the point or points of interpretation or validity is necessary to enable it to give judgment; it is the national court which is in the best position to decide at what stage of the proceedings such a question should be referred. **7.10**

It is, however, desirable that a decision to seek a preliminary ruling should be taken when the national proceedings have reached a stage at which the national court is able to define the factual and legal context of the question, so that the CJEU has available to it all the information necessary to check, where appropriate, that EU law applies to the main proceedings. It may also be in the interests of justice to refer a question for a preliminary ruling only after both sides have been heard. **7.11**

The decision by which a national court or tribunal refers a question to the CJEU for a preliminary ruling may be in any form allowed by national law as regards procedural steps. It must, however, be borne in mind that it is that document which serves as the basis of the proceedings before the CJEU and that it must therefore contain such information as will enable the latter to give a reply which is of assistance to the national court. Moreover, it is only the actual reference for a preliminary ruling which is notified to the interested persons entitled to submit observations to the CJEU, in particular the Member States and the institutions, and which is translated. **7.12**

Owing to the need to translate the reference, it should be drafted simply, clearly, and precisely, avoiding superfluous detail. A maximum of about ten pages is often sufficient to set out in a proper manner the context of a reference for a preliminary ruling. The order for reference must be succinct but sufficiently complete and must contain all the relevant information to give the CJEU and the interested persons entitled to submit observations a clear understanding of the factual and legal context of the main proceedings. In particular, the order for reference must: **7.13**

- include a brief account of the subject matter of the dispute and the relevant findings of fact or, at least, set out the factual situation on which the question referred is based;
- set out the tenor of any applicable national provisions in the Member State and identify, where necessary, the relevant national case law, giving in each case precise references (e.g. a page of an official journal or specific law report, with any internet reference);
- identify the EU law provisions relevant to the case as accurately as possible;
- explain the reasons which prompted the national court to raise the question of the interpretation or validity of the EU law provisions, and the relationship between those provisions and the national provisions applicable to the main proceedings; and
- include, if need be, a summary of the main relevant arguments of the parties to the main proceedings.

---

[2] 2009/C 297/01.
[3] See Annual Report 2011, Court of Justice of the European Union at <http://www.curia.europa.eu>.

7.14 In order to make it easier to read and refer to the document, it is helpful if the different points or paragraphs of the order for reference are numbered. Finally, the referring court may, if it considers itself able, briefly state its view on the answer to be given to the questions referred for a preliminary ruling.

7.15 The question or questions themselves should appear in a separate and clearly identified section of the order for reference, generally at the beginning or the end. It must be possible to understand them without referring to the statement of the grounds for the reference, which will however provide the necessary background for a proper assessment.

7.16 The form of the question should be couched in terms which pose a general question of EU law and if they are not the CJEU may reformulate them. Further scenarios where the CJEU may reformulate the question include where it requires it necessary to furnish the national court with all those elements of EU law which will enable it to give judgment on the dispute before it[4] or to avoid an issue that the CJEU would prefer not to address.

7.17 The CJEU cannot, at the request of one party to the main proceedings, examine questions which have not been submitted to it by the national court. If, in view of the course of the proceedings, the national court were to consider it necessary to obtain further interpretations of EU law, it would be for it to make a fresh reference to the CJEU.[5]

Statements of case or written submissions

7.18 Article 23 of Protocol No. 3 on the Statute of the Court of Justice of the European Union[6] sets out the time period in which parties submit statements of case or written observations.

7.19 First, the decision of the court or tribunal of the Member State is notified to the CJEU by the court or tribunal concerned. The decision is then notified by the Registrar of the CJEU to the parties, to the Member States, and to the Commission, and to the institution, body, office, or agency of the EU which adopted the act the validity or interpretation of which is in dispute.

7.20 Article 23 states:

> Within two months of this notification, the parties, the Member States, the Commission and, where appropriate, the institution, body, office or agency which adopted the act the validity or interpretation of which is in dispute, shall be entitled to submit statements of case or written observations to the Court.

7.21 However, most significant for criminal practitioners is the fourth paragraph of Article 267 TFEU which provides that the CJEU 'shall act with the minimum of delay' if a question is raised in a case pending before a court or tribunal of a Member State with regard to a person in custody.

7.22 Article 23a of the Protocol sets out 'an expedited or accelerated procedure and, for references for a preliminary ruling relating to the area of freedom, security and justice, an urgent procedure.'

7.23 As Article 23a makes clear, the 'urgent' preliminary ruling procedure is applicable only to the areas covered by Title V of Part Three of the TFEU, which relates to the area of freedom,

---

4 Case 28/85 *Deghillage v Caisse Primaire d'Assurance Maladie* [1986] ECR 991, para. 13.
5 Case C-189-95 *Franzen* [1997] ECR I-5909, para. 79.
6 [2008] OJ C 115, p 210.

security, and justice. Alternatively, an 'accelerated' procedure is available in respect of direct actions and other references for preliminary rulings.

The Rules of Procedure[7] provide for shortened time limits in both cases. In the case of the accelerated procedure, the statements of case or written observations are to be submitted within a period prescribed by the President, which shall not be less than 15 days.[8] Under the urgent procedure, the decision to deal with the reference will proscribe the period within which the parties or entities may lodge statements of case or written observations and the Chamber may, in cases of extreme urgency, decide to omit the written part of the procedure.[9] In both cases, the presentation by the Advocate-General of a formal Opinion is dispensed with, albeit that the Chamber rules after 'hearing' the Advocate-General.   **7.24**

The urgent preliminary ruling procedure simplifies the various stages of the proceedings before the CJEU, but its application entails significant constraints for the CJEU and for the parties and other interested persons participating in the procedure, particularly the Member States. As a result, it should only be requested where it is absolutely necessary for the Court to give its ruling on the reference as quickly as possible. One example of such a case would be where a person is deprived of their liberty and the answer to the question raised is decisive as to the assessment of that person's legal situation. The CJEU decides whether the procedure is to be applied. This is generally taken only on a reasoned request from the referring court. Exceptionally, the CJEU may decide of its own motion to deal with a reference under this procedure, where that appears to be required.   **7.25**

The first case that was heard by the CJEU under the urgent procedure was *Inga Rinau*,[10] which concerned the recognition in Lithuania of a judgment delivered in Germany awarding custody of a child to the father in that country and ordering the child to be returned. The reference was received on 14 May 2008 and the judgment was delivered two months later on 11 July 2008. In a second judgment, *Goicoechea*,[11] concerning an extradition request under a European Arrest Warrant, the judgment was delivered just six weeks after the request for a reference was made.[12] This compares with an average of over 19 months for a preliminary ruling to be delivered in 2007.[13]   **7.26**

However, this procedure appears to have been used sparingly. In 2011, just two applications out of a total of five were granted under the urgent preliminary ruling procedure and two applications were granted from a total of eight under the expedited and accelerated procedures.   **7.27**

Transitional regime

Article 10(1)–(3) of Protocol No. 36 provides that the powers of the CJEU in relation to acts adopted before the entry into force of the Treaty of Lisbon under Title VI of the TEU, in the field of police cooperation and judicial cooperation in criminal matters, and which have not   **7.28**

---

[7] [2008] OJ L 24, p 39.
[8] Rules of Procedure, Art. 104a.
[9] Rules of Procedure, Art. 104b.
[10] Case C-195/08 PPU [2008] ECR I-5271.
[11] Case C-195/08 PPU [2008] ECR I-5271. See also Case C-388/08 PPU *Leymann and Pustovarov* [2008] ECR I-9621.
[12] See Panos Koutrakos, 'Speeding Up the Preliminary Reference Procedure—Fast But Not Too Fast' (2008) 33(5) ELRev 617–18 for an assessment of the impact of this procedure.
[13] See Annual Report 2007, Court of Justice of the European Union at <http://www.curia.europa.eu>.

since been amended, are to remain the same for a maximum period of five years from the date of entry into force of the Treaty of Lisbon (1 December 2009).

7.29 During that period, such acts may, therefore, form the subject matter of a reference for a preliminary ruling only where the order for a reference is made by a court of a Member State which has accepted the jurisdiction of the CJEU, it being a matter for each State to determine whether the right to refer a question to the CJEU is to be available to all its national courts or is to be reserved to the courts of last instance.

The requesting body

7.30 Article 267 TFEU provides that it is 'a court or tribunal' that requests a preliminary ruling. In *Dorsch Consult Ingenieurgesellschaft v Bundesbaugesellschaft Berlin*,[14] the CJEU said that in determining whether a body is a court or tribunal:

> the Court takes account of a number of factors, such as whether the body is established by law, whether it is permanent, whether its jurisdiction is compulsory, whether its procedure is inter partes, whether it applies rules of law and whether it is independent.

7.31 Whilst this may be clear in criminal cases from the magistrates' court or the Crown Court, the analysis is more complex in matters such as disciplinary tribunals. For example, in *Broekmeulen v Huisarts Registratie Commissie*[15] the CJEU had to consider whether a body that determined who can practise as a medical professional amounted to a court or tribunal. In finding that it was, the CJEU noted the absence of any right of appeal to the ordinary courts, the fact that it operates with the consent of the public authorities and with their cooperation, and that after an adversarial procedure it delivers decisions which are in fact recognised as final.

7.32 This decision is to be distinguished, for example, from the case of an arbitrator appointed under private contract, who would not be entitled to make a reference.[16]

C. Jurisdiction of the Court in Preliminary Rulings

7.33 National courts may bring issues of EU law before the CJEU whenever they feel it necessary to do so, even if the point has already been considered by the CJEU.[17]

7.34 However, the question of jurisdiction arises when EU law is used in areas of national competence rather than EU competence. EU law may be applied in this area for several reasons—where decisions are taken at a national level to extend the scope of application of a piece of EU legislation;[18] where private actors contract in a way that relies on damages stipulated by EU legislation;[19] or where the same rule is a source of both EU and national law, such as an international agreement adopted jointly by the EU and its Member States.[20] The willingness

---

[14] Case C-54/96 [1997] ECR I-4961, para. 23.
[15] Case 246/80 [1981] ECR 2311.
[16] Case 102/81 *Nordsee v Reederei Mond* [1982] ECR 1095.
[17] Case 283/81 *CILFIT v Ministry of Health* [1982] ECR 3415, para. 15.
[18] Case 166/84 *Thomasdünger v Oberfinanzdirektion Frankfurt am Main* [1985] ECR 3001.
[19] Case C-88/91 *Federazione Italiana dei consorzi Agrari v Azidenda di Stato per gli Interventi nel mercato Agricolo* [1992] ECR I-4035.
[20] Case C-53/96 *Hermès International v FHT Marketing Choice BV* [1998] ECR I-3603.

of the CJEU to accept jurisdiction in areas of national competence has changed over time and has previously been a source of controversy between the CJEU and the Advocates-General.

The case of *Dzodzi v Belgium*[21] is considered the starting point in this jurisprudence. In **7.35** *Dzodzi*, the CJEU held that 'the Court gives its preliminary ruling without, in principle, having to look into the circumstances in which the national courts were prompted to submit the questions and envisage applying the provision of EU law which they have asked the Court to interpret.' As a consequence of this, the field in which the EU law is applied—national or EU competence—is not a relevant consideration for the CJEU.

In applying this rule, the CJEU is confined to considering provisions of EU law only. In its **7.36** reply to the national court, the CJEU cannot take account of the general scheme of the provisions of domestic law which, while referring to EU law, define the extent of that reference. Any consideration of the limits which a national legislature may have placed in the application of the EU law to purely internal situations is a matter for domestic law and falls within the exclusive jurisdiction of the courts of the Member State.

A shift of the CJEU's position can be seen in *Kleinwort Benson v City of Glasgow District* **7.37** *Council*.[22] This case is seen as limiting the extent to which the CJEU will accept jurisdiction in matters that concern national law.

In *Kleinwort Benson*, the Court of Appeal made a reference to the CJEU on a matter concern- **7.38** ing the Civil Jurisdiction and Judgments Act 1982 which provided for the allocation of civil jurisdiction between England, Scotland, Wales, and Northern Ireland. The Act contained a Schedule that was modelled on the Brussels Convention on Jurisdiction and Enforcement of Judgments in Civil and Commercial Matters 1968 as amended by the Convention of 1978 on the Accession of Denmark, Ireland and the United Kingdom.

The CJEU considered that it had no jurisdiction to give a preliminary ruling. The CJEU **7.39** noted that the relevant Schedule in dispute took the Convention as a model only and did not reproduce it in identical terms. The Act expressly provided for the adoption of modifications designed to produce a divergence between any provision in the Schedule and a corresponding Convention provision as interpreted by the CJEU. By a specific section of the Act, the national courts were only required to have regard to, rather than apply, the CJEU's case law concerning the interpretation of the corresponding provisions.

The test set out in *Kleinwort Benson* appears to be whether the provisions of EU law have **7.40** been 'rendered applicable as such'[23] by the law of the Contracting State concerned. This was not the case in the matter before the CJEU, in which there was no 'direct and unconditional renvoi to provisions of Community law so as to incorporate them into the domestic legal order' and its interpretation 'would not be binding on the national court'.[24]

This decision appears to have been weakened by two subsequent cases[25] which seem to **7.41** place fewer restrictions on jurisdiction. In these cases the CJEU held that, whilst it did have

---

[21] Joined Cases C-297/88 and C-197/89 [1990] ECR I-3763. Whilst this is considered the starting point it was actually preceded by *Thomasdünger*, n. 18.
[22] Case C-346/93 [1995] ECR I-615.
[23] Case C-346/93 [1995] ECR I-615, para. 19.
[24] Case C-346/93 [1995] ECR I-615, paras 16 and 23.
[25] Case C-28/95 *Leur-Bloem v Inspecteur der Belastingdienst 2* [1997] ECR I-4161 and Case C-130/95 *Giloy v Hauptzollamt Frankfurt am Main-Ost* [1997] ECR I-4291.

jurisdiction to interpret EU law outside its normal field of application, this would only be possible if the provisions of domestic law and the relevant contractual terms which incorporated EU provisions, clearly did not limit the application of the latter. This, in effect, requires a direct and unconditional reference to EU law (only one of the two principal requirements set out in *Kleinwort Benson*).

7.42 The CJEU's decision in other cases appears to place emphasis on the second requirement set out in *Kleinwort Benson*—that the decision must be binding on the national court. In *BIAO*,[26] the CJEU considered that it had jurisdiction on the basis that any interpretation given by the CJEU will be treated by the referring court as binding, noting:

> the German Government argues and the order for reference moreover acknowledges, that any interpretation given by the Court . . . would be binding for the resolution of the dispute in the main proceeding by the referring court.[27]

7.43 There is therefore a tension between these different tests for jurisdiction, from the low threshold outlined in *Dzodzi* to the various tests imposed in *Kleinwort Benson* which have been adopted to different extents in subsequent cases.

7.44 It is useful to look at the question of jurisdiction in a criminal context, in order to identify a scenario where a criminal offence appears to conflict with EU law.

7.45 In *Vajnai*,[28] reference was made for a preliminary ruling concerning the interpretation of the principle of non-discrimination as a fundamental principle of EU law. The reference was made in the course of criminal proceedings brought against an individual for a violation of Article 269/B of the Hungarian Criminal Code which sanctions the use of 'totalitarian symbols'.

7.46 This provision makes it unlawful to distribute, use in public, or publicly exhibit various symbols including the swastika, hammer and sickle, and five-point red star. The prosecution had been brought against the President of the Hungarian Workers' Party for displaying on his clothing a red star. The defendant was successfully prosecuted in the Central District Court and appealed against his conviction. The Metropolitan Court made a reference for a preliminary ruling and the question that arose was whether a provision in one Member State prohibiting the use of symbols of the international labour movement on pain of criminal prosecution (whereas the display of those symbols on the territory of another Member State does not give rise to any sanction) is discriminatory.

7.47 In posing this question, the national court asked whether the principle of non-discrimination contained within Article 6 TEU, Council Directive 2000/43/EC of 29 June 2000 implementing the principle of equal treatment between persons irrespective of racial or ethnic origin, or Articles 10, 11, and 12 of the Charter of Fundamental Rights of the European Union, proclaimed on 7 December 2000 in Nice, precludes a national provision imposing sanctions of the use in public of such symbols.

7.48 The CJEU held that the situation of the defendant was not connected in any way with any of the situations contemplated by the provisions of the Treaties and the Hungarian provisions

---

[26] Case C-306/99 [2003] ECR I-1.
[27] Case C-306/99 [2003] ECR I-1, para. 92.
[28] Case C-328/04 *Vajnai* [2005] ECR I-8577.

applied in the main proceedings were outside the scope of EU law. Therefore the CJEU had no jurisdiction to answer the question that had been referred.

This case was, perhaps more appropriately, also pursued before the European Court of **7.49**
Human Rights,[29] which held that there had been a violation of the freedom of expression enshrined in Article 10 ECHR and that such interference was not necessary in a democratic society.

Discretionary and mandatory references

By virtue of Article 267(2), a court or tribunal enjoys discretion in deciding whether to **7.50**
request a preliminary ruling unless there is 'no judicial remedy under national law'. Thus, a court of first instance may make a request but is not obliged to make such a request.

There are various factors that a court or tribunal may consider in the exercise of its discre- **7.51**
tion.[30] For example, it may refuse to make a request in the belief that it is possible to detect a clear, general approach to a particular question of construction from the judgments of the CJEU.[31] Conversely, in *R v The Pharmaceutical Society of Great Britain*,[32] Kerr LJ noted that he would expect the House of Lords to feel bound to make a reference and therefore concluded that an immediate reference by the Court of Appeal 'will obviously save considerable time and costs'.

In *Commissioners of Customs and Excise v Samex ApS* Bingham J noted: **7.52**

> I am very conscious of the advantages enjoyed by the Court of Justice. It has a panoramic view of the Community and its institutions, a detailed knowledge of the Treaties and of much subordinate legislation made under them, and an intimate familiarity with the functioning of the Community market which no national judge denied the collective experience of the Court of Justice could hope to achieve.[33]

In addition to this knowledge base, Bingham J noted favourably the CJEU's ability to receive **7.53**
submissions from EU institutions; its capacity to deal with the different languages used in the texts; and its understanding of the broader view of what the orderly development of the EU requires.

Guidelines for the exercise of discretion were suggested by Lord Denning MR in *H.P. Bulmer* **7.54**
Ltd v J. Bollinger SA,[34] which emphasised the complete discretion of a judge at first instance and the ability for an aggrieved party to appeal to the Court of Appeal and then to the House of Lords (where, if a point of interpretation arises, it is assumed to be worthy of reference to the CJEU). A seemingly wider interpretation was given by Sir Thomas Bingham MR in *R v Stock Exchange, ex p Else (1982) Ltd* who stated:

> I understand the correct approach in principle of a national court (other than a final court of appeal) to be quite clear: if the facts have been found and the Community law issue is critical to the court's final decision, the appropriate course is ordinarily to refer the issue to the Court

---

[29] *Vajnai v Hungary* (App. No. 33629/06).
[30] See Anthony Arnull, 'The Law Lords and the European Union: Swimming with the Incoming Tide' (2010) 35 ELRev 57 for the changing approach of the House of Lords and Supreme Court.
[31] *Pickstone and Others v Freemans Plc* [1987] 2 CMLR 572.
[32] [1987] 3 CMLR 951, 972.
[33] [1983] 3 CMLR 194, 210.
[34] [1974] Ch 401.

of Justice unless the national court can with complete confidence resolve the issue itself. In considering whether it can with complete confidence resolve the issue itself the national court must be fully mindful of the differences between national and Community legislation, of the pitfalls which face a national court venturing into what may be an unfamiliar field, of the need for uniform interpretation throughout the Community and of the great advantages enjoyed by the Court of Justice in construing Community instruments. If the national court has any real doubt, it should ordinarily refer.[35]

7.55 As noted earlier, the Information Notice on references from national courts for a preliminary ruling now provides guidance as to the point in proceedings in which it is desirable to make a reference to the CJEU (see **7.07**). However, it is well established that the national court is in principle the sole judge of whether such a reference is necessary and of the relevance of the question referred.[36]

7.56 In circumstances where a matter has reached a court or tribunal against whose decisions there is no judicial remedy, the court or tribunal is obliged to refer the question to the CJEU. Article 267(3) therefore appears to lay down a mandatory stage at which a reference must be made.

7.57 On a practical note, it is important to be aware of the stage at which no judicial remedy is available under the law of England and Wales. In *Chiron Corporation v Murex Diagnostics*,[37] the Court of Appeal held that the essence of a preliminary ruling is that it must precede the judgment of the referring court. Once the domestic court has given judgment and its order has been drawn up, it is *functus officio* and has no power to make a reference. Furthermore, the possibility of making an application to the Supreme Court for leave to appeal amounted to a 'judicial remedy'.

7.58 Therefore, if leave is granted by the Court of Appeal to the Supreme Court, it is the Supreme Court that may then make a reference. Where leave to appeal is refused, the Supreme Court will decide whether to make a reference before refusing leave or will grant leave and consider whether a reference is required at a later stage.

7.59 However, despite the apparent obligation on the highest courts to make a reference, the courts still have the option of not referring in certain circumstances, as set out in the leading case of *CILFIT v Ministry of Health*. The CJEU held:

> A court or tribunal against whose decisions there is no judicial remedy under national law is required, where a question of community law is raised before it, to comply with its obligation to bring the matter before the court of justice, unless it has established that the question raised is irrelevant or that the community provision in question has already been interpreted by the court or that the correct application of community law is so obvious as to leave no scope for any reasonable doubt. The existence of such a possibility must be assessed in the light of the specific characteristics of community law, the particular difficulties to which its interpretation gives rise and the risk of divergences in judicial decisions within the community.[38]

---

[35] [1993] 2 WLR 70, 545.
[36] Case 297/88 *Dzodzi v Belgium* [1990] ECR I-3763.
[37] [1995] All ER (EC) 88. This has been endorsed by the Court of Justice in Case C-99/00 *Lyckeskog* [2002] ECR I-4839.
[38] Case 283/81 [1982] ECR 3415, para. 21.

There are therefore three circumstances in which, in a matter where there is no judicial rem- **7.60**
edy, a court or tribunal may refuse to refer a question to the CJEU:

(a) Where a decision on a question of EU law is not necessary to enable the court or tribunal
to give judgment. Accordingly, those courts or tribunals are not obliged to refer to the
CJEU a question concerning the interpretation of EU law raised before them if that
question is not relevant, that is to say, if the answer to that question, regardless of what it
may be, can in no way affect the outcome of the case. This is also the case where the issue
to be clarified has a purely academic value or is entirely hypothetical.[39]

(b) Where an interpretation has previously been given by the CJEU thereby depriving the
obligation of its purpose and emptying it of its substance. This is especially the case when
the question raised is materially identical with a question which has already been the
subject of a preliminary ruling in a similar case. The same effect may be produced where
previous decisions of the CJEU have already dealt with the point of law in question,
irrespective of the nature of the proceedings which led to those decisions, even though
the questions at issue are not strictly identical. This doctrine is known as *acte éclairé*.

(c) Where the correct application of EU law may be so obvious as to leave no scope for any
reasonable doubt as to the manner in which the question raised is to be resolved. Before
it comes to the conclusion that such is the case, the national court or tribunal must be
convinced that the matter is equally obvious to the courts of the other Member States
and to the CJEU. This doctrine is known as *acte clair*.

In addition, there is no obligation for the court or tribunal to refer when giving judgment in **7.61**
interim proceedings, provided that the parties would be entitled to institute full proceedings,
or require that they are instituted, on the substance of the case and that the relevant question
will be re-examined and referred to the CJEU at that stage.[40]

If a court of last instance breaches Article 267(3) by failing to refer a question which does not **7.62**
fall within the exceptions noted above, it could render the Member State liable in damages
to an individual who has thereby been deprived of their EU rights,[41] albeit that the relevant
test is a high threshold to overcome.

D. The Effect of a Preliminary Ruling

The purpose of a preliminary ruling is to decide a question of law and the ruling from the **7.63**
CJEU is binding on the national court as to the interpretation of the EU provisions and acts
in question.[42]

This is also enshrined in section 3(1) of the European Communities Act 1972 which states: **7.64**

For the purposes of all legal proceedings any question as to the meaning or effect of any of
the Treaties, or as to the validity, meaning or effect of any EU instrument, shall be treated as
a question of law (and, if not referred to the European Court, be for determination as such
in accordance with the principles laid down by and any relevant decision of the European
Court).

---

[39] Case 104/79 *Foglia v Novello (No. 1)* [1980] ECR 745.
[40] Case 102/77 *Hoffmann-La Roche v Centrafarm* [1978] ECR I-1139.
[41] Case C-224/01 *Kobler v Austria* [2003] ECR I-10239.
[42] Case 52/76 *Benedetti v Munari* [1977] ECR 163.

E. Preliminary Rulings in Criminal Cases

7.65   The first reference for a preliminary ruling made by the House of Lords was in the criminal case of *R v Henn and Darby*.[43] This concerned the importation of pornographic articles of Danish origin into England from Holland, the latter being a Member State of the European Economic Community.

7.66   The appellants were charged, inter alia, with 'being knowingly concerned in the fraudulent evasion of the prohibition on importation of [indecent or obscene articles] imposed by section 42 of the Customs Consolidation Act 1876 and contrary to section 304 of the Customs and Excise Act 1952.' This prohibits the importation into the customs territory of the UK of indecent or obscene articles, and provides that articles imported contrary to the prohibition shall be forfeited and may be destroyed or otherwise disposed of as the Commissioners of Customs may direct.

7.67   One matter that arose at trial concerned the interpretation of Article 36 TEC[44] which states:

> The provisions of Articles 28 and 29 [prohibition on restrictions] shall not preclude prohibitions or restrictions on imports, exports or goods in transit justified on grounds of public morality, public policy or public security; the protection of health and life of humans, animals or plants; the protection of national treasures possessing artistic, historic or archaeological value; or the protection of industrial and commercial property. Such prohibitions or restrictions shall not, however, constitute a means of arbitrary discrimination or a disguised restriction on trade between Member States.

7.68   The trial judge and the Court of Appeal refused to refer the matter to the CJEU. However, the House of Lords in granting the appellants leave to appeal, stayed the proceedings and referred to the CJEU for a preliminary ruling. This would determine the following questions:

(1) Is the law of a Member State which prohibits the import into that State of pornographic articles a measure having equivalent effect to a quantitative restriction on imports within the meaning of Article 30 TEC?

(2) If so, does the first sentence of Article 36 upon its true construction mean that a Member State may lawfully impose prohibitions on the importation of goods from another Member State which are of an indecent or obscene character as understood by the laws of that Member State?

(3) In particular, (i) is the Member State entitled to maintain such prohibitions in order to prevent, to guard against, or to reduce the likelihood of breaches of the domestic law of all constituent parts of the customs territory of the State? (ii) is the Member State entitled to maintain such prohibitions having regard to the national standards and characteristics of that State as demonstrated by the domestic laws of the constituent parts of the customs territory of that State including the law imposing the prohibition, notwithstanding variations between the laws of the constituent parts?

(4) If a prohibition on the importation of goods is justifiable on grounds of public morality or public policy, and imposed with that purpose, can that prohibition nevertheless

---

[43]   [1981] AC 850.
[44]   Article 30 EC/Art. 36 TFEU.

amount to a means of arbitrary discrimination or a disguised restriction on trade contrary to Article 36?

(5) Independently of the questions posed, may a Member State lawfully impose prohibitions on the importation of such goods from another Member State by reference to obligations arising from the Geneva Convention 1923, for the suppression of the traffic in obscene publications and the Universal Postal Union bearing in mind the provisions of Article 234 of the Treaty?

On the reference, the CJEU held: **7.69**

(1) That any law of a Member State which prohibited the importation of pornographic material constituted a measure having the equivalent effect to a quantitative restriction and accordingly was prima facie in conflict with Article 30 TEC.

(2) That the power to impose prohibitions on the importation from other Member States of articles of an indecent or obscene character on the grounds of public morality was within the powers reserved to Member States under the first sentence of Article 36 of the Treaty; moreover, for those purposes, each Member State could determine the requirements of public morality in accordance with its own scale of values and select the appropriate form of legislation; and the existence of variations in the laws of different constituent parts of a Member State did not preclude the application of the appropriate domestic law to the whole of the Member State's territory.

(3) That if a prohibition on the importation of certain goods were justified on grounds of public morality in accordance with the first sentence in Article 36 of the Treaty and if it were imposed for that purpose, the enforcement of the prohibition could not, in the absence of a lawful trade in the goods in question in the Member State, constitute a means of arbitrary discrimination or a disguised restriction on trade contrary to the second sentence in Article 36.

(4) That so far as a Member State availed itself of the reservation relating to public morality in Article 36 of the Treaty, Article 234 did not preclude that State from fulfilling its obligations under the Geneva Convention 1923 for the suppression of traffic in obscene publications and the Universal Postal Union.

In applying the CJEU's answers to the facts of the instant case, the House of Lords dismissed   **7.70**
the appeal. The jury had found that the relevant Articles were of such a character as to fall within the prohibition under the Obscene Publications Act 1959, as amended, of trading in them for gain in England, as well as under the prohibition of importation under the Customs Consolidation Act 1876, it therefore followed that in the present case there had not been any arbitrary discrimination or disguised restriction on trade between Member States within the meaning of Article 36 of the EEC Treaty.

Examples of preliminary rulings outside England and Wales

The following are examples of references for preliminary rulings being made in the context   **7.71**
of criminal proceedings from outside the jurisdiction of England and Wales:

- In *Criminal Proceedings against Gueye*[45] and *Criminal Proceedings against Sanchez*,[46] the CJEU was asked for a preliminary ruling on whether a person who had committed

---

[45] Case C-483/09 [2011].
[46] Case C-1/10 [2011].

domestic violence could be subjected to the mandatory imposition of an injunction to stay away from the victim who themselves opposed the injunction. Both defendants had been found guilty of failing to comply with the restrictions.

The issue concerned the interpretation of Decision 2001/220, which concerns the standing of victims in criminal proceedings. The appeal court asked the CJEU whether (a) the mandatory imposition of the prohibitions in these circumstances was precluded by Article 2, 3, or 8 of the Decision and (b) whether Article 10 enabled Member States, having regard to the particular category of offences committed within the family, to exclude recourse to mediation in all criminal proceedings relating to such offences.

The preliminary ruling held that the aim of the Decision was only that minimum standards should be drawn up for the protection of victims of crimes and that they should be afforded the highest level of protection, particularly in respect of access to justice. It did not impose an obligation to treat the victim in a manner equivalent to a party to the proceedings and the procedural right to be heard under Article 3 did not confer any rights on victims in respect of the choice of punishment. Furthermore, the aim of Article 8 was to ensure a suitable level of protection for victims, it did not enable the victim to influence the penalties which national courts impose. Articles 2, 3, and 8 did not preclude the imposition of such an injunction despite the victim of the crime opposing such a measure. Finally, Article 10 did no more than require Member States to seek to promote mediation in criminal cases for offences which they considered appropriate—the choice of the offences for which this was available was for the Member State to determine.

In *Criminal Proceedings against Gasparini*,[47] the CJEU was asked for a preliminary ruling on whether an acquittal in one Member State on the ground that the prosecution was time-barred came within Article 54 of the Convention implementing the Schengen Agreement to prevent trial of the accused on the same facts in another Member State.

The defendant had been charged with smuggling offences in Spain concerning olive oil from outside the EU. However, he had previously been acquitted of similar charges in Portugal on the ground that the prosecution was time-barred.

Article 54 states:

A person whose trial has been finally disposed of in one Contracting Party may not be prosecuted in another Contracting Party for the same acts provided that, if a penalty has been imposed, it has been enforced, is actually in the process of being enforced or can no longer be enforced under the laws of the sentencing Contracting Party.

The Spanish court referred to the CJEU the following questions: whether Article 54 applied to cases where an accused had been acquitted because of time limitations; to whom Article 54 applied; and whether the goods concerned in such cases could be taken as being in free circulation in other Member States.

The preliminary ruling held that Article 54 prevented a person being prosecuted in a Member State when he had been tried on the same facts in another Member State and the matter had been 'finally disposed of'. This term was not defined in Article 54 and, thus, it could not be restricted to convictions. An acquittal was sufficient to come within the meaning of this term. The application of this Article was not made conditional upon the harmonisation of time limitations and to disregard an acquittal in these circumstances would undermine its objective. The Article applied to all those who had a trial finally

---

[47] Case C-467/04 [2006] ECR I-9199.

disposed of in a Member State. Finally, an acquittal had no effect on the classification of the goods, which could not therefore be deemed to be in free circulation on that basis alone.

• In *Criminal Proceedings against Gozutok* and *Criminal Proceedings against Brugge*,[48] the CJEU was asked for a preliminary ruling on whether further prosecution was similarly barred in one Contracting State when the accused had paid a fine determined by the prosecuting authority in another Member State.

In the first case, a defendant had been prosecuted in the Netherlands for dealing in narcotics and the proceedings were discontinued after paying a fine to the Public Prosecutor's Office. He was subsequently prosecuted and convicted in Germany. In the second case, a German national was being prosecuted in Belgium for an offence of intentional assault and wounding alleged to have been committed in that country. During these proceedings, German criminal proceedings were started and discontinued after the payment of a fine to the Public Prosecutor's Office there. Both of these cases concerned the definition of 'finally disposed of' under Article 54 of the Convention implementing the Schengen Agreement.

The preliminary ruling held that where further prosecution was definitively barred following a procedure in which the accused paid a fine to the prosecuting authority, he was someone whose case had been 'finally disposed of' under Article 54. This procedure (the effect of which was laid down by the applicable national law) was dependent upon the accused's undertaking to perform certain obligations prescribed by the Public Prosecutor and penalised the unlawful conduct that the accused was alleged to have committed. Furthermore, the CJEU held that once the accused had complied with their obligations, the penalty had to be regarded as 'enforced'. The fact that the court was not involved in this process did not cast doubt on the interpretation.

F. Direct Actions and Appeals

Actions before the General Court

The General Court can also hear direct actions by those who consider that the actions of the EU have had an adverse effect on them. These include both actions brought by one Member State against another, in order to enforce compliance with Treaty obligations, but also actions for: judicial review of EU acts seeking to annul those acts; actions to remedy failures by EU institutions to act; or to recover damages in respect of loss suffered as a result of EU action.[49]   **7.72**

The right of an individual to commence proceedings depends on whether the individual has *locus standi*. This is defined in Article 263 (ex Art. 230 EC) as: **7.73**

> Any natural or legal person may . . . institute proceedings against an act addressed to that person or which is of direct and individual concern to them, and against a regulatory act which is of direct concern to them and does not entail implementing measures.

In respect of what is meant by an 'act' addressed to an individual applicant, this is commonly a Commission Decision on a breach of competition law. Prior to being amended by the TFEU, the wording of this condition was 'Decision' addressed to an individual. In practice, acts usually take the form of Decisions.   **7.74**

---

[48] Joined Cases C-187/01 and C-385/01 [2003] ECR I-1345.
[49] Articles 263, 265, and 340 TFEU.

7.75   In relation to what is meant by an act addressed to another person, this will commonly take the form of a Decision addressed to a Member State. Where this is the basis for an applicant's admissibility, the additional condition of direct concern which does not entail an implementation measure comes into effect.

7.76   Direct concern requires an applicant to show that there is an unbroken line of causation between the act complained of and the complaint, or damage. Therefore, where damage is sustained as a result of implementation which is within the discretion of a Member State, the application will not be admissible because the applicant is affected by the implementation of the act as opposed to the act itself.[50]

7.77   The requirement for individual concern is the element of the admissibility test that often prevents an individual from proving admissibility. It is a restrictively applied test. It has been defined in the case law of the Gerneral Court to mean that persons other than those to whom a decision is addressed are only individually concerned if the Decision affects them 'by reason of certain attributes which are peculiar to them or by reason of circumstances in which they are differentiated from all other persons.'[51] The restrictive approach of the General Court has been a matter of dispute, but remains intact.

7.78   The term 'regulatory act' is not defined in the Treaties. The TFEU removed a previous distinction between legislative acts (as a result of legislative procedures of the Council and Parliament) and non-legislative acts (by the Commission under its delegated powers). It will be for the Courts of the EU to determine how the term is defined and this will have a clear impact on the width of admissibility and the ability of individuals to bring direct actions.

7.79   The jurisdiction of the General Court is prescribed in Article 256 TFEU:

> The General Court shall have jurisdiction to hear and determine at first instance actions or proceedings referred to in Articles 263, 265, 268, 270 and 272, with the exception of those assigned to a specialised court set up under Article 257 and those reserved in the Statute for the Court of Justice. The Statute may provide for the General Court to have jurisdiction for other classes of action or proceeding.

7.80   It can hear and determine first instance, direct actions brought by individuals which are referred to in Articles 263, 265, 268, 270, and 272 TFEU, with the exception of those assigned to a specialised court set up in Article 257 or reserved in the Statute for the Court of Justice (see those under Arts 263 and 265 TFEU reserved by Art. 51 of the Statute).

7.81   Article 263 TFEU cases are those which relate to acts of the EU institutions. Article 265 cases relate to cases where it is alleged that the EU institutions have failed to act. Article 268 cases are those where compensation is sought pursuant to Article 340(2) and (3). Article 270 cases are those which can be described as staff cases. Article 272 cases are those brought pursuant to an arbitration clause in a contract concluded by or on behalf of the EU.

7.82   Article 51 of the Statute derogates from the rule set out in Article 256(1), so that at present cases which involve a Member State bringing a direct action against an act or failure to act by the European Council or European Parliament go to the CJEU not the General Court.

---

[50] Case 222/83 *Municipality of Differdange v Commission* [1984] ECR 2889.
[51] Case 25/62 *Plaumann v Commission* [1963] ECR 95 and see also Case 11/82 *Paraiki-Patraiki v Commission* [1985] ECR 207.

Article 51, however, grants to the General Court jurisdiction over actions brought by a Member State against acts or decisions of the European Council in respect of State aid (Art. 108(2)(iii) TFEU), anti-dumping (Art. 207 TFEU), and exercising implementing powers under reference to Article 291(2) TFEU.

Appellate function of the Court of Justice

Article 256(1) TFEU provides a right of appeal from a decision of the General Court to the CJEU on points of law only and subject to conditions. Decisions given by the General Court under this paragraph may be subject to a right of appeal to the Court of Justice on points of law only, under the conditions and within the limits laid down by the Statute. **7.83**

An appeal may, therefore, be brought on a point of law. This includes 'lack of competence of the General Court, a breach of procedure before it which adversely affects the interests of the appellant as well as the infringement of Union law by the General Court': Article 58 of the Statute. There is no right to appeal the quantum of costs ordered or a decision to order a party to pay costs. **7.84**

The CJEU does not have any jurisdiction on appeal to establish facts, or to examine the evidence which was adduced before the General Court to support the facts found by that Court. As was made clear in *Lafarge SA v European Commission*:[52] **7.85**

> Provided that the evidence has been properly obtained and the general principles of law and the rules of procedure in relation to the burden of proof and the taking of evidence have been observed, it is for the General Court alone to assess the value which should be attached to the evidenced produced to it.

If it can be argued that the evidence was distorted, a review of the evidence cannot constitute a point of law.[53] If it is alleged that the evidence has been distorted, the appeal must specify precisely what evidence is said to have been distorted and show the errors in its appraisal that led to the distortion as required by Article 112(1)(c) of the Rules of Procedure.[54] Evidence has been found to be distorted such as to fulfil the test where, without recourse to new evidence, the assessment of the existing evidence was manifestly incorrect.[55] **7.86**

The appellate jurisdiction of the CJEU is one of review only, including review of the issues of law raised before the General Court. Therefore, the point of law may only be argued if it was raised in the General Court. This was also set out clearly in the *Lafarge*[56] case: **7.87**

> To allow a party to put forward for the first time before the Court of Justice a plea in law and arguments which it has not raised before the General Court would be to authorise it to bring before the Court of Justice, whose jurisdiction in appeals is limited, a case of wider ambit than that which came before the General Court.[57]

---

[52] Case C-413/08 P [2010] ECR I-5361, para. 15 and Case C-122/01 P *T. Port v Commission* [2003] ECR I-4261; Case C-167/06 P *Komninou and Others v Commission* [2007] ECR I-147.

[53] Case C-9/95 P *New Holland v Commission* [1988] ECR I-3175.

[54] Cases C-204/00 P, C-205/00 P, C-211/00 P, C213/00 P, C-217/00 P, and C-219/00 P *Aalborg Portland and Others v Commission* [2004] ECR I-123.

[55] Case C-229/05 P *PKK v KNK v Council* [2007] ECR I-439.

[56] Case C-413/08 P *Lafarge v Commission* [2010] ECR I-5361, para. 15.

[57] Case C-266/97 P *VBA v VBG and Others* [2000] ECR I-2135; Case C-167/04 P *JCB Service v Commission* [2006] ECR I-8935.

Conditions/limitations

7.88 Conditions and limitations upon the right to appeal are to be found in the Statute of the Court of Justice.

7.89 First,[58] an appeal must be brought within two months of the notification of the decision appealed against.

7.90 Decisions which can be appealed are either final decisions of the General Court or those which dispose of the substantive issues in part only or dispose of a procedural issue concerning a plea of lack of competence or inadmissibility.[59]

7.91 An appeal can be brought by any party who has been, in whole or in part, unsuccessful in the submissions they made before the General Court. Interveners may also appeal. In the case of interveners who are not either a Member State or an EU institution, there is a requirement that they are directly affected by the decision of the General Court: Article 56 of the Statute. In all cases except those which relate to proceedings between the EU and its servants, a Member State of the EU institution which was not involved in the proceedings before the General Court may intervene on appeal. There is also a right to appeal a decision not to permit a party to intervene; there is a two-week time limit on such appeals.[60]

Procedure of appeal

7.92 Article 59 of the Statute establishes the structure of the procedure that is adopted on appeal. There is a written and an oral part, but subject to the Rules, the CJEU, upon hearing the Advocate-General and the parties, may dispense with the oral procedure.

7.93 An appeal does not have the effect of suspending the decision made by the General Court. However, in cases where the decision of the General Court had the effect of declaring a regulation to be void, the regulation is not void until the two month period for an appeal has expired, or from the date when an appeal has been dismissed.[61]

7.94 Where the CJEU finds that an appeal from the General Court is well founded, it must quash the General Court's decision: Article 61. If this occurs, the Court of Justice has a choice: it may either give final judgment itself or, where the state of the proceedings so permits, refer the case back to the General Court for judgment. In the latter case, the General Court is bound by the decision of the CJEU on the point of law.[62]

7.95 If a well-founded appeal has been brought by a Member State or an EU institution which was not a intervening party in the General Court, the CJEU may, if it considers this necessary, state which of the effects of the decision of the General Court which has been quashed must be considered as definitive in respect of the parties to the litigation.[63]

7.96 General rules about time limits are provided in the Rules of Procedure of the Court of Justice in Title II, Chapter 8, Article 80:

- the day on which a decision or act is done is not counted as part of the time limit (Art. 80(1)(a));

---

[58] Statute, Art. 56.
[59] Statute, Art. 56.
[60] Statute, Art. 57.
[61] Statute, Art. 60.
[62] Statute, Art. 61.
[63] Statute, Art. 61.

- when a limit is expressed in days, weeks, or months, the limit will expire on the same day, day in the week, or day on the month as it began (Art. 80(1)(b));
- it does not include weekends and holidays (Art. 80(1)(d)); but
- where a limit expires on a weekend or holiday, the expiry is extended to the next working day (Art. 80(2)).

Further rules as to procedure of appeals can be found in Title IV of the Rules of Procedure of **7.97** the Court of Justice. Among them are the following:

- an appeal is issued by means of being lodged at the Registry of the General Court or CJEU (Art. 111(1));
- it must be served on all parties (Art. 114);
- any response must be lodged within two months (Art. 115).

What the appeal notice should contain is described in Article 113; what a response should con- **7.98** tain is described in Article 115. There are also rules governing the order of costs of an appeal.[64]

Appeal by Court of Justice of its own motion

The Court of Justice may itself institute an appeal from a decision by the General Court in **7.99** the cases provided for in Article 256(2) and (3) TFEU, if the First Advocate-General consid- ers that there is a serious risk of the unity or consistency of EU law being affected, he may invite the CJEU to review the decision of the General Court.[65]

Once the First Advocate-General has made the proposal, the CJEU then decides whether it **7.100** will review the decision in question on appeal.

The two-month time limit still applies overall, but it is divided between these two stages: the **7.101** invitation by the First Advocate-General must be issued within one month and thereafter the CJEU must make its decision as to whether or not there should be an appeal within a further one month.[66]

Appellate function of the General Court

Article 257(3) TFEU provides a right of appeal from a decision of a specialised court to the **7.102** General Court on points of law only unless the regulation which establishes the specialised court from which the appeal lies expressly provides for a right of appeal on matters of fact.

In addition, there is a further right of appeal in such cases from the General Court to the **7.103** CJEU where there is 'a serious risk of the unity or consistency of Union law being affected'. This right of appeal is exceptional.

As with appeals from the General Court to the CJEU, they are subject to conditions: **7.104**

> Decisions given by the General Court under this paragraph may be subject to a right of appeal to the Court of Justice on points of law only, under the conditions and within the limits laid down by the Statute.

The rules governing the only specialised court in existence at present contain provisions **7.105** governing this route of appeal at Articles 9–13.

---

[64] Rules of Procedure of the Court of Justice, Art. 122.
[65] Statute, Art. 62.
[66] Statute, Art. 61.

GLOSSARY OF EU TERMS

Acte clair　A doctrine of EU law pursuant to which domestic courts may refuse to refer a matter for a **Preliminary Ruling**. It applies where the correct interpretation of EU law is so obvious as to leave no scope for any reasonable doubt as to the manner in which the question raised is to be resolved.

Acte éclairé　A doctrine of EU law pursuant to which domestic courts may refuse to refer a matter for a **Preliminary Ruling**. It applies where an interpretation has previously been given by the **Court of Justice**. The doctrine has especial force when the question raised is materially identical to a question which has already been the subject of a Preliminary Ruling in a similar case. The doctrine also applies where previous decisions of the Court of Justice have already dealt with the point of law in question, irrespective of the nature of the proceedings which led to those decisions, even though the questions at issue are not strictly identical.

Area of Freedom, Security and Justice (AFSJ)　A policy area of **Shared Competence** falling under **Title V TFEU** post-**Treaty of Lisbon**. The AFSJ applies to: border control, immigration, and asylum; judicial cooperation in civil matters; judicial cooperation in criminal matters; and police cooperation.

Charter of Fundamental Human Rights (the Charter)　A statement of certain civil, political, economic, and social rights drawn from a variety of international, European, and national sources. It aims to provide in a single document the rights already recognised within the Union which apply to **Member States** when applying EU law. Following the **Treaty of Lisbon**, the Charter was signed by the Union (in its own right) and now has the same legal force as the Treaties.

Commission　An institution established under the **Treaty of Brussels**. One of the three institutions of the Union with legislative competence (see also the **European Parliament** and the **Council**). Based in Brussels, it comprises one representative from each **Member State**, appointed by the Member States with the approval of the European Parliament. The representatives are independent of the Member States and act in the interests of the Union. The Commission proposes the form and content of Union legislation.

Conferral　A principle of EU law. It provides that the competence of the Union to legislate is voluntarily conferred by its **Member States** (usually under the Treaties).

Contra Legem　Literally: against the law. The principle that, in certain circumstances, a court may make a determination that is contrary to the existing law.

Council　The institution formerly known as the Council of Ministers. It is comprised of the Heads of State of the **Member States** as well as the President of the Council and the President of the **Commission**. The Council is not a legislative body of the Union but serves to direct its political development; as such it is indirectly involved in the legislative process. It consists of representatives of the governments of Member States including ministers. The representatives present in the Council vary depending on the issue under consideration. The Presidency of the Council rotates between the Member States. The Council may invite the Commission to propose legislation.

Council of Europe　An organisation to be distinguished from the Union, the Council of Europe is a wholly separate international organisation, formed in 1949 and now comprised of some 47 States. Parties commit themselves to policy decisions through conventions; the most significant being the **European Convention on Human Rights**.

Council of Ministers　See **Council**.

Court of First Instance (CFI)　See **General Court**.

Court of Justice   A Court of the EU. Based in Luxembourg, it comprises one judge from each **Member State** and eight Advocates-General, who may submit an Opinion to the Court. The justices and the Advocates-General serve for renewable periods of six years with one sitting as President for a renewable period of three years. The Court normally sits as three or five justices but may sit as a **Grand Chamber**. A single judgment is handed down, with no dissenting judgments. See also **General Court** and **Specialised Courts**. Proceedings may be brought by way of **Direct Action** or **Preliminary Ruling**.

Decision   A form of Union legislation, binding on those to whom it is addressed. It may be addressed directly to **Member States** or individuals. Decisions were one of the legislative instruments available under the **Third Pillar**.

Direct Action   Legal proceedings commenced and finally determined in the **General Court** or the **Court of Justice**.

Direct Effect   The legal doctrine pursuant to which certain Union legislation is directly enforceable within **Member States**.

Directive   A form of Union legislation to be implemented by each **Member State** by way of its domestic law. A Directive may have **Direct Effect** in certain circumstances.

Double Jeopardy   The principle in common law jurisdictions that a person cannot be prosecuted twice for the same offence. See also *Ne bis in idem*.

Dual Criminality   The principle that a particular criminal offence exists in materially the same form in two jurisdictions.

EC Treaty (TEC)   The Treaty Establishing the European Community: in effect the **Treaty of Rome**, as renamed following the **Treaty on European Union**. It became the TFEU post-**Treaty of Lisbon**.

ECRIS   The European Criminal Records Information System: software established under two **Directives** in 2009, through which **Member States** can share criminal record information from national databases with other Member States; it is not yet operational.

Enhanced Cooperation   A legislative process under Articles 82(3) and 83(3) **TFEU** whereby **Member States**, if acting in a group of at least nine, may adopt as between themselves Union legislation which has been vetoed by another Member State.

Eurojust   An EU agency established in 2002 to facilitate judicial cooperation. Its purposes are threefold: (a) to coordinate national investigations and prosecutions; (b) to improve cooperation between national authorities, in particular by facilitating judicial cooperation and mutual recognition; (c) to support the effectiveness of national investigations and prosecutions. It deals with large and complex cross-border cases, usually involving more than two **Member States**.

European Arrest Warrant   An arrest warrant valid throughout the **Member States**. Once issued, it requires a Member State to arrest and extradite the subject to the requesting Member State unless certain circumstances apply.

European Atomic Energy Community (Euratom)   One of the early institutions which pre-figured the Union, it was created under the **Treaty of Rome** by France, Germany, Italy, Belgium, the Netherlands, and Luxembourg to oversee the peaceful development of atomic energy.

European Coal and Steel Community (ECSC)   The community of nations formed by France, Germany, Italy, Belgium, the Netherlands, and Luxembourg under the **Treaty of Paris**. The signatories agreed to organise their heavy industry under common management, establishing a common market in coal and steel.

European Commission   See **Commission**.

European Community (EC)   The re-named **EEC** following the **Treaty of European Union**; it was renamed to reflect a wider set of policy aims than economic integration and became part of the **First Pillar**.

European Convention on Human Rights (ECHR)   A declaration of rights and freedoms that came into being in 1953 and was based on the Universal Declaration of Human Rights. It was subscribed to by parties to the **Council of Europe** and established the European Court of Human

Rights. It is given domestic effect under UK law by the Human Rights Act 1998. Note that under the **Treaty of Lisbon**, the Union is obliged to accede to the ECHR in its own right.

European Economic Community (EEC)   An early but narrower incarnation of the Union, created under the **Treaty of Rome** to develop a common market between the founding countries and to foster economic integration. It shared a common set of institutions and comprised the ECSC and **Euratom**. It was renamed as the **European Community** post-**Treaty of European Union** and became part of the core activities of the Union under the **First Pillar**.

European Evidence Warrant   A system requiring **Member States** automatically to recognise search warrants issued in criminal proceedings for certain offences in other Member States. The proposal was adopted in a **Framework Decision** but domestic implementing legislation has not yet been brought into force in the UK.

European Investigation Order   A legislative proposal (currently in the form of a draft **Directive**) to reform the existing regime for obtaining evidence in criminal proceedings between **Member States**. The proposal includes replacing the current **Framework Decision** on the **European Evidence Warrant**.

European Parliament   One of the legislative institutions of the Union. Citizens of the **Member States** elect representatives (MEPs) every five years. It sits in Strasbourg, although meetings of its committees may be held in Brussels and its Secretariat is based in Luxembourg. It may invite the **Commission** to propose legislation in certain circumstances.

European Protection Orders   A measure which, once issued, obliges a **Member State** to take appropriate measures under its domestic law to enforce a judgment passed in another Member State aimed at protecting a victim.

European Union   The economic and political union of **Member States**, as renamed under the **Treaty on European Union**. Pre-**Treaty of Lisbon** it was comprised of the **First Pillar**, **Second Pillar**, and **Third Pillar**.

Europol   A law enforcement agency which handles criminal intelligence and aims to further police cooperation between **Member States**. It was created as the European Police Office in 1998 and is based in The Hague.

Exclusive Competence   One of the divisions of policy competence introduced by the **Treaty of Lisbon**; it relates to areas in which the Union has exclusive competence to make **Directives** and conclude international agreements when provided for in a Union legislative act.

Extradition   The formal legal process by which persons accused or convicted of crime are surrendered from one State to another for trial or punishment.

First Pillar   A core area of Union activity and decision making (including the **EC**, the **ECSC**, and **Euratom**) under the Treaty on European Union. The areas of competence under the First Pillar included economic, social, and environmental policies and matters of immigration, asylum, and visas. The First Pillar was supranational in character and its activities were governed by the **Council**, the **Commission**, the **European Parliament**, and **Court of Justice**. The 'pillar' structure was abandoned post-**Treaty of Lisbon**.

Framework Decision   A type of legislation (replacing **Joint Actions**) used in relation to **Third Pillar** policy and decision making. Framework Decisions required **Member States** to achieve particular results without specifying the mechanism by which to do so. They could be proposed by a **Member State** or by the **Commission**, and were then adopted by decision of the **Council**. Unlike **Directives** there was no scope for Framework Decisions to have **Direct Effect**.

General Court   (Previously the Court of First Instance.) The General Court comprises one judge appointed from each **Member State** for a renewable term of six years. It has jurisdiction to hear and determine at first instance proceedings for the review of legislative acts of the Union institutions. The jurisdiction of the General Court to review the legality of legislative acts is confined to applications made by certain individuals. Where the General Court reviews a legislative act, its decision may be appealed to the **Court of Justice** on a point of law.

Grand Chamber   The **Court of Justice** sitting as a tribunal of 13 justices, chaired by the President.

Hague Programme   The **Council**'s 2004 programme initiative to combat terrorism and cross-border and other serious crime. It aimed to involve more intensive practical cooperation between police and customs authorities of **Member States**.

Joint Action   A method of decision making and policy implementation, introduced by the **Treaty on European Union**. It was used in relation to **Third Pillar** policy areas. It was succeeded by the system of **Framework Decisions**.

Locus standi   Standing to bring legal action; in this context, standing to bring legal proceedings in one of the courts of the Union. See **Court of Justice**, **General Court**, and **Specialised Court**.

Maastricht Treaty   See **Treaty on European Union**.

Member State   A country Member State of the Union. Currently the Member States are: Austria, Belgium, Bulgaria, Cyprus, the Czech Republic, Denmark, Estonia, Finland, France, Germany, Greece, Hungary, Ireland, Italy, Latvia, Lithuania, Luxembourg, Malta, the Netherlands, Poland, Portugal, Romania, Slovakia, Slovenia, Spain, Sweden, the UK.

Merger Treaty   See **Treaty of Brussels**.

Mutual Legal Assistance   The formal systems and practices by which **Member States** (and countries worldwide) cooperate in relation to criminal investigations and proceedings.

Mutual Recognition   The concept of mutual respect for the judicial processes and outcomes of other **Member States** under which the courts of one **Member State** must recognise and enforce the decisions of another, without reviewing the basis on which those decisions were made.

Ne bis in idem   Literally: not twice in the same. The term refers to the Roman law principle that no legal action can be instituted twice in relation to the same cause. In common law jurisdictions, it is frequently expressed as the principle of **Double Jeopardy**.

Official Journal of the European Union (OJ)   The official gazette of record of the Union. Only legislative acts published in the Official Journal are binding. It may be accessed at <http://eur-lex.europa.eu/JOIndex.do>.

OLAF   L'Office européen de lutte antifraude, or the European Anti-Fraud Office. An agency formally attached to the **Commission** which exists to investigate fraud within the Union.

Preliminary Ruling   Proceedings in the **Court of Justice** brought by way of a reference from a domestic court of a **Member State** for a determination on a point of EU law.

Proportionality   A principle of EU law. It provides that where the Union acts (for example, by legislation), the content and form of that action must be no more than is necessary to achieve the objectives of the Treaties. See also **Conferral** and **Subsidiarity**. Note that it is a more narrow concept than that which applies under the **European Convention on Human Rights**.

Prüm Treaty   Signed originally between Belgium, Germany, France, Spain, Luxembourg, the Netherlands, and Austria and since adopted throughout the Union by way of a **Decision**, the Treaty seeks to enhance cooperation between **Member States** by providing for automatic searching or comparison of data on to databases in each country covering DNA, fingerprints, and vehicle registration data. Currently a number of countries (including the UK) have failed to implement it.

Regulation   Union legislation that is binding and enforceable per se in **Member States**; it is legislation that has **Direct Effect**.

Renvoi   In the context of conflict of laws: an aspect of the choice of laws by which the applicable law is determined.

Roadmap   Adopted as part of the **Stockholm Programme**, the Roadmap is a statement of policy which sets out six measures to be implemented for the development of equivalent standards of basic procedural rights for defendants in criminal proceedings across **Member States**.

Schengen (and related terms)   An agreement signed in 1985 at Schengen in Luxembourg between all the then **Member States** of the Union apart from the UK and Ireland: the **Schengen Agreement** was followed in 1990 by the **Convention Implementing the Schengen Agreement**. Following these agreements the **Schengen Area** came into effect in 1995 which abolished the internal borders of the signatory States and created a single external border. Further measures were taken to improve cooperation between the law enforcement and judicial authorities operating within the Schengen Area. The measures are known collectively as the **Schengen Acquis**.

Second Pillar   Created as one of two further areas of decision making (in addition to the **First Pillar**) by the **Treaty on European Union**. The Second Pillar dealt with Common Foreign and Security Policy: viz foreign policy and military matters. Decisions in this area were made intergovernmentally rather than supranationally. The 'pillar' structure was abandoned post-**Treaty of Lisbon**.

Shared Competence   One of the divisions of policy competence introduced by the **Treaty of Lisbon**. Shared Competence applies to policy areas in which the **Member States** cannot exercise competence where the Union has done so. However, where the Union has not acted, or has decided not to act, Member States may exercise their competence. The **AFSJ** is an area of Shared Competence.

Specialised Courts   Article 257 TFEU authorised the creation of certain specialised courts whose decisions will be subject to appeal to the **General Court**. To date, the only specialised court of the Union that has been established is the Civil Service Tribunal.

Stockholm Programme   One of the Union programmes outlining priorities for the **AFSJ**. The Stockholm Programme deals with the period 2010–2014. It focuses on rights in the criminal process for both those who are accused and victims and also a further development in the programme of mutual recognition of court decisions in criminal cases with measures to strengthen mutual trust. It includes the **Roadmap**.

Subsidiarity   A principle of EU law. It provides that the Union may only intervene where it would be more effective that the **Member States** act together, rather than alone; accordingly, Member States are to take action so far as possible alone before the Union intervenes.

Supporting Competence   One of the divisions of policy competence introduced by the **Treaty of Lisbon**. Within an area of Supporting Competence, the Union has no legislative power but can only support, coordinate, or supplement the policies of **Member States**.

Third Pillar   Created as one of two further areas of decision making (in addition to the **First Pillar**) by the **Treaty on European Union**. The Third Pillar dealt with Justice and Home Affairs (later known as Police and Judicial Cooperation in Criminal Matters). It operated intergovernmentally by the **Council** voting unanimously. The **Court of Justice** was excluded from operating its powers in relation to matters falling within the Third Pillar. Policy implementation was frequently by means of **Joint Action** and, later, **Framework Decisions**. The 'pillar' structure was abandoned post-**Treaty of Lisbon**.

Title V TFEU   See **AFSJ**.

Treaty of Brussels (Merger Treaty)   Signed in 1965. Consolidated the institutions of the **ECSC**, **Euratom**, and the **EEC**. The executive bodies of the ECSC and Euratom were subsumed into the **Commission** and the **Council**. The **Court of Justice** and the Parliamentary Assembly (the forerunner of the **European Parliament**), and the Commission and the Council were common to all three communities.

Treaty of Lisbon   Entered into force on 1 December 2009. Abolished the 'pillar' system in favour of a single entity and the consolidation of all the aspects of the European Communities into the legal personality of the **European Union**. Legislation now follows the old **First Pillar** mechanism. Areas of policy are divided into competencies which are either areas of **Exclusive Competence**, **Shared Competence**, or **Supporting Competence**.

Treaty of Paris Signed in 1951 between France, Germany, Italy, Belgium, the Netherlands, and Luxembourg. Established the **European Coal and Steel Community** (ECSC) and created a High Authority, an **Assembly**, a **Council**, and a **Court of Justice**.

Treaty of Rome Entered into by France, Germany, Italy, Belgium, the Netherlands, and Luxembourg in 1957, creating the **European Economic Community** (EEC) and **European Atomic Energy Community** (Euratom). Its full name was the Treaty Establishing the European Economic Community. It was renamed the **TEC** (or **EC Treaty**) under the **Treaty of Maastricht**.

Treaty on European Union (Maastricht Treaty) Signed in 1992, it created the **European Union** and established the **First Pillar**, **Second Pillar**, and **Third Pillar** structure of policy areas. Its objectives included the promotion of economic and social progress, the removal of internal frontiers, the establishment of economic and monetary union, a common foreign policy, strengthening the protection of the rights and interests of the nationals of its **Member States**, and developing close cooperation on justice and home affairs.

Treaty on the Functioning of the European Union (TFEU) This was formerly known as the **EC Treaty** or TEC but renamed under the **Treaty of Lisbon**. Following the abolition of the 'pillar' structure the **European Union** ceased to exist separated from the **European Community**.

Appendices

APPENDIX A

UK Statute
European Communities Act 1972,
sections 2 and 3 (as amended)

2. General implementation of Treaties

(1) All such rights, powers, liabilities, obligations and restrictions from time to time created or arising by or under the Treaties, and all such remedies and procedures from time to time provided for by or under the Treaties, as in accordance with the Treaties are without further enactment to be given legal effect or used in the United Kingdom shall be recognised and available in law, and be enforced, allowed and followed accordingly; and the expression 'enforceable EU right' and similar expressions shall be read as referring to one to which this subsection applies.

(2) Subject to Schedule 2 to this Act, at any time after its passing Her Majesty may by Order in Council, and any designated Minister or department may by order, rules, regulations or scheme, make provision—

    (a) for the purpose of implementing any EU obligation of the United Kingdom, or enabling any such obligation to be implemented, or of enabling any rights enjoyed or to be enjoyed by the United Kingdom under or by virtue of the Treaties to be exercised; or

    (b) for the purpose of dealing with matters arising out of or related to any such obligation or rights or the coming into force, or the operation from time to time, of subsection (1) above;

and in the exercise of any statutory power or duty, including any power to give directions or to legislate by means of orders, rules, regulations or other subordinate instrument, the person entrusted with the power or duty may have regard to the objects of the EU and to any such obligation or rights as aforesaid.

In this subsection 'designated Minister or department' means such Minister of the Crown or government department as may from time to time be designated by Order in Council in relation to any matter or for any purpose, but subject to such restrictions or conditions (if any) as may be specified by the Order in Council.

(3) [Deleted]

(4) The provision that may be made under subsection (2) above includes, subject to Schedule 2 to this Act, any such provision (of any such extent) as might be made by Act of Parliament, and any enactment passed or to be passed, other than one contained in this part of this Act, shall be construed and have effect subject to the foregoing provisions of this section; but, except as may be provided by any Act passed after this Act, Schedule 2 shall have effect in connection with the powers conferred by this and the following sections of this Act to make Orders in Council or orders, rules, regulations or schemes.

(5) [Deleted]

(6) [Deleted]

3. Decisions on, and proof of, Treaties and EU instruments etc.

(1) For the purposes of all legal proceedings any question as to the meaning or effect of any of the Treaties, or as to the validity, meaning or effect of any EU instrument, shall be treated as a question of law (and, if not referred to the European Court, be for determination as such in accordance with the principles laid down by and any relevant decision of the European Court).

(2) Judicial notice shall be taken of the Treaties, of the Official Journal of the European Union and of any decision of, or expression of opinion by, the European Court on any such question as aforesaid; and the Official Journal shall be admissible as evidence of any instrument or other act thereby communicated of the EU or of any EU institution.

(3) Evidence of any instrument issued by a EU institution, including any judgment or order of the European Court, or of any document in the custody of a EU institution, or any entry in or extract from such a document, may be given in any legal proceedings by production of a copy certified as a

true copy by an official of that institution; and any document purporting to be such a copy shall be received in evidence without proof of the official position or handwriting of the person signing the certificate.

(4) Evidence of any EU instrument may also be given in any legal proceedings—

   (a) by production of a copy purporting to be printed by the Queen's Printer;

   (b) where the instrument is in the custody of a government department (including a department of the Government of Northern Ireland), by production of a copy certified on behalf of the department to be a true copy by an officer of the department generally or specially authorised so to do;

and any document purporting to be such a copy as is mentioned in paragraph (b) above of an instrument in the custody of a department shall be received in evidence without proof of the official position or handwriting of the person signing the certificate, or of his authority to do so, or of the document being in the custody of the department.

(5) [Deleted].

APPENDIX B

Treaties

Treaty on the Functioning of
the European Union (TFEU) (extracts)

Part One
Principles

Article 1

1. This Treaty organises the functioning of the Union and determines the areas of, delimitation of, and arrangements for exercising its competences.
2. This Treaty and the Treaty on European Union constitute the Treaties on which the Union is founded. These two Treaties, which have the same legal value, shall be referred to as 'the Treaties'.

TITLE I
CATEGORIES AND AREAS OF UNION COMPETENCE

Article 2

1. When the Treaties confer on the Union exclusive competence in a specific area, only the Union may legislate and adopt legally binding acts, the Member States being able to do so themselves only if so empowered by the Union or for the implementation of Union acts.
2. When the Treaties confer on the Union a competence shared with the Member States in a specific area, the Union and the Member States may legislate and adopt legally binding acts in that area. The Member States shall exercise their competence to the extent that the Union has not exercised its competence. The Member States shall again exercise their competence to the extent that the Union has decided to cease exercising its competence.
3. The Member States shall coordinate their economic and employment policies within arrangements as determined by this Treaty, which the Union shall have competence to provide.
4. The Union shall have competence, in accordance with the provisions of the Treaty on European Union, to define and implement a common foreign and security policy, including the progressive framing of a common defence policy.
5. In certain areas and under the conditions laid down in the Treaties, the Union shall have competence to carry out actions to support, coordinate or supplement the actions of the Member States, without thereby superseding their competence in these areas.

    Legally binding acts of the Union adopted on the basis of the provisions of the Treaties relating to these areas shall not entail harmonisation of Member States' laws or regulations.
6. The scope of and arrangements for exercising the Union's competences shall be determined by the provisions of the Treaties relating to each area.

Article 3

1. The Union shall have exclusive competence in the following areas:
   (a) customs union;
   (b) the establishing of the competition rules necessary for the functioning of the internal market;
   (c) monetary policy for the Member States whose currency is the euro;
   (d) the conservation of marine biological resources under the common fisheries policy;
   (e) common commercial policy.
2. The Union shall also have exclusive competence for the conclusion of an international agreement when its conclusion is provided for in a legislative act of the Union or is necessary to enable the Union

to exercise its internal competence, or in so far as its conclusion may affect common rules or alter their scope.

Article 4

1. The Union shall share competence with the Member States where the Treaties confer on it a competence which does not relate to the areas referred to in Articles 3 and 6.
2. Shared competence between the Union and the Member States applies in the following principal areas:
    (a) internal market;
    (b) social policy, for the aspects defined in this Treaty;
    (c) economic, social and territorial cohesion;
    (d) agriculture and fisheries, excluding the conservation of marine biological resources;
    (e) environment;
    (f) consumer protection;
    (g) transport;
    (h) trans-European networks;
    (i) energy;
    (j) area of freedom, security and justice;
    (k) common safety concerns in public health matters, for the aspects defined in this Treaty.
3. In the areas of research, technological development and space, the Union shall have competence to carry out activities, in particular to define and implement programmes; however, the exercise of that competence shall not result in Member States being prevented from exercising theirs.
4. In the areas of development cooperation and humanitarian aid, the Union shall have competence to carry out activities and conduct a common policy; however, the exercise of that competence shall not result in Member States being prevented from exercising theirs.

Article 5

1. The Member States shall coordinate their economic policies within the Union. To this end, the Council shall adopt measures, in particular broad guidelines for these policies.
    Specific provisions shall apply to those Member States whose currency is the euro.
2. The Union shall take measures to ensure coordination of the employment policies of the Member States, in particular by defining guidelines for these policies.
3. The Union may take initiatives to ensure coordination of Member States' social policies.

Article 6

The Union shall have competence to carry out actions to support, coordinate or supplement the actions of the Member States. The areas of such action shall, at European level, be:
    (a) protection and improvement of human health;
    (b) industry;
    (c) culture;
    (d) tourism;
    (e) education, vocational training, youth and sport;
    (f) civil protection;
    (g) administrative cooperation.

TITLE V
AREA OF FREEDOM, SECURITY AND JUSTICE

CHAPTER 1
GENERAL PROVISIONS

Article 67 (ex Article 61 TEC and ex Article 29 TEU)

1. The Union shall constitute an area of freedom, security and justice with respect for fundamental rights and the different legal systems and traditions of the Member States.

2. It shall ensure the absence of internal border controls for persons and shall frame a common policy on asylum, immigration and external border control, based on solidarity between Member States, which is fair towards third-country nationals. For the purpose of this Title, stateless persons shall be treated as third-country nationals.
3. The Union shall endeavour to ensure a high level of security through measures to prevent and combat crime, racism and xenophobia, and through measures for coordination and cooperation between police and judicial authorities and other competent authorities, as well as through the mutual recognition of judgments in criminal matters and, if necessary, through the approximation of criminal laws.
4. The Union shall facilitate access to justice, in particular through the principle of mutual recognition of judicial and extrajudicial decisions in civil matters.

Article 68

The European Council shall define the strategic guidelines for legislative and operational planning within the area of freedom, security and justice.

Article 69

National Parliaments ensure that the proposals and legislative initiatives submitted under Chapters 4 and 5 comply with the principle of subsidiarity, in accordance with the arrangements laid down by the Protocol on the application of the principles of subsidiarity and proportionality.

Articles 70 and 71 (the latter ex Article 36 TEU) are procedural and thus omitted

Article 72 (ex Article 64(1) TEC and ex Article 33 TEU)

This Title shall not affect the exercise of the responsibilities incumbent upon Member States with regard to the maintenance of law and order and the safeguarding of internal security.

Article 73

It shall be open to Member States to organise between themselves and under their responsibility such forms of cooperation and coordination as they deem appropriate between the competent departments of their administrations responsible for safeguarding national security.

Article 74 (ex Article 66 TEC)

The Council shall adopt measures to ensure administrative cooperation between the relevant departments of the Member States in the areas covered by this Title, as well as between those departments and the Commission. It shall act on a Commission proposal, subject to Article 76, and after consulting the European Parliament.

Article 75 (ex Article 60 TEC)

Where necessary to achieve the objectives set out in Article 67, as regards preventing and combating terrorism and related activities, the European Parliament and the Council, acting by means of regulations in accordance with the ordinary legislative procedure, shall define a framework for administrative measures with regard to capital movements and payments, such as the freezing of funds, financial assets or economic gains belonging to, or owned or held by, natural or legal persons, groups or non-State entities.

The Council, on a proposal from the Commission, shall adopt measures to implement the framework referred to in the first paragraph.

The acts referred to in this Article shall include necessary provisions on legal safeguards.

Article 76

The acts referred to in Chapters 4 and 5, together with the measures referred to in Article 74 which ensure administrative cooperation in the areas covered by these Chapters, shall be adopted:

(a) on a proposal from the Commission, or
(b) on the initiative of a quarter of the Member States.

CHAPTER 4
JUDICAL COOPERATION IN CRIMINAL MATTERS

Article 82 (ex Article 31 TEU)

1. Judicial cooperation in criminal matters in the Union shall be based on the principle of mutual recognition of judgments and judicial decisions and shall include the approximation of the laws and regulations of the Member States in the areas referred to in paragraph 2 and in Article 83.

   The European Parliament and the Council, acting in accordance with the ordinary legislative procedure, shall adopt measures to:

   (a) lay down rules and procedures for ensuring recognition throughout the Union of all forms of judgments and judicial decisions;

   (b) prevent and settle conflicts of jurisdiction between Member States;

   (c) support the training of the judiciary and judicial staff;

   (d) facilitate cooperation between judicial or equivalent authorities of the Member States in relation to proceedings in criminal matters and the enforcement of decisions.

2. To the extent necessary to facilitate mutual recognition of judgments and judicial decisions and police and judicial cooperation in criminal matters having a cross-border dimension, the European Parliament and the Council may, by means of directives adopted in accordance with the ordinary legislative procedure, establish minimum rules. Such rules shall take into account the differences between the legal traditions and systems of the Member States.

   They shall concern:

   (a) mutual admissibility of evidence between Member States;

   (b) the rights of individuals in criminal procedure;

   (c) the rights of victims of crime;

   (d) any other specific aspects of criminal procedure which the Council has identified in advance by a decision; for the adoption of such a decision, the Council shall act unanimously after obtaining the consent of the European Parliament.

   Adoption of the minimum rules referred to in this paragraph shall not prevent Member States from maintaining or introducing a higher level of protection for individuals.

3. Where a member of the Council considers that a draft directive as referred to in paragraph 2 would affect fundamental aspects of its criminal justice system, it may request that the draft directive be referred to the European Council. In that case, the ordinary legislative procedure shall be suspended. After discussion, and in case of a consensus, the European Council shall, within four months of this suspension, refer the draft back to the Council, which shall terminate the suspension of the ordinary legislative procedure.

   Within the same timeframe, in case of disagreement, and if at least nine Member States wish to establish enhanced cooperation on the basis of the draft directive concerned, they shall notify the European Parliament, the Council and the Commission accordingly. In such a case, the authorisation to proceed with enhanced cooperation referred to in Article 20(2) of the Treaty on European Union and Article 329(1) of this Treaty shall be deemed to be granted and the provisions on enhanced cooperation shall apply.

Article 83 (ex Article 31 TEU)

1. The European Parliament and the Council may, by means of directives adopted in accordance with the ordinary legislative procedure, establish minimum rules concerning the definition of criminal offences and sanctions in the areas of particularly serious crime with a cross-border dimension resulting from the nature or impact of such offences or from a special need to combat them on a common basis.

   These areas of crime are the following: terrorism, trafficking in human beings and sexual exploitation of women and children, illicit drug trafficking, illicit arms trafficking, money laundering, corruption, counterfeiting of means of payment, computer crime and organised crime.

   On the basis of developments in crime, the Council may adopt a decision identifying other areas of crime that meet the criteria specified in this paragraph. It shall act unanimously after obtaining the consent of the European Parliament.

2. If the approximation of criminal laws and regulations of the Member States proves essential to ensure the effective implementation of a Union policy in an area which has been subject to harmonisation

measures, directives may establish minimum rules with regard to the definition of criminal offences and sanctions in the area concerned. Such directives shall be adopted by the same ordinary or special legislative procedure as was followed for the adoption of the harmonisation measures in question, without prejudice to Article 76.

3. Where a member of the Council considers that a draft directive as referred to in paragraph 1 or 2 would affect fundamental aspects of its criminal justice system, it may request that the draft directive be referred to the European Council. In that case, the ordinary legislative procedure shall be suspended. After discussion, and in case of a consensus, the European Council shall, within four months of this suspension, refer the draft back to the Council, which shall terminate the suspension of the ordinary legislative procedure.

   Within the same timeframe, in case of disagreement, and if at least nine Member States wish to establish enhanced cooperation on the basis of the draft directive concerned, they shall notify the European Parliament, the Council and the Commission accordingly. In such a case, the authorisation to proceed with enhanced cooperation referred to in Article 20(2) of the Treaty on European Union and Article 329(1) of this Treaty shall be deemed to be granted and the provisions on enhanced cooperation shall apply.

Article 84

The European Parliament and the Council, acting in accordance with the ordinary legislative procedure, may establish measures to promote and support the action of Member States in the field of crime prevention, excluding any harmonisation of the laws and regulations of the Member States.

Article 85 (ex Article 31 TEU)

1. Eurojust's mission shall be to support and strengthen coordination and cooperation between national investigating and prosecuting authorities in relation to serious crime affecting two or more Member States or requiring a prosecution on common bases, on the basis of operations conducted and information supplied by the Member States' authorities and by Europol.

   In this context, the European Parliament and the Council, by means of regulations adopted in accordance with the ordinary legislative procedure, shall determine Eurojust's structure, operation, field of action and tasks. These tasks may include:
   (a) the initiation of criminal investigations, as well as proposing the initiation of prosecutions conducted by competent national authorities, particularly those relating to offences against the financial interests of the Union;
   (b) the coordination of investigations and prosecutions referred to in point (a);
   (c) the strengthening of judicial cooperation, including by resolution of conflicts of jurisdiction and by close cooperation with the European Judicial Network.

   These regulations shall also determine arrangements for involving the European Parliament and national Parliaments in the evaluation of Eurojust's activities.

2. In the prosecutions referred to in paragraph 1, and without prejudice to Article 86, formal acts of judicial procedure shall be carried out by the competent national officials.

Article 86

1. In order to combat crimes affecting the financial interests of the Union, the Council, by means of regulations adopted in accordance with a special legislative procedure, may establish a European Public Prosecutor's Office from Eurojust. The Council shall act unanimously after obtaining the consent of the European Parliament.

   In the absence of unanimity in the Council, a group of at least nine Member States may request that the draft regulation be referred to the European Council. In that case, the procedure in the Council shall be suspended. After discussion, and in case of a consensus, the European Council shall, within four months of this suspension, refer the draft back to the Council for adoption.

   Within the same timeframe, in case of disagreement, and if at least nine Member States wish to establish enhanced cooperation on the basis of the draft regulation concerned, they shall notify the European Parliament, the Council and the Commission accordingly. In such a case, the authorisation to proceed with enhanced cooperation referred to in Article 20(2) of the Treaty on European Union and Article 329(1) of this Treaty shall be deemed to be granted and the provisions on enhanced cooperation shall apply.

2. The European Public Prosecutor's Office shall be responsible for investigating, prosecuting and bringing to judgment, where appropriate in liaison with Europol, the perpetrators of, and accomplices in, offences against the Union's financial interests, as determined by the regulation provided for in paragraph 1. It shall exercise the functions of prosecutor in the competent courts of the Member States in relation to such offences.

3. The regulations referred to in paragraph 1 shall determine the general rules applicable to the European Public Prosecutor's Office, the conditions governing the performance of its functions, the rules of procedure applicable to its activities, as well as those governing the admissibility of evidence, and the rules applicable to the judicial review of procedural measures taken by it in the performance of its functions.

4. The European Council may, at the same time or subsequently, adopt a decision amending paragraph 1 in order to extend the powers of the European Public Prosecutor's Office to include serious crime having a cross-border dimension and amending accordingly paragraph 2 as regards the perpetrators of, and accomplices in, serious crimes affecting more than one Member State. The European Council shall act unanimously after obtaining the consent of the European Parliament and after consulting the Commission.

CHAPTER 5

POLICE COOPERATION

Article 87 (ex Article 30 TEU)

1. The Union shall establish police cooperation involving all the Member States' competent authorities, including police, customs and other specialised law enforcement services in relation to the prevention, detection and investigation of criminal offences.

2. For the purposes of paragraph 1, the European Parliament and the Council, acting in accordance with the ordinary legislative procedure, may establish measures concerning:
   (a) the collection, storage, processing, analysis and exchange of relevant information;
   (b) support for the training of staff, and cooperation on the exchange of staff, on equipment and on research into crime-detection;
   (c) common investigative techniques in relation to the detection of serious forms of organised crime.

3. The Council, acting in accordance with a special legislative procedure, may establish measures concerning operational cooperation between the authorities referred to in this Article. The Council shall act unanimously after consulting the European Parliament.
   [The remainder of the paragraph deals with procedural measures in the absence of unanimity.]

Article 88 (ex Article 30 TEU)

1. Europol's mission shall be to support and strengthen action by the Member States' police authorities and other law enforcement services and their mutual cooperation in preventing and combating serious crime affecting two or more Member States, terrorism and forms of crime which affect a common interest covered by a Union policy.

2. The European Parliament and the Council, by means of regulations adopted in accordance with the ordinary legislative procedure, shall determine Europol's structure, operation, field of action and tasks. These tasks may include:
   (a) the collection, storage, processing, analysis and exchange of information, in particular that forwarded by the authorities of the Member States or third countries or bodies;
   (b) the coordination, organisation and implementation of investigative and operational action carried out jointly with the Member States' competent authorities or in the context of joint investigative teams, where appropriate in liaison with Eurojust.
   These regulations shall also lay down the procedures for scrutiny of Europol's activities by the European Parliament, together with national Parliaments.

3. Any operational action by Europol must be carried out in liaison and in agreement with the authorities of the Member State or States whose territory is concerned. The application of coercive measures shall be the exclusive responsibility of the competent national authorities.

Article 89 (ex Article 32 TEU)

The Council, acting in accordance with a special legislative procedure, shall lay down the conditions and limitations under which the competent authorities of the Member States referred to in

Articles 82 and 87 may operate in the territory of another Member State in liaison and in agreement with the authorities of that State. The Council shall act unanimously after consulting the European Parliament.

CHAPTER 2

LEGAL ACTS OF THE UNION, ADOPTION PROCEDURES
AND OTHER PROVISIONS

Section 1
The Legal Acts of the Union

Article 288 (ex Article 249 TEC)

To exercise the Union's competences, the institutions shall adopt regulations, directives, decisions, recommendations and opinions.

A regulation shall have general application. It shall be binding in its entirety and directly applicable in all Member States.

A directive shall be binding, as to the result to be achieved, upon each Member State to which it is addressed, but shall leave to the national authorities the choice of form and methods.

A decision shall be binding in its entirety. A decision which specifies those to whom it is addressed shall be binding only on them.

Recommendations and opinions shall have no binding force.

Article 289

1. The ordinary legislative procedure shall consist in the joint adoption by the European Parliament and the Council of a regulation, directive or decision on a proposal from the Commission. This procedure is defined in Article 294.
2. In the specific cases provided for by the Treaties, the adoption of a regulation, directive or decision by the European Parliament with the participation of the Council, or by the latter with the participation of the European Parliament, shall constitute a special legislative procedure.
3. Legal acts adopted by legislative procedure shall constitute legislative acts.
4. In the specific cases provided for by the Treaties, legislative acts may be adopted on the initiative of a group of Member States or of the European Parliament, on a recommendation from the European Central Bank or at the request of the Court of Justice or the European Investment Bank.

Article 290

1. A legislative act may delegate to the Commission the power to adopt non-legislative acts of general application to supplement or amend certain non-essential elements of the legislative act.

   The objectives, content, scope and duration of the delegation of power shall be explicitly defined in the legislative acts. The essential elements of an area shall be reserved for the legislative act and accordingly shall not be the subject of a delegation of power.
2. Legislative acts shall explicitly lay down the conditions to which the delegation is subject; these conditions may be as follows:
   (a) the European Parliament or the Council may decide to revoke the delegation;
   (b) the delegated act may enter into force only if no objection has been expressed by the European Parliament or the Council within a period set by the legislative act.

   For the purposes of (a) and (b), the European Parliament shall act by a majority of its component members, and the Council by a qualified majority.
3. The adjective 'delegated' shall be inserted in the title of delegated acts.

Article 291

1. Member States shall adopt all measures of national law necessary to implement legally binding Union acts.

213

2. Where uniform conditions for implementing legally binding Union acts are needed, those acts shall confer implementing powers on the Commission, or, in duly justified specific cases and in the cases provided for in Articles 24 and 26 of the Treaty on European Union, on the Council.
3. For the purposes of paragraph 2, the European Parliament and the Council, acting by means of regulations in accordance with the ordinary legislative procedure, shall lay down in advance the rules and general principles concerning mechanisms for control by Member States of the Commission's exercise of implementing powers.
4. The word 'implementing' shall be inserted in the title of implementing acts.

Article 292

The Council shall adopt recommendations. It shall act on a proposal from the Commission in all cases where the Treaties provide that it shall adopt acts on a proposal from the Commission. It shall act unanimously in those areas in which unanimity is required for the adoption of a Union act. The Commission, and the European Central Bank in the specific cases provided for in the Treaties, shall adopt recommendations.

Protocol (No 2)
on the application of the principles of subsidiarity and proportionality

Protocol (No 3)
on the Statute of the Court of Justice of the European Union

THE HIGH CONTRACTING PARTIES

DESIRING to lay down the Statute of the Court of Justice of the European Union provided for in Article 281 of the Treaty on the Functioning of the European Union,

HAVE AGREED UPON the following provisions, which shall be annexed to the Treaty on European Union, the Treaty on the Functioning of the European Union and the Treaty establishing the European Atomic Energy Community:

Article 1

The Court of Justice of the European Union shall be constituted and shall function in accordance with the provisions of the Treaties, of the Treaty establishing the European Atomic Energy Community (EAEC Treaty) and of this Statute.

TITLE I
JUDGES AND ADVOCATES-GENERAL

TITLE II
ORGANISATION OF THE COURT OF JUSTICE

Article 9

When, every three years, the Judges are partially replaced, 14 and 13 Judges shall be replaced alternately.

When, every three years, the Advocates-General are partially replaced, four Advocates-General shall be replaced on each occasion.

Article 10

The Registrar shall take an oath before the Court of Justice to perform his duties impartially and conscientiously and to preserve the secrecy of the deliberations of the Court of Justice.

Article 11

The Court of Justice shall arrange for replacement of the Registrar on occasions when he is prevented from attending the Court of Justice.

Article 12

Officials and other servants shall be attached to the Court of Justice to enable it to function. They shall be responsible to the Registrar under the authority of the President.

Article 13

At the request of the Court of Justice, the European Parliament and the Council may, acting in accordance with the ordinary legislative procedure, provide for the appointment of Assistant Rapporteurs and lay down the rules governing their service. The Assistant Rapporteurs may be required, under conditions laid down in the Rules of Procedure, to participate in preparatory inquiries in cases pending before the Court and to cooperate with the Judge who acts as Rapporteur.

The Assistant Rapporteurs shall be chosen from persons whose independence is beyond doubt and who possess the necessary legal qualifications; they shall be appointed by the Council, acting by a simple majority. They shall take an oath before the Court to perform their duties impartially and conscientiously and to preserve the secrecy of the deliberations of the Court.

Article 14

The Judges, the Advocates-General and the Registrar shall be required to reside at the place where the Court of Justice has its seat.

Article 15

The Court of Justice shall remain permanently in session. The duration of the judicial vacations shall be determined by the Court with due regard to the needs of its business.

Article 16

The Court of Justice shall form chambers consisting of three and five Judges. The Judges shall elect the Presidents of the chambers from among their number. The Presidents of the chambers of five Judges shall be elected for three years. They may be re-elected once.

The Grand Chamber shall consist of 13 Judges. It shall be presided over by the President of the Court. The Presidents of the chambers of five Judges and other Judges appointed in accordance with the conditions laid down in the Rules of Procedure shall also form part of the Grand Chamber.

The Court shall sit in a Grand Chamber when a Member State or an institution of the Union that is party to the proceedings so requests.

The Court shall sit as a full Court where cases are brought before it pursuant to Article 228(2), Article 245(2), Article 247 or Article 286(6) of the Treaty on the Functioning of the European Union.

Moreover, where it considers that a case before it is of exceptional importance, the Court may decide, after hearing the Advocate-General, to refer the case to the full Court.

Article 17

Decisions of the Court of Justice shall be valid only when an uneven number of its members is sitting in the deliberations.

Decisions of the chambers consisting of either three or five Judges shall be valid only if they are taken by three Judges.

Decisions of the Grand Chamber shall be valid only if nine Judges are sitting.

Decisions of the full Court shall be valid only if 15 Judges are sitting.

In the event of one of the Judges of a chamber being prevented from attending, a Judge of another chamber may be called upon to sit in accordance with conditions laid down in the Rules of Procedure.

Article 18

No Judge or Advocate-General may take part in the disposal of any case in which he has previously taken part as agent or adviser or has acted for one of the parties, or in which he has been called upon to pronounce as a member of a court or tribunal, of a commission of inquiry or in any other capacity.

If, for some special reason, any Judge or Advocate-General considers that he should not take part in the judgment or examination of a particular case, he shall so inform the President. If, for some special reason, the President considers that any Judge or Advocate-General should not sit or make submissions in a particular case, he shall notify him accordingly.

Any difficulty arising as to the application of this Article shall be settled by decision of the Court of Justice.

A party may not apply for a change in the composition of the Court or of one of its chambers on the grounds of either the nationality of a Judge or the absence from the Court or from the chamber of a Judge of the nationality of that party.

TITLE III
PROCEDURE BEFORE THE COURT OF JUSTICE

Article 19

The Member States and the institutions of the Union shall be represented before the Court of Justice by an agent appointed for each case; the agent may be assisted by an adviser or by a lawyer.

The States, other than the Member States, which are parties to the Agreement on the European Economic Area and also the EFTA Surveillance Authority referred to in that Agreement shall be represented in same manner.

Other parties must be represented by a lawyer.

Only a lawyer authorised to practise before a court of a Member State or of another State which is a party to the Agreement on the European Economic Area may represent or assist a party before the Court.

Such agents, advisers and lawyers shall, when they appear before the Court, enjoy the rights and immunities necessary to the independent exercise of their duties, under conditions laid down in the Rules of Procedure.

As regards such advisers and lawyers who appear before it, the Court shall have the powers normally accorded to courts of law, under conditions laid down in the Rules of Procedure.

University teachers being nationals of a Member State whose law accords them a right of audience shall have the same rights before the Court as are accorded by this Article to lawyers.

Article 20

The procedure before the Court of Justice shall consist of two parts: written and oral.

The written procedure shall consist of the communication to the parties and to the institutions of the Union whose decisions are in dispute, of applications, statements of case, defences and observations, and of replies, if any, as well as of all papers and documents in support or of certified copies of them.

Communications shall be made by the Registrar in the order and within the time laid down in the Rules of Procedure.

The oral procedure shall consist of the reading of the report presented by a Judge acting as Rapporteur, the hearing by the Court of agents, advisers and lawyers and of the submissions of the Advocate-General, as well as the hearing, if any, of witnesses and experts.

Where it considers that the case raises no new point of law, the Court may decide, after hearing the Advocate-General, that the case shall be determined without a submission from the Advocate- General.

Article 21

A case shall be brought before the Court of Justice by a written application addressed to the Registrar. The application shall contain the applicant's name and permanent address and the description of the signatory, the name of the party or names of the parties against whom the application is made, the subject-matter of the dispute, the form of order sought and a brief statement of the pleas in law on which the application is based.

The application shall be accompanied, where appropriate, by the measure the annulment of which is sought or, in the circumstances referred to in Article 265 of the Treaty on the Functioning of the European Union, by documentary evidence of the date on which an institution was, in accordance with those Articles, requested to act. If the documents are not submitted with the application, the Registrar shall ask the party concerned to produce them within a reasonable period, but in that event the rights of the party shall not lapse even if such documents are produced after the time limit for bringing proceedings.

Article 22

A case governed by Article 18 of the EAEC Treaty shall be brought before the Court of Justice by an appeal addressed to the Registrar. The appeal shall contain the name and permanent address of the applicant and the description of the signatory, a reference to the decision against which the appeal is brought, the names of the respondents, the subject-matter of the dispute, the submissions and a brief statement of the grounds on which the appeal is based.

The appeal shall be accompanied by a certified copy of the decision of the Arbitration Committee which is contested.

If the Court rejects the appeal, the decision of the Arbitration Committee shall become final.

If the Court annuls the decision of the Arbitration Committee, the matter may be re-opened, where appropriate, on the initiative of one of the parties in the case, before the Arbitration Committee. The latter shall conform to any decisions on points of law given by the Court.

Article 23

In the cases governed by Article 267 of the Treaty on the Functioning of the European Union, the decision of the court or tribunal of a Member State which suspends its proceedings and refers a case to the Court of Justice shall be notified to the Court by the court or tribunal concerned. The decision shall then be notified by the Registrar of the Court to the parties, to the Member States and to the Commission, and to the institution, body, office or agency of the Union which adopted the act the validity or interpretation of which is in dispute.

Within two months of this notification, the parties, the Member States, the Commission and, where appropriate, the institution, body, office or agency which adopted the act the validity or interpretation of which is in dispute, shall be entitled to submit statements of case or written observations to the Court.

In the cases governed by Article 267 of the Treaty on the Functioning of the European Union, the decision of the national court or tribunal shall, moreover, be notified by the Registrar of the Court to the States, other than the Member States, which are parties to the Agreement on the European Economic Area and also to the EFTA Surveillance Authority referred to in that Agreement which may, within two months of notification, where one of the fields of application of that Agreement is concerned, submit statements of case or written observations to the Court.

Where an agreement relating to a specific subject matter, concluded by the Council and one or more non-member States, provides that those States are to be entitled to submit statements of case or written observations where a court or tribunal of a Member State refers to the Court of Justice for a preliminary ruling a question falling within the scope of the agreement, the decision of the national court or tribunal containing that question shall also be notified to the non-member States concerned. Within two months from such notification, those States may lodge at the Court statements of case or written observations.

Article 23a[1]

The Rules of Procedure may provide for an expedited or accelerated procedure and, for references for a preliminary ruling relating to the area of freedom, security and justice, an urgent procedure.

Those procedures may provide, in respect of the submission of statements of case or written observations, for a shorter period than that provided for by Article 23, and, in derogation from the fourth paragraph of Article 20, for the case to be determined without a submission from the Advocate General.

---

[1] Article inserted by Decision 2008/79/EC, Euratom (OJ L 24, 29.1.2008, p. 42).

In addition, the urgent procedure may provide for restriction of the parties and other interested persons mentioned in Article 23, authorised to submit statements of case or written observations and, in cases of extreme urgency, for the written stage of the procedure to be omitted.

Article 24

The Court of Justice may require the parties to produce all documents and to supply all information which the Court considers desirable. Formal note shall be taken of any refusal.

The Court may also require the Member States and institutions, bodies, offices and agencies not being parties to the case to supply all information which the Court considers necessary for the proceedings.

Article 25

The Court of Justice may at any time entrust any individual, body, authority, committee or other organisation it chooses with the task of giving an expert opinion.

Article 26

Witnesses may be heard under conditions laid down in the Rules of Procedure.

Article 27

With respect to defaulting witnesses the Court of Justice shall have the powers generally granted to courts and tribunals and may impose pecuniary penalties under conditions laid down in the Rules of Procedure.

Article 28

Witnesses and experts may be heard on oath taken in the form laid down in the Rules of Procedure or in the manner laid down by the law of the country of the witness or expert.

Article 29

The Court of Justice may order that a witness or expert be heard by the judicial authority of his place of permanent residence.

The order shall be sent for implementation to the competent judicial authority under conditions laid down in the Rules of Procedure. The documents drawn up in compliance with the letters rogatory shall be returned to the Court under the same conditions.

The Court shall defray the expenses, without prejudice to the right to charge them, where appropriate, to the parties.

Article 30

A Member State shall treat any violation of an oath by a witness or expert in the same manner as if the offence had been committed before one of its courts with jurisdiction in civil proceedings. At the instance of the Court of Justice, the Member State concerned shall prosecute the offender before its competent court.

Article 31

The hearing in court shall be public, unless the Court of Justice, of its own motion or on application by the parties, decides otherwise for serious reasons.

Article 32

During the hearings the Court of Justice may examine the experts, the witnesses and the parties themselves. The latter, however, may address the Court of Justice only through their representatives.

Article 33

Minutes shall be made of each hearing and signed by the President and the Registrar.

Article 34

The case list shall be established by the President.

Article 35

The deliberations of the Court of Justice shall be and shall remain secret.

Article 36

Judgments shall state the reasons on which they are based. They shall contain the names of the Judges who took part in the deliberations.

Article 37

Judgments shall be signed by the President and the Registrar. They shall be read in open court.

Article 38

The Court of Justice shall adjudicate upon costs.

Article 39

The President of the Court of Justice may, by way of summary procedure, which may, in so far as necessary, differ from some of the rules contained in this Statute and which shall be laid down in the Rules of Procedure, adjudicate upon applications to suspend execution, as provided for in Article 278 of the Treaty on the Functioning of the European Union and Article 157 of the EAEC Treaty, or to prescribe interim measures pursuant to Article 279 of the Treaty on the Functioning of the European Union, or to suspend enforcement in accordance with the fourth paragraph of Article 299 of the Treaty on the Functioning of the European Union or the third paragraph of Article 164 of the EAEC Treaty.

Should the President be prevented from attending, his place shall be taken by another Judge under conditions laid down in the Rules of Procedure.

The ruling of the President or of the Judge replacing him shall be provisional and shall in no way prejudice the decision of the Court on the substance of the case.

Article 40

Member States and institutions of the Union may intervene in cases before the Court of Justice.

The same right shall be open to the bodies, offices and agencies of the Union and to any other person which can establish an interest in the result of a case submitted to the Court. Natural or legal persons shall not intervene in cases between Member States, between institutions of the Union or between Member States and institutions of the Union.

Without prejudice to the second paragraph, the States, other than the Member States, which are parties to the Agreement on the European Economic Area, and also the EFTA Surveillance Authority referred to in that Agreement, may intervene in cases before the Court where one of the fields of application of that Agreement is concerned.

An application to intervene shall be limited to supporting the form of order sought by one of the parties.

Article 41

Where the defending party, after having been duly summoned, fails to file written submissions in defence, judgment shall be given against that party by default. An objection may be lodged against the judgment within one month of it being notified. The objection shall not have the effect of staying enforcement of the judgment by default unless the Court of Justice decides otherwise.

Article 42

Member States, institutions, bodies, offices and agencies of the Union and any other natural or legal persons may, in cases and under conditions to be determined by the Rules of Procedure, institute third-party proceedings to contest a judgment rendered without their being heard, where the judgment is prejudicial to their rights.

Article 43

If the meaning or scope of a judgment is in doubt, the Court of Justice shall construe it on application by any party or any institution of the Union establishing an interest therein.

Article 44

An application for revision of a judgment may be made to the Court of Justice only on discovery of a fact which is of such a nature as to be a decisive factor, and which, when the judgment was given, was unknown to the Court and to the party claiming the revision.

The revision shall be opened by a judgment of the Court expressly recording the existence of a new fact, recognising that it is of such a character as to lay the case open to revision and declaring the application admissible on this ground.

No application for revision may be made after the lapse of 10 years from the date of the judgment.

Article 45

Periods of grace based on considerations of distance shall be determined by the Rules of Procedure.

No right shall be prejudiced in consequence of the expiry of a time limit if the party concerned proves the existence of unforeseeable circumstances or of *force majeure*.

Article 46

Proceedings against the Union in matters arising from non-contractual liability shall be barred after a period of five years from the occurrence of the event giving rise thereto. The period of limitation shall be interrupted if proceedings are instituted before the Court of Justice or if prior to such proceedings an application is made by the aggrieved party to the relevant institution of the Union. In the latter event the proceedings must be instituted within the period of two months provided for in Article 263 of the Treaty on the Functioning of the European Union; the provisions of the second paragraph of Article 265 of the Treaty on the Functioning of the European Union shall apply where appropriate.

This Article shall also apply to proceedings against the European Central Bank regarding non- contractual liability.

TITLE IV
GENERAL COURT

Article 47

The first paragraph of Article 9, Articles 14 and 15, the first, second, fourth and fifth paragraphs of Article 17 and Article 18 shall apply to the General Court and its members.

The fourth paragraph of Article 3 and Articles 10, 11 and 14 shall apply to the Registrar of the General Court *mutatis mutandis*.

Article 48

The General Court shall consist of 27 Judges.

Article 49

The Members of the General Court may be called upon to perform the task of an Advocate-General.

It shall be the duty of the Advocate-General, acting with complete impartiality and independence, to make, in open court, reasoned submissions on certain cases brought before the General Court in order to assist the General Court in the performance of its task.

The criteria for selecting such cases, as well as the procedures for designating the Advocates-General, shall be laid down in the Rules of Procedure of the General Court.

A Member called upon to perform the task of Advocate-General in a case may not take part in the judgment of the case.

Article 50

The General Court shall sit in chambers of three or five Judges. The Judges shall elect the Presidents of the chambers from among their number. The Presidents of the chambers of five Judges shall be elected for three years. They may be re-elected once.

The composition of the chambers and the assignment of cases to them shall be governed by the Rules of Procedure. In certain cases governed by the Rules of Procedure, the General Court may sit as a full court or be constituted by a single Judge.

The Rules of Procedure may also provide that the General Court may sit in a Grand Chamber in cases and under the conditions specified therein.

Article 51

By way of derogation from the rule laid down in Article 256(1) of the Treaty on the Functioning of the European Union, jurisdiction shall be reserved to the Court of Justice in the actions referred to in Articles 263 and 265 of the Treaty on the Functioning of the European Union when they are brought by a Member State against:

(a) an act of or failure to act by the European Parliament or the Council, or by those institutions acting jointly, except for:
   - decisions taken by the Council under the third subparagraph of Article 108(2) of the Treaty on the Functioning of the European Union;
   - acts of the Council adopted pursuant to a Council regulation concerning measures to protect trade within the meaning of Article 207 of the Treaty on the Functioning of the European Union;
   - acts of the Council by which the Council exercises implementing powers in accordance with the second paragraph of Article 291 of the Treaty on the Functioning of the European Union;

(b) against an act of or failure to act by the Commission under the first paragraph of Article 331 of the Treaty on the Functioning of the European Union.

Jurisdiction shall also be reserved to the Court of Justice in the actions referred to in the same Articles when they are brought by an institution of the Union against an act of or failure to act by the European Parliament, the Council, both those institutions acting jointly, or the Commission, or brought by an institution of the Union against an act of or failure to act by the European Central Bank.

Article 52

The President of the Court of Justice and the President of the General Court shall determine, by common accord, the conditions under which officials and other servants attached to the Court of Justice shall render their services to the General Court to enable it to function. Certain officials or other servants shall be responsible to the Registrar of the General Court under the authority of the President of the General Court.

Article 53

The procedure before the General Court shall be governed by Title III.

Such further and more detailed provisions as may be necessary shall be laid down in its Rules of Procedure. The Rules of Procedure may derogate from the fourth paragraph of Article 40 and from Article 41 in order to take account of the specific features of litigation in the field of intellectual property.

Notwithstanding the fourth paragraph of Article 20, the Advocate-General may make his reasoned submissions in writing.

Article 54

Where an application or other procedural document addressed to the General Court is lodged by mistake with the Registrar of the Court of Justice, it shall be transmitted immediately by that Registrar to the Registrar of the General Court; likewise, where an application or other procedural document addressed to the Court of Justice is lodged by mistake with the Registrar of the General Court, it shall be transmitted immediately by that Registrar to the Registrar of the Court of Justice.

Where the General Court finds that it does not have jurisdiction to hear and determine an action in respect of which the Court of Justice has jurisdiction, it shall refer that action to the Court of Justice; likewise, where the Court of Justice finds that an action falls within the jurisdiction of the General Court, it shall refer that action to the General Court, whereupon that Court may not decline jurisdiction.

Where the Court of Justice and the General Court are seised of cases in which the same relief is sought, the same issue of interpretation is raised or the validity of the same act is called in question, the General Court may, after hearing the parties, stay the proceedings before it until such time as the Court of Justice has delivered judgment or, where the action is one brought pursuant to Article 263 of the Treaty on the Functioning of the European Union, may decline jurisdiction so as to allow the Court of Justice to rule on such actions. In the same circumstances, the Court of Justice may also decide to stay the proceedings before it; in that event, the proceedings before the General Court shall continue.

Where a Member State and an institution of the Union are challenging the same act, the General Court shall decline jurisdiction so that the Court of Justice may rule on those applications.

Article 55

Final decisions of the General Court, decisions disposing of the substantive issues in part only or disposing of a procedural issue concerning a plea of lack of competence or inadmissibility, shall be notified by the Registrar of the General Court to all parties as well as all Member States and the institutions of the Union even if they did not intervene in the case before the General Court.

Article 56

An appeal may be brought before the Court of Justice, within two months of the notification of the decision appealed against, against final decisions of the General Court and decisions of that Court disposing of the substantive issues in part only or disposing of a procedural issue concerning a plea of lack of competence or inadmissibility.

Such an appeal may be brought by any party which has been unsuccessful, in whole or in part, in its submissions. However, interveners other than the Member States and the institutions of the Union may bring such an appeal only where the decision of the General Court directly affects them.

With the exception of cases relating to disputes between the Union and its servants, an appeal may also be brought by Member States and institutions of the Union which did not intervene in the proceedings before the General Court. Such Member States and institutions shall be in the same position as Member States or institutions which intervened at first instance.

Article 57

Any person whose application to intervene has been dismissed by the General Court may appeal to the Court of Justice within two weeks from the notification of the decision dismissing the application.

The parties to the proceedings may appeal to the Court of Justice against any decision of the General Court made pursuant to Article 278 or Article 279 or the fourth paragraph of Article 299 of the Treaty on the Functioning of the European Union or Article 157 or the third paragraph of Article 164 of the EAEC Treaty within two months from their notification.

The appeal referred to in the first two paragraphs of this Article shall be heard and determined under the procedure referred to in Article 39.

Article 58

An appeal to the Court of Justice shall be limited to points of law. It shall lie on the grounds of lack of competence of the General Court, a breach of procedure before it which adversely affects the interests of the appellant as well as the infringement of Union law by the General Court.

No appeal shall lie regarding only the amount of the costs or the party ordered to pay them.

Article 59

Where an appeal is brought against a decision of the General Court, the procedure before the Court of Justice shall consist of a written part and an oral part. In accordance with conditions laid down in the Rules of Procedure, the Court of Justice, having heard the Advocate-General and the parties, may dispense with the oral procedure.

Article 60

Without prejudice to Articles 278 and 279 of the Treaty on the Functioning of the European Union or Article 157 of the EAEC Treaty, an appeal shall not have suspensory effect.

By way of derogation from Article 280 of the Treaty on the Functioning of the European Union, decisions of the General Court declaring a regulation to be void shall take effect only as from the date of expiry of the period referred to in the first paragraph of Article 56 of this Statute or, if an appeal shall have been brought within that period, as from the date of dismissal of the appeal, without prejudice, however, to the right of a party to apply to the Court of Justice, pursuant to Articles 278 and 279 of the Treaty on the Functioning of the European Union or Article 157 of the EAEC Treaty, for the suspension of the effects of the regulation which has been declared void or for the prescription of any other interim measure.

Article 61

If the appeal is well founded, the Court of Justice shall quash the decision of the General Court. It may itself give final judgment in the matter, where the state of the proceedings so permits, or refer the case back to the General Court for judgment.

Where a case is referred back to the General Court, that Court shall be bound by the decision of the Court of Justice on points of law.

When an appeal brought by a Member State or an institution of the Union, which did not intervene in the proceedings before the General Court, is well founded, the Court of Justice may, if it considers this necessary, state which of the effects of the decision of the General Court which has been quashed shall be considered as definitive in respect of the parties to the litigation.

Article 62

In the cases provided for in Article 256(2) and (3) of the Treaty on the Functioning of the European Union, where the First Advocate-General considers that there is a serious risk of the unity or consistency of Union law being affected, he may propose that the Court of Justice review the decision of the General Court.

The proposal must be made within one month of delivery of the decision by the General Court. Within one month of receiving the proposal made by the First Advocate-General, the Court of Justice shall decide whether or not the decision should be reviewed.

Article 62a

The Court of Justice shall give a ruling on the questions which are subject to review by means of an urgent procedure on the basis of the file forwarded to it by the General Court.

Those referred to in Article 23 of this Statute and, in the cases provided for in Article 256(2) of the EC Treaty, the parties to the proceedings before the General Court shall be entitled to lodge statements or written observations with the Court of Justice relating to questions which are subject to review within a period prescribed for that purpose.

The Court of Justice may decide to open the oral procedure before giving a ruling.

Article 62b

In the cases provided for in Article 256(2) of the Treaty on the Functioning of the European Union, without prejudice to Articles 278 and 279 of the Treaty on the Functioning of the European Union, proposals for review and decisions to open the review procedure shall not have suspensory effect. If the Court of Justice finds that the decision of the General Court affects the unity or consistency of Union law, it shall refer the case back to the General Court which shall be bound by the points of law decided by the Court of Justice; the Court of Justice may state which of the effects of the decision of the General Court are to be considered as definitive in respect of the parties to the litigation. If, however, having regard to the result of the review, the outcome of the proceedings flows from the findings of fact on which the decision of the General Court was based, the Court of Justice shall give final judgment.

In the cases provided for in Article 256(3) of the Treaty on the Functioning of the European Union, in the absence of proposals for review or decisions to open the review procedure, the answer(s) given by the General Court to the questions submitted to it shall take effect upon expiry of the periods prescribed for that purpose in the second paragraph of Article 62. Should a review procedure be opened, the answer(s) subject to review shall take effect following that procedure, unless the Court of Justice decides otherwise. If the Court of Justice finds that the decision of the General Court affects the unity or consistency of Union law, the answer given by the Court of Justice to the questions subject to review shall be substituted for that given by the General Court.

TITLE IVA
SPECIALISED COURTS

Article 62c

The provisions relating to the jurisdiction, composition, organisation and procedure of the specialised courts established under Article 257 of the Treaty on the Functioning of the European Union are set out in an Annex to this Statute.

TITLE V
FINAL PROVISIONS

Article 63

The Rules of Procedure of the Court of Justice and of the General Court shall contain any provisions necessary for applying and, where required, supplementing this Statute.

Article 64

The rules governing the language arrangements applicable at the Court of Justice of the European Union shall be laid down by a regulation of the Council acting unanimously. This regulation shall be adopted either at the request of the Court of Justice and after consultation of the Commission and the European Parliament, or on a proposal from the Commission and after consultation of the Court of Justice and of the European Parliament.

Until those rules have been adopted, the provisions of the Rules of Procedure of the Court of Justice and of the Rules of Procedure of the General Court governing language arrangements shall continue to apply. By way of derogation from Articles 253 and 254 of the Treaty on the Functioning of the European Union, those provisions may only be amended or repealed with the unanimous consent of the Council.

Annex I
The European Union Civil Service Tribunal

Protocol (No 21)
On the position of the United Kingdom and Ireland in respect of the area of freedom, security and justice

THE HIGH CONTRACTING PARTIES,

DESIRING to settle certain questions relating to the United Kingdom and Ireland,

HAVING REGARD to the Protocol on the application of certain aspects of Article 26 of the Treaty on the Functioning of the European Union to the United Kingdom and to Ireland,

HAVE AGREED UPON the following provisions, which shall be annexed to the Treaty on European Union and the Treaty on the Functioning of the European Union:

Article 1

Subject to Article 3, the United Kingdom and Ireland shall not take part in the adoption by the Council of proposed measures pursuant to Title V of Part Three of the Treaty on the Functioning of the European Union. The unanimity of the members of the Council, with the exception of the representatives of the governments of the United Kingdom and Ireland, shall be necessary for decisions of the Council which must be adopted unanimously.

For the purposes of this Article, a qualified majority shall be defined in accordance with Article 238(3) of the Treaty on the Functioning of the European Union.

Article 2

In consequence of Article 1 and subject to Articles 3, 4 and 6, none of the provisions of Title V of Part Three of the Treaty on the Functioning of the European Union, no measure adopted pursuant to that Title, no provision of any international agreement concluded by the Union pursuant to that Title, and no decision of the Court of Justice interpreting any such provision or measure shall be binding upon or applicable in the United Kingdom or Ireland; and no such provision, measure or decision shall in any way affect the competences, rights and obligations of those States; and no such provision, measure or decision shall in any way affect the Community or Union *acquis* nor form part of Union law as they apply to the United Kingdom or Ireland.

Article 3

1. The United Kingdom or Ireland may notify the President of the Council in writing, within three months after a proposal or initiative has been presented to the Council pursuant to Title V of Part Three of the Treaty on the Functioning of the European Union, that it wishes to take part in the adoption and application of any such proposed measure, whereupon that State shall be entitled to do so.

   The unanimity of the members of the Council, with the exception of a member which has not made such a notification, shall be necessary for decisions of the Council which must be adopted unanimously. A measure adopted under this paragraph shall be binding upon all Member States which took part in its adoption.

   Measures adopted pursuant to Article 70 of the Treaty on the Functioning of the European Union shall lay down the conditions for the participation of the United Kingdom and Ireland in the evaluations concerning the areas covered by Title V of Part Three of that Treaty.

   For the purposes of this Article, a qualified majority shall be defined in accordance with Article 238(3) of the Treaty on the Functioning of the European Union.

2. If after a reasonable period of time a measure referred to in paragraph 1 cannot be adopted with the United Kingdom or Ireland taking part, the Council may adopt such measure in accordance with Article 1 without the participation of the United Kingdom or Ireland. In that case Article 2 applies.

Article 4

The United Kingdom or Ireland may at any time after the adoption of a measure by the Council pursuant to Title V of Part Three of the Treaty on the Functioning of the European Union notify its intention to the Council and to the Commission that it wishes to accept that measure. In that case, the procedure provided for in Article 331(1) of the Treaty on the Functioning of the European Union shall apply *mutatis mutandis*.

Article 4a

1. The provisions of this Protocol apply for the United Kingdom and Ireland also to measures proposed or adopted pursuant to Title V of Part Three of the Treaty on the Functioning of the European Union amending an existing measure by which they are bound.

2. However, in cases where the Council, acting on a proposal from the Commission, determines that the non-participation of the United Kingdom or Ireland in the amended version of an existing measure makes the application of that measure inoperable for other Member States or the Union, it may urge them to make a notification under Article 3 or 4. For the purposes of Article 3, a further period of two months starts to run as from the date of such determination by the Council.

   If at the expiry of that period of two months from the Council's determination the United Kingdom or Ireland has not made a notification under Article 3 or Article 4, the existing measure shall no longer be binding upon or applicable to it, unless the Member State concerned has made a notification under Article 4 before the entry into force of the amending measure. This shall take effect from the date of entry into force of the amending measure or of expiry of the period of two months, whichever is the later.

   For the purpose of this paragraph, the Council shall, after a full discussion of the matter, act by a qualified majority of its members representing the Member States participating or having participated in the adoption of the amending measure. A qualified majority of the Council shall be defined in accordance with Article 238(3)(a) of the Treaty on the Functioning of the European Union.

3. The Council, acting by a qualified majority on a proposal from the Commission, may determine that the United Kingdom or Ireland shall bear the direct financial consequences, if any, necessarily and unavoidably incurred as a result of the cessation of its participation in the existing measure.

4. This Article shall be without prejudice to Article 4.

Article 5

A Member State which is not bound by a measure adopted pursuant to Title V of Part Three of the Treaty on the Functioning of the European Union shall bear no financial consequences of that measure other than administrative costs entailed for the institutions, unless all members of the Council, acting unanimously after consulting the European Parliament, decide otherwise.

Article 6

Where, in cases referred to in this Protocol, the United Kingdom or Ireland is bound by a measure adopted by the Council pursuant to Title V of Part Three of the Treaty on the Functioning of the European Union, the relevant provisions of the Treaties shall apply to that State in relation to that measure.

Article 6a

The United Kingdom and Ireland shall not be bound by the rules laid down on the basis of Article 16 of the Treaty on the Functioning of the European Union which relate to the processing of personal data by the Member States when carrying out activities which fall within the scope of Chapter 4 or Chapter 5 of Title V of Part Three of that Treaty where the United Kingdom and Ireland are not bound by the rules governing the forms of judicial cooperation in criminal matters or police cooperation which require compliance with the provisions laid down on the basis of Article 16.

Article 7

Articles 3, 4 and 4*a* shall be without prejudice to the Protocol on the Schengen *acquis* integrated into the framework of the European Union.

Articles 8 and 9 relate to Ireland

Protocol (No 30)
On the application of the Charter of Fundamental Rights of the European Union to Poland and to the United Kingdom

THE HIGH CONTRACTING PARTIES,

WHEREAS in Article 6 of the Treaty on European Union, the Union recognises the rights, freedoms and principles set out in the Charter of Fundamental Rights of the European Union,

WHEREAS the Charter is to be applied in strict accordance with the provisions of the aforementioned Article 6 and Title VII of the Charter itself,

WHEREAS the aforementioned Article 6 requires the Charter to be applied and interpreted by the courts of Poland and of the United Kingdom strictly in accordance with the explanations referred to in that Article,

WHEREAS the Charter contains both rights and principles,

WHEREAS the Charter contains both provisions which are civil and political in character and those which are economic and social in character,

WHEREAS the Charter reaffirms the rights, freedoms and principles recognised in the Union and makes those rights more visible, but does not create new rights or principles,

RECALLING the obligations devolving upon Poland and the United Kingdom under the Treaty on European Union, the Treaty on the Functioning of the European Union, and Union law generally,

NOTING the wish of Poland and the United Kingdom to clarify certain aspects of the application of the Charter,

DESIROUS therefore of clarifying the application of the Charter in relation to the laws and administrative action of Poland and of the United Kingdom and of its justiciability within Poland and within the United Kingdom,

REAFFIRMING that references in this Protocol to the operation of specific provisions of the Charter are strictly without prejudice to the operation of other provisions of the Charter,

REAFFIRMING that this Protocol is without prejudice to the application of the Charter to other Member States,

REAFFIRMING that this Protocol is without prejudice to other obligations devolving upon Poland and the United Kingdom under the Treaty on European Union, the Treaty on the Functioning of the European Union, and Union law generally,

HAVE AGREED UPON the following provisions, which shall be annexed to the Treaty on European Union and to the Treaty on the Functioning of the European Union:

Article 1

1. The Charter does not extend the ability of the Court of Justice of the European Union, or any court or tribunal of Poland or of the United Kingdom, to find that the laws, regulations or administrative provisions, practices or action of Poland or of the United Kingdom are inconsistent with the fundamental rights, freedoms and principles that it reaffirms.
2. In particular, and for the avoidance of doubt, nothing in Title IV of the Charter creates justiciable rights applicable to Poland or the United Kingdom except in so far as Poland or the United Kingdom has provided for such rights in its national law.

Article 2

To the extent that a provision of the Charter refers to national laws and practices, it shall only apply to Poland or the United Kingdom to the extent that the rights or principles that it contains are recognised in the law or practices of Poland or of the United Kingdom.

Treaty on European Union (TEU) (extracts)
TITLE I
COMMON PROVISIONS

Article 1 (ex Article 1 TEU)[1]

By this Treaty, the HIGH CONTRACTING PARTIES establish among themselves a EUROPEAN UNION, hereinafter called 'the Union', on which the Member States confer competences to attain objectives they have in common.

This Treaty marks a new stage in the process of creating an ever closer union among the peoples of Europe, in which decisions are taken as openly as possible and as closely as possible to the citizen.

The Union shall be founded on the present Treaty and on the Treaty on the Functioning of the European Union (hereinafter referred to as 'the Treaties'). Those two Treaties shall have the same legal value. The Union shall replace and succeed the European Community.

Article 2

The Union is founded on the values of respect for human dignity, freedom, democracy, equality, the rule of law and respect for human rights, including the rights of persons belonging to minorities. These values are common to the Member States in a society in which pluralism, non-discrimination, tolerance, justice, solidarity and equality between women and men prevail.

Article 3 (ex Article 2 TEU)

1. The Union's aim is to promote peace, its values and the well-being of its peoples.
2. The Union shall offer its citizens an area of freedom, security and justice without internal frontiers, in which the free movement of persons is ensured in conjunction with appropriate measures with respect to external border controls, asylum, immigration and the prevention and combating of crime.

---

[1] These references are merely indicative. For more ample information, please refer to the table of equivalences between the old and the new numbering of the Treaties, at <http://www.oup.com/uk/orc/bin/9780199581597/01student/table/eulaw_table.pdf>.

3. The Union shall establish an internal market. It shall work for the sustainable development of Europe based on balanced economic growth and price stability, a highly competitive social market economy, aiming at full employment and social progress, and a high level of protection and improvement of the quality of the environment. It shall promote scientific and technological advance.

   It shall combat social exclusion and discrimination, and shall promote social justice and protection, equality between women and men, solidarity between generations and protection of the rights of the child.

   It shall promote economic, social and territorial cohesion, and solidarity among Member States.

   It shall respect its rich cultural and linguistic diversity, and shall ensure that Europe's cultural heritage is safeguarded and enhanced.

4. The Union shall establish an economic and monetary union whose currency is the euro.

5. In its relations with the wider world, the Union shall uphold and promote its values and interests and contribute to the protection of its citizens. It shall contribute to peace, security, the sustainable development of the Earth, solidarity and mutual respect among peoples, free and fair trade, eradication of poverty and the protection of human rights, in particular the rights of the child, as well as to the strict observance and the development of international law, including respect for the principles of the United Nations Charter.

6. The Union shall pursue its objectives by appropriate means commensurate with the competences which are conferred upon it in the Treaties.

Article 4

1. In accordance with Article 5, competences not conferred upon the Union in the Treaties remain with the Member States.

2. The Union shall respect the equality of Member States before the Treaties as well as their national identities, inherent in their fundamental structures, political and constitutional, inclusive of regional and local self-government. It shall respect their essential State functions, including ensuring the territorial integrity of the State, maintaining law and order and safeguarding national security. In particular, national security remains the sole responsibility of each Member State.

3. Pursuant to the principle of sincere cooperation, the Union and the Member States shall, in full mutual respect, assist each other in carrying out tasks which flow from the Treaties.

   The Member States shall take any appropriate measure, general or particular, to ensure fulfilment of the obligations arising out of the Treaties or resulting from the acts of the institutions of the Union.

   The Member States shall facilitate the achievement of the Union's tasks and refrain from any measure which could jeopardise the attainment of the Union's objectives.

Article 5 (ex Article 5 TEC)

1. The limits of Union competences are governed by the principle of conferral. The use of Union competences is governed by the principles of subsidiarity and proportionality.

2. Under the principle of conferral, the Union shall act only within the limits of the competences conferred upon it by the Member States in the Treaties to attain the objectives set out therein. Competences not conferred upon the Union in the Treaties remain with the Member States.

3. Under the principle of subsidiarity, in areas which do not fall within its exclusive competence, the Union shall act only if and in so far as the objectives of the proposed action cannot be sufficiently achieved by the Member States, either at central level or at regional and local level, but can rather, by reason of the scale or effects of the proposed action, be better achieved at Union level.

   The institutions of the Union shall apply the principle of subsidiarity as laid down in the Protocol on the application of the principles of subsidiarity and proportionality. National Parliaments ensure compliance with the principle of subsidiarity in accordance with the procedure set out in that Protocol.

4. Under the principle of proportionality, the content and form of Union action shall not exceed what is necessary to achieve the objectives of the Treaties.

   The institutions of the Union shall apply the principle of proportionality as laid down in the Protocol on the application of the principles of subsidiarity and proportionality.

Article 6 (ex Article 6 TEU)

1. The Union recognises the rights, freedoms and principles set out in the Charter of Fundamental Rights of the European Union of 7 December 2000, as adapted at Strasbourg, on 12 December 2007, which shall have the same legal value as the Treaties.

The provisions of the Charter shall not extend in any way the competences of the Union as defined in the Treaties.

The rights, freedoms and principles in the Charter shall be interpreted in accordance with the general provisions in Title VII of the Charter governing its interpretation and application and with due regard to the explanations referred to in the Charter, that set out the sources of those provisions.

2. The Union shall accede to the European Convention for the Protection of Human Rights and Fundamental Freedoms. Such accession shall not affect the Union's competences as defined in the Treaties.

3. Fundamental rights, as guaranteed by the European Convention for the Protection of Human Rights and Fundamental Freedoms and as they result from the constitutional traditions common to the Member States, shall constitute general principles of the Union's law.

Article 7 (ex Article 7 TEU)

[Measures relating to breach of Article 2 by a Member State.]

Charter of Fundamental Rights of the European Union

Preamble

The peoples of Europe, in creating an ever closer union among them, are resolved to share a peaceful future based on common values.

Conscious of its spiritual and moral heritage, the Union is founded on the indivisible, universal values of human dignity, freedom, equality and solidarity; it is based on the principles of democracy and the rule of law. It places the individual at the heart of its activities, by establishing the citizenship of the Union and by creating an area of freedom, security and justice.

The Union contributes to the preservation and to the development of these common values while respecting the diversity of the cultures and traditions of the peoples of Europe as well as the national identities of the Member States and the organisation of their public authorities at national, regional and local levels; it seeks to promote balanced and sustainable development and ensures free movement of persons, services, goods and capital, and the freedom of establishment.

To this end, it is necessary to strengthen the protection of fundamental rights in the light of changes in society, social progress and scientific and technological developments by making those rights more visible in a Charter.

This Charter reaffirms, with due regard for the powers and tasks of the Union and for the principle of subsidiarity, the rights as they result, in particular, from the constitutional traditions and international obligations common to the Member States, the European Convention for the Protection of Human Rights and Fundamental Freedoms, the Social Charters adopted by the Union and by the Council of Europe and the case-law of the Court of Justice of the European Union and of the European Court of Human Rights. In this context the Charter will be interpreted by the courts of the Union and the Member States with due regard to the explanations prepared under the authority of the Praesidium of the Convention which drafted the Charter and updated under the responsibility of the Praesidium of the European Convention.

Enjoyment of these rights entails responsibilities and duties with regard to other persons, to the human community and to future generations.

The Union therefore recognises the rights, freedoms and principles set out hereafter.

TITLE I
DIGNITY

Article 1
Human dignity

Human dignity is inviolable. It must be respected and protected.

Article 2
Right to life

1. Everyone has the right to life.
2. No one shall be condemned to the death penalty, or executed.

Article 3
Right to the integrity of the person

1. Everyone has the right to respect for his or her physical and mental integrity.
2. In the fields of medicine and biology, the following must be respected in particular:
   (a) the free and informed consent of the person concerned, according to the procedures laid down by law;
   (b) the prohibition of eugenic practices, in particular those aiming at the selection of persons;
   (c) the prohibition on making the human body and its parts as such a source of financial gain;
   (d) the prohibition of the reproductive cloning of human beings.

Article 4
Prohibition of torture and inhuman or degrading treatment or punishment

No one shall be subjected to torture or to inhuman or degrading treatment or punishment.

Article 5
Prohibition of slavery and forced labour

1. No one shall be held in slavery or servitude.
2. No one shall be required to perform forced or compulsory labour.
3. Trafficking in human beings is prohibited.

TITLE II
FREEDOMS

Article 6
Right to liberty and security

Everyone has the right to liberty and security of person.

Article 7
Respect for private and family life

Everyone has the right to respect for his or her private and family life, home and communications.

Article 8
Protection of personal data

1. Everyone has the right to the protection of personal data concerning him or her.
2. Such data must be processed fairly for specified purposes and on the basis of the consent of the person concerned or some other legitimate basis laid down by law. Everyone has the right of access to data which has been collected concerning him or her, and the right to have it rectified.
3. Compliance with these rules shall be subject to control by an independent authority.

Article 9
Right to marry and right to found a family

The right to marry and the right to found a family shall be guaranteed in accordance with the national laws governing the exercise of these rights.

Article 10
Freedom of thought, conscience and religion

1. Everyone has the right to freedom of thought, conscience and religion. This right includes freedom to change religion or belief and freedom, either alone or in community with others and in public or in private, to manifest religion or belief, in worship, teaching, practice and observance.

2. The right to conscientious objection is recognised, in accordance with the national laws governing the exercise of this right.

Article 11
Freedom of expression and information

1. Everyone has the right to freedom of expression. This right shall include freedom to hold opinions and to receive and impart information and ideas without interference by public authority and regardless of frontiers.
2. The freedom and pluralism of the media shall be respected.

Article 12
Freedom of assembly and of association

1. Everyone has the right to freedom of peaceful assembly and to freedom of association at all levels, in particular in political, trade union and civic matters, which implies the right of everyone to form and to join trade unions for the protection of his or her interests.
2. Political parties at Union level contribute to expressing the political will of the citizens of the Union.

Article 13
Freedom of the arts and sciences

The arts and scientific research shall be free of constraint. Academic freedom shall be respected.

Article 14
Right to education

1. Everyone has the right to education and to have access to vocational and continuing training.
2. This right includes the possibility to receive free compulsory education.
3. The freedom to found educational establishments with due respect for democratic principles and the right of parents to ensure the education and teaching of their children in conformity with their religious, philosophical and pedagogical convictions shall be respected, in accordance with the national laws governing the exercise of such freedom and right.

Article 15
Freedom to choose an occupation and right to engage in work

1. Everyone has the right to engage in work and to pursue a freely chosen or accepted occupation.
2. Every citizen of the Union has the freedom to seek employment, to work, to exercise the right of establishment and to provide services in any Member State.
3. Nationals of third countries who are authorised to work in the territories of the Member States are entitled to working conditions equivalent to those of citizens of the Union.

Article 16
Freedom to conduct a business

The freedom to conduct a business in accordance with Union law and national laws and practices is recognised.

Article 17
Right to property

1. Everyone has the right to own, use, dispose of and bequeath his or her lawfully acquired possessions. No one may be deprived of his or her possessions, except in the public interest and in the cases and under the conditions provided for by law, subject to fair compensation being paid in good time for their loss. The use of property may be regulated by law in so far as is necessary for the general interest.
2. Intellectual property shall be protected.

Article 18
Right to asylum

The right to asylum shall be guaranteed with due respect for the rules of the Geneva Convention of 28 July 1951 and the Protocol of 31 January 1967 relating to the status of refugees and in accordance with the Treaty on European Union and the Treaty on the Functioning of the European Union (hereinafter referred to as 'the Treaties').

Article 19
Protection in the event of removal, expulsion or extradition

1. Collective expulsions are prohibited.
2. No one may be removed, expelled or extradited to a State where there is a serious risk that he or she would be subjected to the death penalty, torture or other inhuman or degrading treatment or punishment.

TITLE III
EQUALITY

Article 20
Equality before the law

Everyone is equal before the law.

Article 21
Non-discrimination

1. Any discrimination based on any ground such as sex, race, colour, ethnic or social origin, genetic features, language, religion or belief, political or any other opinion, membership of a national minority, property, birth, disability, age or sexual orientation shall be prohibited.
2. Within the scope of application of the Treaties and without prejudice to any of their specific provisions, any discrimination on grounds of nationality shall be prohibited.

Article 22
Cultural, religious and linguistic diversity

The Union shall respect cultural, religious and linguistic diversity.

Article 23
Equality between women and men

Equality between women and men must be ensured in all areas, including employment, work and pay.

The principle of equality shall not prevent the maintenance or adoption of measures providing for specific advantages in favour of the under-represented sex.

Article 24
The rights of the child

1. Children shall have the right to such protection and care as is necessary for their well-being. They may express their views freely. Such views shall be taken into consideration on matters which concern them in accordance with their age and maturity.
2. In all actions relating to children, whether taken by public authorities or private institutions, the child's best interests must be a primary consideration.
3. Every child shall have the right to maintain on a regular basis a personal relationship and direct contact with both his or her parents, unless that is contrary to his or her interests.

Article 25
The rights of the elderly

The Union recognises and respects the rights of the elderly to lead a life of dignity and independence and to participate in social and cultural life.

Article 26
Integration of persons with disabilities

The Union recognises and respects the right of persons with disabilities to benefit from measures designed to ensure their independence, social and occupational integration and participation in the life of the community.

TITLE IV
SOLIDARITY

TITLE V
CITIZENS' RIGHTS

Articles 39 and 40 address the right to vote and stand for election.

Article 41
Right to good administration

1. Every person has the right to have his or her affairs handled impartially, fairly and within a reasonable time by the institutions, bodies, offices and agencies of the Union.
2. This right includes:
   (a) the right of every person to be heard, before any individual measure which would affect him or her adversely is taken;
   (b) the right of every person to have access to his or her file, while respecting the legitimate interests of confidentiality and of professional and business secrecy;
   (c) the obligation of the administration to give reasons for its decisions.
3. Every person has the right to have the Union make good any damage caused by its institutions or by its servants in the performance of their duties, in accordance with the general principles common to the laws of the Member States.
4. Every person may write to the institutions of the Union in one of the languages of the Treaties and must have an answer in the same language.

Article 42
Right of access to documents

Any citizen of the Union, and any natural or legal person residing or having its registered office in a Member State, has a right of access to documents of the institutions, bodies, offices and agencies of the Union, whatever their medium.

Article 43
European Ombudsman

Any citizen of the Union and any natural or legal person residing or having its registered office in a Member State has the right to refer to the European Ombudsman cases of maladministration in the activities of the institutions, bodies, offices or agencies of the Union, with the exception of the Court of Justice of the European Union acting in its judicial role.

Article 44
Right to petition

Any citizen of the Union and any natural or legal person residing or having its registered office in a Member State has the right to petition the European Parliament.

Article 45
Freedom of movement and of residence

1. Every citizen of the Union has the right to move and reside freely within the territory of the Member States.
2. Freedom of movement and residence may be granted, in accordance with the Treaties, to nationals of third countries legally resident in the territory of a Member State.

Article 46
Diplomatic and consular protection

Every citizen of the Union shall, in the territory of a third country in which the Member State of which he or she is a national is not represented, be entitled to protection by the diplomatic or consular authorities of any Member State, on the same conditions as the nationals of that Member State.

TITLE VI
JUSTICE

Article 47
Right to an effective remedy and to a fair trial

Everyone whose rights and freedoms guaranteed by the law of the Union are violated has the right to an effective remedy before a tribunal in compliance with the conditions laid down in this Article.

Everyone is entitled to a fair and public hearing within a reasonable time by an independent and impartial tribunal previously established by law. Everyone shall have the possibility of being advised, defended and represented.

Legal aid shall be made available to those who lack sufficient resources in so far as such aid is necessary to ensure effective access to justice.

Article 48
Presumption of innocence and right of defence

1. Everyone who has been charged shall be presumed innocent until proved guilty according to law.
2. Respect for the rights of the defence of anyone who has been charged shall be guaranteed.

Article 49
Principles of legality and proportionality of criminal offences and penalties

1. No one shall be held guilty of any criminal offence on account of any act or omission which did not constitute a criminal offence under national law or international law at the time when it was committed. Nor shall a heavier penalty be imposed than the one that was applicable at the time the criminal offence was committed. If, subsequent to the commission of a criminal offence, the law provides for a lighter penalty, that penalty shall be applicable.
2. This Article shall not prejudice the trial and punishment of any person for any act or omission which, at the time when it was committed, was criminal according to the general principles recognised by the community of nations.
3. The severity of penalties must not be disproportionate to the criminal offence.

Article 50
Right not to be tried or punished twice in criminal proceedings for the same criminal offence

No one shall be liable to be tried or punished again in criminal proceedings for an offence for which he or she has already been finally acquitted or convicted within the Union in accordance with the law.

TITLE VII
GENERAL PROVISIONS GOVERNING THE INTERPRETATION AND APPLICATION OF THE CHARTER

Article 51
Field of application

1. The provisions of this Charter are addressed to the institutions, bodies, offices and agencies of the Union with due regard for the principle of subsidiarity and to the Member States only when they are implementing Union law. They shall therefore respect the rights, observe the principles and promote the application thereof in accordance with their respective powers and respecting the limits of the powers of the Union as conferred on it in the Treaties.
2. The Charter does not extend the field of application of Union law beyond the powers of the Union or establish any new power or task for the Union, or modify powers and tasks as defined in the Treaties.

Article 52
Scope and interpretation of rights and principles

1. Any limitation on the exercise of the rights and freedoms recognised by this Charter must be provided for by law and respect the essence of those rights and freedoms. Subject to the principle of proportionality, limitations may be made only if they are necessary and genuinely meet objectives of general interest recognised by the Union or the need to protect the rights and freedoms of others.
2. Rights recognised by this Charter for which provision is made in the Treaties shall be exercised under the conditions and within the limits defined by those Treaties.
3. In so far as this Charter contains rights which correspond to rights guaranteed by the Convention for the Protection of Human Rights and Fundamental Freedoms, the meaning and scope of those rights shall be the same as those laid down by the said Convention. This provision shall not prevent Union law providing more extensive protection.
4. In so far as this Charter recognises fundamental rights as they result from the constitutional traditions common to the Member States, those rights shall be interpreted in harmony with those traditions.
5. The provisions of this Charter which contain principles may be implemented by legislative and executive acts taken by institutions, bodies, offices and agencies of the Union, and by acts of Member States when they are implementing Union law, in the exercise of their respective powers. They shall be judicially cognisable only in the interpretation of such acts and in the ruling on their legality.
6. Full account shall be taken of national laws and practices as specified in this Charter.
7. The explanations drawn up as a way of providing guidance in the interpretation of this Charter shall be given due regard by the courts of the Union and of the Member States.

Article 53
Level of protection

Nothing in this Charter shall be interpreted as restricting or adversely affecting human rights and fundamental freedoms as recognised, in their respective fields of application, by Union law and international law and by international agreements to which the Union or all the Member States are party, including the European Convention for the Protection of Human Rights and Fundamental Freedoms, and by the Member States' constitutions.

Article 54
Prohibition of abuse of rights

Nothing in this Charter shall be interpreted as implying any right to engage in any activity or to perform any act aimed at the destruction of any of the rights and freedoms recognised in this Charter or at their limitation to a greater extent than is provided for herein.

The above text adapts the wording of the Charter proclaimed on 7 December 2000, and will replace it as from the date of entry into force of the Treaty of Lisbon.

APPENDIX C

Decisions and Directives

Corruption in the private sector— Council Framework Decision 2003/568/JHA

Council Framework Decision 2003/568/JHA of 22 July 2003 on combating corruption in the private sector

[Early paras of the preamble dealing with history and earlier measures are omitted.]

(9) Member States attach particular importance to combating corruption in both the public and the private sector, in the belief that in both those sectors it poses a threat to a law-abiding society as well as distorting competition in relation to the purchase of goods or commercial services and impeding sound economic development. In that context the Member States which have not yet ratified the European Union Convention of 26 May 1997 and the Council of Europe Convention of 27 January 1999 will consider how to do so as soon as possible.

(10) The aim of this Framework Decision is in particular to ensure that both active and passive corruption in the private sector are criminal offences in all Member States, that legal persons may also be held responsible for such offences, and that these offences incur effective, proportionate and dissuasive penalties,

HAS ADOPTED THIS FRAMEWORK DECISION:

Article 1
Definitions

For the purposes of this Framework Decision:

- 'legal person' means any entity having such status under the applicable national law, except for States or other public bodies acting in the exercise of State authority and for public international organisations,
- 'breach of duty' shall be understood in accordance with national law. The concept of breach of duty in national law should cover as a minimum any disloyal behaviour constituting a breach of a statutory duty, or, as the case may be, a breach of professional regulations or instructions, which apply within the business of a person who in any capacity directs or works for a private sector entity.

Article 2
Active and passive corruption in the private sector

1. Member States shall take the necessary measures to ensure that the following intentional conduct constitutes a criminal offence, when it is carried out in the course of business activities:
   (a) promising, offering or giving, directly or through an intermediary, to a person who in any capacity directs or works for a private-sector entity an undue advantage of any kind, for that person or for a third party, in order that that person should perform or refrain from performing any act, in breach of that person's duties;
   (b) directly or through an intermediary, requesting or receiving an undue advantage of any kind, or accepting the promise of such an advantage, for oneself or for a third party, while in any capacity directing or working for a private-sector entity, in order to perform or refrain from performing any act, in breach of one's duties.

2. Paragraph 1 applies to business activities within profit and non-profit entities.
3. A Member State may declare that it will limit the scope of paragraph 1 to such conduct which involves, or could involve, a distortion of competition in relation to the purchase of goods or commercial services.
4. Declarations referred to in paragraph 3 shall be communicated to the Council at the time of the adoption of this Framework Decision and shall be valid for five years as from 22 July 2005.

5. The Council shall review this Article in due time before 22 July 2010 with a view to considering whether it shall be possible to renew declarations made under paragraph 3.

Article 3
Instigation, aiding and abetting

Member States shall take the necessary measures to ensure that instigating, aiding and abetting the conduct referred to in Article 2 constitute criminal offences.

Article 4
Penalties and other sanctions

1. Each Member State shall take the necessary measures to ensure that the conduct referred to in Articles 2 and 3 is punishable by effective, proportionate and dissuasive criminal penalties.
2. Each Member State shall take the necessary measures to ensure that the conduct referred to in Article 2 is punishable by a penalty of a maximum of at least one to three years of imprisonment.
3. Each Member State shall take the necessary measures in accordance with its constitutional rules and principles to ensure that where a natural person in relation to a certain business activity has been convicted of the conduct referred to in Article 2, that person may, where appropriate, at least in cases where he or she had a leading position in a company within the business concerned, be temporarily prohibited from carrying on this particular or comparable business activity in a similar position or capacity, if the facts established give reason to believe there to be a clear risk of abuse of position or of office by active or passive corruption.

Article 5
Liability of legal persons

1. Each Member State shall take the necessary measures to ensure that legal persons can be held liable for offences referred to in Articles 2 and 3 committed for their benefit by any person, acting either individually or as part of an organ of the legal person, who has a leading position within the legal person, based on:
   (a) a power of representation of the legal person;
   (b) an authority to take decisions on behalf of the legal person; or
   (c) an authority to exercise control within the legal person.
2. Apart from the cases provided for in paragraph 1, each Member State shall take the necessary measures to ensure that a legal person can be held liable where the lack of supervision or control by a person referred to in paragraph 1 has made possible the commission of an offence of the type referred to in Articles 2 and 3 for the benefit of that legal person by a person under its authority.
3. Liability of a legal person under paragraphs 1 and 2 shall not exclude criminal proceedings against natural persons who are involved as perpetrators, instigators or accessories in an offence of the type referred to in Articles 2 and 3.

Article 6
Penalties for legal persons

1. Each Member State shall take the necessary measures to ensure that a legal person held liable pursuant to Article 5(1) is punishable by effective, proportionate and dissuasive penalties, which shall include criminal or non-criminal fines and may include other penalties such as:
   (a) exclusion from entitlement to public benefits or aid;
   (b) temporary or permanent disqualification from the practice of commercial activities;
   (c) placing under judicial supervision; or
   (d) a judicial winding-up order.
2. Each Member State shall take the necessary measures to ensure that a legal person held liable pursuant to Article 5(2) is punishable by penalties or measures which are effective, proportionate and dissuasive.

Article 7
Jurisdiction

1. Each Member State shall take the necessary measures to establish its jurisdiction with regard to the offences referred to in Articles 2 and 3, where the offence has been committed:

(a) in whole or in part within its territory;

(b) by one of its nationals; or

(c) for the benefit of a legal person that has its head office in the territory of that Member State.

2. Any Member State may decide that it will not apply the jurisdiction rules in paragraph 1(b) and (c), or will apply them only in specific cases or circumstances, where the offence has been committed outside its territory.

3. Any Member State which, under its domestic law, does not as yet surrender its own nationals shall take the necessary measures to establish its jurisdiction with regard to the offences referred to in Articles 2 and 3, when committed by its own nationals outside its territory.

4. Member States which decide to apply paragraph 2 shall inform the General Secretariat of the Council and the Commission accordingly, where appropriate with an indication of the specific cases or circumstances in which the decision applies.

Article 8
Repeal

Joint Action 98/742/JHA shall be repealed.

Article 9
Implementation

1. Member States shall take the necessary measures to comply with the provisions of this Framework Decision before 22 July 2005.

2. By the same date, Member States shall transmit to the General Secretariat of the Council and the Commission the text of the provisions transposing into their national law the obligations imposed on them under this Framework Decision. On the basis of a report established using this information and a written report from the Commission, the Council shall before 22 October 2005 assess the extent to which Member States have complied with the provisions of this Framework Decision.

Cybercrime—Council Framework Decision 2005/222/JHA

Council Framework Decision 2005/222/JHA of 24 February 2005 on attacks against information systems

THE COUNCIL OF THE EUROPEAN UNION,

Having regard to the Treaty on European Union, and in particular Articles 29, 30(1)(a), 31(1)(e) and 34(2)(b) thereof,

Having regard to the proposal from the Commission,

Having regard to the opinion of the European Parliament,[1]

Whereas:

(1) The objective of this Framework Decision is to improve cooperation between judicial and other competent authorities, including the police and other specialised law enforcement services of the Member States, through approximating rules on criminal law in the Member States in the area of attacks against information systems.

(2) There is evidence of attacks against information systems, in particular as a result of the threat from organised crime, and increasing concern at the potential of terrorist attacks against information systems which form part of the critical infrastructure of the Member States. This constitutes a threat to the achievement of a safer information society and an area of freedom, security and justice, and therefore requires a response at the level of the European Union.

(3) An effective response to those threats requires a comprehensive approach to network and information security, as underlined in the eEurope Action Plan, in the Communication by the Commission 'Network and Information Security: Proposal for a European Policy Approach' and in the Council Resolution of 28 January 2002 on a common approach and specific actions in the area of network and information security.[2]

---

[1] OJ C 300 E, 11.12.2003, p. 26.
[2] OJ C 43, 16.2.2002, p. 2.

(4) The need to further increase awareness of the problems related to information security and provide practical assistance has also been stressed in the European Parliament Resolution of 5 September 2001.

(5) Significant gaps and differences in Member States' laws in this area may hamper the fight against organised crime and terrorism, and may complicate effective police and judicial cooperation in the area of attacks against information systems. The transnational and borderless character of modern information systems means that attacks against such systems are often trans-border in nature, thus underlining the urgent need for further action to approximate criminal laws in this area.

(6) The Action Plan of the Council and the Commission on how to best implement the provisions of the Treaty of Amsterdam on an area of freedom, security and justice,[3] the Tampere European Council on 15 to 16 October 1999, the Santa Maria da Feira European Council on 19 to 20 June 2000, the Commission in the 'Scoreboard' and the European Parliament in its Resolution of 19 May 2000 indicate or call for legislative action against high technology crime, including common definitions, incriminations and sanctions.

(7) It is necessary to complement the work performed by international organisations, in particular the Council of Europe's work on approximating criminal law and the G8's work on transnational cooperation in the area of high tech crime, by providing a common approach in the European Union in this area. This call was further elaborated by the Communication from the Commission to the Council, the European Parliament, the Economic and Social Committee and the Committee of the Regions on 'Creating a Safer Information Society by Improving the Security of Information Infrastructures and Combating Computer-related Crime'.

(8) Criminal law in the area of attacks against information systems should be approximated in order to ensure the greatest possible police and judicial cooperation in the area of criminal offences related to attacks against information systems, and to contribute to the fight against organised crime and terrorism.

(9) All Member States have ratified the Council of Europe Convention of 28 January 1981 for the protection of individuals with regard to automatic processing of personal data. The personal data processed in the context of the implementation of this Framework Decision should be protected in accordance with the principles of the said Convention.

(10) Common definitions in this area, particularly of information systems and computer data, are important to ensure a consistent approach in Member States in the application of this Framework Decision.

(11) There is a need to achieve a common approach to the constituent elements of criminal offences by providing for common offences of illegal access to an information system, illegal system interference and illegal data interference.

(12) In the interest of combating computer-related crime, each Member State should ensure effective judicial cooperation in respect of offences based on the types of conduct referred to in Articles 2, 3, 4 and 5.

(13) There is a need to avoid over-criminalisation, particularly of minor cases, as well as a need to avoid criminalising right-holders and authorised persons.

(14) There is a need for Member States to provide for penalties for attacks against information systems. The penalties thus provided for shall be effective, proportionate and dissuasive.

(15) It is appropriate to provide for more severe penalties when an attack against an information system is committed within the framework of a criminal organisation, as defined in the Joint Action 98/733 JHA of 21 December 1998 on making it a criminal offence to participate in a criminal organisation in the Member State of the European Union.[4] It is also appropriate to provide for more severe penalties where such an attack has caused serious damages or has affected essential interests.

(16) Measures should also be foreseen for the purposes of cooperation between Member States with a view to ensuring effective action against attacks against information systems. Member States should therefore make use of the existing network of operational contact points referred to in the Council Recommendation of 25 June 2001 on contact points maintaining a 24-hour service for combating high-tech crime,[5] for the exchange of information.

---

[3] OJ C 19, 23.1.1999, p. 1.
[4] OJ L 351, 29.12.1998, p. 1.
[5] OJ C 187, 3.7.2001, p. 5.

(17) Since the objectives of this Framework Decision, ensuring that attacks against information systems be sanctioned in all Member States by effective, proportionate and dissuasive criminal penalties and improving and encouraging judicial cooperation by removing potential complications, cannot be sufficiently achieved by the Member States, as rules have to be common and compatible, and can therefore be better achieved at the level of the Union, the Union may adopt measures, in accordance with the principle of subsidiarity as set out in Article 5 of the EC Treaty. In accordance with the principle of proportionality, as set out in that Article, this Framework Decision does not go beyond what is necessary in order to achieve those objectives.

(18) This Framework Decision respects the fundamental rights and observes the principles recognised by Article 6 of the Treaty on European Union and reflected in the Charter of Fundamental Rights of the European Union, and notably Chapters II and VI thereof,

HAS ADOPTED THIS FRAMEWORK DECISION:

Article 1
Definitions

For the purposes of this Framework Decision, the following definitions shall apply:

(a) 'information system' means any device or group of inter-connected or related devices, one or more of which, pursuant to a program, performs automatic processing of computer data, as well as computer data stored, processed, retrieved or transmitted by them for the purposes of their operation, use, protection and maintenance;

(b) 'computer data' means any representation of facts, information or concepts in a form suitable for processing in an information system, including a program suitable for causing an information system to perform a function;

(c) 'legal person' means any entity having such status under the applicable law, except for States or other public bodies in the exercise of State authority and for public international organisations;

(d) 'without right' means access or interference not authorised by the owner, other right holder of the system or part of it, or not permitted under the national legislation.

Article 2
Illegal access to information systems

1. Each Member State shall take the necessary measures to ensure that the intentional access without right to the whole or any part of an information system is punishable as a criminal offence, at least for cases which are not minor.

2. Each Member State may decide that the conduct referred to in paragraph 1 is incriminated only where the offence is committed by infringing a security measure.

Article 3
Illegal system interference

Each Member State shall take the necessary measures to ensure that the intentional serious hindering or interruption of the functioning of an information system by inputting, transmitting, damaging, deleting, deteriorating, altering, suppressing or rendering inaccessible computer data is punishable as a criminal offence when committed without right, at least for cases which are not minor.

Article 4
Illegal data interference

Each Member State shall take the necessary measures to ensure that the intentional deletion, damaging, deterioration, alteration, suppression or rendering inaccessible of computer data on an information system is punishable as a criminal offence when committed without right, at least for cases which are not minor.

Article 5
Instigation, aiding and abetting and attempt

1. Each Member State shall ensure that the instigation of aiding and abetting an offence referred to in Articles 2, 3 and 4 is punishable as a criminal offence.

2. Each Member State shall ensure that the attempt to commit the offences referred to in Articles 2, 3 and 4 is punishable as a criminal offence.

3. Each Member State may decide not to apply paragraph 2 for the offences referred to in Article 2.

Article 6
Penalties

[Similar terms to Art. 4 of Framework Decision 2003/568/JHA.]

Article 7
Aggravating circumstances

1. Each Member State shall take the necessary measures to ensure that the offence referred to in Article 2(2) and the offence referred to in Articles 3 and 4 are punishable by criminal penalties of a maximum of at least between two and five years of imprisonment when committed within the framework of a criminal organisation as defined in Joint Action 98/733/JHA apart from the penalty level referred to therein.

2. A Member State may also take the measures referred to in paragraph 1 when the offence has caused serious damages or has affected essential interests.

Article 8
Liability of legal persons

[Similar terms to Art. 5 of Framework Decision 2003/568/JHA.]

Article 9
Penalties for legal persons

[Similar terms to Art. 6 of Framework Decision 2003/568/JHA.]

Article 10
Jurisdiction

1. Each Member State shall establish its jurisdiction with regard to the offences referred to in Articles 2, 3, 4 and 5 where the offence has been committed:
   (a) in whole or in part within its territory; or
   (b) by one of its nationals; or
   (c) for the benefit of a legal person that has its head office in the territory of that Member State.

2. When establishing its jurisdiction in accordance with paragraph (1)(a), each Member State shall ensure that the jurisdiction includes cases where:
   (a) the offender commits the offence when physically present on its territory, whether or not the offence is against an information system on its territory; or
   (b) the offence is against an information system on its territory, whether or not the offender commits the offence when physically present on its territory.

3. A Member State which, under its law, does not as yet extradite or surrender its own nationals shall take the necessary measures to establish its jurisdiction over and to prosecute, where appropriate, the offences referred to in Articles 2, 3, 4 and 5, when committed by one of its nationals outside its territory.

4. Where an offence falls within the jurisdiction of more than one Member State and when any of the States concerned can validly prosecute on the basis of the same facts, the Member States concerned shall cooperate in order to decide which of them will prosecute the offenders with the aim, if possible, of centralising proceedings in a single Member State. To this end, the Member States may have recourse to any body or mechanism established within the European Union in order to facilitate cooperation between their judicial authorities and the coordination of their action. Sequential account may be taken of the following factors:
   - the Member State shall be that in the territory of which the offences have been committed according to paragraph 1(a) and paragraph 2,
   - the Member State shall be that of which the perpetrator is a national,
   - the Member State shall be that in which the perpetrator has been found.

5. A Member State may decide not to apply, or to apply only in specific cases or circumstances, the jurisdiction rules set out in paragraphs 1(b) and 1(c).

6. Member States shall inform the General Secretariat of the Council and the Commission where they decide to apply paragraph 5, where appropriate with an indication of the specific cases or circumstances in which the decision applies.

Article 11
Exchange of information

1. For the purpose of exchange of information relating to the offences referred to in Articles 2, 3, 4 and 5, and in accordance with data protection rules, Member States shall ensure that they make use of the existing network of operational points of contact available 24 hours a day and seven days a week.

2. Each Member State shall inform the General Secretariat of the Council and the Commission of its appointed point of contact for the purpose of exchanging information on offences relating to attacks against information systems. The General Secretariat shall forward that information to the other Member States.

Article 12
Implementation

1. Member States shall take the necessary measures to comply with the provisions of this Framework Decision by 16 March 2007.

2. By 16 March 2007 Member States shall transmit to the General Secretariat of the Council and to the Commission the text of any provisions transposing into their national law the obligations imposed on them under this Framework Decision. By 16 September 2007, on the basis of a report established on the basis of information and a written report by the Commission, the Council shall assess the extent to which Member States have complied with the provisions of this Framework Decision.

Drug trafficking—Council Framework Decision 2004/757/JHA

Council Framework Decision 2004/757/JHA of 25 October 2004 laying down minimum provisions on the constituent elements of criminal acts and penalties in the field of illicit drug trafficking

THE COUNCIL OF THE EUROPEAN UNION,

Having regard to the Treaty on European Union, and in particular Article 31(e) and Article 34(2)(b) thereof,

Having regard to the proposal from the Commission,[1]

Having regard to the opinion of the European Parliament,[2]

Whereas:

(1) Illicit drug trafficking poses a threat to health, safety and the quality of life of citizens of the European Union, and to the legal economy, stability and security of the Member States.

(2) The need for legislative action to tackle illicit drug trafficking has been recognised in particular in the Action Plan of the Council and the Commission on how best to implement the provisions of the Amsterdam Treaty on an area of freedom, security and justice,[3] adopted by the Justice and Home Affairs Council in Vienna on 3 December 1998, the conclusions of the Tampere European Council of 15 and 16 October 1999, in particular point 48 thereof, the European Union's Drugs Strategy (2000–2004) endorsed by the Helsinki European Council from 10 to 12 December 1999 and the European Union's Action Plan on Drugs (2000–2004) endorsed by the European Council in Santa Maria da Feira on 19 and 20 June 2000.

---

[1] OJ C 304 E, 30.10.2001, p. 172.
[2] Opinion of 9 March 2004 (not yet published in the Official Journal).
[3] OJ C 19, 23.1.1999, p. 1.

(3) It is necessary to adopt minimum rules relating to the constituent elements of the offences of illicit trafficking in drugs and precursors which will allow a common approach at European Union level to the fight against such trafficking.

(4) By virtue of the principle of subsidiarity, European Union action should focus on the most serious types of drug offence. The exclusion of certain types of behaviour as regards personal consumption from the scope of this Framework Decision does not constitute a Council guideline on how Member States should deal with these other cases in their national legislation.

(5) Penalties provided for by the Member States should be effective, proportionate and dissuasive, and include custodial sentences. To determine the level of penalties, factual elements such as the quantities and the type of drugs trafficked, and whether the offence was committed within the framework of a criminal organisation, should be taken into account.

(6) Member States should be allowed to make provision for reducing the penalties when the offender has supplied the competent authorities with valuable information.

(7) It is necessary to take measures to enable the confiscation of the proceeds of the offences referred to in this Framework Decision.

(8) Measures should be taken to ensure that legal persons can be held liable for the criminal offences referred to by this Framework Decision which are committed for their benefit.

(9) The effectiveness of the efforts made to tackle illicit drug trafficking depends essentially on the harmonisation of the national measures implementing this Framework Decision,

HAS DECIDED AS FOLLOWS:

Article 1
Definitions

For the purposes of this Framework Decision:

1. 'drugs': shall mean any of the substances covered by the following United Nations Conventions:
   (a) the 1961 Single Convention on Narcotic Drugs (as amended by the 1972 Protocol);
   (b) the 1971 Vienna Convention on Psychotropic Substances. It shall also include the substances subject to controls under Joint Action 97/396/JHA of 16 June 1997 concerning the information exchange risk assessment and the control of new synthetic drugs;[4]
2. 'precursors': shall mean any substance scheduled in the Community legislation giving effect to the obligations deriving from Article 12 of the United Nations Convention against Illicit Traffic in Narcotic Drugs and Psychotropic Substances of 20 December 1988;
3. 'legal person': shall mean any legal entity having such status under the applicable national law, except for States or other public bodies acting in the exercise of their sovereign rights and for public international organisations.

Article 2
Crimes linked to trafficking in drugs and precursors

1. Each Member State shall take the necessary measures to ensure that the following intentional conduct when committed without right is punishable:
   (a) the production, manufacture, extraction, preparation, offering, offering for sale, distribution, sale, delivery on any terms whatsoever, brokerage, dispatch, dispatch in transit, transport, importation or exportation of drugs;
   (b) the cultivation of opium poppy, coca bush or cannabis plant;
   (c) the possession or purchase of drugs with a view to conducting one of the activities listed in (a);
   (d) the manufacture, transport or distribution of precursors, knowing that they are to be used in or for the illicit production or manufacture of drugs.
2. The conduct described in paragraph 1 shall not be included in the scope of this Framework Decision when it is committed by its perpetrators exclusively for their own personal consumption as defined by national law.

---

[4] OJ L 167, 25.6.1997, p. 1.

Article 3
Incitement, aiding and abetting and attempt

1. Each Member State shall take the necessary measures to make incitement to commit, aiding and abetting or attempting one of the offences referred to in Article 2 a criminal offence.
2. A Member State may exempt from criminal liability the attempt to offer or prepare drugs referred to in Article 2(1)(a) and the attempt to possess drugs referred to in Article 2(1)(c).

Article 4
Penalties

1. Each Member State shall take the measures necessary to ensure that the offences defined in Articles 2 and 3 are punishable by effective, proportionate and dissuasive criminal penalties.
   Each Member State shall take the necessary measures to ensure that the offences referred to in Article 2 are punishable by criminal penalties of a maximum of at least between one and three years of imprisonment.
2. Each Member State shall take the necessary measures to ensure that the offences referred to in Article 2(1)(a), (b) and (c) are punishable by criminal penalties of a maximum of at least between 5 and 10 years of imprisonment in each of the following circumstances:
   (a) the offence involves large quantities of drugs;
   (b) the offence either involves those drugs which cause the most harm to health, or has resulted in significant damage to the health of a number of persons.
3. Each Member State shall take the necessary measures to ensure that the offences referred to in paragraph 2 are punishable by criminal penalties of a maximum of at least 10 years of deprivation of liberty, where the offence was committed within the framework of a criminal organisation as defined in Joint Action 98/733/JHA of 21 December 1998 on making it a criminal offence to participate in a criminal organisation in the Member States of the European Union.[5]
4. Each Member State shall take the necessary measures to ensure that the offences referred to in Article 2(1)(d) are punishable by criminal penalties of a maximum of at least between 5 and 10 years of deprivation of liberty, where the offence was committed within the framework of a criminal organisation as defined in Joint Action 98/733/JHA and the precursors are intended to be used in or for the production or manufacture of drugs under the circumstances referred to in paragraphs 2(a) or (b).
5. Without prejudice to the rights of victims and of other bona fide third parties, each Member State shall take the necessary measures to enable the confiscation of substances which are the object of offences referred to in Articles 2 and 3, instrumentalities used or intended to be used for these offences and proceeds from these offences or the confiscation of property the value of which corresponds to that of such proceeds, substances or instrumentalities.
   The terms 'confiscation', 'instrumentalities', 'proceeds' and 'property' shall have the same meaning as in Article 1 of the 1990 Council of Europe Convention on Laundering, Search, Seizure and Confiscation of the Proceeds from Crime.

Article 5
Particular circumstances

Notwithstanding Article 4, each Member State may take the necessary measures to ensure that the penalties referred to in Article 4 may be reduced if the offender:

(a) renounces criminal activity relating to trafficking in drugs and precursors, and
(b) provides the administrative or judicial authorities with information which they would not otherwise have been able to obtain, helping them to:
   (i) prevent or mitigate the effects of the offence,
   (ii) identify or bring to justice the other offenders,
   (iii) find evidence, or
   (iv) prevent further offences referred to in Articles 2 and 3.

---

[5] OJ L 351, 29.12.1998, p. 1.

Article 6
Liability of legal persons

[Similar terms to Art. 5 of Framework Decision 2003/568/JHA.]

Article 7
Sanctions for legal persons

1. Member States shall take the necessary measures to ensure that a legal person held liable pursuant to Article 6(1) is punishable by effective, proportionate and dissuasive sanctions, which shall include criminal or non-criminal fines and may include other sanctions, such as:
   (a) exclusion from entitlement to tax relief or other benefits or public aid;
   (b) temporary or permanent disqualification from the pursuit of commercial activities;
   (c) placing under judicial supervision;
   (d) a judicial winding-up order;
   (e) temporary or permanent closure of establishments used for committing the offence;
   (f) in accordance with Article 4(5), the confiscation of substances which are the object of offences referred to in Articles 2 and 3, instrumentalities used or intended to be used for these offences and proceeds from these offences or the confiscation of property the value of which corresponds to that of such proceeds, substances or instrumentalities.
2. Each Member State shall take the necessary measures to ensure that a legal person held liable pursuant to Article 6(2) is punishable by effective, proportionate and dissuasive sanctions or measures.

Article 8
Jurisdiction and prosecution

[Similar terms to Art. 7 of Framework Decision 2003/568/JHA.]

Article 9
Implementation and reports

1. Member States shall take the necessary measures to comply with the provisions of this Framework Decision by 12 May 2006.
2. By the deadline referred to in paragraph 1, Member States shall transmit to the General Secretariat of the Council and to the Commission the text of the provisions transposing into their national law the obligations imposed on them under this Framework Decision. The Commission shall, by 12 May 2009, submit a report to the European Parliament and to the Council on the functioning of the implementation of the Framework Decision, including its effects on judicial cooperation in the field of illicit drug trafficking. Following this report, the Council shall assess, at the latest within six months after submission of the report, whether Member States have taken the necessary measures to comply with this Framework Decision.

Environmental crime—Environmental Protection (Criminal Enforcement) Directive 2008/99/EC

Directive 2008/99/EC of the European Parliament and of the Council of 19 November 2008 on the protection of the environment through criminal law (Text with EEA relevance)

THE EUROPEAN PARLIAMENT AND THE COUNCIL OF THE EUROPEAN UNION,

Having regard to the Treaty establishing the European Community, and in particular Article 175(1) thereof,

Having regard to the proposal from the Commission,

Having regard to the opinion of the European Economic and Social Committee[1],

After consulting the Committee of the Regions,

Acting in accordance with the procedure laid down in Article 251 of the Treaty[2],

---

[1] OJ C 10, 15.1.2008, p. 47.
[2] Opinion of the European Parliament of 21 May 2008 (not yet published in the Official Journal) and Council Decision of 24 October 2008.

Whereas:

(1) According to Article 174(2) of the Treaty, Community policy on the environment must aim at a high level of protection.

(2) The Community is concerned at the rise in environmental offences and at their effects, which are increasingly extending beyond the borders of the States in which the offences are committed. Such offences pose a threat to the environment and therefore call for an appropriate response.

(3) Experience has shown that the existing systems of penalties have not been sufficient to achieve complete compliance with the laws for the protection of the environment. Such compliance can and should be strengthened by the availability of criminal penalties, which demonstrate a social disapproval of a qualitatively different nature compared to administrative penalties or a compensation mechanism under civil law.

(4) Common rules on criminal offences make it possible to use effective methods of investigation and assistance within and between Member States.

(5) In order to achieve effective protection of the environment, there is a particular need for more dissuasive penalties for environmentally harmful activities, which typically cause or are likely to cause substantial damage to the air, including the stratosphere, to soil, water, animals or plants, including to the conservation of species.

(6) Failure to comply with a legal duty to act can have the same effect as active behaviour and should therefore also be subject to corresponding penalties.

(7) Therefore, such conduct should be considered a criminal offence throughout the Community when committed intentionally or with serious negligence.

(8) The legislation listed in the Annexes to this Directive contains provisions which should be subject to criminal law measures in order to ensure that the rules on environmental protection are fully effective.

(9) The obligations under this Directive only relate to the provisions of the legislation listed in the Annexes to this Directive which entail an obligation for Member States, when implementing that legislation, to provide for prohibitive measures.

(10) This Directive obliges Member States to provide for criminal penalties in their national legislation in respect of serious infringements of provisions of Community law on the protection of the environment. This Directive creates no obligations regarding the application of such penalties, or any other available system of law enforcement, in individual cases.

(11) This Directive is without prejudice to other systems of liability for environmental damage under Community law or national law.

(12) As this Directive provides for minimum rules, Member States are free to adopt or maintain more stringent measures regarding the effective criminal law protection of the environment. Such measures must be compatible with the Treaty.

(13) Member States should provide information to the Commission on the implementation of this Directive, in order to enable it to evaluate the effect of this Directive.

(14) Since the objective of this Directive, namely to ensure a more effective protection of the environment, cannot be sufficiently achieved by the Member States and can therefore, by reason of the scale and effects of this Directive, be better achieved at Community level, the Community may adopt measures, in accordance with the principle of subsidiarity as set out in Article 5 of the Treaty. In accordance with the principle of proportionality, as set out in that Article, this Directive does not go beyond what is necessary in order to achieve that objective.

(15) Whenever subsequent legislation on environmental matters is adopted, it should specify where appropriate that this Directive will apply. Where necessary, Article 3 should be amended.

(16) This Directive respects the fundamental rights and observes the principles as recognised in particular by the Charter of Fundamental Rights of the European Union,

HAVE ADOPTED THIS DIRECTIVE:

Article 1
Subject matter

This Directive establishes measures relating to criminal law in order to protect the environment more effectively.

Article 2
Definitions

For the purpose of this Directive:
(a) 'unlawful' means infringing:
  (i) the legislation adopted pursuant to the EC Treaty and listed in Annex A; or
  (ii) with regard to activities covered by the Euratom Treaty, the legislation adopted pursuant to the Euratom Treaty and listed in Annex B; or
  (iii) a law, an administrative regulation of a Member State or a decision taken by a competent authority of a Member State that gives effect to the Community legislation referred to in (i) or (ii);
(b) 'protected wild fauna and flora species' are:

  (i) for the purposes of Article 3(f), those listed in:
    – Annex IV to Council Directive 92/43/EEC of 21 May 1992 on the conservation of natural habitats and of wild fauna and flora[3],
    – Annex I to, and referred to in Article 4(2) of, Council Directive 79/409/EEC of 2 April 1979 on the conservation of wild birds [4];
  (ii) for the purposes of Article 3(g), those listed in Annex A or B to Council Regulation (EC) No 338/97 of 9 December 1996 on the protection of species of wild fauna and flora by regulating trade therein[5];
(c) 'habitat within a protected site' means any habitat of species for which an area is classified as a special protection area pursuant to Article 4(1) or (2) of Directive 79/409/EEC, or any natural habitat or a habitat of species for which a site is designated as a special area of conservation pursuant to Article 4(4) of Directive 92/43/EEC;
(d) 'legal person' means any legal entity having such status under the applicable national law, except for States or public bodies exercising State authority and for public international organisations.

Article 3
Offences

Member States shall ensure that the following conduct constitutes a criminal offence, when unlawful and committed intentionally or with at least serious negligence:
(a) the discharge, emission or introduction of a quantity of materials or ionising radiation into air, soil or water, which causes or is likely to cause death or serious injury to any person or substantial damage to the quality of air, the quality of soil or the quality of water, or to animals or plants;
(b) the collection, transport, recovery or disposal of waste, including the supervision of such operations and the after-care of disposal sites, and including action taken as a dealer or a broker (waste management), which causes or is likely to cause death or serious injury to any person or substantial damage to the quality of air, the quality of soil or the quality of water, or to animals or plants;
(c) the shipment of waste, where this activity falls within the scope of Article 2(35) of Regulation (EC) No 1013/2006 of the European Parliament and of the Council of 14 June 2006 on shipments of waste[6] and is undertaken in a non-negligible quantity, whether executed in a single shipment or in several shipments which appear to be linked;
(d) the operation of a plant in which a dangerous activity is carried out or in which dangerous substances or preparations are stored or used and which, outside the plant, causes or is likely to cause death or serious injury to any person or substantial damage to the quality of air, the quality of soil or the quality of water, or to animals or plants;
(e) the production, processing, handling, use, holding, storage, transport, import, export or disposal of nuclear materials or other hazardous radioactive substances which causes or is likely to cause death or serious injury to any person or substantial damage to the quality of air, the quality of soil or the quality of water, or to animals or plants;

---

[3] OJ L 206, 22.7.1992, p. 7.
[4] OJ L 103, 25.4.1979, p. 1.
[5] OJ L 61, 3.3.1997, p. 1.
[6] OJ L 190, 12.7.2006, p. 1.

(f) the killing, destruction, possession or taking of specimens of protected wild fauna or flora species, except for cases where the conduct concerns a negligible quantity of such specimens and has a negligible impact on the conservation status of the species;

(g) trading in specimens of protected wild fauna or flora species or parts or derivatives thereof, except for cases where the conduct concerns a negligible quantity of such specimens and has a negligible impact on the conservation status of the species;

(h) any conduct which causes the significant deterioration of a habitat within a protected site;

(i) the production, importation, exportation, placing on the market or use of ozone-depleting substances.

Article 4
Inciting, aiding and abetting

[In similar terms to Art. 3 of Framework Decision 2003/568/JHA.]

Article 5
Penalties

Member States shall take the necessary measures to ensure that the offences referred to in Articles 3 and 4 are punishable by effective, proportionate and dissuasive criminal penalties.

Article 6
Liability of legal persons

[Similar terms to Art. 5 of Framework Decision 2003/568/JHA.]

Article 7
Penalties for legal persons

Member States shall take the necessary measures to ensure that legal persons held liable pursuant to Article 6 are punishable by effective, proportionate and dissuasive penalties.

Article 8
Transposition

1. Member States shall bring into force the laws, regulations and administrative provisions necessary to comply with this Directive before 26 December 2010.

    When Member States adopt these measures, they shall contain a reference to this Directive or be accompanied by such a reference on the occasion of their official publication. Member States shall determine how such reference is to be made.

2. Member States shall communicate to the Commission the text of the main provisions of national law which they adopt in the field covered by this Directive and a table indicating the correlation between those provisions and this Directive.

Article 9
ANNEX A

List of Community legislation adopted pursuant to the EC Treaty, the infringement of which constitutes unlawful conduct pursuant to Article 2(a)(i) of this Directive

- Council Directive 70/220/EEC of 20 March 1970 on the approximation of the laws of the Member States on measures to be taken against air pollution by emissions from motor vehicles,
- Council Directive 72/306/EEC of 2 August 1972 on the approximation of the laws of the Member States relating to the measures to be taken against the emission of pollutants from diesel engines for use in vehicles,
- Council Directive 75/439/EEC of 16 June 1975 on the disposal of waste oils,
- Council Directive 76/160/EEC of 8 December 1975 concerning the quality of bathing water,
- Council Directive 76/769/EEC of 27 July 1976 on the approximation of the laws, regulations and administrative provisions of the Member States relating to restrictions on the marketing and use of certain dangerous substances and preparations,

- Council Directive 77/537/EEC of 28 June 1977 on the approximation of the laws of the Member States relating to the measures to be taken against the emission of pollutants from diesel engines for use in wheeled agricultural or forestry tractors,
- Council Directive 78/176/EEC of 20 February 1978 on waste from the titanium dioxide industry,
- Council Directive 79/117/EEC of 21 December 1978 prohibiting the placing on the market and use of plant protection products containing certain active substances,
- Council Directive 79/409/EEC of 2 April 1979 on the conservation of wild birds,
- Council Directive 82/176/EEC of 22 March 1982 on limit values and quality objectives for mercury discharges by the chlor-alkali electrolysis industry,
- Council Directive 83/513/EEC of 26 September 1983 on limit values and quality objectives for cadmium discharges,
- Council Directive 84/156/EEC of 8 March 1984 on limit values and quality objectives for mercury discharges by sectors other than the chlor-alkali electrolysis industry,
- Council Directive 84/360/EEC of 28 June 1984 on the combating of air pollution from industrial plants,
- Council Directive 84/491/EEC of 9 October 1984 on limit values and quality objectives for discharges of hexachlorocyclohexane,
- Council Directive 85/203/EEC of 7 March 1985 on air quality standards for nitrogen dioxide,
- Council Directive 86/278/EEC of 12 June 1986 on the protection of the environment, and in particular of the soil, when sewage sludge is used in agriculture,
- Council Directive 86/280/EEC of 12 June 1986 on limit values and quality objectives for discharges of certain dangerous substances included in List I of the Annex to Directive 76/464/EEC,
- Council Directive 87/217/EEC of 19 March 1987 on the prevention and reduction of environmental pollution by asbestos,
- Council Directive 90/219/EEC of 23 April 1990 on the contained use of genetically modified micro-organisms,
- Council Directive 91/271/EEC of 21 May 1991 concerning urban waste-water treatment,
- Council Directive 91/414/EEC of 15 July 1991 concerning the placing of plant protection products on the market,
- Council Directive 91/676/EEC of 12 December 1991 concerning the protection of waters against pollution caused by nitrates from agricultural sources,
- Council Directive 91/689/EEC of 12 December 1991 on hazardous waste,
- Council Directive 92/43/EEC of 21 May 1992 on the conservation of natural habitats and of wild fauna and flora,
- Council Directive 92/112/EEC of 15 December 1992 on procedures for harmonising the programmes for the reduction and eventual elimination of pollution caused by waste from the titanium dioxide industry,
- Directive 94/25/EC of the European Parliament and of the Council of 16 June 1994 on the approximation of the laws, regulations and administrative provisions of the Member States relating to recreational craft: the provisions amended by Directive 2003/44/EC,
- European Parliament and Council Directive 94/62/EC of 20 December 1994 on packaging and packaging waste,
- European Parliament and Council Directive 94/63/EC of 20 December 1994 on the control of volatile organic compound (VOC) emissions resulting from the storage of petrol and its distribution from terminals to service stations,
- Council Directive 96/49/EC of 23 July 1996 on the approximation of the laws of the Member States with regard to the transport of dangerous goods by rail,
- Council Directive 96/59/EC of 16 September 1996 on the disposal of polychlorinated biphenyls and polychlorinated terphenyls (PCB/PCT),
- Council Directive 96/62/EC of 27 September 1996 on ambient air quality assessment and management,
- Council Directive 96/82/EC of 9 December 1996 on the control of major-accident hazards involving dangerous substances,

- Directive 97/68/EC of the European Parliament and of the Council of 16 December 1997 on the approximation of the laws of the Member States relating to measures against the emission of gaseous and particulate pollutants from internal combustion engines to be installed in non-road mobile machinery,
- Council Regulation (EC) No 338/97 of 9 December 1996 on the protection of species of wild fauna and flora by regulating trade therein,
- Directive 98/8/EC of the European Parliament and of the Council of 16 February 1998 concerning the placing of biocidal products on the market,
- Directive 98/70/EC of the European Parliament and of the Council of 13 October 1998 relating to the quality of petrol and diesel fuels,
- Council Directive 98/83/EC of 3 November 1998 on the quality of water intended for human consumption,
- Council Directive 1999/13/EC of 11 March 1999 on the limitation of emissions of volatile organic compounds due to the use of organic solvents in certain activities and installations,
- Council Directive 1999/30/EC of 22 April 1999 relating to limit values for sulphur dioxide, nitrogen dioxide and oxides of nitrogen, particulate matter and lead in ambient air,
- Council Directive 1999/31/EC of 26 April 1999 on the landfill of waste,
- Council Directive 1999/32/EC of 26 April 1999 relating to a reduction in the sulphur content of certain liquid fuels,
- Directive 2000/53/EC of the European Parliament and of the Council of 18 September 2000 on end of life vehicles,
- Directive 2000/60/EC of the European Parliament and of the Council of 23 October 2000 establishing a framework for Community action in the field of water policy,
- Directive 2000/69/EC of the European Parliament and of the Council of 16 November 2000 relating to limit values for benzene and carbon monoxide in ambient air,
- Directive 2000/76/EC of the European Parliament and of the Council of 4 December 2000 on the incineration of waste,
- Regulation (EC) No 2037/2000 of the European Parliament and of the Council of 29 June 2000 on substances that deplete the ozone layer,
- Directive 2001/18/EC of the European Parliament and of the Council of 12 March 2001 on the deliberate release into the environment of genetically modified organisms,
- Directive 2001/80/EC of the European Parliament and of the Council of 23 October 2001 on the limitation of emissions of certain pollutants into the air from large combustion plants,
- Directive 2002/3/EC of the European Parliament and of the Council of 12 February 2002 relating to ozone in ambient air,
- Directive 2002/95/EC of the European Parliament and of the Council of 27 January 2003 on the restriction of the use of certain hazardous substances in electrical and electronic equipment,
- Directive 2002/96/EC of the European Parliament and of the Council of 27 January 2003 on waste electrical and electronic equipment (WEEE),
- Directive 2004/107/EC of the European Parliament and of the Council of 15 December 2004 relating to arsenic, cadmium, mercury, nickel and polycyclic aromatic hydrocarbons in ambient air,
- Regulation (EC) No 648/2004 of the European Parliament and of the Council of 31 March 2004 on detergents,
- Regulation (EC) No 850/2004 of the European Parliament and of the Council of 29 April 2004 on persistent organic pollutants,
- Directive 2005/55/EC of the European Parliament and of the Council of 28 September 2005 on the approximation of the laws of the Member States relating to the measures to be taken against the emission of gaseous and particulate pollutants from compression-ignition engines for use in vehicles, and the emission of gaseous pollutants from positive-ignition engines fuelled with natural gas or liquefied petroleum gas for use in vehicles,
- Commission Directive 2005/78/EC of 14 November 2005 implementing Directive 2005/55/EC of the European Parliament and of the Council on the approximation of the laws of the Member States relating to the measures to be taken against the emission of gaseous and particulate pollutants from compression-ignition engines for use in vehicles, and the emission of gaseous pollutants from positive

ignition engines fuelled with natural gas or liquefied petroleum gas for use in vehicles and amending Annexes I, II, III, IV and VI thereto,

• Directive 2006/7/EC of the European Parliament and of the Council of 15 February 2006 concerning the management of bathing water quality,

• Directive 2006/11/EC of the European Parliament and of the Council of 15 February 2006 on pollution caused by certain dangerous substances discharged into the aquatic environment of the Community,

• Directive 2006/12/EC of the European Parliament and of the Council of 5 April 2006 on waste,

• Directive 2006/21/EC of the European Parliament and of the Council of 15 March 2006 on the management of waste from extractive industries,

• Directive 2006/40/EC of the European Parliament and of the Council of 17 May 2006 relating to emissions from air conditioning systems in motor vehicles,

• Directive 2006/44/EC of the European Parliament and of the Council of 6 September 2006 on the quality of fresh waters needing protection or improvement in order to support fish life,

• Directive 2006/66/EC of the European Parliament and of the Council of 6 September 2006 on batteries and accumulators and waste batteries and accumulators,

• Directive 2006/118/EC of the European Parliament and of the Council of 12 December 2006 on the protection of groundwater against pollution and deterioration,

• Regulation (EC) No 842/2006 of the European Parliament and of the Council of 17 May 2006 on certain fluorinated greenhouse gases,

• Regulation (EC) No 1013/2006 of the European Parliament and of the Council of 14 June 2006 on shipments of waste,

• Regulation (EC) No 715/2007 of the European Parliament and of the Council of 20 June 2007 on type approval of motor vehicles with respect to emissions from light passenger and commercial vehicles (Euro 5 and Euro 6) and on access to vehicle repair and maintenance information,

• Commission Regulation (EC) No 1418/2007 of 29 November 2007 concerning the export for recovery of certain waste listed in Annex III or IIIA to Regulation (EC) No 1013/2006 of the European Parliament and of the Council to certain countries to which the OECD Decision on the control of transboundary movements of wastes does not apply,

• Directive 2008/1/EC of the European Parliament and of the Council of 15 January 2008 concerning integrated pollution prevention and control.

Annex B

List of Community Legislation adopted pursuant to the Euratom Treaty, the infringement of which constitutes unlawful conduct pursuant to Article 2(a)(ii) of this Directive

• Council Directive 96/29/Euratom of 13 May 1996 laying down basic safety standards for the protection of the health of workers and the general public against the dangers arising from ionising radiation;

• Council Directive 2003/122/Euratom of 22 December 2003 on the control of high-activity sealed radioactive sources and orphan sources;

• Council Directive 2006/117/Euratom of 20 November 2006 on the supervision and control of shipments of radioactive waste and spent fuel.

Extradition—Council Framework Decision 2002/584/JHA

Council Framework Decision of 13 June 2002 on the European arrest warrant and the surrender procedures between Member States (2002/584/JHA)

THE COUNCIL OF THE EUROPEAN UNION,

Having regard to the Treaty on European Union, and in particular Article 31(a) and (b) and Article 34(2)(b) thereof,

Having regard to the proposal from the Commission[1],

Having regard to the opinion of the European Parliament[2],

Whereas:

(1) According to the Conclusions of the Tampere European Council of 15 and 16 October 1999, and in particular point 35 thereof, the formal extradition procedure should be abolished among the Member States in respect of persons who are fleeing from justice after having been finally sentenced and extradition procedures should be speeded up in respect of persons suspected of having committed an offence.

(2) The programme of measures to implement the principle of mutual recognition of criminal decisions envisaged in point 37 of the Tampere European Council Conclusions and adopted by the Council on 30 November 2000[3], addresses the matter of mutual enforcement of arrest warrants.

(3) All or some Member States are parties to a number of conventions in the field of extradition, including the European Convention on extradition of 13 December 1957 and the European Convention on the suppression of terrorism of 27 January 1977. The Nordic States have extradition laws with identical wording.

(4) In addition, the following three Conventions dealing in whole or in part with extradition have been agreed upon among Member States and form part of the Union acquis: the Convention of 19 June 1990 implementing the Schengen Agreement of 14 June 1985 on the gradual abolition of checks at their common borders[4] (regarding relations between the Member States which are parties to that Convention), the Convention of 10 March 1995 on simplified extradition procedure between the Member States of the European Union[5] and the Convention of 27 September 1996 relating to extradition between the Member States of the European Union[6].

(5) The objective set for the Union to become an area of freedom, security and justice leads to abolishing extradition between Member States and replacing it by a system of surrender between judicial authorities. Further, the introduction of a new simplified system of surrender of sentenced or suspected persons for the purposes of execution or prosecution of criminal sentences makes it possible to remove the complexity and potential for delay inherent in the present extradition procedures. Traditional cooperation relations which have prevailed up till now between Member States should be replaced by a system of free movement of judicial decisions in criminal matters, covering both pre-sentence and final decisions, within an area of freedom, security and justice.

(6) The European arrest warrant provided for in this Framework Decision is the first concrete measure in the field of criminal law implementing the principle of mutual recognition which the European Council referred to as the 'cornerstone' of judicial cooperation.

(7) Since the aim of replacing the system of multilateral extradition built upon the European Convention on Extradition of 13 December 1957 cannot be sufficiently achieved by the Member States acting unilaterally and can therefore, by reason of its scale and effects, be better achieved at Union level, the Council may adopt measures in accordance with the principle of subsidiarity as referred to in Article 2 of the Treaty on European Union and Article 5 of the Treaty establishing the European Community. In accordance with the principle of proportionality, as set out in the latter Article, this Framework Decision does not go beyond what is necessary in order to achieve that objective.

(8) Decisions on the execution of the European arrest warrant must be subject to sufficient controls, which means that a judicial authority of the Member State where the requested person has been arrested will have to take the decision on his or her surrender.

(9) The role of central authorities in the execution of a European arrest warrant must be limited to practical and administrative assistance.

(10) The mechanism of the European arrest warrant is based on a high level of confidence between Member States. Its implementation may be suspended only in the event of a serious and persistent breach by one of the Member States of the principles set out in Article 6(1) of the Treaty on European Union,

---

[1] OJ C 332 E, 27.11.2001, p. 305.
[2] Opinion delivered on 9 January 2002 (not yet published in the Official Journal).
[3] OJ C 12 E, 15.1.2001, p. 10.
[4] OJ L 239, 22.9.2000, p. 19.
[5] OJ C 78, 30.3.1995, p. 2.
[6] OJ C 313, 13.10.1996, p. 12.

determined by the Council pursuant to Article 7(1) of the said Treaty with the consequences set out in Article 7(2) thereof.

(11) In relations between Member States, the European arrest warrant should replace all the previous instruments concerning extradition, including the provisions of Title III of the Convention implementing the Schengen Agreement which concern extradition.

(12) This Framework Decision respects fundamental rights and observes the principles recognised by Article 6 of the Treaty on European Union and reflected in the Charter of Fundamental Rights of the European Union[7], in particular Chapter VI thereof. Nothing in this Framework Decision may be interpreted as prohibiting refusal to surrender a person for whom a European arrest warrant has been issued when there are reasons to believe, on the basis of objective elements, that the said arrest warrant has been issued for the purpose of prosecuting or punishing a person on the grounds of his or her sex, race, religion, ethnic origin, nationality, language, political opinions or sexual orientation, or that that person's position may be prejudiced for any of these reasons.

This Framework Decision does not prevent a Member State from applying its constitutional rules relating to due process, freedom of association, freedom of the press and freedom of expression in other media.

(13) No person should be removed, expelled or extradited to a State where there is a serious risk that he or she would be subjected to the death penalty, torture or other inhuman or degrading treatment or punishment.

(14) Since all Member States have ratified the Council of Europe Convention of 28 January 1981 for the protection of individuals with regard to automatic processing of personal data, the personal data processed in the context of the implementation of this Framework Decision should be protected in accordance with the principles of the said Convention,

HAS ADOPTED THIS FRAMEWORK DECISION:

CHAPTER 1
GENERAL PRINCIPLES

Article 1

Definition of the European arrest warrant and obligation to execute it

1. The European arrest warrant is a judicial decision issued by a Member State with a view to the arrest and surrender by another Member State of a requested person, for the purposes of conducting a criminal prosecution or executing a custodial sentence or detention order.
2. Member States shall execute any European arrest warrant on the basis of the principle of mutual recognition and in accordance with the provisions of this Framework Decision.
3. This Framework Decision shall not have the effect of modifying the obligation to respect fundamental rights and fundamental legal principles as enshrined in Article 6 of the Treaty on European Union.

Article 2
Scope of the European arrest warrant

1. A European arrest warrant may be issued for acts punishable by the law of the issuing Member State by a custodial sentence or a detention order for a maximum period of at least 12 months or, where a sentence has been passed or a detention order has been made, for sentences of at least four months.
2. The following offences, if they are punishable in the issuing Member State by a custodial sentence or a detention order for a maximum period of at least three years and as they are defined by the law of the issuing Member State, shall, under the terms of this Framework Decision and without verification of the double criminality of the act, give rise to surrender pursuant to a European arrest warrant:
    – participation in a criminal organisation,
    – terrorism,
    – trafficking in human beings,
    – sexual exploitation of children and child pornography,
    – illicit trafficking in narcotic drugs and psychotropic substances,

---

[7] OJ C 364, 18.12.2000, p. 1.

- illicit trafficking in weapons, munitions and explosives,
- corruption,
- fraud, including that affecting the financial interests of the European Communities within the meaning of the Convention of 26 July 1995 on the protection of the European Communities' financial interests,
- laundering of the proceeds of crime,
- counterfeiting currency, including of the euro,
- computer-related crime,
- environmental crime, including illicit trafficking in endangered animal species and in endangered plant species and varieties,
- facilitation of unauthorised entry and residence,
- murder, grievous bodily injury,
- illicit trade in human organs and tissue,
- kidnapping, illegal restraint and hostage-taking,
- racism and xenophobia,
- organised or armed robbery,
- illicit trafficking in cultural goods, including antiques and works of art,
- swindling,
- racketeering and extortion,
- counterfeiting and piracy of products,
- forgery of administrative documents and trafficking therein,
- forgery of means of payment,
- illicit trafficking in hormonal substances and other growth promoters,
- illicit trafficking in nuclear or radioactive materials,
- trafficking in stolen vehicles,
- rape,
- arson,
- crimes within the jurisdiction of the International Criminal Court,
- unlawful seizure of aircraft/ships,
- sabotage.

3. The Council may decide at any time, acting unanimously after consultation of the European Parliament under the conditions laid down in Article 39(1) of the Treaty on European Union (TEU), to add other categories of offence to the list contained in paragraph 2. The Council shall examine, in the light of the report submitted by the Commission pursuant to Article 34(3), whether the list should be extended or amended.

4. For offences other than those covered by paragraph 2, surrender may be subject to the condition that the acts for which the European arrest warrant has been issued constitute an offence under the law of the executing Member State, whatever the constituent elements or however it is described.

Article 3
Grounds for mandatory non-execution of the European arrest warrant

The judicial authority of the Member State of execution (hereinafter 'executing judicial authority') shall refuse to execute the European arrest warrant in the following cases:

1. if the offence on which the arrest warrant is based is covered by amnesty in the executing Member State, where that State had jurisdiction to prosecute the offence under its own criminal law;

2. if the executing judicial authority is informed that the requested person has been finally judged by a Member State in respect of the same acts provided that, where there has been sentence, the sentence has been served or is currently being served or may no longer be executed under the law of the sentencing Member State;

3. if the person who is the subject of the European arrest warrant may not, owing to his age, be held criminally responsible for the acts on which the arrest warrant is based under the law of the executing State.

Article 4
Grounds for optional non-execution of the European arrest warrant

The executing judicial authority may refuse to execute the European arrest warrant:

1. if, in one of the cases referred to in Article 2(4), the act on which the European arrest warrant is based does not constitute an offence under the law of the executing Member State; however, in relation to taxes or duties, customs and exchange, execution of the European arrest warrant shall not be refused on the ground that the law of the executing Member State does not impose the same kind of tax or duty or does not contain the same type of rules as regards taxes, duties and customs and exchange regulations as the law of the issuing Member State;
2. where the person who is the subject of the European arrest warrant is being prosecuted in the executing Member State for the same act as that on which the European arrest warrant is based;
3. where the judicial authorities of the executing Member State have decided either not to prosecute for the offence on which the European arrest warrant is based or to halt proceedings, or where a final judgment has been passed upon the requested person in a Member State, in respect of the same acts, which prevents further proceedings;
4. where the criminal prosecution or punishment of the requested person is statute-barred according to the law of the executing Member State and the acts fall within the jurisdiction of that Member State under its own criminal law;
5. if the executing judicial authority is informed that the requested person has been finally judged by a third State in respect of the same acts provided that, where there has been a sentence, the sentence has been served or is currently being served or may no longer be executed under the law of the sentencing country;
6. if the European arrest warrant has been issued for the purposes of execution of a custodial sentence or detention order, where the requested person is staying in, or is a national or a resident of the executing Member State and that State undertakes to execute the sentence or detention order in accordance with its domestic law;
7. where the European arrest warrant relates to offences which:
    (a) are regarded by the law of the executing Member State as having been committed in whole or in part in the territory of the executing Member State or in a place treated as such; or
    (b) have been committed outside the territory of the issuing Member State and the law of the executing Member State does not allow prosecution for the same offences when committed outside its territory.

Article 5
Guarantees to be given by the issuing Member State in particular cases

The execution of the European arrest warrant by the executing judicial authority may, by the law of the executing Member State, be subject to the following conditions:

1. where the European arrest warrant has been issued for the purposes of executing a sentence or a detention order imposed by a decision rendered in absentia and if the person concerned has not been summoned in person or otherwise informed of the date and place of the hearing which led to the decision rendered in absentia, surrender may be subject to the condition that the issuing judicial authority gives an assurance deemed adequate to guarantee the person who is the subject of the European arrest warrant that he or she will have an opportunity to apply for a retrial of the case in the issuing Member State and to be present at the judgment;
2. if the offence on the basis of which the European arrest warrant has been issued is punishable by custodial life sentence or life-time detention order, the execution of the said arrest warrant may be subject to the condition that the issuing Member State has provisions in its legal system for a review of the penalty or measure imposed, on request or at the latest after 20 years, or for the application of measures of clemency to which the person is entitled to apply for under the law or practice of the issuing Member State, aiming at a non-execution of such penalty or measure;
3. where a person who is the subject of a European arrest warrant for the purposes of prosecution is a national or resident of the executing Member State, surrender may be subject to the condition that the person, after being heard, is returned to the executing Member State in order to serve there the custodial sentence or detention order passed against him in the issuing Member State.

Article 6
Determination of the competent judicial authorities

1. The issuing judicial authority shall be the judicial authority of the issuing Member State which is competent to issue a European arrest warrant by virtue of the law of that State.

2. The executing judicial authority shall be the judicial authority of the executing Member State which is competent to execute the European arrest warrant by virtue of the law of that State.
3. Each Member State shall inform the General Secretariat of the Council of the competent judicial authority under its law.

Article 7
Recourse to the central authority

1. Each Member State may designate a central authority or, when its legal system so provides, more than one central authority to assist the competent judicial authorities.
2. A Member State may, if it is necessary as a result of the organisation of its internal judicial system, make its central authority(ies) responsible for the administrative transmission and reception of European arrest warrants as well as for all other official correspondence relating thereto.
   Member State wishing to make use of the possibilities referred to in this Article shall communicate to the General Secretariat of the Council information relating to the designated central authority or central authorities. These indications shall be binding upon all the authorities of the issuing Member State.

Article 8
Content and form of the European arrest warrant

1. The European arrest warrant shall contain the following information set out in accordance with the form contained in the Annex:
   (a) the identity and nationality of the requested person;
   (b) the name, address, telephone and fax numbers and e-mail address of the issuing judicial authority;
   (c) evidence of an enforceable judgment, an arrest warrant or any other enforceable judicial decision having the same effect, coming within the scope of Articles 1 and 2;
   (d) the nature and legal classification of the offence, particularly in respect of Article 2;
   (e) a description of the circumstances in which the offence was committed, including the time, place and degree of participation in the offence by the requested person;
   (f) the penalty imposed, if there is a final judgment, or the prescribed scale of penalties for the offence under the law of the issuing Member State;
   (g) if possible, other consequences of the offence.
2. The European arrest warrant must be translated into the official language or one of the official languages of the executing Member State. Any Member State may, when this Framework Decision is adopted or at a later date, state in a declaration deposited with the General Secretariat of the Council that it will accept a translation in one or more other official languages of the Institutions of the European Communities.

CHAPTER 2

SURRENDER PROCEDURE

Article 9
Transmission of a European arrest warrant

1. When the location of the requested person is known, the issuing judicial authority may transmit the European arrest warrant directly to the executing judicial authority.
2. The issuing judicial authority may, in any event, decide to issue an alert for the requested person in the Schengen Information System (SIS).
3. Such an alert shall be effected in accordance with the provisions of Article 95 of the Convention of 19 June 1990 implementing the Schengen Agreement of 14 June 1985 on the gradual abolition of controls at common borders. An alert in the Schengen Information System shall be equivalent to a European arrest warrant accompanied by the information set out in Article 8(1).
   For a transitional period, until the SIS is capable of transmitting all the information described in Article 8, the alert shall be equivalent to a European arrest warrant pending the receipt of the original in due and proper form by the executing judicial authority.

Article 10
Detailed procedures for transmitting a European arrest warrant

1. If the issuing judicial authority does not know the competent executing judicial authority, it shall make the requisite enquiries, including through the contact points of the European Judicial Network[8], in order to obtain that information from the executing Member State.
2. If the issuing judicial authority so wishes, transmission may be effected via the secure telecommunications system of the European Judicial Network.
3. If it is not possible to call on the services of the SIS, the issuing judicial authority may call on Interpol to transmit a European arrest warrant.
4. The issuing judicial authority may forward the European arrest warrant by any secure means capable of producing written records under conditions allowing the executing Member State to establish its authenticity.
5. All difficulties concerning the transmission or the authenticity of any document needed for the execution of the European arrest warrant shall be dealt with by direct contacts between the judicial authorities involved, or, where appropriate, with the involvement of the central authorities of the Member States.
6. If the authority which receives a European arrest warrant is not competent to act upon it, it shall automatically forward the European arrest warrant to the competent authority in its Member State and shall inform the issuing judicial authority accordingly.

Article 11
Rights of a requested person

1. When a requested person is arrested, the executing competent judicial authority shall, in accordance with its national law, inform that person of the European arrest warrant and of its contents, and also of the possibility of consenting to surrender to the issuing judicial authority.
2. A requested person who is arrested for the purpose of the execution of a European arrest warrant shall have a right to be assisted by a legal counsel and by an interpreter in accordance with the national law of the executing Member State.

Article 12
Keeping the person in detention

When a person is arrested on the basis of a European arrest warrant, the executing judicial authority shall take a decision on whether the requested person should remain in detention, in accordance with the law of the executing Member State. The person may be released provisionally at any time in conformity with the domestic law of the executing Member State, provided that the competent authority of the said Member State takes all the measures it deems necessary to prevent the person absconding.

Article 13
Consent to surrender

1. If the arrested person indicates that he or she consents to surrender, that consent and, if appropriate, express renunciation of entitlement to the 'speciality rule', referred to in Article 27(2), shall be given before the executing judicial authority, in accordance with the domestic law of the executing Member State.
2. Each Member State shall adopt the measures necessary to ensure that consent and, where appropriate, renunciation, as referred to in paragraph 1, are established in such a way as to show that the person concerned has expressed them voluntarily and in full awareness of the consequences. To that end, the requested person shall have the right to legal counsel.
3. The consent and, where appropriate, renunciation, as referred to in paragraph 1, shall be formally recorded in accordance with the procedure laid down by the domestic law of the executing Member State.
4. In principle, consent may not be revoked. Each Member State may provide that consent and, if appropriate, renunciation may be revoked, in accordance with the rules applicable under its domestic law.

---

[8] Council Joint Action 98/428/JHA of 29 June 1998 on the creation of a European Judicial Network (OJ L 191, 7.7.1998, p. 4).

In this case, the period between the date of consent and that of its revocation shall not be taken into consideration in establishing the time limits laid down in Article 17. A Member State which wishes to have recourse to this possibility shall inform the General Secretariat of the Council accordingly when this Framework Decision is adopted and shall specify the procedures whereby revocation of consent shall be possible and any amendment to them.

Article 14
Hearing of the requested person

Where the arrested person does not consent to his or her surrender as referred to in Article 13, he or she shall be entitled to be heard by the executing judicial authority, in accordance with the law of the executing Member State.

Article 15
Surrender decision

1. The executing judicial authority shall decide, within the time-limits and under the conditions defined in this Framework Decision, whether the person is to be surrendered.
2. If the executing judicial authority finds the information communicated by the issuing Member State to be insufficient to allow it to decide on surrender, it shall request that the necessary supplementary information, in particular with respect to Articles 3 to 5 and Article 8, be furnished as a matter of urgency and may fix a time limit for the receipt thereof, taking into account the need to observe the time limits set in Article 17.
3. The issuing judicial authority may at any time forward any additional useful information to the executing judicial authority.

Article 16
Decision in the event of multiple requests

1. If two or more Member States have issued European arrest warrants for the same person, the decision on which of the European arrest warrants shall be executed shall be taken by the executing judicial authority with due consideration of all the circumstances and especially the relative seriousness and place of the offences, the respective dates of the European arrest warrants and whether the warrant has been issued for the purposes of prosecution or for execution of a custodial sentence or detention order.
2. The executing judicial authority may seek the advice of Eurojust[9] when making the choice referred to in paragraph 1.
3. In the event of a conflict between a European arrest warrant and a request for extradition presented by a third country, the decision on whether the European arrest warrant or the extradition request takes precedence shall be taken by the competent authority of the executing Member State with due consideration of all the circumstances, in particular those referred to in paragraph 1 and those mentioned in the applicable convention.
4. This Article shall be without prejudice to Member States' obligations under the Statute of the International Criminal Court.

Article 17
Time limits and procedures for the decision to execute the European arrest warrant

1. A European arrest warrant shall be dealt with and executed as a matter of urgency.
2. In cases where the requested person consents to his surrender, the final decision on the execution of the European arrest warrant should be taken within a period of 10 days after consent has been given.
3. In other cases, the final decision on the execution of the European arrest warrant should be taken within a period of 60 days after the arrest of the requested person.
4. Where in specific cases the European arrest warrant cannot be executed within the time limits laid down in paragraphs 2 or 3, the executing judicial authority shall immediately inform the issuing judicial authority thereof, giving the reasons for the delay. In such case, the time limits may be extended by a further 30 days.

---

[9] Council Decision 2002/187/JHA of 28 February 2002 setting up Eurojust with a view to reinforcing the fight against serious crime (OJ L 63, 6.3.2002, p. 1).

5. As long as the executing judicial authority has not taken a final decision on the European arrest warrant, it shall ensure that the material conditions necessary for effective surrender of the person remain fulfilled.

6. Reasons must be given for any refusal to execute a European arrest warrant.

7. Where in exceptional circumstances a Member State cannot observe the time limits provided for in this Article, it shall inform Eurojust, giving the reasons for the delay. In addition, a Member State which has experienced repeated delays on the part of another Member State in the execution of European arrest warrants shall inform the Council with a view to evaluating the implementation of this Framework Decision at Member State level.

Article 18
Situation pending the decision

1. Where the European arrest warrant has been issued for the purpose of conducting a criminal prosecution, the executing judicial authority must:
   (a) either agree that the requested person should be heard according to Article 19;
   (b) or agree to the temporary transfer of the requested person.

2. The conditions and the duration of the temporary transfer shall be determined by mutual agreement between the issuing and executing judicial authorities.

3. In the case of temporary transfer, the person must be able to return to the executing Member State to attend hearings concerning him or her as part of the surrender procedure.

Article 19
Hearing the person pending the decision

1. The requested person shall be heard by a judicial authority, assisted by another person designated in accordance with the law of the Member State of the requesting court.

2. The requested person shall be heard in accordance with the law of the executing Member State and with the conditions determined by mutual agreement between the issuing and executing judicial authorities.

3. The competent executing judicial authority may assign another judicial authority of its Member State to take part in the hearing of the requested person in order to ensure the proper application of this Article and of the conditions laid down.

Article 20
Privileges and immunities

1. Where the requested person enjoys a privilege or immunity regarding jurisdiction or execution in the executing Member State, the time limits referred to in Article 17 shall not start running unless, and counting from the day when, the executing judicial authority is informed of the fact that the privilege or immunity has been waived.

   The executing Member State shall ensure that the material conditions necessary for effective surrender are fulfilled when the person no longer enjoys such privilege or immunity.

2. Where power to waive the privilege or immunity lies with an authority of the executing Member State, the executing judicial authority shall request it to exercise that power forthwith. Where power to waive the privilege or immunity lies with an authority of another State or international organisation, it shall be for the issuing judicial authority to request it to exercise that power.

Article 21
Competing international obligations

This Framework Decision shall not prejudice the obligations of the executing Member State where the requested person has been extradited to that Member State from a third State and where that person is protected by provisions of the arrangement under which he or she was extradited concerning speciality. The executing Member State shall take all necessary measures for requesting forthwith the consent of the State from which the requested person was extradited so that he or she can be surrendered to the Member State which issued the European arrest warrant. The time limits referred to in Article 17 shall not start running until the day on which these speciality rules cease to apply. Pending the decision of the State from which the requested person was extradited, the executing Member State will ensure that the material conditions necessary for effective surrender remain fulfilled.

Article 22
Notification of the decision

The executing judicial authority shall notify the issuing judicial authority immediately of the decision on the action to be taken on the European arrest warrant.

Article 23
Time limits for surrender of the person

1. The person requested shall be surrendered as soon as possible on a date agreed between the authorities concerned.
2. He or she shall be surrendered no later than 10 days after the final decision on the execution of the European arrest warrant.
3. If the surrender of the requested person within the period laid down in paragraph 2 is prevented by circumstances beyond the control of any of the Member States, the executing and issuing judicial authorities shall immediately contact each other and agree on a new surrender date. In that event, the surrender shall take place within 10 days of the new date thus agreed.
4. The surrender may exceptionally be temporarily postponed for serious humanitarian reasons, for example if there are substantial grounds for believing that it would manifestly endanger the requested person's life or health. The execution of the European arrest warrant shall take place as soon as these grounds have ceased to exist. The executing judicial authority shall immediately inform the issuing judicial authority and agree on a new surrender date. In that event, the surrender shall take place within 10 days of the new date thus agreed.
5. Upon expiry of the time limits referred to in paragraphs 2 to 4, if the person is still being held in custody he shall be released.

Article 24
Postponed or conditional surrender

1. The executing judicial authority may, after deciding to execute the European arrest warrant, postpone the surrender of the requested person so that he or she may be prosecuted in the executing Member State or, if he or she has already been sentenced, so that he or she may serve, in its territory, a sentence passed for an act other than that referred to in the European arrest warrant.
2. Instead of postponing the surrender, the executing judicial authority may temporarily surrender the requested person to the issuing Member State under conditions to be determined by mutual agreement between the executing and the issuing judicial authorities. The agreement shall be made in writing and the conditions shall be binding on all the authorities in the issuing Member State.

Article 25
Transit

1. Each Member State shall, except when it avails itself of the possibility of refusal when the transit of a national or a resident is requested for the purpose of the execution of a custodial sentence or detention order, permit the transit through its territory of a requested person who is being surrendered provided that it has been given information on:
   (a) the identity and nationality of the person subject to the European arrest warrant;
   (b) the existence of a European arrest warrant;
   (c) the nature and legal classification of the offence;
   (d) the description of the circumstances of the offence, including the date and place.
   Where a person who is the subject of a European arrest warrant for the purposes of prosecution is a national or resident of the Member State of transit, transit may be subject to the condition that the person, after being heard, is returned to the transit Member State to serve the custodial sentence or detention order passed against him in the issuing Member State.
2. Each Member State shall designate an authority responsible for receiving transit requests and the necessary documents, as well as any other official correspondence relating to transit requests. Member States shall communicate this designation to the General Secretariat of the Council.
3. The transit request and the information set out in paragraph 1 may be addressed to the authority designated pursuant to paragraph 2 by any means capable of producing a written record. The Member State of transit shall notify its decision by the same procedure.

4. This Framework Decision does not apply in the case of transport by air without a scheduled stopover. However, if an unscheduled landing occurs, the issuing Member State shall provide the authority designated pursuant to paragraph 2 with the information provided for in paragraph 1.

5. Where a transit concerns a person who is to be extradited from a third State to a Member State this Article will apply mutatis mutandis. In particular the expression 'European arrest warrant' shall be deemed to be replaced by 'extradition request'.

CHAPTER 3

EFFECTS OF THE SURRENDER

Article 26

Deduction of the period of detention served in the executing Member State

1. The issuing Member State shall deduct all periods of detention arising from the execution of a European arrest warrant from the total period of detention to be served in the issuing Member State as a result of a custodial sentence or detention order being passed.

2. To that end, all information concerning the duration of the detention of the requested person on the basis of the European arrest warrant shall be transmitted by the executing judicial authority or the central authority designated under Article 7 to the issuing judicial authority at the time of the surrender.

Article 27

Possible prosecution for other offences

1. Each Member State may notify the General Secretariat of the Council that, in its relations with other Member States that have given the same notification, consent is presumed to have been given for the prosecution, sentencing or detention with a view to the carrying out of a custodial sentence or detention order for an offence committed prior to his or her surrender, other than that for which he or she was surrendered, unless in a particular case the executing judicial authority states otherwise in its decision on surrender.

2. Except in the cases referred to in paragraphs 1 and 3, a person surrendered may not be prosecuted, sentenced or otherwise deprived of his or her liberty for an offence committed prior to his or her surrender other than that for which he or she was surrendered.

3. Paragraph 2 does not apply in the following cases:
   (a) when the person having had an opportunity to leave the territory of the Member State to which he or she has been surrendered has not done so within 45 days of his or her final discharge, or has returned to that territory after leaving it;
   (b) the offence is not punishable by a custodial sentence or detention order;
   (c) the criminal proceedings do not give rise to the application of a measure restricting personal liberty;
   (d) when the person could be liable to a penalty or a measure not involving the deprivation of liberty, in particular a financial penalty or a measure in lieu thereof, even if the penalty or measure may give rise to a restriction of his or her personal liberty;
   (e) when the person consented to be surrendered, where appropriate at the same time as he or she renounced the speciality rule, in accordance with Article 13;
   (f) when the person, after his/her surrender, has expressly renounced entitlement to the speciality rule with regard to specific offences preceding his/her surrender. Renunciation shall be given before the competent judicial authorities of the issuing Member State and shall be recorded in accordance with that State's domestic law. The renunciation shall be drawn up in such a way as to make clear that the person has given it voluntarily and in full awareness of the consequences. To that end, the person shall have the right to legal counsel;
   (g) where the executing judicial authority which surrendered the person gives its consent in accordance with paragraph 4.

4. A request for consent shall be submitted to the executing judicial authority, accompanied by the information mentioned in Article 8(1) and a translation as referred to in Article 8(2). Consent shall be given when the offence for which it is requested is itself subject to surrender in accordance with the provisions of this Framework Decision. Consent shall be refused on the grounds referred to in Article 3

and otherwise may be refused only on the grounds referred to in Article 4. The decision shall be taken no later than 30 days after receipt of the request.

For the situations mentioned in Article 5 the issuing Member State must give the guarantees provided for therein.

Article 28
Surrender or subsequent extradition

1. Each Member State may notify the General Secretariat of the Council that, in its relations with other Member States which have given the same notification, the consent for the surrender of a person to a Member State other than the executing Member State pursuant to a European arrest warrant issued for an offence committed prior to his or her surrender is presumed to have been given, unless in a particular case the executing judicial authority states otherwise in its decision on surrender.

2. In any case, a person who has been surrendered to the issuing Member State pursuant to a European arrest warrant may, without the consent of the executing Member State, be surrendered to a Member State other than the executing Member State pursuant to a European arrest warrant issued for any offence committed prior to his or her surrender in the following cases:
   (a) where the requested person, having had an opportunity to leave the territory of the Member State to which he or she has been surrendered, has not done so within 45 days of his final discharge, or has returned to that territory after leaving it;
   (b) where the requested person consents to be surrendered to a Member State other than the executing Member State pursuant to a European arrest warrant. Consent shall be given before the competent judicial authorities of the issuing Member State and shall be recorded in accordance with that State's national law. It shall be drawn up in such a way as to make clear that the person concerned has given it voluntarily and in full awareness of the consequences. To that end, the requested person shall have the right to legal counsel;
   (c) where the requested person is not subject to the speciality rule, in accordance with Article 27(3) (a), (e), (f) and (g).

3. The executing judicial authority consents to the surrender to another Member State according to the following rules:
   (a) the request for consent shall be submitted in accordance with Article 9, accompanied by the information mentioned in Article 8(1) and a translation as stated in Article 8(2);
   (b) consent shall be given when the offence for which it is requested is itself subject to surrender in accordance with the provisions of this Framework Decision;
   (c) the decision shall be taken no later than 30 days after receipt of the request;
   (d) consent shall be refused on the grounds referred to in Article 3 and otherwise may be refused only on the grounds referred to in Article 4.
   For the situations referred to in Article 5, the issuing Member State must give the guarantees provided for therein.

4. Notwithstanding paragraph 1, a person who has been surrendered pursuant to a European arrest warrant shall not be extradited to a third State without the consent of the competent authority of the Member State which surrendered the person. Such consent shall be given in accordance with the Conventions by which that Member State is bound, as well as with its domestic law.

Article 29
Handing over of property

1. At the request of the issuing judicial authority or on its own initiative, the executing judicial authority shall, in accordance with its national law, seize and hand over property which:
   (a) may be required as evidence, or
   (b) has been acquired by the requested person as a result of the offence.

2. The property referred to in paragraph 1 shall be handed over even if the European arrest warrant cannot be carried out owing to the death or escape of the requested person.

3. If the property referred to in paragraph 1 is liable to seizure or confiscation in the territory of the executing Member State, the latter may, if the property is needed in connection with pending criminal proceedings, temporarily retain it or hand it over to the issuing Member State, on condition that it is returned.

4. Any rights which the executing Member State or third parties may have acquired in the property referred to in paragraph 1 shall be preserved. Where such rights exist, the issuing Member State shall return the property without charge to the executing Member State as soon as the criminal proceedings have been terminated.

Article 30
Expenses

1. Expenses incurred in the territory of the executing Member State for the execution of a European arrest warrant shall be borne by that Member State.
2. All other expenses shall be borne by the issuing Member State.

CHAPTER 4
GENERAL AND FINAL PROVISIONS

Article 31
Relation to other legal instruments

1. Without prejudice to their application in relations between Member States and third States, this Framework Decision shall, from 1 January 2004, replace the corresponding provisions of the following conventions applicable in the field of extradition in relations between the Member States:
   (a) the European Convention on Extradition of 13 December 1957, its additional protocol of 15 October 1975, its second additional protocol of 17 March 1978, and the European Convention on the suppression of terrorism of 27 January 1977 as far as extradition is concerned;
   (b) the Agreement between the 12 Member States of the European Communities on the simplification and modernisation of methods of transmitting extradition requests of 26 May 1989;
   (c) the Convention of 10 March 1995 on simplified extradition procedure between the Member States of the European Union;
   (d) the Convention of 27 September 1996 relating to extradition between the Member States of the European Union;
   (e) Title III, Chapter 4 of the Convention of 19 June 1990 implementing the Schengen Agreement of 14 June 1985 on the gradual abolition of checks at common borders.
2. Member States may continue to apply bilateral or multilateral agreements or arrangements in force when this Framework Decision is adopted in so far as such agreements or arrangements allow the objectives of this Framework Decision to be extended or enlarged and help to simplify or facilitate further the procedures for surrender of persons who are the subject of European arrest warrants.

   Member States may conclude bilateral or multilateral agreements or arrangements after this Framework Decision has come into force in so far as such agreements or arrangements allow the prescriptions of this Framework Decision to be extended or enlarged and help to simplify or facilitate further the procedures for surrender of persons who are the subject of European arrest warrants, in particular by fixing time limits shorter than those fixed in Article 17, by extending the list of offences laid down in Article 2(2), by further limiting the grounds for refusal set out in Articles 3 and 4, or by lowering the threshold provided for in Article 2(1) or (2).

   The agreements and arrangements referred to in the second subparagraph may in no case affect relations with Member States which are not parties to them.

   Member States shall, within three months from the entry into force of this Framework Decision, notify the Council and the Commission of the existing agreements and arrangements referred to in the first subparagraph which they wish to continue applying.

   Member States shall also notify the Council and the Commission of any new agreement or arrangement as referred to in the second subparagraph, within three months of signing it.
3. Where the conventions or agreements referred to in paragraph 1 apply to the territories of Member States or to territories for whose external relations a Member State is responsible to which this Framework Decision does not apply, these instruments shall continue to govern the relations existing between those territories and the other Members States.

Article 32
Transitional provision

1. Extradition requests received before 1 January 2004 will continue to be governed by existing instruments relating to extradition. Requests received after that date will be governed by the rules

adopted by Member States pursuant to this Framework Decision. However, any Member State may, at the time of the adoption of this Framework Decision by the Council, make a statement indicating that as executing Member State it will continue to deal with requests relating to acts committed before a date which it specifies in accordance with the extradition system applicable before 1 January 2004. The date in question may not be later than 7 August 2002. The said statement will be published in the Official Journal of the European Communities. It may be withdrawn at any time.

Article 34
Implementation

1. Member States shall take the necessary measures to comply with the provisions of this Framework Decision by 31 December 2003.
2. Member States shall transmit to the General Secretariat of the Council and to the Commission the text of the provisions transposing into their national law the obligations imposed on them under this Framework Decision. When doing so, each Member State may indicate that it will apply immediately this Framework Decision in its relations with those Member States which have given the same notification.

   The General Secretariat of the Council shall communicate to the Member States and to the Commission the information received pursuant to Article 7(2), Article 8(2), Article 13(4) and Article 25(2). It shall also have the information published in the Official Journal of the European Communities.
3. On the basis of the information communicated by the General Secretariat of the Council, the Commission shall, by 31 December 2004 at the latest, submit a report to the European Parliament and to the Council on the operation of this Framework Decision, accompanied, where necessary, by legislative proposals.
4. The Council shall in the second half of 2003 conduct a review, in particular of the practical application, of the provisions of this Framework Decision by the Member States as well as the functioning of the Schengen Information System.

Annex

European Arrest Warrant[10]

This warrant has been issued by a competent judicial authority. I request that the person mentioned below be arrested and surrendered for the purposes of conducting a criminal prosecution or executing a custodial sentence or detention order.

Fraud and counterfeiting—Council Framework Decision 2001/413/JHA; Council Framework Decision 2000/383/JHA as amended by Council Framework Decision 2001/888/JHA

Council Framework Decision of 28 May 2001 combating fraud and counterfeiting of non-cash means of payment (2001/413/JHA)

THE COUNCIL OF THE EUROPEAN UNION,

Having regard to the Treaty on European Union, and in particular Article 34(2)(b) thereof,

Having regard to the initiative of the Commission[1],

Having regard to the opinion of the European Parliament[2],

---

[10] This warrant must be written in, or translated into, one of the official languages of the executing Member State, when that State is known, or any other language accepted by that State.

[1] OJ C 376 E, 28.12.1999, p. 20.

[2] OJ C 121, 24.4.2001, p. 105.

Whereas:

(1) Fraud and counterfeiting of non-cash means of payment often operate on an international scale.

(2) The work developed by various international organisations (i.e. the Council of Europe, the Group of Eight, the OECD, Interpol and the UN) is important but needs to be complemented by action of the European Union.

(3) The Council considers that the seriousness and development of certain forms of fraud regarding non-cash means of payment require comprehensive solutions. Recommendation No 18 of the Action Plan to combat organised crime[3], approved by the Amsterdam European Council on 16 and 17 June 1997, as well as point 46 of the Action Plan of the Council and the Commission on how to implement the provisions of the Treaty of Amsterdam on an area of freedom, security and justice[4], approved by the Vienna European Council on 11 and 12 December 1998, call for an action on this subject.

(4) Since the objectives of this Framework Decision, namely to ensure that fraud and counterfeiting involving all forms of non-cash means of payment are recognised as criminal offences and are subject to effective, proportionate and dissuasive sanctions in all Member States cannot be sufficiently achieved by the Member States in view of the international dimension of those offences and can therefore be better achieved at Union level, the Union may adopt measures, in accordance with the principle of subsidiarity as set out in Article 5 of the Treaty establishing the European Community. In accordance with the principle of proportionality, as set out in that Article, this Framework Decision does not go beyond what is necessary in order to achieve those objectives.

(5) This Framework Decision should assist in the fight against fraud and counterfeiting involving non-cash means of payment together with other instruments already agreed by the Council such as Joint Action 98/428/JHA on the creation of a European Judicial Network[5], Joint Action 98/733/JHA on making it a criminal offence to participate in a criminal organisation in the Member States of the European Union[6], Joint Action 98/699/JHA on money laundering, the identification, tracing, freezing, seizing and confiscation of instrumentalities and the proceeds from crime[7], as well as the Decision of 29 April 1999 extending Europol's mandate to deal with forgery of money and means of payment[8].

(6) The Commission submitted to the Council, on 1 July 1998, the Communication entitled 'A framework for action combating fraud and counterfeit of non-cash means of payment' which advocates a Union Policy covering both preventive and repressive aspects of the problem.

(7) The Communication contains a Draft Joint Action which is one element of that comprehensive approach, and constitutes the starting point for this Framework Decision.

(8) It is necessary that a description of the different forms of behaviour requiring criminalisation in relation to fraud and counterfeiting of non-cash means of payment cover the whole range of activities that together constitute the menace of organised crime in this regard.

(9) It is necessary that these forms of behaviour be classified as criminal offences in all Member States, and that effective, proportionate and dissuasive sanctions be provided for natural and legal persons having committed, or being liable for, such offences.

(10) By giving protection by penal law primarily to payment instruments that are provided with a special form of protection against imitation or abuse, the intention is to encourage operators to provide that protection to payment instruments issued by them, and thereby to add an element of prevention to the instrument.

(11) It is necessary that Member States afford each other the widest measure of mutual assistance, and that they consult each other when two or more Member States have jurisdiction over the same offence,

HAS ADOPTED THIS FRAMEWORK DECISION:

---

[3] OJ C 251, 15.8.1997, p. 1.
[4] OJ C 19, 23.1.1999, p. 1.
[5] OJ L 191, 7.7.1998, p. 4.
[6] OJ L 351, 29.12.1998, p. 1.
[7] OJ L 333, 9.12.1998, p. 1.
[8] OJ C 149, 28.5.1999, p. 16.

Article 1
Definitions

For the purpose of this Framework Decision:

(a) 'Payment instrument' shall mean a corporeal instrument, other than legal tender (bank notes and coins), enabling, by its specific nature, alone or in conjunction with another (payment) instrument, the holder or user to transfer money or monetary value, as for example credit cards, eurocheque cards, other cards issued by financial institutions, travellers' cheques, eurocheques, other cheques and bills of exchange, which is protected against imitation or fraudulent use, for example through design, coding or signature;

(b) 'Legal person' shall mean any entity having such status under the applicable law, except for States or other public bodies in the exercise of State authority and for public international organisations.

Article 2
Offences related to payment instruments

Each Member State shall take the necessary measures to ensure that the following conduct is a criminal offence when committed intentionally, at least in respect of credit cards, eurocheque cards, other cards issued by financial institutions, travellers cheques, eurocheques, other cheques and bills of exchange:

(a) theft or other unlawful appropriation of a payment instrument;

(b) counterfeiting or falsification of a payment instrument in order for it to be used fraudulently;

(c) receiving, obtaining, transporting, sale or transfer to another person or possession of a stolen or otherwise unlawfully appropriated, or of a counterfeited or falsified payment instrument in order for it to be used fraudulently;

(d) fraudulent use of a stolen or otherwise unlawfully appropriated, or of a counterfeited or falsified payment instrument;

Article 3
Offences related to computers

Each Member State shall take the necessary measures to ensure that the following conduct is a criminal offence when committed intentionally:

performing or causing a transfer of money or monetary value and thereby causing an unauthorised loss of property for another person, with the intention of procuring an unauthorised economic benefit for the person committing the offence or for a third party, by:

– without right introducing, altering, deleting or suppressing computer data, in particular identification data, or

– without right interfering with the functioning of a computer programme or system.

Article 4
Offences related to specifically adapted devices

Each Member State shall take the necessary measures to ensure that the following conduct is established as a criminal offence when committed intentionally:

the fraudulent making, receiving, obtaining, sale or transfer to another person or possession of:

– instruments, articles, computer programmes and any other means peculiarly adapted for the commission of any of the offences described under Article 2(b);

– computer programmes the purpose of which is the commission of any of the offences described under Article 3.

Article 5
Participation, instigation and attempt

Each Member State shall take the necessary measures to ensure that participating in and instigating the conduct referred to in Articles 2, 3 and 4, or attempting the conduct referred to in Article 2(a), (b) and (d) and Article 3, are punishable.

Article 6
Penalties

[Similar terms to Art. 4 of Framework Decision 2003/568/JHA.]

Article 7
Liability of legal persons

[Similar terms to Art. 5 of Framework Decision 2003/568/JHA.]

Article 8
Sanctions for legal persons

[Similar terms to Art. 6 of Framework Decision 2003/568/JHA.]

Article 9
Jurisdiction

Article 10
Extradition and prosecution

1. (a) Any Member State which, under its law, does not extradite its own nationals shall take the necessary measures to establish its jurisdiction over the offences provided for in Articles 2, 3, 4 and 5 when committed by its own nationals outside its territory.
   (b) Each Member State shall, when one of its nationals is alleged to have committed, in another Member State, an offence involving the conduct described in Articles 2, 3, 4 or 5, and it does not extradite that person to that other Member State solely on the ground of his nationality, submit the case to its competent authorities for the purpose of prosecution if appropriate. In order to enable prosecution to take place, the files, information and exhibits relating to the offence shall be forwarded in accordance with the procedures laid down in Article 6(2) of the European Convention on Extradition of 13 December 1957. The requesting Member State shall be informed of the prosecution initiated and of its outcome.
2. For the purpose of this Article, a 'national' of a Member State shall be construed in accordance with any declaration made by that State under Article 6(1)(b) and (c) of the European Convention on Extradition.

Article 11
Cooperation between Member States

1. In accordance with the applicable conventions, multilateral or bilateral agreements or arrangements, Member States shall afford each other the widest measure of mutual assistance in respect of proceedings relating to the offences provided for in this Framework Decision.
2. Where several Member States have jurisdiction in respect of offences envisaged by this Framework Decision, they shall consult one another with a view to coordinating their action in order to prosecute effectively.

Article 12
Exchange of information

1. Member States shall designate operational contact points or may use existing operational structures for the exchange of information and for other contacts between Member States for the purposes of applying this Framework Decision.
2. Each Member State shall inform the General Secretariat of the Council and the Commission of its department or departments acting as contact points in accordance with paragraph 1. The General Secretariat shall notify the other Member States of these contact points.

Article 14
Implementation

1. Member States shall bring into force the measures necessary to comply with this Framework Decision by 2 June 2003.
2. By 2 June 2003, Member States shall forward to the General Secretariat of the Council and to the Commission the text of the provisions transposing into their national law the obligations imposed upon them under this Framework Decision. The Council shall, by 2 September 2003, on the basis of a report established on the basis of this information and a written report by the Commission, assess the extent to which Member States have taken the necessary measures in order to comply with this Framework Decision.

Council framework Decision of 29 May 2000 on increasing protection by criminal penalties and other sanctions against counterfeiting in connection with the introduction of the euro (2000/383/JHA)

THE COUNCIL OF THE EUROPEAN UNION,

Having regard to the Treaty on European Union, and in particular Article 31(e) and Article 34(2)(b) thereof,

Having regard to the initiative by the Federal Republic of Germany[1],

Having regard to the opinion of the European Parliament[2],

Whereas:

[Paras dealing with history are here omitted.]

(7) The worldwide importance of the euro means it will be particularly open to the risk of counterfeiting.

(8) Account should be taken of the fact that there is already evidence of fraudulent activity with regard to the euro.

(9) It should be ensured that the euro is protected in an appropriate way in all Member States by efficient criminal law measures, even before the currency starts to be put into circulation as from 1 January 2002, in order to defend the necessary credibility of the new currency and thereby avoid serious economic consequences.

(10) Account should be taken of the Council resolution of 28 May 1999 on increasing protection by penal sanctions against counterfeiting in connection with the introduction of the euro[3] with its guidelines for a binding legal instrument,

HAS ADOPTED THIS FRAMEWORK DECISION:

Article 1
Definitions

For the purposes of this framework Decision:

- 'Convention' means the International Convention of 20 April 1929 for the Suppression of Counterfeiting Currency and its Protocol[4],
- 'currency' means paper money (including banknotes) and metallic money, the circulation of which is legally authorised including euro banknotes and euro coins, the circulation of which is legally authorised pursuant to Regulation (EC) 974/98,
- 'legal person' shall mean any entity having such status under the applicable national law, except for States or other public bodies in the exercise of State authority and for public international organisations.

Article 2
Relation to the Convention

1. The purpose of this framework Decision is to supplement the provisions and to facilitate the application of the Convention by the Member States in accordance with the following provisions.
2. To this end, the Member States that have not yet done so undertake to accede to the Convention.
3. The obligations under the Convention shall remain unaffected.

Article 3
General offences

1. Each Member State shall take the necessary measures to ensure that the following conduct is punishable:

---

[1] OJ C 322, 10.11.1999, p. 6.
[2] Opinion delivered on 17 February 2000 (not yet published in the Official Journal).
[3] OJ C 171, 18.6.1999, p. 1.
[4] No 2623, p. 372. League of Nations Treaty Series 1931. Signed in Geneva on 20 April 1929.

(a) any fraudulent making or altering of currency, whatever means are employed;

(b) the fraudulent uttering of counterfeit currency;

(c) the import, export, transport, receiving, or obtaining of counterfeit currency with a view to uttering the same and with knowledge that it is counterfeit;

(d) the fraudulent making, receiving, obtaining or possession of

- instruments, articles, computer programs and any other means peculiarly adapted for the counterfeiting or altering of currency, or
- holograms or other components of currency which serve to protect against counterfeiting.

2. Each Member State shall take the necessary measures to ensure that participating in and instigating the conduct referred to in paragraph 1, and attempting the conduct referred to in points (a) to (c) of paragraph 1, are punishable.

Article 4
Additional offences

Each Member State shall take the necessary measures to ensure that the conduct referred to in Article 3 is punishable also with respect to banknotes or coins being manufactured or having been manufactured by use of legal facilities or materials in violation of the rights or the conditions under which the competent authorities may issue currency, without these authorities' agreement.

Article 5
Currency not issued but designated for circulation

Each Member State shall take the necessary measures to ensure that the conduct referred to in Articles 3 and 4 is punishable if:

(a) it relates to the future banknotes and coins of the euro and is committed before 1 January 2002;

(b) it relates to banknotes and coins which are not yet issued but are designated for circulation, and are of a currency which is legal tender.

Article 6
Penalties

1. Each Member State shall take the necessary measures to ensure that the conduct referred to in Articles 3 to 5 is punishable by effective, proportionate and dissuasive criminal penalties, including penalties involving deprivation of liberty which can give rise to extradition.

2. The offences of fraudulent making or altering of currency provided for in Article 3(1)(a) shall be punishable by terms of imprisonment, the maximum being not less than eight years.

Article 7
Jurisdiction

[Similar terms to Art. 7 of Framework Decision 2003/568/JHA.]

Article 8
Liability of legal persons

1. Each Member State shall take the necessary measures to ensure that legal persons can be held liable for the offences referred to in Articles 3 to 5 committed for their benefit by any person, acting either individually or as part of an organ of the legal person, who has a leading position within the legal person, based on:
   - a power of representation of the legal person, or
   - an authority to take decisions on behalf of the legal person, or
   - an authority to exercise control within the legal person,
   - as well as for involvement as accessories or instigators in such offences or the attempted commission of the offences referred to in Article 3(1)(a) and (b).

2. Apart from the cases already provided for in paragraph 1, each Member State shall take the necessary measures to ensure that a legal person can be held liable where the lack of supervision or control by a person referred to in paragraph 1 has rendered possible the commission of an offence referred to in Articles 3 to 5 for the benefit of that legal person by a person under its authority.

3. Liability of a legal person under paragraphs 1 and 2 shall not exclude criminal proceedings against natural persons who are perpetrators, instigators or accessories in an offence referred to in Articles 3 to 5.

Article 9
Sanctions for legal persons
[Similar terms to Art. 6 of Framework Decision 2003/568/JHA.]

Article 11
Implementation
1. Member States shall take the necessary measures to comply with this framework Decision by 31 December 2000 as far as Article 5(a) is concerned and not later than 29 May 2001 as far as the other provisions are concerned.
2. By the same dates, the Member States shall transmit to the General Secretariat of the Council, the Commission and the European Central Bank the text of the provisions transposing into their national law the obligations imposed on them under this framework Decision. The Council will, by 30 June 2001 at the latest, on the basis of a report established on the basis of this information and a written report by the Commission, assess the extent to which Member States have taken the necessary measures in order to comply with this framework Decision.

Council Framework Decision of 6 December 2001 amending Framework Decision 2000/383/JHA on increasing protection by criminal penalties and other sanctions against counterfeiting in connection with the introduction of the euro (2001/888/JHA)

THE COUNCIL OF THE EUROPEAN UNION,

Having regard to the Treaty on European Union, and in particular Article 31(e) and Article 34(2)(b) thereof,

Having regard to the initiative of the Kingdom of Sweden[1],

Having regard to the Opinion of the European Parliament,

Whereas:

(1) The Council adopted on 29 May 2000 Framework Decision 2000/383/JHA on increasing protection by criminal penalties and other sanctions against counterfeiting in connection with the introduction of the euro[2].

(2) The measures in Framework Decision 2000/383/JHA should be supplemented by a provision on the recognition of previous convictions regarding offences referred to in that Framework Decision,

HAS ADOPTED THIS FRAMEWORK DECISION:

Article 1

The following Article shall be inserted after Article 9 of Framework Decision 2000/383/JHA:
'*Article 9a*

Recognition of previous convictions

Every Member State shall recognise the principle of the recognition of previous convictions under the conditions prevailing under its domestic law and, under those same conditions, shall recognise for the purpose of establishing habitual criminality final sentences handed down in another Member State for the offences referred to in Articles 3 to 5 of this Framework Decision, or the offences referred to in Article 3 of the Convention, irrespective of the currency counterfeited.'

Article 2
Implementation
1. Member States shall take the necessary measures to comply with this Framework Decision by 31 December 2002.
2. By 31 December 2002, the Member States shall transmit to the General Secretariat of the Council, the Commission and the European Central Bank the text of the provisions transposing into their national law the obligations imposed on them under this Framework Decision.

---

[1] OJ C 225, 10.8.2001, p. 9.
[2] OJ L 140, 14.6.2000, p. 1.

Human trafficking—Council Framework Decision 2002/629/JHA

Council Framework Decision of 19 July 2002 on combating trafficking in human beings (2002/629/JHA)

THE COUNCIL OF THE EUROPEAN UNION,

Having regard to the Treaty on European Union, and in particular Article 29, Article 31(e) and Article 34(2)(b) thereof,

Having regard to the proposal of the Commission[1],

Having regard to the opinion of the European Parliament[2],

Whereas:

(1) The Action Plan of the Council and the Commission on how best to implement the provisions of the Treaty of Amsterdam on an area of freedom, security and justice[3], the Tampere European Council on 15 and 16 October 1999, the Santa Maria da Feira European Council on 19 and 20 June 2000, as listed in the Scoreboard, and the European Parliament in its Resolution of 19 May 2000 on the communication from the Commission 'for further actions in the fight against trafficking in women' indicate or call for legislative action against trafficking in human beings, including common definitions, incriminations and sanctions.

(2) Council Joint Action 97/154/JHA of 24 February 1997 concerning action to combat trafficking in human beings and sexual exploitation of children[4] needs to be followed by further legislative action addressing the divergence of legal approaches in the Member States and contributing to the development of an efficient judicial and law enforcement cooperation against trafficking in human beings.

(3) Trafficking in human beings comprises serious violations of fundamental human rights and human dignity and involves ruthless practices such as the abuse and deception of vulnerable persons, as well as the use of violence, threats, debt bondage and coercion.

(4) The UN protocol to prevent, suppress and punish trafficking in persons, especially women and children, supplementing the UN Convention against transnational organised crimes, represents a decisive step towards international cooperation in this field.

(5) Children are more vulnerable and are therefore at greater risk of falling victim to trafficking.

(6) The important work performed by international organisations, in particular the UN, must be complemented by that of the European Union.

(7) It is necessary that the serious criminal offence of trafficking in human beings be addressed not only through individual action by each Member State but by a comprehensive approach in which the definition of constituent elements of criminal law common to all Member States, including effective, proportionate and dissuasive sanctions, forms an integral part. In accordance with the principles of subsidiarity and proportionality, this Framework Decision confines itself to the minimum required in order to achieve those objectives at European level and does not go beyond what is necessary for that purpose.

(8) It is necessary to introduce sanctions on perpetrators sufficiently severe to allow for trafficking in human beings to be included within the scope of instruments already adopted for the purpose of combating organised crime such as Council Joint Action 98/699/JHA of 3 December 1998 on money laundering, the identification, tracing, freezing, seizing and confiscation of the instrumentalities and the proceeds from crime[5] and Council Joint Action 98/733/JHA of 21 December 1998 on making it a criminal offence to participate in a criminal organisation in the Member States of the European Union[6].

---

[1] OJ C 62 E, 27.2.2001, p. 324.
[2] OJ C 35 E, 28.2.2002, p. 114.
[3] OJ C 19, 23.1.1999, p. 1.
[4] OJ L 63, 4.3.1997, p. 2.
[5] OJ L 333, 9.12.1998, p. 1. Joint Action as last amended by Framework Decision 2001/500/JHA (OJ L 182, 5.7.2001, p. 1).
[6] OJ L 351, 29.12.1998, p. 1.

(9) This Framework Decision should contribute to the fight against and prevention of trafficking in human beings by complementing the instruments adopted in this area such as Council Joint Action 96/700/JHA of 29 November 1996 establishing an incentive and exchange programme for persons responsible for combating trade in human beings and sexual exploitation of children (STOP)[7], Council Joint Action 96/748/JHA of 16 December 1996 extending the mandate given to the Europol Drugs Unit[8] Decision No 293/2000/EC of the European Parliament and of the Council of 24 January 2000 adopting a programme of Community action (the Daphne programme) (2000 to 2003) on preventive measures to fight violence against children, young persons and women[9], Council Joint Action 98/428/JHA of 29 June 1998 on the creation of a European Judicial Network[10], Council Joint Action 96/277/JHA of 22 April 1996 concerning a framework for the exchange of liaison magistrates to improve judicial cooperation between the Member States of the European Union[11] and Council Joint Action 98/427/JHA of 29 June 1998 on good practice in mutual legal assistance in criminal matters[12].

(10)   Council Joint Action 97/154/JHA should accordingly cease to apply in so far as it concerns trafficking in human beings,

HAS ADOPTED THIS FRAMEWORK DECISION:

Article 1
Offences concerning trafficking in human beings for the purposes of labour exploitation or sexual exploitation

1.   Each Member State shall take the necessary measures to ensure that the following acts are punishable: the recruitment, transportation, transfer, harbouring, subsequent reception of a person, including exchange or transfer of control over that person, where:
    (a) use is made of coercion, force or threat, including abduction, or
    (b) use is made of deceit or fraud, or
    (c) there is an abuse of authority or of a position of vulnerability, which is such that the person has no real and acceptable alternative but to submit to the abuse involved, or
    (d) payments or benefits are given or received to achieve the consent of a person having control over another person
    for the purpose of exploitation of that person's labour or services, including at least forced or compulsory labour or services, slavery or practices similar to slavery or servitude, or
    for the purpose of the exploitation of the prostitution of others or other forms of sexual exploitation, including pornography.
2.   The consent of a victim of trafficking in human beings to the exploitation, intended or actual, shall be irrelevant where any of the means set forth in paragraph 1 have been used.
3.   When the conduct referred to in paragraph 1 involves a child, it shall be a punishable trafficking offence even if none of the means set forth in paragraph 1 have been used.
4.   For the purpose of this Framework Decision, 'child' shall mean any person below 18 years of age.

Article 2
Instigation, aiding, abetting and attempt

Each Member State shall take the necessary measures to ensure that the instigation of, aiding, abetting or attempt to commit an offence referred to in Article 1 is punishable.

Article 3
Penalties

1.   Each Member State shall take the necessary measures to ensure that an offence referred to in Articles 1 and 2 is punishable by effective, proportionate and dissuasive criminal penalties, which may entail extradition.

---

[7]   OJ L 322, 12.12.1996, p. 7.
[8]   OJ L 342, 31.12.1996, p. 4.
[9]   OJ L 34, 9.2.2000, p. 1.
[10] OJ L 191, 7.7.1998, p. 4.
[11] OJ L 105, 27.4.1996, p. 1.
[12] OJ L 191, 7.7.1998, p. 1.

2. Each Member State shall take the necessary measures to ensure that an offence referred to in Article 1 is punishable by terms of imprisonment with a maximum penalty that is not less than eight years where it has been committed in any of the following circumstances:

   (a) the offence has deliberately or by gross negligence endangered the life of the victim;

   (b) the offence has been committed against a victim who was particularly vulnerable. A victim shall be considered to have been particularly vulnerable at least when the victim was under the age of sexual majority under national law and the offence has been committed for the purpose of the exploitation of the prostitution of others or other forms of sexual exploitation, including pornography;

   (c) the offence has been committed by use of serious violence or has caused particularly serious harm to the victim;

   (d) the offence has been committed within the framework of a criminal organisation as defined in Joint Action 98/733/JHA, apart from the penalty level referred to therein.

Article 4
Liability of legal persons

[Similar terms to Art. 5 of Framework Decision 2003/568/JHA.]

Article 5
Sanctions on legal persons

Each Member State shall take the necessary measures to ensure that a legal person held liable pursuant to Article 4 is punishable by effective, proportionate and dissuasive sanctions, which shall include criminal or non-criminal fines and may include other sanctions, such as:

(a) exclusion from entitlement to public benefits or aid, or

(b) temporary or permanent disqualification from the practice of commercial activities, or

(c) placing under judicial supervision, or

(d) a judicial winding-up order, or

(e) temporary or permanent closure of establishments which have been used for committing the offence.

Article 6
Jurisdiction and prosecution

[Similar terms to Art. 7 of Framework Decision 2003/568/JHA.]

Article 7
Protection of and assistance to victims

1. Member States shall establish that investigations into or prosecution of offences covered by this Framework Decision shall not be dependent on the report or accusation made by a person subjected to the offence, at least in cases where Article 6(1)(a) applies.

2. Children who are victims of an offence referred to in Article 1 should be considered as particularly vulnerable victims pursuant to Article 2(2), Article 8(4) and Article 14(1) of Council Framework Decision 2001/220/JHA of 15 March 2001 on the standing of victims in criminal proceedings[13].

3. Where the victim is a child, each Member State shall take the measures possible to ensure appropriate assistance for his or her family. In particular, each Member State shall, where appropriate and possible, apply Article 4 of Framework Decision 2001/220/JHA to the family referred to.

Article 9
Application of Joint Action 97/154/JHA

Joint Action 97/154/JHA shall cease to apply in so far as it concerns trafficking in human beings.

Article 10
Implementation

1. Member States shall take the necessary measures to comply with this Framework Decision before 1 August 2004.

---

[13] OJ L 82, 22.3.2001, p. 1.

2. By the date referred to in paragraph 1, Member States shall transmit to the General Secretariat of the Council and to the Commission the text of the provisions transposing into their national law the obligations imposed on them under this Framework Decision. The Council will, by 1 August 2005 at the latest, on the basis of a report established on the basis of this information and a written report transmitted by the Commission, assess the extent to which Member States have taken the necessary measures in order to comply with this Framework Decision.

Money laundering—Council Framework Decision 2001/500/JHA

Council Framework Decision of 26 June 2001 on money laundering, the identification, tracing, freezing, seizing and confiscation of instrumentalities and the proceeds of crime (2001/500/JHA)

THE COUNCIL OF THE EUROPEAN UNION,

Having regard to the Treaty on European Union, and in particular Article 31(a), (c) and (e) and Article 34(2)(b) thereof,

Having regard to the initiative of the French Republic,

Having regard to the opinion of the European Parliament,

Whereas:

(1) On 3 December 1998 the Council adopted Joint Action 98/699/JHA on money laundering, the identification, tracing, freezing, seizing and confiscation of instrumentalities and the proceeds from crime[1].

(2) Account should be taken of the Presidency conclusions of the European Council meeting in Tampere on 15 and 16 October 1999, and of the Presidency conclusions of the European Council meeting in Vienna on 11 and 12 December 1998.

(3) The European Council, noting that serious forms of crime increasingly have tax and duty aspects, calls on Member States to provide full mutual legal assistance in the investigation and prosecution of this type of crime.

(4) The European Council calls for the approximation of criminal law and procedures on money laundering (in particular, confiscating funds), adding that the scope of criminal activities which constitute principal offences for money laundering should be uniform and sufficiently broad in all Member States.

(5) The European Council in Tampere considered that, with regard to national criminal law, efforts to agree on common definitions, incriminations and sanctions should be focused in the first instance on a limited number of sectors of particular relevance, such as financial crime.

(6) The European Council in Tampere noted that money laundering is at the very heart of organised crime and should be rooted out wherever it occurs. The European Council is determined to ensure that concrete steps are taken to trace, freeze, seize and confiscate the proceeds of crime.

(7) Member States have subscribed to the principles of the 1990 Council of Europe Convention on Laundering, Search, Seizure and Confiscation of the Proceeds from Crime, hereinafter referred to as 'the 1990 Convention',

HAS ADOPTED THIS FRAMEWORK DECISION:

Article 1
Reservations in respect of the 1990 Convention

In order to enhance action against organised crime, Member States shall take the necessary steps not to make or uphold reservations in respect of the following articles of the 1990 Convention:

(a) Article 2, in so far as the offence is punishable by deprivation of liberty or a detention order for a maximum of more than one year.

---

[1] OJ L 333, 9.12.1998, p. 1.

However, Member States may uphold reservations on Article 2 of the 1990 Convention in respect of the confiscation of the proceeds from tax offences for the sole purpose of their being able to confiscate such proceeds, both nationally and through international cooperation, under national, Community and international tax-debt recovery legislation;

(b) Article 6, in so far as serious offences are concerned. Such offences shall in any event include offences which are punishable by deprivation of liberty or a detention order for a maximum of more than one year or, as regards those States which have a minimum threshold for offences in their legal system, offences punishable by deprivation of liberty or a detention order for a minimum of more than six months.

Article 2
Penalties

Each Member State shall take the necessary steps consistent with its system of penalties to ensure that the offences referred to in Article 6(1)(a) and (b) of the 1990 Convention, as they result from the Article 1(b) of this framework Decision, are punishable by deprivation of liberty for a maximum of not less than 4 years.

Article 3
Value confiscation

Each Member State shall take the necessary steps to ensure that its legislation and procedures on the confiscation of the proceeds of crime also allow, at least in cases where these proceeds cannot be seized, for the confiscation of property the value of which corresponds to such proceeds, both in purely domestic proceedings and in proceedings instituted at the request of another Member State, including requests for the enforcement of foreign confiscation orders. However, Member States may exclude the confiscation of property the value of which corresponds to the proceeds of crime in cases in which that value would be less than EUR 4000.

The words 'property', 'proceeds' and 'confiscation' shall have the same meaning as in Article 1 of the 1990 Convention.

Article 4
Processing of requests for mutual assistance

Member States shall take the necessary steps to ensure that all requests from other Member States which relate to asset identification, tracing, freezing or seizing and confiscation are processed with the same priority as is given to such measures in domestic proceedings.

Article 5
Repeal of existing provisions

Articles 1, 3, 5(1) and 8(2) of Joint Action 98/699/JHA are hereby repealed.

Article 6
Implementation

1. Member States shall adopt the measures necessary to comply with the provisions of this framework Decision by 31 December 2002.
2. By 1 March 2003, Member States shall forward to the General Secretariat of the Council and to the Commission the text of the provisions transposing into their national law the obligations arising for them from this framework Decision and, where appropriate, the notifications made pursuant to Article 40(2) of the 1990 Convention. On the basis of this information and a written report from the Commission, the Council shall ascertain, by 31 December 2003, to what extent Member States have taken the measures necessary to comply with this framework Decision.

Organised crime—Council Framework Decision 2008/841/JHA

Council Framework Decision 2008/841/JHA of 24 October 2008 on the fight against organised crime

THE COUNCIL OF THE EUROPEAN UNION,

Having regard to the Treaty on European Union, and in particular Articles 29, 31(1)(e) and 34(2)(b) thereof,

Having regard to the proposal of the Commission,

Having regard to the opinion of the European Parliament[1],

Whereas:

(1) The objective of the Hague Programme is to improve the common capability of the Union and the Member States for the purpose, among others, of combating transnational organised crime. This objective is to be pursued by, in particular, the approximation of legislation. Closer cooperation between the Member States of the European Union is needed in order to counter the dangers and proliferation of criminal organisations and to respond effectively to citizens' expectations and Member States' own requirements. In this respect point 14 of the conclusions of the Brussels European Council of 4 and 5 November 2004 states that the citizens of Europe expect the European Union, while guaranteeing respect for fundamental freedoms and rights, to take a more effective, combined approach to cross-border problems such as organised crime.

(2) In its Communication of 29 March 2004 on measures to be taken to combat terrorism and other forms of serious crime, the Commission considered that the facilities available for combating organised crime in the EU needed to be strengthened and stated that it would draw up a Framework Decision to replace Joint Action 98/733/JHA of 21 December 1998 on making it a criminal offence to participate in a criminal organisation in the Member States of the European Union[2].

(3) Point 3.3.2 of the Hague Programme states that the approximation of substantive criminal law serves the purpose of facilitating mutual recognition of judgments and judicial decisions and police and judicial cooperation in criminal matters and concerns areas of particularly serious crime with cross-border dimensions and that priority should be given to areas of crime that are specifically mentioned in the Treaties. The definition of offences relating to participation in a criminal organisation should therefore be approximated in the Member States. Thus, this Framework Decision should encompass crimes which are typically committed in a criminal organisation. It should provide, moreover, for the imposition of penalties corresponding to the seriousness of those offences, on natural and legal persons who committed them or are responsible for their commission.

(4) The obligations arising by virtue of Article 2(a) should be without prejudice to Member States' freedom to classify other groups of persons as criminal organisations, for example, groups whose purpose is not financial or other material gain.

(5) The obligations arising by virtue of Article 2(a) should be without prejudice to the Member States' freedom to interpret the term 'criminal activities' as implying the carrying out of material acts.

(6) The European Union should build on the important work done by international organisations, in particular the United Nations Convention Against Transnational Organised Crime (the 'Palermo Convention'), which was concluded, on behalf of the European Community, by Council Decision 2004/579/EC[3].

(7) Since the objectives of this Framework Decision cannot be sufficiently achieved by the Member States, and can therefore, by reason of the scale of the action, be better achieved at Union level, the Union may adopt measures, in accordance with the principle of subsidiarity as set out in Article 5 of the Treaty establishing European Community, as applied by the second paragraph of Article 2 of the Treaty on European Union. In accordance with the principle of proportionality this Framework Decision does not go beyond what is necessary to achieve those objectives.

(8) This Framework Decision respects the fundamental rights and principles recognised by the Charter of Fundamental Rights of the European Union, and in particular Articles 6 and 49 thereof. Nothing in this Framework Decision is intended to reduce or restrict national rules relating to fundamental rights or freedoms such as due process, the right to strike, freedom of assembly, of association, of the press or of

---

[1] Opinion delivered following non-compulsory consultation (not yet published in the Official Journal).
[2] OJ L 351, 29.12.1998, p. 1.
[3] OJ L 261, 6.8.2004, p. 69.

expression, including the right of everyone to form and to join trade unions with others for the protection of his or her interests and the related right to demonstrate.

(9) Joint Action 98/733/JHA should therefore be repealed,

HAS ADOPTED THIS FRAMEWORK DECISION:

Article 1
Definitions

For the purposes of this Framework Decision:

1. 'criminal organisation' means a structured association, established over a period of time, of more than two persons acting in concert with a view to committing offences which are punishable by deprivation of liberty or a detention order of a maximum of at least four years or a more serious penalty, to obtain, directly or indirectly, a financial or other material benefit;
2. 'structured association' means an association that is not randomly formed for the immediate commission of an offence, nor does it need to have formally defined roles for its members, continuity of its membership, or a developed structure.

Article 2
Offences relating to participation in a criminal organisation

Each Member State shall take the necessary measures to ensure that one or both of the following types of conduct related to a criminal organisation are regarded as offences:

(a) conduct by any person who, with intent and with knowledge of either the aim and general activity of the criminal organisation or its intention to commit the offences in question, actively takes part in the organisation's criminal activities, including the provision of information or material means, the recruitment of new members and all forms of financing of its activities, knowing that such participation will contribute to the achievement of the organisation's criminal activities;
(b) conduct by any person consisting in an agreement with one or more persons that an activity should be pursued, which if carried out, would amount to the commission of offences referred to in Article 1, even if that person does not take part in the actual execution of the activity.

Article 3
Penalties

1. Each Member State shall take the necessary measures to ensure that:
   (a) the offence referred to in Article 2(a) is punishable by a maximum term of imprisonment of at least between two and five years; or
   (b) the offence referred to in Article 2(b) is punishable by the same maximum term of imprisonment as the offence at which the agreement is aimed, or by a maximum term of imprisonment of at least between two and five years.
2. Each Member State shall take the necessary measures to ensure that the fact that offences referred to in Article 2, as determined by this Member State, have been committed within the framework of a criminal organisation, may be regarded as an aggravating circumstance.

Article 4
Special circumstances

Each Member State may take the necessary measures to ensure that the penalties referred to in Article 3 may be reduced or that the offender may be exempted from penalties if he, for example:

(a) renounces criminal activity; and
(b) provides the administrative or judicial authorities with information which they would not otherwise have been able to obtain, helping them to:
   (i) prevent, end or mitigate the effects of the offence;
   (ii) identify or bring to justice the other offenders;
   (iii) find evidence;
   (iv) deprive the criminal organisation of illicit resources or of the proceeds of its criminal activities; or
   (v) prevent further offences referred to in Article 2 from being committed.

Article 5
Liability of legal persons

[Similar terms to Art. 5 of Framework Decision 2003/568/JHA.]

Article 6
Penalties for legal persons

[Similar terms to Art. 6 of Framework Decision 2003/568/JHA.]

Article 7
Jurisdiction and coordination of prosecution

1. Each Member State shall ensure that its jurisdiction covers at least the cases in which the offences referred to in Article 2 were committed:
   (a) in whole or in part within its territory, wherever the criminal organisation is based or pursues its criminal activities;
   (b) by one of its nationals; or
   (c) for the benefit of a legal person established in the territory of that Member State.
      A Member State may decide that it will not apply, or that it will apply only in specific cases or circumstances, the jurisdiction rules set out in (b) and (c) where the offences referred to in Article 2 are committed outside its territory.
2. When an offence referred to in Article 2 falls within the jurisdiction of more than one Member State and when any one of the States concerned can validly prosecute on the basis of the same facts, the Member States concerned shall cooperate in order to decide which of them will prosecute the offenders, with the aim, if possible, of centralising proceedings in a single Member State. To this end, Member States may have recourse to Eurojust or any other body or mechanism established within the European Union in order to facilitate cooperation between their judicial authorities and the coordination of their action. Special account shall be taken of the following factors:
   (a) the Member State in the territory of which the acts were committed;
   (b) the Member State of which the perpetrator is a national or resident;
   (c) the Member State of the origin of the victims;
   (d) the Member State in the territory of which the perpetrator was found.
3. A Member State which, under its law, does not as yet extradite or surrender its own nationals shall take the necessary measures to establish its jurisdiction over and, where appropriate, to prosecute the offence referred to in Article 2, when committed by one of its nationals outside its territory.
4. This Article shall not exclude the exercise of jurisdiction in criminal matters as laid down by a Member State in accordance with its national legislation.

Article 8
Absence of requirement of a report or accusation by victims

Member States shall ensure that investigations into, or prosecution of, offences referred to in Article 2 are not dependent on a report or accusation made by a person subjected to the offence, at least as regards acts committed in the territory of the Member State.

Article 9
Repeal of existing provisions

Joint Action 98/733/JHA is hereby repealed.

References to participation in a criminal organisation within the meaning of Joint Action 98/733/JHA in measures adopted pursuant to Title VI of the Treaty on European Union and the Treaty establishing the European Community shall be construed as references to participation in a criminal organisation within the meaning of this Framework Decision.

Article 10
Implementation and reports

1. Member States shall take the necessary measures to comply with the provisions of this Framework Decision before 11 May 2010.
2. The Member States shall transmit to the General Secretariat of the Council and to the Commission, before 11 May 2010, the text of the provisions transposing into their national law the obligations imposed

on them under this Framework Decision. On the basis of a report established using this information and a written report transmitted by the Commission, the Council shall, before 11 November 2012, assess the extent to which Member States have complied with the provisions of this Framework Decision.

Racism and xenophobia—Council Framework Decision 2008/913/JHA

Council Framework Decision 2008/913/JHA of 28 November 2008 on combating certain forms and expressions of racism and xenophobia by means of criminal law

THE COUNCIL OF THE EUROPEAN UNION,

Having regard to the Treaty on European Union, and in particular Articles 29, 31 and 34(2)(b) thereof,

Having regard to the proposal from the Commission,

Having regard to the Opinion of the European Parliament[1],

Whereas:

(1) Racism and xenophobia are direct violations of the principles of liberty, democracy, respect for human rights and fundamental freedoms and the rule of law, principles upon which the European Union is founded and which are common to the Member States.

(2) The Action Plan of the Council and the Commission on how best to implement the provisions of the Treaty of Amsterdam on an area of freedom, security and justice[2] the Conclusions of the Tampere European Council of 15 and 16 October 1999, the Resolution of the European Parliament of 20 September 2000 on the European Union's position at the World Conference Against Racism and the current situation in the Union[3] and the Communication from the Commission to the Council and the European Parliament on the biannual update of the Scoreboard to review progress on the creation of an area of 'freedom, security and justice' in the European Union (second half of 2000) call for action in this field. In the Hague Programme of 4 and 5 November 2004, the Council recalls its firm commitment to oppose any form of racism, anti-Semitism and xenophobia as already expressed by the European Council in December 2003.

(3) Council Joint Action 96/443/JHA of 15 July 1996 concerning action to combat racism and xenophobia[4] should be followed by further legislative action addressing the need for further approximation of law and regulations of Member States and for overcoming obstacles for efficient judicial cooperation which are mainly based on the divergence of legal approaches in the Member States.

(4) According to the evaluation of Joint Action 96/443/JHA and work carried out in other international fora, such as the Council of Europe, some difficulties have still been experienced regarding judicial cooperation and therefore there is a need for further approximation of Member States' criminal laws in order to ensure the effective implementation of comprehensive and clear legislation to combat racism and xenophobia.

(5) Racism and xenophobia constitute a threat against groups of persons which are the target of such behaviour. It is necessary to define a common criminal-law approach in the European Union to this phenomenon in order to ensure that the same behaviour constitutes an offence in all Member States and that effective, proportionate and dissuasive penalties are provided for natural and legal persons having committed or being liable for such offences.

(6) Member States acknowledge that combating racism and xenophobia requires various kinds of measures in a comprehensive framework and may not be limited to criminal matters. This Framework Decision is limited to combating particularly serious forms of racism and xenophobia by means of criminal law. Since the Member States' cultural and legal traditions are, to some extent, different, particularly in this field, full harmonisation of criminal laws is currently not possible.

---

[1] Opinion of 29 November 2007 (not yet published in the Official Journal).
[2] OJ C 19, 23.1.1999, p. 1.
[3] OJ C 146, 17.5.2001, p. 110.
[4] OJ L 185, 24.7.1996, p. 5.

(7) In this Framework Decision 'descent' should be understood as referring mainly to persons or groups of persons who descend from persons who could be identified by certain characteristics (such as race or colour), but not necessarily all of these characteristics still exist. In spite of that, because of their descent, such persons or groups of persons may be subject to hatred or violence.

(8) 'Religion' should be understood as broadly referring to persons defined by reference to their religious convictions or beliefs.

(9) 'Hatred' should be understood as referring to hatred based on race, colour, religion, descent or national or ethnic origin.

(10) This Framework Decision does not prevent a Member State from adopting provisions in national law which extend Article 1(1)(c) and (d) to crimes directed against a group of persons defined by other criteria than race, colour, religion, descent or national or ethnic origin, such as social status or political convictions.

(11) It should be ensured that investigations and prosecutions of offences involving racism and xenophobia are not dependent on reports or accusations made by victims, who are often particularly vulnerable and reluctant to initiate legal proceedings.

(12) Approximation of criminal law should lead to combating racist and xenophobic offences more effectively, by promoting a full and effective judicial cooperation between Member States. The difficulties which may exist in this field should be taken into account by the Council when reviewing this Framework Decision with a view to considering whether further steps in this area are necessary.

(13) Since the objective of this Framework Decision, namely ensuring that racist and xenophobic offences are sanctioned in all Member States by at least a minimum level of effective, proportionate and dissuasive criminal penalties, cannot be sufficiently achieved by the Member States individually, since such rules have to be common and compatible and since this objective can therefore be better achieved at the level of the European Union, the Union may adopt measures, in accordance with the principle of subsidiarity as referred to in Article 2 of the Treaty on European Union and as set out in Article 5 of the Treaty establishing the European Community. In accordance with the principle of proportionality, as set out in the latter Article, this Framework Decision does not go beyond what is necessary in order to achieve that objective.

(14) This Framework Decision respects the fundamental rights and observes the principles recognised by Article 6 of the Treaty on European Union and by the European Convention for the Protection of Human Rights and Fundamental Freedoms, in particular Articles 10 and 11 thereof, and reflected in the Charter of Fundamental Rights of the European Union, and notably Chapters II and VI thereof.

(15) Considerations relating to freedom of association and freedom of expression, in particular freedom of the press and freedom of expression in other media have led in many Member States to procedural guarantees and to special rules in national law as to the determination or limitation of liability.

(16) Joint Action 96/443/JHA should be repealed since, with the entry into force of the Treaty of Amsterdam, Council Directive 2000/43/EC of 29 June 2000 implementing the principle of equal treatment between persons irrespective of racial or ethnic origin[5] and this Framework Decision, it becomes obsolete,

HAS ADOPTED THIS FRAMEWORK DECISION:

Article 1
Offences concerning racism and xenophobia

1. Each Member State shall take the measures necessary to ensure that the following intentional conduct is punishable:
    (a) publicly inciting to violence or hatred directed against a group of persons or a member of such a group defined by reference to race, colour, religion, descent or national or ethnic origin;
    (b) the commission of an act referred to in point (a) by public dissemination or distribution of tracts, pictures or other material;
    (c) publicly condoning, denying or grossly trivialising crimes of genocide, crimes against humanity and war crimes as defined in Articles 6, 7 and 8 of the Statute of the International Criminal Court,

---

5   OJ L 180, 19.7.2000, p. 22.

directed against a group of persons or a member of such a group defined by reference to race, colour, religion, descent or national or ethnic origin when the conduct is carried out in a manner likely to incite to violence or hatred against such a group or a member of such a group;

(d) publicly condoning, denying or grossly trivialising the crimes defined in Article 6 of the Charter of the International Military Tribunal appended to the London Agreement of 8 August 1945, directed against a group of persons or a member of such a group defined by reference to race, colour, religion, descent or national or ethnic origin when the conduct is carried out in a manner likely to incite to violence or hatred against such a group or a member of such a group.

2. For the purpose of paragraph 1, Member States may choose to punish only conduct which is either carried out in a manner likely to disturb public order or which is threatening, abusive or insulting.

3. For the purpose of paragraph 1, the reference to religion is intended to cover, at least, conduct which is a pretext for directing acts against a group of persons or a member of such a group defined by reference to race, colour, descent, or national or ethnic origin.

4. Any Member State may, on adoption of this Framework Decision or later, make a statement that it will make punishable the act of denying or grossly trivialising the crimes referred to in paragraph 1(c) and/or (d) only if the crimes referred to in these paragraphs have been established by a final decision of a national court of this Member State and/or an international court, or by a final decision of an international court only.

Article 2
Instigation, aiding and abetting

1. Each Member State shall take the measures necessary to ensure that instigating the conduct referred to in Article 1(1)(c) and (d) is punishable.

2. Each Member State shall take the measures necessary to ensure that aiding and abetting in the commission of the conduct referred to in Article 1 is punishable.

Article 3
Criminal penalties

1. Each Member State shall take the necessary measures to ensure that the conduct referred to in Articles 1 and 2 is punishable by effective, proportionate and dissuasive criminal penalties.

2. Each Member State shall take the necessary measures to ensure that the conduct referred to in Article 1 is punishable by criminal penalties of a maximum of at least between 1 and 3 years of imprisonment.

Article 4
Racist and xenophobic motivation

For offences other than those referred to in Articles 1 and 2, Member States shall take the necessary measures to ensure that racist and xenophobic motivation is considered an aggravating circumstance, or, alternatively that such motivation may be taken into consideration by the courts in the determination of the penalties.

Article 5
Liability of legal persons

[Similar terms to Art. 5 of Framework Decision 2003/568/JHA.]

Article 6
Penalties for legal persons

[Similar terms to Art. 6 of Framework Decision 2003/568/JHA.]

Article 7
Constitutional rules and fundamental principles

1. This Framework Decision shall not have the effect of modifying the obligation to respect fundamental rights and fundamental legal principles, including freedom of expression and association, as enshrined in Article 6 of the Treaty on European Union.

2. This Framework Decision shall not have the effect of requiring Member States to take measures in contradiction to fundamental principles relating to freedom of association and freedom of expression, in particular freedom of the press and the freedom of expression in other media as they result

from constitutional traditions or rules governing the rights and responsibilities of, and the procedural guarantees for, the press or other media where these rules relate to the determination or limitation of liability.

Article 8
Initiation of investigation or prosecution

Each Member State shall take the necessary measures to ensure that investigations into or prosecution of the conduct referred to in Articles 1 and 2 shall not be dependent on a report or an accusation made by a victim of the conduct, at least in the most serious cases where the conduct has been committed in its territory.

Article 9
Jurisdiction

[Similar terms to Art. 7 of Framework Decision 2003/568/JHA.]

Article 10
Implementation and review

1. Member States shall take the necessary measures to comply with the provisions of this Framework Decision by 28 November 2010.
2. By the same date Member States shall transmit to the General Secretariat of the Council and to the Commission the text of the provisions transposing into their national law the obligations imposed on them under this Framework Decision. On the basis of a report established using this information by the Council and a written report from the Commission, the Council shall, by 28 November 2013, assess the extent to which Member States have complied with the provisions of this Framework Decision.
3. Before 28 November 2013, the Council shall review this Framework Decision. For the preparation of this review, the Council shall ask Member States whether they have experienced difficulties in judicial cooperation with regard to the conduct under Article 1(1). In addition, the Council may request Eurojust to submit a report, on whether differences between national legislations have resulted in any problems regarding judicial cooperation between the Member States in this area.

Article 11
Repeal of Joint Action 96/443/JHA

Joint Action 96/443/JHA is hereby repealed.

Rights in criminal proceedings—The 'Roadmap' for strengthening procedural rights of suspected or accused persons in criminal proceedings; Directive 2010/64/EU on the right to interpretation and translation in criminal proceedings; Directive 2012/13/EU on the right to information in criminal proceedings

The 'Roadmap' for strengthening procedural rights of suspected or accused persons in criminal proceedings
(2009/C 295/01, OJ C 295/1)

The order of the rights indicated in this Roadmap is indicative. It is emphasised that the explanations provided below merely serve to give an indication of the proposed action, and do not aim to regulate the precise scope and content of the measures concerned in advance.

Measure A: Translation and Interpretation

Short explanation:

The suspected or accused person must be able to understand what is happening and to make him/herself understood. A suspected or accused person who does not speak or understand the language that is used in the proceedings will need an interpreter and translation of essential procedural documents. Particular attention should also be paid to the needs of suspected or accused persons with hearing impediments.

Measure B: Information on Rights and Information about the Charges

Short explanation:

A person that is suspected or accused of a crime should get information on his/her basic rights orally or, where appropriate, in writing, e.g. by way of a Letter of Rights. Furthermore, that person should also receive information promptly about the nature and cause of the accusation against him or her. A person who has been charged should be entitled, at the appropriate time, to the information necessary for the preparation of his or her defence, it being understood that this should not prejudice the due course of the criminal proceedings.

Measure C: Legal Advice and Legal Aid

Short explanation:

The right to legal advice (through a legal counsel) for the suspected or accused person in criminal proceedings at the earliest appropriate stage of such proceedings is fundamental in order to safeguard the fairness of the proceedings; the right to legal aid should ensure effective access to the aforementioned right to legal advice.

Measure D: Communication with Relatives, Employers and Consular Authorities

Short explanation:

A suspected or accused person who is deprived of his or her liberty shall be promptly informed of the right to have at least one person, such as a relative or employer, informed of the deprivation of liberty, it being understood that this should not prejudice the due course of the criminal proceedings. In addition, a suspected or accused person who is deprived of his or her liberty in a State other than his or her own shall be informed of the right to have the competent consular authorities informed of the deprivation of liberty.

Measure E: Special Safeguards for Suspected or Accused Persons who are Vulnerable

Short explanation:

In order to safeguard the fairness of the proceedings, it is important that special attention is shown to suspected or accused persons who cannot understand or follow the content or the meaning of the proceedings, owing, for example, to their age, mental or physical condition.

Measure F: A Green Paper on Pre-Trial Detention

Short explanation:

The time that a person can spend in detention before being tried in court and during the court proceedings varies considerably between the Member States. Excessively long periods of pre-trial detention are detrimental for the individual, can prejudice the judicial cooperation between the Member States and do not represent the values for which the European Union stands. Appropriate measures in this context should be examined in a Green Paper. EN 4.12.2009 Official Journal of the European Union C 295/3.

Directive 2010/64/EU of the European Parliament and of the Council of 20 October 2010 on the right to interpretation and translation in criminal proceedings

THE EUROPEAN PARLIAMENT AND THE COUNCIL OF THE EUROPEAN UNION,

Having regard to the Treaty on the Functioning of the European Union, and in particular point (b) of the second subparagraph of Article 82(2) thereof,

Having regard to the initiative of the Kingdom of Belgium, the Federal Republic of Germany, the Republic of Estonia, the Kingdom of Spain, the French Republic, the Italian Republic, the Grand-Duchy of Luxembourg, the Republic of Hungary, the Republic of Austria, the Portuguese Republic, Romania, the Republic of Finland and the Kingdom of Sweden[1],

After transmission of the draft legislative act to the national parliaments,

---

[1] OJ C 69, 18.3.2010, p. 1.

Acting in accordance with the ordinary legislative procedure[2],

Whereas:

(1) The Union has set itself the objective of maintaining and developing an area of freedom, security and justice. According to the Presidency Conclusions of the European Council in Tampere of 15 and 16 October 1999, and in particular point 33 thereof, the principle of mutual recognition of judgments and other decisions of judicial authorities should become the cornerstone of judicial cooperation in civil and criminal matters within the Union because enhanced mutual recognition and the necessary approximation of legislation would facilitate cooperation between competent authorities and the judicial protection of individual rights.

(2) On 29 November 2000, the Council, in accordance with the Tampere Conclusions, adopted a programme of measures to implement the principle of mutual recognition of decisions in criminal matters[3]. The introduction to the programme states that mutual recognition is 'designed to strengthen cooperation between Member States but also to enhance the protection of individual rights'.

(3) The implementation of the principle of mutual recognition of decisions in criminal matters presupposes that Member States have trust in each other's criminal justice systems. The extent of mutual recognition is very much dependent on a number of parameters, which include mechanisms for safeguarding the rights of suspected or accused persons and common minimum standards necessary to facilitate the application of the principle of mutual recognition.

(4) Mutual recognition of decisions in criminal matters can operate effectively only in a spirit of trust in which not only judicial authorities but all actors in the criminal process consider decisions of the judicial authorities of other Member States as equivalent to their own, implying not only trust in the adequacy of other Member States' rules, but also trust that those rules are correctly applied.

(5) Article 6 of the European Convention for the Protection of Human Rights and Fundamental Freedoms (hereinafter the ECHR) and Article 47 of the Charter of Fundamental Rights of the European Union (hereinafter the Charter) enshrine the right to a fair trial. Article 48(2) of the Charter guarantees respect for the right of defence. This Directive respects those rights and should be implemented accordingly.

(6) Although all the Member States are party to the ECHR, experience has shown that that alone does not always provide a sufficient degree of trust in the criminal justice systems of other Member States.

(7) Strengthening mutual trust requires a more consistent implementation of the rights and guarantees set out in Article 6 of the ECHR. It also requires, by means of this Directive and other measures, further development within the Union of the minimum standards set out in the ECHR and the Charter.

(8) Article 82(2) of the Treaty on the Functioning of the European Union provides for the establishment of minimum rules applicable in the Member States so as to facilitate mutual recognition of judgments and judicial decisions and police and judicial cooperation in criminal matters having a cross-border dimension. Point (b) of the second subparagraph of Article 82(2) refers to 'the rights of individuals in criminal procedure' as one of the areas in which minimum rules may be established.

(9) Common minimum rules should lead to increased confidence in the criminal justice systems of all Member States, which, in turn, should lead to more efficient judicial cooperation in a climate of mutual trust. Such common minimum rules should be established in the fields of interpretation and translation in criminal proceedings.

(10) On 30 November 2009, the Council adopted a resolution on a Roadmap for strengthening procedural rights of suspected or accused persons in criminal proceeding.[4] Taking a step-by-step approach, the Roadmap called for the adoption of measures regarding the right to translation and interpretation (measure A), the right to information on rights and information about the charges (measure B), the right to legal advice and legal aid (measure C), the right to communication with relatives, employers and consular authorities (measure D), and special safeguards for suspected or accused persons who are vulnerable (measure E).

(11) In the Stockholm programme, adopted on 10 December 2009, the European Council welcomed the Roadmap and made it part of the Stockholm programme (point 2.4). The European Council underlined the non-exhaustive character of the Roadmap, by inviting the Commission to examine further elements of

---

[2] Position of the European Parliament of 16 June 2010 (not yet published in the Official Journal) and decision of the Council of 7 October 2010.

[3] OJ C 12, 15.1.2001, p. 10.

[4] OJ C 295, 4.12.2009, p. 1.

minimum procedural rights for suspected and accused persons, and to assess whether other issues, for instance the presumption of innocence, need to be addressed, in order to promote better cooperation in that area.

(12) This Directive relates to measure A of the Roadmap. It lays down common minimum rules to be applied in the fields of interpretation and translation in criminal proceedings with a view to enhancing mutual trust among Member States.

(13) This Directive draws on the Commission proposal for a Council Framework Decision on the right to interpretation and to translation in criminal proceedings of 8 July 2009, and on the Commission proposal for a Directive of the European Parliament and of the Council on the right to interpretation and translation in criminal proceedings of 9 March 2010.

(14) The right to interpretation and translation for those who do not speak or understand the language of the proceedings is enshrined in Article 6 of the ECHR, as interpreted in the case-law of the European Court of Human Rights. This Directive facilitates the application of that right in practice. To that end, the aim of this Directive is to ensure the right of suspected or accused persons to interpretation and translation in criminal proceedings with a view to ensuring their right to a fair trial.

(15) The rights provided for in this Directive should also apply, as necessary accompanying measures, to the execution of a European arrest warrant[5] within the limits provided for by this Directive. Executing Members States should provide, and bear the costs of, interpretation and translation for the benefit of the requested persons who do not speak or understand the language of the proceedings.

(16) In some Member States an authority other than a court having jurisdiction in criminal matters has competence for imposing sanctions in relation to relatively minor offences. That may be the case, for example, in relation to traffic offences which are committed on a large scale and which might be established following a traffic control. In such situations, it would be unreasonable to require that the competent authority ensure all the rights under this Directive. Where the law of a Member State provides for the imposition of a sanction regarding minor offences by such an authority and there is a right of appeal to a court having jurisdiction in criminal matters, this Directive should therefore apply only to the proceedings before that court following such an appeal.

(17) This Directive should ensure that there is free and adequate linguistic assistance, allowing suspected or accused persons who do not speak or understand the language of the criminal proceedings fully to exercise their right of defence and safeguarding the fairness of the proceedings.

(18) Interpretation for the benefit of the suspected or accused persons should be provided without delay. However, where a certain period of time elapses before interpretation is provided, that should not constitute an infringement of the requirement that interpretation be provided without delay, as long as that period of time is reasonable in the circumstances.

(19) Communication between suspected or accused persons and their legal counsel should be interpreted in accordance with this Directive. Suspected or accused persons should be able, inter alia, to explain their version of the events to their legal counsel, point out any statements with which they disagree and make their legal counsel aware of any facts that should be put forward in their defence.

(20) For the purposes of the preparation of the defence, communication between suspected or accused persons and their legal counsel in direct connection with any questioning or hearing during the proceedings, or with the lodging of an appeal or other procedural applications, such as an application for bail, should be interpreted where necessary in order to safeguard the fairness of the proceedings.

(21) Member States should ensure that there is a procedure or mechanism in place to ascertain whether suspected or accused persons speak and understand the language of the criminal proceedings and whether they need the assistance of an interpreter. Such procedure or mechanism implies that competent authorities verify in any appropriate manner, including by consulting the suspected or accused persons concerned, whether they speak and understand the language of the criminal proceedings and whether they need the assistance of an interpreter.

(22) Interpretation and translation under this Directive should be provided in the native language of the suspected or accused persons or in any other language that they speak or understand in order to allow them fully to exercise their right of defence, and in order to safeguard the fairness of the proceedings.

---

[5] Council Framework Decision 2002/584/JHA of 13 June 2002 on the European arrest warrant and the surrender procedures between Member States (OJ L 190, 18.7.2002, p. 1).

(23) The respect for the right to interpretation and translation contained in this Directive should not compromise any other procedural right provided under national law.

(24) Member States should ensure that control can be exercised over the adequacy of the interpretation and translation provided when the competent authorities have been put on notice in a given case.

(25) The suspected or accused persons or the persons subject to proceedings for the execution of a European arrest warrant should have the right to challenge the finding that there is no need for interpretation, in accordance with procedures in national law. That right does not entail the obligation for Member States to provide for a separate mechanism or complaint procedure in which such finding may be challenged and should not prejudice the time limits applicable to the execution of a European arrest warrant.

(26) When the quality of the interpretation is considered insufficient to ensure the right to a fair trial, the competent authorities should be able to replace the appointed interpreter.

(27) The duty of care towards suspected or accused persons who are in a potentially weak position, in particular because of any physical impairments which affect their ability to communicate effectively, underpins a fair administration of justice. The prosecution, law enforcement and judicial authorities should therefore ensure that such persons are able to exercise effectively the rights provided for in this Directive, for example by taking into account any potential vulnerability that affects their ability to follow the proceedings and to make themselves understood, and by taking appropriate steps to ensure those rights are guaranteed.

(28) When using videoconferencing for the purpose of remote interpretation, the competent authorities should be able to rely on the tools that are being developed in the context of European e-Justice (e.g. information on courts with videoconferencing equipment or manuals).

(29) This Directive should be evaluated in the light of the practical experience gained. If appropriate, it should be amended so as to improve the safeguards which it lays down.

(30) Safeguarding the fairness of the proceedings requires that essential documents, or at least the relevant passages of such documents, be translated for the benefit of suspected or accused persons in accordance with this Directive. Certain documents should always be considered essential for that purpose and should therefore be translated, such as any decision depriving a person of his liberty, any charge or indictment, and any judgment. It is for the competent authorities of the Member States to decide, on their own motion or upon a request of suspected or accused persons or of their legal counsel, which other documents are essential to safeguard the fairness of the proceedings and should therefore be translated as well.

(31) Member States should facilitate access to national databases of legal translators and interpreters where such databases exist. In that context, particular attention should be paid to the aim of providing access to existing databases through the e-Justice portal, as planned in the multiannual European e-Justice action plan 2009–2013 of 27 November 2008[6].

(32) This Directive should set minimum rules. Member States should be able to extend the rights set out in this Directive in order to provide a higher level of protection also in situations not explicitly dealt with in this Directive. The level of protection should never fall below the standards provided by the ECHR or the Charter as interpreted in the case-law of the European Court of Human Rights or the Court of Justice of the European Union.

(33) The provisions of this Directive that correspond to rights guaranteed by the ECHR or the Charter should be interpreted and implemented consistently with those rights, as interpreted in the relevant case-law of the European Court of Human Rights and the Court of Justice of the European Union.

(34) Since the objective of this Directive, namely establishing common minimum rules, cannot be sufficiently achieved by the Member States and can therefore, by reason of its scale and effects, be better achieved at Union level, the Union may adopt measures in accordance with the principle of subsidiarity as set out in Article 5 of the Treaty on European Union. In accordance with the principle of proportionality, as set out in that Article, this Directive does not go beyond what is necessary in order to achieve that objective.

(35) In accordance with Article 3 of the Protocol (No 21) on the position of the United Kingdom and Ireland in respect of the Area of Freedom, Security and Justice, annexed to the Treaty on European Union

---

6   OJ C 75, 31.3.2009, p. 1.

and to the Treaty on the Functioning of the European Union, those Member States have notified their wish to take part in the adoption and application of this Directive.

(36) In accordance with Articles 1 and 2 of the Protocol (No 22) on the position of Denmark, annexed to the Treaty on European Union and to the Treaty on the Functioning of the European Union, Denmark is not taking part in the adoption of this Directive and is not bound by it or subject to its application,

HAVE ADOPTED THIS DIRECTIVE:

Article 1
Subject matter and scope

1. This Directive lays down rules concerning the right to interpretation and translation in criminal proceedings and proceedings for the execution of a European arrest warrant.
2. The right referred to in paragraph 1 shall apply to persons from the time that they are made aware by the competent authorities of a Member State, by official notification or otherwise, that they are suspected or accused of having committed a criminal offence until the conclusion of the proceedings, which is understood to mean the final determination of the question whether they have committed the offence, including, where applicable, sentencing and the resolution of any appeal.
3. Where the law of a Member State provides for the imposition of a sanction regarding minor offences by an authority other than a court having jurisdiction in criminal matters, and the imposition of such a sanction may be appealed to such a court, this Directive shall apply only to the proceedings before that court following such an appeal.
4. This Directive does not affect national law concerning the presence of legal counsel during any stage of the criminal proceedings, nor does it affect national law concerning the right of access of a suspected or accused person to documents in criminal proceedings.

Article 2
Right to interpretation

1. Member States shall ensure that suspected or accused persons who do not speak or understand the language of the criminal proceedings concerned are provided, without delay, with interpretation during criminal proceedings before investigative and judicial authorities, including during police questioning, all court hearings and any necessary interim hearings.
2. Member States shall ensure that, where necessary for the purpose of safeguarding the fairness of the proceedings, interpretation is available for communication between suspected or accused persons and their legal counsel in direct connection with any questioning or hearing during the proceedings or with the lodging of an appeal or other procedural applications.
3. The right to interpretation under paragraphs 1 and 2 includes appropriate assistance for persons with hearing or speech impediments.
4. Member States shall ensure that a procedure or mechanism is in place to ascertain whether suspected or accused persons speak and understand the language of the criminal proceedings and whether they need the assistance of an interpreter.
5. Member States shall ensure that, in accordance with procedures in national law, suspected or accused persons have the right to challenge a decision finding that there is no need for interpretation and, when interpretation has been provided, the possibility to complain that the quality of the interpretation is not sufficient to safeguard the fairness of the proceedings.
6. Where appropriate, communication technology such as videoconferencing, telephone or the Internet may be used, unless the physical presence of the interpreter is required in order to safeguard the fairness of the proceedings.
7. In proceedings for the execution of a European arrest warrant, the executing Member State shall ensure that its competent authorities provide persons subject to such proceedings who do not speak or understand the language of the proceedings with interpretation in accordance with this Article.
8. Interpretation provided under this Article shall be of a quality sufficient to safeguard the fairness of the proceedings, in particular by ensuring that suspected or accused persons have knowledge of the case against them and are able to exercise their right of defence.

Article 3
Right to translation of essential documents

1. Member States shall ensure that suspected or accused persons who do not understand the language of the criminal proceedings concerned are, within a reasonable period of time, provided with a written

translation of all documents which are essential to ensure that they are able to exercise their right of defence and to safeguard the fairness of the proceedings.

2. Essential documents shall include any decision depriving a person of his liberty, any charge or indictment, and any judgment.

3. The competent authorities shall, in any given case, decide whether any other document is essential. Suspected or accused persons or their legal counsel may submit a reasoned request to that effect.

4. There shall be no requirement to translate passages of essential documents which are not relevant for the purposes of enabling suspected or accused persons to have knowledge of the case against them.

5. Member States shall ensure that, in accordance with procedures in national law, suspected or accused persons have the right to challenge a decision finding that there is no need for the translation of documents or passages thereof and, when a translation has been provided, the possibility to complain that the quality of the translation is not sufficient to safeguard the fairness of the proceedings.

6. In proceedings for the execution of a European arrest warrant, the executing Member State shall ensure that its competent authorities provide any person subject to such proceedings who does not understand the language in which the European arrest warrant is drawn up, or into which it has been translated by the issuing Member State, with a written translation of that document.

7. As an exception to the general rules established in paragraphs 1, 2, 3 and 6, an oral translation or oral summary of essential documents may be provided instead of a written translation on condition that such oral translation or oral summary does not prejudice the fairness of the proceedings.

8. Any waiver of the right to translation of documents referred to in this Article shall be subject to the requirements that suspected or accused persons have received prior legal advice or have otherwise obtained full knowledge of the consequences of such a waiver, and that the waiver was unequivocal and given voluntarily.

9. Translation provided under this Article shall be of a quality sufficient to safeguard the fairness of the proceedings, in particular by ensuring that suspected or accused persons have knowledge of the case against them and are able to exercise their right of defence.

Article 4

Costs of interpretation and translation

Member States shall meet the costs of interpretation and translation resulting from the application of Articles 2 and 3, irrespective of the outcome of the proceedings.

Article 5

Quality of the interpretation and translation

1. Member States shall take concrete measures to ensure that the interpretation and translation provided meets the quality required under Article 2(8) and Article 3(9).

2. In order to promote the adequacy of interpretation and translation and efficient access thereto, Member States shall endeavour to establish a register or registers of independent translators and interpreters who are appropriately qualified. Once established, such register or registers shall, where appropriate, be made available to legal counsel and relevant authorities.

3. Member States shall ensure that interpreters and translators be required to observe confidentiality regarding interpretation and translation provided under this Directive.

Article 6

Training

Without prejudice to judicial independence and differences in the organisation of the judiciary across the Union, Member States shall request those responsible for the training of judges, prosecutors and judicial staff involved in criminal proceedings to pay special attention to the particularities of communicating with the assistance of an interpreter so as to ensure efficient and effective communication.

Article 7

Record-keeping

Member States shall ensure that when a suspected or accused person has been subject to questioning or hearings by an investigative or judicial authority with the assistance of an interpreter pursuant to Article 2, when an oral translation or oral summary of essential documents has been provided in the presence of such an authority pursuant to Article 3(7), or when a person has waived the right to translation pursuant to Article 3(8), it will be noted that these events have occurred, using the recording procedure in accordance with the law of the Member State concerned.

Article 8
Non-regression

Nothing in this Directive shall be construed as limiting or derogating from any of the rights and procedural safeguards that are ensured under the European Convention for the Protection of Human Rights and Fundamental Freedoms, the Charter of Fundamental Rights of the European Union, other relevant provisions of international law or the law of any Member State which provides a higher level of protection.

Article 9
Transposition

1. Member States shall bring into force the laws, regulations and administrative provisions necessary to comply with this Directive by 27 October 2013.
2. Member States shall transmit the text of those measures to the Commission.
3. When Member States adopt those measures, they shall contain a reference to this Directive or be accompanied by such a reference on the occasion of their official publication. The methods of making such reference shall be laid down by the Member States.

Article 10
Report

The Commission shall, by 27 October 2014, submit a report to the European Parliament and to the Council, assessing the extent to which the Member States have taken the necessary measures in order to comply with this Directive, accompanied, if necessary, by legislative proposals.

Directive 2012/13/EU of the European Parliament and of the Council of 22 May 2012 on the right to information in criminal proceedings

THE EUROPEAN PARLIAMENT AND THE COUNCIL OF THE EUROPEAN UNION,

Having regard to the Treaty on the Functioning of the European Union, and in particular Article 82(2) thereof,

Having regard to the proposal from the European Commission,

After transmission of the draft legislative act to the national parliaments,

Having regard to the opinion of the European Economic and Social Committee[1],

After consulting the Committee of the Regions,

Acting in accordance with the ordinary legislative procedure[2],

Whereas:

(1) The Union has set itself the objective of maintaining and developing an area of freedom, security and justice. According to the Presidency Conclusions of the European Council in Tampere of 15 and 16 October 1999, and in particular point 33 thereof, the principle of mutual recognition of judgments and other decisions of judicial authorities should become the cornerstone of judicial cooperation in both civil and criminal matters within the Union because enhanced mutual recognition and the necessary approximation of legislation would facilitate cooperation between competent authorities and the judicial protection of individual rights.

(2) On 29 November 2000, the Council, in accordance with the Tampere conclusions, adopted a programme of measures to implement the principle of mutual recognition of decisions in criminal matters[3].

---

[1] [1] OJ C 54, 19.2.2011, p. 48.
[2] Position of the European Parliament of 13 December 2011 (not yet published in the Official Journal) and decision of the Council of 26 April 2012.
[3] OJ C 12, 15.1.2001, p. 10.

The introduction to the programme states that mutual recognition is 'designed to strengthen cooperation between Member States but also to enhance the protection of individual rights'.

(3) The implementation of the principle of mutual recognition of decisions in criminal matters presupposes that Member States trust in each other's criminal justice systems. The extent of mutual recognition is very much dependent on a number of parameters, which include mechanisms for safeguarding the rights of suspects or accused persons and common minimum standards necessary to facilitate the application of the principle of mutual recognition.

(4) Mutual recognition of decisions in criminal matters can operate effectively only in a spirit of trust in which not only judicial authorities but all actors in the criminal process consider decisions of the judicial authorities of other Member States as equivalent to their own, implying not only trust in the adequacy of other Member States' rules, but also trust that those rules are correctly applied.

(5) Article 47 of the Charter of Fundamental Rights of the European Union (hereinafter 'the Charter') and Article 6 of the European Convention for the Protection of Human Rights and Fundamental Freedoms (hereinafter 'the ECHR') enshrine the right to a fair trial. Article 48(2) of the Charter guarantees respect for the rights of the defence.

(6) Article 6 of the Charter and Article 5 ECHR enshrine the right to liberty and security of person. Any restrictions on that right must not exceed those permitted in accordance with Article 5 ECHR and inferred from the case-law of the European Court of Human Rights.

(7) Although all the Member States are party to the ECHR, experience has shown that that alone does not always provide a sufficient degree of trust in the criminal justice systems of other Member States.

(8) Strengthening mutual trust requires detailed rules on the protection of the procedural rights and guarantees arising from the Charter and from the ECHR.

(9) Article 82(2) of the Treaty on the Functioning of the European Union provides for the establishment of minimum rules applicable in the Member States so as to facilitate mutual recognition of judgments and judicial decisions and police and judicial cooperation in criminal matters having a cross-border dimension. That Article refers to 'the rights of individuals in criminal procedure' as one of the areas in which minimum rules may be established.

(10) Common minimum rules should lead to increased confidence in the criminal justice systems of all Member States, which, in turn, should lead to more efficient judicial cooperation in a climate of mutual trust. Such common minimum rules should be established in the field of information in criminal proceedings.

(11) On 30 November 2009, the Council adopted a resolution on a Roadmap for strengthening procedural rights of suspected or accused persons in criminal proceedings [4] (hereinafter 'the Roadmap'). Taking a step-by-step approach, the Roadmap called for the adoption of measures regarding the right to translation and interpretation (measure A), the right to information on rights and information about the charges (measure B), the right to legal advice and legal aid (measure C), the right to communication with relatives, employers and consular authorities (measure D), and special safeguards for suspects or accused persons who are vulnerable (measure E). The Roadmap emphasises that the order of the rights is only indicative and thus implies that it may be changed in accordance with priorities. The Roadmap is designed to operate as a whole; only when all its component parts have been implemented will its benefits be felt in full.

(12) On 11 December 2009, the European Council welcomed the Roadmap and made it part of the Stockholm Programme—An open and secure Europe serving and protecting citizens [5] (point 2.4). The European Council underlined the non-exhaustive character of the Roadmap, by inviting the Commission to examine further elements of minimum procedural rights for suspects and accused persons, and to assess whether other issues, for instance the presumption of innocence, need to be addressed, in order to promote better cooperation in that area.

(13) The first measure adopted pursuant to the Roadmap, measure A, was Directive 2010/64/EU of the European Parliament and of the Council of 20 October 2010 on the right to interpretation and translation in criminal proceedings [6].

---

[4] OJ C 295, 4.12.2009, p. 1.
[5] OJ C 115, 4.5.2010, p. 1.
[6] OJ L 280, 26.10.2010, p. 1.

(14) This Directive relates to measure B of the Roadmap. It lays down common minimum standards to be applied in the field of information about rights and about the accusation to be given to persons suspected or accused of having committed a criminal offence, with a view to enhancing mutual trust among Member States. This Directive builds on the rights laid down in the Charter, and in particular Articles 6, 47 and 48 thereof, by building upon Articles 5 and 6 ECHR as interpreted by the European Court of Human Rights. In this Directive, the term 'accusation' is used to describe the same concept as the term 'charge' used in Article 6(1) ECHR.

(15) In its Communication of 20 April 2010 entitled 'Delivering an area of freedom, security and justice for Europe's citizens—Action Plan Implementing the Stockholm Programme', the Commission announced that it would present a proposal on the right to information on rights and information about charges in 2010.

(16) This Directive should apply to suspects and accused persons regardless of their legal status, citizenship or nationality.

(17) In some Member States an authority other than a court having jurisdiction in criminal matters has competence for imposing sanctions in relation to relatively minor offences. That may be the case, for example, in relation to traffic offences which are committed on a large scale and which might be established following a traffic control. In such situations, it would be unreasonable to require that the competent authority ensure all the rights under this Directive. Where the law of a Member State provides for the imposition of a sanction regarding minor offences by such an authority and there is either a right of appeal or the possibility for the case to be otherwise referred to a court having jurisdiction in criminal matters, this Directive should therefore apply only to the proceedings before that court following such an appeal or referral.

(18) The right to information about procedural rights, which is inferred from the case-law of the European Court of Human Rights, should be explicitly established by this Directive.

(19) The competent authorities should inform suspects or accused persons promptly of those rights, as they apply under national law, which are essential to safeguarding the fairness of the proceedings, either orally or in writing, as provided for by this Directive. In order to allow the practical and effective exercise of those rights, the information should be provided promptly in the course of the proceedings and at the latest before the first official interview of the suspect or accused person by the police or by another competent authority.

(20) This Directive lays down minimum rules with respect to the information on rights of suspects or accused persons. This is without prejudice to information to be given on other procedural rights arising out of the Charter, the ECHR, national law and applicable Union law as interpreted by the relevant courts and tribunals. Once the information about a particular right has been provided, the competent authorities should not be required to reiterate it, unless the specific circumstances of the case or the specific rules laid down in national law so require.

(21) References in this Directive to suspects or accused persons who are arrested or detained should be understood to refer to any situation where, in the course of criminal proceedings, suspects or accused persons are deprived of liberty within the meaning of Article 5(1)(c) ECHR, as interpreted by the case-law of the European Court of Human Rights.

(22) Where suspects or accused persons are arrested or detained, information about applicable procedural rights should be given by means of a written Letter of Rights drafted in an easily comprehensible manner so as to assist those persons in understanding their rights. Such a Letter of Rights should be provided promptly to each arrested person when deprived of liberty by the intervention of law enforcement authorities in the context of criminal proceedings. It should include basic information concerning any possibility to challenge the lawfulness of the arrest, obtaining a review of the detention, or requesting provisional release where, and to the extent that, such a right exists in national law. To help Member States draw up such a Letter of Rights, a model is provided in Annex I. That model is indicative and may be subject to review in the context of the Commission's report on the implementation of this Directive and also once all the Roadmap measures have entered into force. The Letter of Rights may include other relevant procedural rights that apply in Member States.

(23) Specific conditions and rules relating to the right of suspects or accused persons to have another person informed about their arrest or detention are to be determined by the Member States in their national law. As set out in the Roadmap, the exercise of that right should not prejudice the due course of the criminal proceedings.

(24) This Directive is without prejudice to the provisions of national law concerning safety of persons remaining in detention facilities.

(25) Member States should ensure that, when providing information in accordance with this Directive, suspects or accused persons are provided, where necessary, with translations or interpretation into a language that they understand, in accordance with the standards set out in Directive 2010/64/EU.

(26) When providing suspects or accused persons with information in accordance with this Directive, competent authorities should pay particular attention to persons who cannot understand the content or meaning of the information, for example because of their youth or their mental or physical condition.

(27) Persons accused of having committed a criminal offence should be given all the information on the accusation necessary to enable them to prepare their defence and to safeguard the fairness of the proceedings.

(28) The information provided to suspects or accused persons about the criminal act they are suspected or accused of having committed should be given promptly, and at the latest before their first official interview by the police or another competent authority, and without prejudicing the course of ongoing investigations. A description of the facts, including, where known, time and place, relating to the criminal act that the persons are suspected or accused of having committed and the possible legal classification of the alleged offence should be given in sufficient detail, taking into account the stage of the criminal proceedings when such a description is given, to safeguard the fairness of the proceedings and allow for an effective exercise of the rights of the defence.

(29) Where, in the course of the criminal proceedings, the details of the accusation change to the extent that the position of suspects or accused persons is substantially affected, this should be communicated to them where necessary to safeguard the fairness of the proceedings and in due time to allow for an effective exercise of the rights of the defence.

(30) Documents and, where appropriate, photographs, audio and video recordings, which are essential to challenging effectively the lawfulness of an arrest or detention of suspects or accused persons in accordance with national law, should be made available to suspects or accused persons or to their lawyers at the latest before a competent judicial authority is called to decide upon the lawfulness of the arrest or detention in accordance with Article 5(4) ECHR, and in due time to allow the effective exercise of the right to challenge the lawfulness of the arrest or detention.

(31) For the purpose of this Directive, access to the material evidence, as defined in national law, whether for or against the suspect or accused person, which is in the possession of the competent authorities in relation to the specific criminal case, should include access to materials such as documents, and where appropriate photographs and audio and video recordings. Such materials may be contained in a case file or otherwise held by competent authorities in any appropriate way in accordance with national law.

(32) Access to the material evidence in the possession of the competent authorities, whether for or against the suspect or accused person, as provided for under this Directive, may be refused, in accordance with national law, where such access may lead to a serious threat to the life or fundamental rights of another person or where refusal of such access is strictly necessary to safeguard an important public interest. Any refusal of such access must be weighed against the rights of the defence of the suspect or accused person, taking into account the different stages of the criminal proceedings. Restrictions on such access should be interpreted strictly and in accordance with the principle of the right to a fair trial under the ECHR and as interpreted by the case-law of the European Court of Human Rights.

(33) The right of access to the materials of a case should be without prejudice to the provisions of national law on the protection of personal data and the whereabouts of protected witnesses.

(34) Access to the materials of the case, as provided for by this Directive, should be provided free of charge, without prejudice to provisions of national law providing for fees to be paid for documents to be copied from the case file or for sending materials to the persons concerned or to their lawyer.

(35) Where information is provided in accordance with this Directive, the competent authorities should take note of this in accordance with existing recording procedures under national law and should not be subject to any additional obligation to introduce new mechanisms or to any additional administrative burden.

(36) Suspects or accused persons or their lawyers should have the right to challenge, in accordance with national law, the possible failure or refusal of the competent authorities to provide information or to disclose certain materials of the case in accordance with this Directive. That right does not entail the obligation for Member States to provide for a specific appeal procedure, a separate mechanism, or a complaint procedure in which such failure or refusal may be challenged.

(37) Without prejudice to judicial independence and to differences in the organisation of the judiciary across the Union, Member States should provide or encourage the provision of adequate training with respect to the objectives of this Directive to the relevant officials in Member States.

(38) Member States should undertake all the necessary action to comply with this Directive. A practical and effective implementation of some of the provisions such as the obligation to provide suspects or accused persons with information about their rights in simple and accessible language could be achieved by different means including non-legislative measures such as appropriate training for the competent authorities or by a Letter of Rights drafted in simple and non-technical language so as to be easily understood by a lay person without any knowledge of criminal procedural law.

(39) The right to written information about rights on arrest provided for in this Directive should also apply, mutatis mutandis, to persons arrested for the purpose of the execution of a European Arrest Warrant under Council Framework Decision 2002/584/JHA of 13 June 2002 on the European arrest warrant and the surrender procedures between Member States[7]. To help Member States draw up a Letter of Rights for such persons, a model is provided in Annex II. That model is indicative and may be subject to review in the context of the Commission's report on implementation of this Directive and also once all the Roadmap measures have come into force.

(40) This Directive sets minimum rules. Member States may extend the rights set out in this Directive in order to provide a higher level of protection also in situations not explicitly dealt with in this Directive. The level of protection should never fall below the standards provided by the ECHR as interpreted in the case-law of the European Court of Human Rights.

(41) This Directive respects fundamental rights and observes the principles recognised by the Charter. In particular, this Directive seeks to promote the right to liberty, the right to a fair trial and the rights of the defence. It should be implemented accordingly.

(42) The provisions of this Directive that correspond to rights guaranteed by the ECHR should be interpreted and implemented consistently with those rights, as interpreted in the case-law of the European Court of Human Rights.

(43) Since the objective of this Directive, namely establishing common minimum standards relating to the right to information in criminal proceedings, cannot be achieved by Member States acting unilaterally, at national, regional or local level, and can therefore, by reason of its scale and effects, be better achieved at Union level, the Union may adopt measures in accordance with the principle of subsidiarity as set out in Article 5 of the Treaty on European Union. In accordance with the principle of proportionality, as set out in that Article, this Directive does not go beyond what is necessary in order to achieve that objective.

(44) In accordance with Article 3 of the Protocol (No 21) on the position of the United Kingdom and Ireland in respect of the Area of Freedom, Security and Justice, annexed to the Treaty on European Union and to the Treaty on the Functioning of the European Union, those Member States have notified their wish to take part in the adoption and application of this Directive.

(45) In accordance with Articles 1 and 2 of the Protocol (No 22) on the position of Denmark, annexed to the Treaty on European Union and to the Treaty on the Functioning of the European Union, Denmark is not taking part in the adoption of this Directive and is not bound by it or subject to its application,

HAVE ADOPTED THIS DIRECTIVE:

[Terms of Decision are set out in Chapter 5.]

---

[7] OJ L 190, 18.7.2002, p. 1.

ANNEX I
Indicative model Letter of Rights

The sole purpose of this model is to assist national authorities in drawing up their Letter of Rights at national level. Member States are not bound to use this model. When preparing their Letter of Rights, Member States may amend this model in order to align it with their national rules and add further useful information. The Member State's Letter of Rights must be given upon arrest or detention. This however does not prevent Member States from providing suspects or accused persons with written information in other situations during criminal proceedings.

You have the following rights when you are arrested or detained:

A. ASSISTANCE OF A LAWYER/ENTITLEMENT TO LEGAL AID

You have the right to speak confidentially to a lawyer. A lawyer is independent from the police. Ask the police if you need help to get in contact with a lawyer, the police shall help you. In certain cases the assistance may be free of charge. Ask the police for more information.

B. INFORMATION ABOUT THE ACCUSATION

You have the right to know why you have been arrested or detained and what you are suspected or accused of having done.

C. INTERPRETATION AND TRANSLATION

If you do not speak or understand the language spoken by the police or other competent authorities, you have the right to be assisted by an interpreter, free of charge. The interpreter may help you to talk to your lawyer and must keep the content of that communication confidential. You have the right to translation of at least the relevant passages of essential documents, including any order by a judge allowing your arrest or keeping you in custody, any charge or indictment and any judgment. You may in some circumstances be provided with an oral translation or summary.

D. RIGHT TO REMAIN SILENT

While questioned by the police or other competent authorities, you do not have to answer questions about the alleged offence. Your lawyer can help you to decide on that.

E. ACCESS TO DOCUMENTS

When you are arrested and detained, you (or your lawyer) have the right to access essential documents you need to challenge the arrest or detention. If your case goes to court, you (or your lawyer) have the right to access the material evidence for or against you.

F. INFORMING SOMEONE ELSE ABOUT YOUR ARREST OR DETENTION/ INFORMING YOUR CONSULATE OR EMBASSY

When you are arrested or detained, you should tell the police if you want someone to be informed of your detention, for example a family member or your employer. In certain cases the right to inform another person of your detention may be temporarily restricted. In such cases the police will inform you of this.

If you are a foreigner, tell the police if you want your consular authority or embassy to be informed of your detention. Please also tell the police if you want to contact an official of your consular authority or embassy.

G. URGENT MEDICAL ASSISTANCE

When you are arrested or detained, you have the right to urgent medical assistance. Please let the police know if you are in need of such assistance.

H. PERIOD OF DEPRIVATION OF LIBERTY

After your arrest you may be deprived of liberty or detained for a maximum period of . . . [fill in applicable number of hours/days]. At the end of that period you must either be released or be heard by a judge who will decide on your further detention. Ask your lawyer or the judge for information about the possibility to challenge your arrest, to review the detention or to ask for provisional release.

ANNEX II

Indicative model Letter of Rights for persons arrested on the basis of a European Arrest Warrant

The sole purpose of this model is to assist national authorities in drawing up their Letter of Rights at national level. Member States are not bound to use this model. When preparing their Letter of Rights, Member States may amend this model in order to align it with their national rules and add further useful information.

You have been arrested on the basis of a European Arrest Warrant. You have the following rights:

A. INFORMATION ABOUT THE EUROPEAN ARREST WARRANT

You have the right to be informed about the content of the European Arrest Warrant on the basis of which you have been arrested.

B. ASSISTANCE OF A LAWYER

You have the right to speak confidentially to a lawyer. A lawyer is independent from the police. Ask the police if you need help to get in contact with a lawyer, the police shall help you. In certain cases the assistance may be free of charge. Ask the police for more information.

C. INTERPRETATION AND TRANSLATION

If you do not speak or understand the language spoken by the police or other competent authorities, you have the right to be assisted by an interpreter, free of charge. The interpreter may help you to talk to your lawyer and must keep the content of that communication confidential. You have the right to a translation of the European Arrest Warrant in a language you understand. You may in some circumstances be provided with an oral translation or summary.

D. POSSIBILITY TO CONSENT

You may consent or not consent to being surrendered to the State seeking you. Your consent would speed up the proceedings. [Possible addition of certain Member States: It may be difficult or even impossible to change this decision at a later stage.] Ask the authorities or your lawyer for more information.

E. HEARING

If you do not consent to your surrender, you have the right to be heard by a judicial authority.

Sex exploitation of children—Council Framework Decision 2004/68/JHA

Council Framework Decision 2004/68/JHA of 22 December 2003 on combating the sexual exploitation of children and child pornography

THE COUNCIL OF THE EUROPEAN UNION,

Having regard to the Treaty on European Union, and in particular Article 29, Article 31(1)(e) and Article 34(2)(b) thereof,

Having regard to the proposal from the Commission[1],

Having regard to the opinion of the European Parliament[2],

Whereas:

(1) The Action Plan of the Council and the Commission on how best to implement the provisions of the Treaty of Amsterdam on an area of freedom, security and justice[3], the conclusions of the Tampere European Council and the Resolution of the European Parliament of 11 April 2000 include or call for legislative action against sexual exploitation of children and child pornography, including common definitions, charges and penalties.

(2) Council Joint Action 97/154/JHA of 24 February 1997 concerning action to combat trafficking in human beings and sexual exploitation of children[4] and Council Decision 2000/375/JHA of 29 May 2000 to combat child pornography on the Internet[5] need to be followed by further legislative action addressing the divergence of legal approaches in the Member States and contributing to the development of efficient judicial and law enforcement cooperation against sexual exploitation of children and child pornography.

(3) The European Parliament, in its Resolution of 30 March 2000 on the Commission Communication on the implementation of measures to combat child sex tourism, reiterates that child sex tourism is a criminal act closely linked to those of sexual exploitation of children and of child pornography, and requests the Commission to submit to the Council a proposal for a framework Decision establishing minimum rules relating to the constituent elements of these criminal acts.

(4) Sexual exploitation of children and child pornography constitute serious violations of human rights and of the fundamental right of a child to a harmonious upbringing and development.

(5) Child pornography, a particularly serious form of sexual exploitation of children, is increasing and spreading through the use of new technologies and the Internet.

(6) The important work performed by international organisations must be complemented by that of the European Union.

(7) It is necessary that serious criminal offences such as the sexual exploitation of children and child pornography be addressed by a comprehensive approach in which the constituent elements of criminal law common to all Member States, including effective, proportionate and dissuasive sanctions, form an integral part together with the widest possible judicial cooperation.

(8) In accordance with the principles of subsidiarity and proportionality, this framework Decision confines itself to the minimum required in order to achieve those objectives at European level and does not go beyond what is necessary for that purpose.

(9) Penalties must be introduced against the perpetrators of such offences which are sufficiently stringent to bring sexual exploitation of children and child pornography within the scope of instruments already adopted for the purpose of combating organised crime, such as Council Joint Action 98/699/JHA of 3 December 1998 on money laundering, the identification, tracing, freezing, seizing and confiscation of the instrumentalities and the proceeds from crime[6] and Council Joint Action 98/733/JHA of 21 December 1998 on making it a criminal offence to participate in a criminal organisation in the Member States of the European Union[7].

(10) The specific characteristics of the combat against the sexual exploitation of children must lead Member States to lay down effective, proportionate and dissuasive sanctions in national law. Such sanctions should also be adjusted in line with the activity carried on by legal persons.

(11) Victims who are children should be questioned according to their age and stage of development for the purpose of investigation and prosecution of offences falling under this framework Decision.

---

[1] OJ C 62 E, 27.2.2001, p. 327.
[2] OJ C 53 E, 28.2.2002, p. 108.
[3] OJ C 19, 23.1.1999, p. 1.
[4] OJ L 63, 4.3.1997, p. 2.
[5] OJ L 138, 9.6.2000, p. 1.
[6] OJ L 333, 9.12.1998, p. 1. Joint Action as amended by framework Decision 2001/500/JHA (OJ L 182, 5.7.2001, p. 1).
[7] OJ L 351, 29.12.1998, p. 1.

(12) This framework Decision is without prejudice to the powers of the Community.

(13) This framework Decision should contribute to the fight against sexual exploitation of children and child pornography by complementing the instruments adopted by the Council, such as Joint Action 96/700/JHA of 29 November 1996 establishing an incentive and exchange programme for persons responsible for combating trade in human beings and sexual exploitation of children[8], Joint Action 96/748/JHA of 16 December 1996 extending the mandate given to the Europol Drugs Unit[9], Joint Action 98/428/JHA of 29 June 1998 on the creation of a European Judicial Network[10], Joint Action 96/277/JHA of 22 April 1996 concerning a framework for the exchange of liaison magistrates to improve judicial cooperation between the Member States of the European Union[11], and Joint Action 98/427/JHA of 29 June 1998 on good practice in mutual legal assistance in criminal matters[12], as well as acts adopted by the European Council and the Council, such as Decision No 276/1999/EC of the European Parliament and of the Council of 25 January 1999 adopting a multiannual Community action plan on promoting safer use of the Internet by combating illegal and harmful content on global networks[13], and Decision No 293/2000/EC of the European Parliament and of the Council of 24 January 2000 adopting a programme of Community action (the Daphne programme) (2000 to 2003) on preventive measures to fight violence against children, young persons and women[14],

HAS ADOPTED THIS FRAMEWORK DECISION:

Article 1
Definitions

For the purposes of this framework Decision:

(a) 'child' shall mean any person below the age of 18 years;

(b) 'child pornography' shall mean pornographic material that visually depicts or represents:

    (i) a real child involved or engaged in sexually explicit conduct, including lascivious exhibition of the genitals or the pubic area of a child; or

    (ii) a real person appearing to be a child involved or engaged in the conduct mentioned in (i); or

    (iii) realistic images of a non-existent child involved or engaged in the conduct mentioned in (i);

(c) 'computer system' shall mean any device or group of inter-connected or related devices, one or more of which, pursuant to a programme, perform automatic processing of data;

(d) 'legal person' shall mean any entity having such status under the applicable law, except for States or other public bodies in the exercise of State authority and for public international organisations.

Article 2
Offences concerning sexual exploitation of children

Each Member State shall take the necessary measures to ensure that the following intentional conduct is punishable:

(a) coercing a child into prostitution or into participating in pornographic performances, or profiting from or otherwise exploiting a child for such purposes;

(b) recruiting a child into prostitution or into participating in pornographic performances;

(c) engaging in sexual activities with a child, where

    (i) use is made of coercion, force or threats;

    (ii) money or other forms of remuneration or consideration is given as payment in exchange for the child engaging in sexual activities; or

    (iii) abuse is made of a recognised position of trust, authority or influence over the child.

---

[8] OJ L 322, 12.12.1996, p. 7.
[9] OJ L 342, 31.12.1996, p. 4.
[10] OJ L 191, 7.7.1998, p. 4.
[11] OJ L 105, 27.4.1996, p. 1.
[12] OJ L 191, 7.7.1998, p. 1.
[13] OJ L 33, 6.2.1999, p. 1.
[14] OJ L 34, 9.2.2000, p. 1.

Article 3
Offences concerning child pornography

1. Each Member State shall take the necessary measures to ensure that the following intentional conduct whether undertaken by means of a computer system or not, when committed without right is punishable:
   (a) production of child pornography;
   (b) distribution, dissemination or transmission of child pornography;
   (c) supplying or making available child pornography;
   (d) acquisition or possession of child pornography.
2. A Member State may exclude from criminal liability conduct relating to child pornography:
   (a) referred to in Article 1(b)(ii) where a real person appearing to be a child was in fact 18 years of age or older at the time of the depiction;
   (b) referred to in Article 1(b)(i) and (ii) where, in the case of production and possession, images of children having reached the age of sexual consent are produced and possessed with their consent and solely for their own private use. Even where the existence of consent has been established, it shall not be considered valid, if for example superior age, maturity, position, status, experience or the victim's dependency on the perpetrator has been abused in achieving the consent;
   (c) referred to in Article 1(b)(iii), where it is established that the pornographic material is produced and possessed by the producer solely for his or her own private use, as far as no pornographic material as referred to in Article 1(b)(i) and (ii) has been used for the purpose of its production, and provided that the act involves no risk for the dissemination of the material.

Article 4
Instigation, aiding, abetting and attempt

1. Each Member State shall take the necessary measures to ensure that the instigation of, or aiding or abetting in the commission of an offence referred to in Articles 2 and 3 is punishable.
2. Each Member State shall take the necessary measures to ensure that attempts to commit the conduct referred to in Article 2 and Article 3(1)(a) and (b), are punishable.

Article 5
Penalties and aggravating circumstances

1. Subject to paragraph 4, each Member State shall take the necessary measures to ensure that the offences referred to in Articles 2, 3 and 4 are punishable by criminal penalties of a maximum of at least between one and three years of imprisonment.
2. Subject to paragraph 4, each Member State shall take the necessary measures to ensure that the following offences are punishable with criminal penalties of a maximum of at least between five and ten years of imprisonment:
   (a) the offences referred to in Article 2(a), consisting in 'coercing a child into prostitution or into participating in pornographic performances', and the offences referred to in Article 2(c)(i);
   (b) the offences referred to in Article 2(a), consisting in 'profiting from or otherwise exploiting a child for such purposes', and the offences referred to in Article 2(b), in both cases as far as they refer to prostitution, where at least one of the following circumstances may apply:
      – the victim is a child below the age of sexual consent under national law,
      – the offender has deliberately or by recklessness endangered the life of the child,
      – the offences involve serious violence or caused serious harm to the child,
      – the offences are committed within the framework of a criminal organisation within the meaning of Joint Action 98/733/JHA, irrespective of the level of the penalty referred to in that Joint Action;
      – the offences referred to in Article 2(a), consisting in 'profiting from or otherwise exploiting a child for such purposes', and the offences referred to in Article 2(b), in both cases as far as they refer to pornographic performances, Article 2(c)(ii) and (iii), Article 3(1)(a), (b) and (c), where the victim is a child below the age of sexual consent under national law and at least one of the circumstances referred to under the second, third and fourth indent under point (b) of this paragraph may apply.
3. Each Member State shall take the necessary measures to ensure that a natural person, who has been convicted of one of the offences referred to in Articles 2, 3 or 4, may, if appropriate, be temporarily or permanently prevented from exercising professional activities related to the supervision of children.

4. Each Member State may provide for other sanctions, including non-criminal sanctions or measures, concerning conduct relating to child pornography referred to in Article 1(b)(iii).

Article 6
Liability of legal persons

[Similar terms to Art. 5 of Framework Decision 2003/568/JHA.]

Article 7
Sanctions on legal persons

[Similar terms to Art. 6 of Framework Decision 2003/568/JHA.]

Article 8
Jurisdiction and prosecution

1. Each Member State shall take the necessary measures to establish its jurisdiction over the offences referred to in Articles 2, 3 and 4 where:
   (a) the offence is committed in whole or in part within its territory;
   (b) the offender is one of its nationals; or
   (c) the offence is committed for the benefit of a legal person established in the territory of that Member State.
2. A Member State may decide that it will not apply, or that it will apply only in specific cases or circumstances, the jurisdiction rules set out in paragraphs 1(b) and 1(c) where the offence is committed outside its territory.
3. A Member State which, under its laws, does not extradite its own nationals shall take the necessary measures to establish its jurisdiction over and to prosecute, where appropriate, an offence referred to in Articles 2, 3 and 4 when it is committed by one of its own nationals outside its territory.
4. Member States shall inform the General Secretariat of the Council and the Commission accordingly where they decide to apply paragraph 2, where appropriate with an indication of the specific cases or circumstances in which the decision applies.
5. Each Member State shall ensure that its jurisdiction includes situations where an offence under Article 3 and, insofar as it is relevant, under Article 4, is committed by means of a computer system accessed from its territory, whether or not the computer system is on its territory.
6. Each Member State shall take the necessary measures to enable the prosecution, in accordance with national law, of at least the most serious of the offences referred to in Article 2 after the victim has reached the age of majority.

Article 9
Protection of and assistance to victims

1. Member States shall establish that investigations into or prosecution of offences covered by this framework Decision shall not be dependent on the report or accusation made by a person subjected to the offence, at least in cases where Article 8(1)(a) applies.
2. Victims of an offence referred to in Article 2 should be considered as particularly vulnerable victims pursuant to Article 2(2), Article 8(4) and Article 14(1) of Council framework Decision 2001/220/JHA of 15 March 2001 on the standing of victims in criminal proceedings[15].
3. Each Member State shall take all measures possible to ensure appropriate assistance for the victim's family. In particular, each Member State shall, where appropriate and possible, apply Article 4 of that framework Decision to the family referred therein.

Article 11

Repeal of Joint Action 97/154/JHA

Joint Action 97/154/JHA is hereby repealed.

---

[15] OJ L 82, 22.3.2001, p. 1.

Article 12

Implementation

1. Member States shall take the necessary measures to comply with this framework Decision by 20 January 2006 at the latest.
2. By 20 January 2006 the Member States shall transmit to the General Secretariat of the Council and to the Commission the text of the provisions transposing into their national legislation the obligations imposed on them under this framework Decision. By 20 January 2008 on the basis of a report established using this information and a written report from the Commission, the Council shall assess the extent to which the Member States have complied with the provisions of this framework Decision.

Ship pollution—Council Framework Decision 2005/667/JHA

Council Framework Decision 2005/667/JHA of 12 July 2005 to strengthen the criminal-law framework for the enforcement of the law against ship-source pollution

THE COUNCIL OF THE EUROPEAN UNION,

Having regard to the Treaty on European Union, and in particular Articles 31(1)(e) and 34(2)(b) thereof,

Having regard to the proposal from the Commission,

Having regard to the opinion of the European Parliament[1],

Whereas:

(1) The Action Plan of the Council and the Commission on how best to implement the provisions of the Treaty of Amsterdam on an area of freedom, security and justice[2] and the conclusions of the Tampere European Council of 15 and 16 October 1999, and in particular point 48 thereof, call for proposals for legislation to combat environmental crime, in particular common penalties and comparable procedural guarantees.

(2) The fight against intentional or seriously negligent ship-source pollution constitutes one of the Union's priorities. Points 32 to 34 of the conclusions of the Copenhagen European Council of 12 and 13 December 2002 and the statement of the JHA Council of 19 December 2002 following the shipwreck of the tanker Prestige, in particular, express the Union's determination to adopt all the measures needed to avoid recurrence of such damage.

(3) To this end, as the Commission stated in its Communication to the European Parliament and the Council on improving safety at sea in response to the Prestige accident, the legislation of the Member States should be approximated.

(4) The purpose of Directive 2005/35/EC of the European Parliament and of the Council of 7 September 2005 on ship-source pollution and on the introduction of penalties for infringements[3] and this framework Decision, which supplements Directive 2005/35/EC with detailed rules in criminal matters, is to carry out this approximation.

(5) This framework Decision, based on Article 34 of the Treaty on the European Union, is the correct instrument for imposing on the Member States the obligation to provide for criminal penalties.

(6) Due to the specific nature of the conduct, common penalties with regard to legal persons should be introduced.

(7) The 1982 United Nations Convention on the Law of the Sea, signed by all the Member States and with the European Community as a party, is particularly important in the context of cooperation.

(8) The best possible cooperation should be organised between Member States to guarantee the swift transmission of information from one Member State to another. Contact points should be designated and identified.

---

[1] Opinion of the European Parliament of 13 January 2004 (OJ C 92, 16.4.2004, p. 19).
[2] OJ C 19, 23.1.1999, p. 1.
[3] See page 11 of this Official Journal.

(9) Since the objectives of this framework Decision cannot be achieved adequately by the Member States and can therefore, by reason of the cross-border character of the damage which may be caused by the behaviour concerned, be better achieved at Union level, the Union may adopt measures, in accordance with the principle of subsidiarity as set out in Article 5 of the Treaty establishing the European Community. In accordance with the principle of proportionality, as set out in that Article, this framework Decision does not go beyond what is necessary in order to achieve those objectives.

(10) This framework Decision respects the fundamental rights and observes the principles recognised by Article 6 of the Treaty of the European Union and reflected in the Charter of Fundamental Rights of the European Union.

(11) This framework Decision does not contain an explicit obligation for Member States bordering straits used for international navigation subject to the regime for transit passage, as laid down in Part III, section 2 of the 1982 United Nations Convention on the Law of the Sea, to establish jurisdiction with regard to offences committed in such straits. The jurisdiction with regard to offences should be established in accordance with international law and in particular Article 34 of the 1982 United Nations Convention on the Law of the Sea.

(12) The practical application of the measures taken by the Member States in implementing this framework Decision, should be monitored by the Commission which should in five years from the date of implementation of this framework Decision, present a report to the Council. This report may include appropriate proposals,

HAS ADOPTED THIS FRAMEWORK DECISION:

Article 1
Definitions

For the purposes of this framework Decision, the definitions provided for in Article 2 of Directive 2005/35/EC shall apply.

Article 2
Criminal offences

1. Subject to Article 4(2) of this framework Decision, each Member State shall take the measures necessary to ensure that an infringement within the meaning of Articles 4 and 5 of Directive 2005/35/EC shall be regarded as a criminal offence.
2. Paragraph 1 shall not apply to crew members in respect of infringements that occur in straits used for international navigation, exclusive economic zones and on the high seas where the conditions set out in Annex I, Regulation 11(b) or in Annex II, Regulation 6(b), of the Marpol 73/78 Convention are satisfied.

Article 3
Aiding, abetting and inciting

Each Member State shall, in accordance with national law, take the measures necessary to ensure that aiding, abetting or inciting an offence referred to in Article 2 is punishable.

Article 4
Penalties

1. Each Member State shall take the measures necessary to ensure that the offences referred to in Articles 2 and 3 are punishable by effective, proportionate and dissuasive criminal penalties which shall include, at least for serious cases, criminal penalties of a maximum of at least between one and three years of imprisonment.
2. In minor cases, where the act committed does not cause a deterioration of the quality of the water, a Member State may provide for penalties of a different type from those laid down in paragraph 1.
3. The criminal penalties provided for in paragraph 1 may be accompanied by other penalties or measures, in particular fines, or the disqualification for a natural person from engaging in an activity requiring official authorisation or approval, or founding, managing or directing a company or a foundation, where the facts having led to his/her conviction show an obvious risk that the same kind of criminal activity may be pursued again.

4. Each Member State shall take the measures necessary to ensure that the intentionally committed offence referred to in Article 2 is punishable by a maximum of at least between five and ten years of imprisonment where the offence caused significant and widespread damage to water quality, to animal or vegetable species or to parts of them and the death or serious injury of persons.

5. Each Member State shall take the measures necessary to ensure that the intentionally committed offence referred to in Article 2 is punishable by a maximum of at least between two and five years of imprisonment where:
   (a) the offence caused significant and widespread damage to water quality, to animal or vegetable species or to parts of them; or
   (b) the offence was committed within the framework of a criminal organisation within the meaning of Council Joint Action 98/733/JHA of 21 December 1998 on making it a criminal offence to participate in a criminal organisation in the Member States of the European Union[4], irrespective of the level of the penalty referred to in that Joint Action.

6. Each Member State shall take the measures necessary to ensure that the offence referred to in Article 2, when committed with serious negligence, is punishable by a maximum of at least between two and five years of imprisonment where the offence caused significant and widespread damage to water quality, to animal or vegetable species or to parts of them and the death or serious injury of persons.

7. Each Member State shall take the measures necessary to ensure that the offence referred to in Article 2, when committed with serious negligence, is punishable by a maximum of at least between one and three years of imprisonment where the offence caused significant and widespread damage to water quality, to animal or vegetable species or to parts of them.

8. Regarding custodial penalties, this Article shall apply without prejudice to international law and in particular Article 230 of the 1982 United Nations Convention on the Law of the Sea.

Article 5
Liability of legal persons
[Similar terms to Art. 5 of Framework Decision 2003/568/JHA.]

Article 6
Penalties against legal persons

1. Each Member State shall take the measures necessary to ensure that a legal person held liable pursuant to Article 5(1) is punishable by effective, proportionate and dissuasive penalties. The penalties:
   (a) Shall include criminal or non-criminal fines, which, at least for cases where the legal person is held liable for offences referred to in Article 2, are:
      (i) of a maximum of at least between EUR 150000 and EUR 300000;
      (ii) of a maximum of at least between EUR 750000 and EUR 1500000 in the most serious cases, including at least the intentionally committed offences covered by Article 4(4) and (5).
   (b) may, for all cases, include penalties other than fines, such as:
      (i) exclusion from entitlement to public benefits or aid;
      (ii) temporary or permanent disqualification from engaging in commercial activities;
      (iii) placing under judicial supervision;
      (iv) a judicial winding-up order;
      (v) the obligation to adopt specific measures in order to eliminate the consequences of the offence which led to the liability of the legal person.

2. For the purpose of the implementation of paragraph 1(a), and without prejudice to the first sentence of paragraph 1, Member States in which the euro has not been adopted shall apply the exchange rate between the euro and their currency as published in the Official Journal of the European Union on 12 July 2005.

3. A Member State may implement paragraph 1(a) by applying a system, whereby the fine is proportionate to the turnover of the legal person, to the financial advantage achieved or envisaged by the commission of the offence, or to any other value indicating the financial situation of the legal person, provided that such system allows for maximum fines, which are at least equivalent to the minimum for the maximum fines established in paragraph 1(a).

---

[4] OJ L 351, 29.12.1998, p. 1.

4. A Member State that implements the framework Decision in accordance with paragraph 3 shall notify the General Secretariat of the Council and the Commission that it intends to do so.
5. Each Member State shall take the measures necessary to ensure that a legal person held liable pursuant to Article 5(2) is punishable by effective, proportionate and dissuasive penalties or measures.

Article 7
Jurisdiction

1. Each Member State shall take the measures necessary to establish its jurisdiction, so far as permitted by international law, with regard to the offences referred to in Articles 2 and 3 where the offence has been committed:
   (a) fully or in part in its territory;
   (b) in its exclusive economic zone or in an equivalent zone established in accordance with international law;
   (c) on board of a ship flying its flag;
   (d) by one of its nationals if the offence is punishable under criminal law where it was committed or if the place where it was committed does not fall under any territorial jurisdiction;
   (e) for the benefit of a legal person with a registered office in its territory;
   (f) outside of its territory but has caused or is likely to cause pollution in its territory or its economic zone, and the ship is voluntarily within a port or at an offshore terminal of the Member State;
   (g) on the high seas, and the ship is voluntarily within a port or at an offshore terminal of the Member State.
2. Any Member State may decide that it will not apply, or that it will apply only in specific cases or circumstances, the jurisdiction rules set out in:
   (a) paragraph 1(d);
   (b) paragraph 1(e).
3. Member States shall inform the General Secretariat of the Council accordingly where they decide to apply paragraph 2, where appropriate with an indication of the specific cases or circumstances in which the decision applies.
4. When an offence is subject to the jurisdiction of more than one Member State, the relevant Member States shall strive to coordinate their actions appropriately, in particular concerning the conditions for prosecution and the detailed arrangements for mutual assistance.
5. The following connecting factors shall be taken into account:
   (a) the Member State in whose territory, exclusive economic zone or equivalent zone the offence was committed;
   (b) the Member State in whose territory, exclusive economic zone or equivalent zone the effects of the offence are felt;
   (c) the Member State in whose territory, exclusive economic zone or equivalent zone a ship from which the offence was committed is in transit;
   (d) the Member State of which the perpetrator of the offence is a national or a resident;
   (e) the Member State in whose territory the legal person on whose behalf the offence was committed has its registered office;
   (f) the Member State of the flag of the ship from which the offence was committed.
6. For the application of this Article, the territory includes the area referred to in Article 3(1)(a) and (b) of Directive 2005/35/EC.

Article 8
Notification of information

1. Where a Member State is informed of the commission of an offence to which Article 2 applies or of the risk of the commission of such an offence which causes or is likely to cause imminent pollution, it shall immediately inform such other Member States as are likely to be exposed to this damage, and the Commission.
2. Where a Member State is informed of the commission of an offence to which Article 2 applies or of the risk of the commission of such an offence which is likely to fall within the jurisdiction of a Member State, it shall immediately inform that other Member State.
3. Member States shall without delay notify the flag State or any other State concerned of measures taken pursuant to this framework Decision, and in particular Article 7.

Article 9
Designation of contact points

1. Each Member State shall designate existing contact points, or, if necessary, create new contact points, in particular for the exchange of information as referred to in Article 8.
2. Each Member State shall inform the Commission which of its departments acts or act as contact points in accordance with paragraph 1. The Commission shall notify the other Member States of these contact points.

Article 10
Territorial scope

This framework Decision shall have the same territorial scope as Directive 2005/35/EC.

Article 11
Implementation

Terrorism—Council Framework Decision 2002/475/JHA and Council Framework Decision 2008/919/JHA
Council Framework Decision of 13 June 2002 on combating terrorism (2002/475/JHA)

THE COUNCIL OF THE EUROPEAN UNION,

Having regard to the Treaty establishing the European Union, and in particular Article 29, Article 31(e) and Article 34(2)(b) thereof,

Having regard to the proposal from the Commission[1],

Having regard to the opinion of the European Parliament[2],

Whereas:

(1) The European Union is founded on the universal values of human dignity, liberty, equality and solidarity, respect for human rights and fundamental freedoms. It is based on the principle of democracy and the principle of the rule of law, principles which are common to the Member States.

(2) Terrorism constitutes one of the most serious violations of those principles. The La Gomera Declaration adopted at the informal Council meeting on 14 October 1995 affirmed that terrorism constitutes a threat to democracy, to the free exercise of human rights and to economic and social development.

(3) All or some Member States are party to a number of conventions relating to terrorism. The Council of Europe Convention of 27 January 1977 on the Suppression of Terrorism does not regard terrorist offences as political offences or as offences connected with political offences or as offences inspired by political motives. The United Nations has adopted the Convention for the suppression of terrorist bombings of 15 December 1997 and the Convention for the suppression of financing terrorism of 9 December 1999. A draft global Convention against terrorism is currently being negotiated within the United Nations.

(4) At European Union level, on 3 December 1998 the Council adopted the Action Plan of the Council and the Commission on how best to implement the provisions of the Treaty of Amsterdam on an area of freedom, security and justice[3]. Account should also be taken of the Council Conclusions of 20 September 2001 and of the Extraordinary European Council plan of action to combat terrorism of 21 September 2001. Terrorism was referred to in the conclusions of the Tampere European Council of 15 and 16 October 1999, and of the Santa María da Feira European Council of 19 and 20 June 2000. It was also mentioned in the Commission communication to the Council and the European Parliament on the biannual update of the scoreboard to review progress on the creation of an area of 'freedom, security and justice' in the European Union (second half of 2000). Furthermore, on 5 September 2001 the European Parliament adopted a recommendation on the role of the European Union in combating terrorism. It should,

---

[1] OJ C 332 E, 27.11.2001, p. 300.
[2] Opinion delivered on 6 February 2002 (not yet published in the Official Journal).
[3] OJ C 19, 23.1.1999, p. 1.

moreover, be recalled that on 30 July 1996 twenty-five measures to fight against terrorism were advocated by the leading industrialised countries (G7) and Russia meeting in Paris.

(5) The European Union has adopted numerous specific measures having an impact on terrorism and organised crime, such as the Council Decision of 3 December 1998 instructing Europol to deal with crimes committed or likely to be committed in the course of terrorist activities against life, limb, personal freedom or property[4]; Council Joint Action 96/610/JHA of 15 October 1996 concerning the creation and maintenance of a Directory of specialised counter-terrorist competences, skills and expertise to facilitate counter-terrorism cooperation between the Member States of the European Union[5]; Council Joint Action 98/428/JHA of 29 June 1998 on the creation of a European Judicial Network[6], with responsibilities in terrorist offences, in particular Article 2; Council Joint Action 98/733/JHA of 21 December 1998 on making it a criminal offence to participate in a criminal organisation in the Member States of the European Union[7]; and the Council Recommendation of 9 December 1999 on cooperation in combating the financing of terrorist groups[8].

(6) The definition of terrorist offences should be approximated in all Member States, including those offences relating to terrorist groups. Furthermore, penalties and sanctions should be provided for natural and legal persons having committed or being liable for such offences, which reflect the seriousness of such offences.

(7) Jurisdictional rules should be established to ensure that the terrorist offence may be effectively prosecuted.

(8) Victims of terrorist offences are vulnerable, and therefore specific measures are necessary with regard to them.

(9) Given that the objectives of the proposed action cannot be sufficiently achieved by the Member States unilaterally, and can therefore, because of the need for reciprocity, be better achieved at the level of the Union, the Union may adopt measures, in accordance with the principle of subsidiarity. In accordance with the principle of proportionality, this Framework Decision does not go beyond what is necessary in order to achieve those objectives.

(10) This Framework Decision respects fundamental rights as guaranteed by the European Convention for the Protection of Human Rights and Fundamental Freedoms and as they emerge from the constitutional traditions common to the Member States as principles of Community law. The Union observes the principles recognised by Article 6(2) of the Treaty on European Union and reflected in the Charter of Fundamental Rights of the European Union, notably Chapter VI thereof. Nothing in this Framework Decision may be interpreted as being intended to reduce or restrict fundamental rights or freedoms such as the right to strike, freedom of assembly, of association or of expression, including the right of everyone to form and to join trade unions with others for the protection of his or her interests and the related right to demonstrate.

(11) Actions by armed forces during periods of armed conflict, which are governed by international humanitarian law within the meaning of these terms under that law, and, inasmuch as they are governed by other rules of international law, actions by the armed forces of a State in the exercise of their official duties are not governed by this Framework Decision,

HAS ADOPTED THIS FRAMEWORK DECISION:

Article 1
Terrorist offences and fundamental rights and principles

1. Each Member State shall take the necessary measures to ensure that the intentional acts referred to below in points (a) to (i), as defined as offences under national law, which, given their nature or context, may seriously damage a country or an international organisation where committed with the aim of:
   – seriously intimidating a population, or
   – unduly compelling a Government or international organisation to perform or abstain from performing any act, or

---

[4] OJ C 26, 30.1.1999, p. 22.
[5] OJ L 273, 25.10.1996, p. 1.
[6] OJ L 191, 7.7.1998, p. 4.
[7] OJ L 351, 29.12.1998, p. 1.
[8] OJ C 373, 23.12.1999, p. 1.

- seriously destabilising or destroying the fundamental political, constitutional, economic or social structures of a country or an international organisation,
- shall be deemed to be terrorist offences:
  - (a) attacks upon a person's life which may cause death;
  - (b) attacks upon the physical integrity of a person;
  - (c) kidnapping or hostage taking;
  - (d) causing extensive destruction to a Government or public facility, a transport system, an infrastructure facility, including an information system, a fixed platform located on the continental shelf, a public place or private property likely to endanger human life or result in major economic loss;
  - (e) seizure of aircraft, ships or other means of public or goods transport;
  - (f) manufacture, possession, acquisition, transport, supply or use of weapons, explosives or of nuclear, biological or chemical weapons, as well as research into, and development of, biological and chemical weapons;
  - (g) release of dangerous substances, or causing fires, floods or explosions the effect of which is to endanger human life;
  - (h) interfering with or disrupting the supply of water, power or any other fundamental natural resource the effect of which is to endanger human life;
  - (i) threatening to commit any of the acts listed in (a) to (h).
2. This Framework Decision shall not have the effect of altering the obligation to respect fundamental rights and fundamental legal principles as enshrined in Article 6 of the Treaty on European Union.

Article 2
Offences relating to a terrorist group

1. For the purposes of this Framework Decision, 'terrorist group' shall mean: a structured group of more than two persons, established over a period of time and acting in concert to commit terrorist offences. 'Structured group' shall mean a group that is not randomly formed for the immediate commission of an offence and that does not need to have formally defined roles for its members, continuity of its membership or a developed structure.
2. Each Member State shall take the necessary measures to ensure that the following intentional acts are punishable:
   (a) directing a terrorist group;
   (b) participating in the activities of a terrorist group, including by supplying information or material resources, or by funding its activities in any way, with knowledge of the fact that such participation will contribute to the criminal activities of the terrorist group.

Article 3
Offences linked to terrorist activities

Each Member State shall take the necessary measures to ensure that terrorist-linked offences include the following acts:

(a) aggravated theft with a view to committing one of the acts listed in Article 1(1);
(b) extortion with a view to the perpetration of one of the acts listed in Article 1(1);
(c) drawing up false administrative documents with a view to committing one of the acts listed in Article 1(1)(a) to (h) and Article 2(2)(b).

Article 4
Inciting, aiding or abetting, and attempting

1. Each Member State shall take the necessary measures to ensure that inciting or aiding or abetting an offence referred to in Article 1(1), Articles 2 or 3 is made punishable.
2. Each Member State shall take the necessary measures to ensure that attempting to commit an offence referred to in Article 1(1) and Article 3, with the exception of possession as provided for in Article 1(1)(f) and the offence referred to in Article 1(1)(i), is made punishable.

Article 5
Penalties

1. Each Member State shall take the necessary measures to ensure that the offences referred to in Articles 1 to 4 are punishable by effective, proportionate and dissuasive criminal penalties, which may entail extradition.

2. Each Member State shall take the necessary measures to ensure that the terrorist offences referred to in Article 1(1) and offences referred to in Article 4, inasmuch as they relate to terrorist offences, are punishable by custodial sentences heavier than those imposable under national law for such offences in the absence of the special intent required pursuant to Article 1(1), save where the sentences imposable are already the maximum possible sentences under national law.

3. Each Member State shall take the necessary measures to ensure that offences listed in Article 2 are punishable by custodial sentences, with a maximum sentence of not less than fifteen years for the offence referred to in Article 2(2)(a), and for the offences listed in Article 2(2)(b) a maximum sentence of not less than eight years. In so far as the offence referred to in Article 2(2)(a) refers only to the act in Article 1(1)(i), the maximum sentence shall not be less than eight years.

Article 6
Particular circumstances

Each Member State may take the necessary measures to ensure that the penalties referred to in Article 5 may be reduced if the offender:

(a) renounces terrorist activity, and

(b) provides the administrative or judicial authorities with information which they would not otherwise have been able to obtain, helping them to:
  (i) prevent or mitigate the effects of the offence;
  (ii) identify or bring to justice the other offenders;
  (iii) find evidence; or
  (iv) prevent further offences referred to in Articles 1 to 4.

Article 7
Liability of legal persons

[Similar terms to Art. 5 of Framework Decision 2003/568/JHA.]

Article 8
Penalties for legal persons

Each Member State shall take the necessary measures to ensure that a legal person held liable pursuant to Article 7 is punishable by effective, proportionate and dissuasive penalties, which shall include criminal or non-criminal fines and may include other penalties, such as:

(a) exclusion from entitlement to public benefits or aid;

(b) temporary or permanent disqualification from the practice of commercial activities;

(c) placing under judicial supervision;

(d) a judicial winding-up order;

(e) temporary or permanent closure of establishments which have been used for committing the offence.

Article 9
Jurisdiction and prosecution

1. Each Member State shall take the necessary measures to establish its jurisdiction over the offences referred to in Articles 1 to 4 where:
  (a) the offence is committed in whole or in part in its territory. Each Member State may extend its jurisdiction if the offence is committed in the territory of a Member State;
  (b) the offence is committed on board a vessel flying its flag or an aircraft registered there;
  (c) the offender is one of its nationals or residents;
  (d) the offence is committed for the benefit of a legal person established in its territory;
  (e) the offence is committed against the institutions or people of the Member State in question or against an institution of the European Union or a body set up in accordance with the Treaty establishing the European Community or the Treaty on European Union and based in that Member State.

2. When an offence falls within the jurisdiction of more than one Member State and when any of the States concerned can validly prosecute on the basis of the same facts, the Member States concerned shall cooperate in order to decide which of them will prosecute the offenders with the aim, if

possible, of centralising proceedings in a single Member State. To this end, the Member States may have recourse to any body or mechanism established within the European Union in order to facilitate cooperation between their judicial authorities and the coordination of their action. Sequential account shall be taken of the following factors:

– the Member State shall be that in the territory of which the acts were committed,
– the Member State shall be that of which the perpetrator is a national or resident,
– the Member State shall be the Member State of origin of the victims,
– the Member State shall be that in the territory of which the perpetrator was found.

3. Each Member State shall take the necessary measures also to establish its jurisdiction over the offences referred to in Articles 1 to 4 in cases where it refuses to hand over or extradite a person suspected or convicted of such an offence to another Member State or to a third country.

4. Each Member State shall ensure that its jurisdiction covers cases in which any of the offences referred to in Articles 2 and 4 has been committed in whole or in part within its territory, wherever the terrorist group is based or pursues its criminal activities.

5. This Article shall not exclude the exercise of jurisdiction in criminal matters as laid down by a Member State in accordance with its national legislation.

Article 10
Protection of, and assistance to, victims

1. Member States shall ensure that investigations into, or prosecution of, offences covered by this Framework Decision are not dependent on a report or accusation made by a person subjected to the offence, at least if the acts were committed on the territory of the Member State.

2. In addition to the measures laid down in the Council Framework Decision 2001/220/JHA of 15 March 2001 on the standing of victims in criminal proceedings[9], each Member State shall, if necessary, take all measures possible to ensure appropriate assistance for victims' families.

Article 11
Implementation and reports

1. Member States shall take the necessary measures to comply with this Framework Decision by 31 December 2002.

2. By 31 December 2002, Member States shall forward to the General Secretariat of the Council and to the Commission the text of the provisions transposing into their national law the obligations imposed on them under this Framework Decision. On the basis of a report drawn up from that information and a report from the Commission, the Council shall assess, by 31 December 2003, whether Member States have taken the necessary measures to comply with this Framework Decision.

3. The Commission report shall specify, in particular, transposition into the criminal law of the Member States of the obligation referred to in Article 5(2).

Council Framework Decision 2008/919/JHA of 28 November 2008 amending Framework Decision 2002/475/JHA on combating terrorism

THE COUNCIL OF THE EUROPEAN UNION,

Having regard to the Treaty on European Union, and in particular Article 29, Article 31(1)(e) and Article 34(2)(b) thereof,

Having regard to the proposal from the Commission,

Having regard to the opinion of the European Parliament[1],

Whereas:

(1) Terrorism constitutes one of the most serious violations of the universal values of human dignity, liberty, equality and solidarity, respect for human rights and fundamental freedoms on which the European

---

[9] OJ L 82, 22.3.2001, p. 1.
[1] Not yet published in the Official Journal.

Union is founded. It also represents one of the most serious attacks on democracy and the rule of law, principles which are common to the Member States and on which the European Union is based.

(2) Council Framework Decision 2002/475/JHA of 13 June 2002 on combating terrorism[2] is the basis of the counter-terrorist policy of the European Union. The achievement of a legal framework common to all Member States, and in particular, of a harmonised definition of terrorist offences, has allowed the counter-terrorism policy of the European Union to develop and expand, subject to the respect of fundamental rights and the rule of law.

(3) The terrorist threat has grown and rapidly evolved in recent years, with changes in the modus operandi of terrorist activists and supporters including the replacement of structured and hierarchical groups by semi-autonomous cells loosely tied to each other. Such cells inter-link international networks and increasingly rely on the use of new technologies, in particular the Internet.

(4) The Internet is used to inspire and mobilise local terrorist networks and individuals in Europe and also serves as a source of information on terrorist means and methods, thus functioning as a 'virtual training camp'. Activities of public provocation to commit terrorist offences, recruitment for terrorism and training for terrorism have multiplied at very low cost and risk.

(5) The Hague Programme on strengthening freedom, security and justice in the European Union, adopted by the European Council on 5 November 2004, underlines that effective prevention and combating of terrorism in full compliance with fundamental rights requires Member States not to confine their activities to maintaining their own security, but to focus also on the security of the Union as a whole.

(6) The Council and Commission Action Plan implementing the Hague Programme on strengthening freedom, security and justice in the European Union[3], recalls that a global response is required to address terrorism and that the expectations that citizens have of the Union cannot be ignored, nor can the Union fail to respond to them. In addition, it states that attention must focus on different aspects of prevention, preparedness and response to further enhance, and where necessary complement, Member States' capabilities to fight terrorism, concentrating particularly on recruitment, financing, risk analysis, protection of critical infrastructures and consequence management.

(7) This Framework Decision provides for the criminalisation of offences linked to terrorist activities in order to contribute to the more general policy objective of preventing terrorism through reducing the dissemination of those materials which might incite persons to commit terrorist attacks.

(8) United Nations Security Council Resolution 1624 (2005) calls upon States to take measures that are necessary and appropriate, and in accordance with their obligations under international law, to prohibit by law incitement to commit a terrorist act or acts and to prevent such conduct. The report of the Secretary-General of the United Nations 'Uniting against terrorism: recommendations for a global counter-terrorism strategy' of 27 April 2006, interprets the above-mentioned Resolution as providing for a basis for the criminalisation of incitement to terrorist acts and recruitment, including through the Internet. The United Nations Global Counter-Terrorism Strategy of 8 September 2006 mentions that the Member States of the UN resolve to explore ways and means to coordinate efforts at the international and regional level to counter terrorism in all its forms and manifestations on the Internet.

(9) The Council of Europe Convention on the Prevention of Terrorism establishes the obligations of States parties thereto to criminalise public provocation to commit a terrorist offence and recruitment and training for terrorism, when committed unlawfully and intentionally.

(10) The definition of terrorist offences, including offences linked to terrorist activities, should be further approximated in all Member States, so that it covers public provocation to commit a terrorist offence, recruitment for terrorism and training for terrorism, when committed intentionally.

(11) Penalties should be provided for natural persons having intentionally committed or legal persons held liable for public provocation to commit terrorist offences, recruitment for terrorism and training for terrorism. These forms of behaviour should be equally punishable in all Member States irrespective of whether they are committed through the Internet or not.

---

[2] OJ L 164, 22.6.2002, p. 3.
[3] OJ C 198, 12.8.2005, p. 1.

(12) Given that the objectives of this Framework Decision cannot be sufficiently achieved by the Member States unilaterally, and can therefore, because of the need for European-wide harmonised rules, be better achieved at the level of the Union, the Union may adopt measures, in accordance with the principle of subsidiarity, as set out in Article 5 of the EC Treaty and referred to in Article 2 of the EU Treaty. In accordance with the principle of proportionality, as set out in Article 5 of the EC Treaty, this Framework Decision does not go beyond what is necessary in order to achieve those objectives.

(13) The Union observes the principles recognised by Article 6(2) of the EU Treaty and reflected in the Charter of Fundamental Rights of the European Union, notably Chapters II and VI thereof. Nothing in this Framework Decision may be interpreted as being intended to reduce or restrict fundamental rights or freedoms such as freedom of expression, assembly, or of association, the right to respect for private and family life, including the right to respect of the confidentiality of correspondence.

(14) Public provocation to commit terrorist offences, recruitment for terrorism and training for terrorism are intentional crimes. Therefore, nothing in this Framework Decision may be interpreted as being intended to reduce or restrict the dissemination of information for scientific, academic or reporting purposes. The expression of radical, polemic or controversial views in the public debate on sensitive political questions, including terrorism, falls outside the scope of this Framework Decision and, in particular, of the definition of public provocation to commit terrorist offences.

(15) The implementation of the criminalisation under this Framework Decision should be proportional to the nature and circumstances of the offence, with respect to the legitimate aims pursued and to their necessity in a democratic society, and should exclude any form of arbitrariness or discrimination,

HAS ADOPTED THIS FRAMEWORK DECISION:

Article 1
Amendments

Framework Decision 2002/475/JHA shall be amended as follows:

1. Article 3 shall be replaced by the following:

'Article 3
Offences linked to terrorist activities

1. For the purposes of this Framework Decision:
   (a) 'public provocation to commit a terrorist offence' shall mean the distribution, or otherwise making available, of a message to the public, with the intent to incite the commission of one of the offences listed in Article 1(1)(a) to (h), where such conduct, whether or not directly advocating terrorist offences, causes a danger that one or more such offences may be committed;
   (b) 'recruitment for terrorism' shall mean soliciting another person to commit one of the offences listed in Article 1(1)(a) to (h), or in Article 2(2);
   (c) 'training for terrorism' shall mean providing instruction in the making or use of explosives, firearms or other weapons or noxious or hazardous substances, or in other specific methods or techniques, for the purpose of committing one of the offences listed in Article 1(1)(a) to (h), knowing that the skills provided are intended to be used for this purpose.
2. Each Member State shall take the necessary measures to ensure that offences linked to terrorist activities include the following intentional acts:
   (a) public provocation to commit a terrorist offence;
   (b) recruitment for terrorism;
   (c) training for terrorism;
   (d) aggravated theft with a view to committing one of the offences listed in Article 1(1);
   (e) extortion with a view to the perpetration of one of the offences listed in Article 1(1);
   (f) drawing up false administrative documents with a view to committing one of the offences listed in Article 1(1)(a) to (h) and Article 2(2)(b).
3. For an act as set out in paragraph 2 to be punishable, it shall not be necessary that a terrorist offence be actually committed.'
2. Article 4 shall be replaced by the following:

'Article 4

Aiding or abetting, inciting and attempting

1. Each Member State shall take the necessary measures to ensure that aiding or abetting an offence referred to in Article 1(1), Articles 2 or 3 is made punishable.

2. Each Member State shall take the necessary measures to ensure that inciting an offence referred to in Article 1(1), Article 2 or Article 3(2)(d) to (f) is made punishable.

3. Each Member State shall take the necessary measures to ensure that attempting to commit an offence referred to in Article 1(1) and Article 3(2)(d) to (f), with the exception of possession as provided for in Article 1(1)(f) and the offence referred to in Article 1(1)(i), is made punishable.

4. Each Member State may decide to take the necessary measures to ensure that attempting to commit an offence referred to in Article 3(2)(b) and (c) is made punishable.'

Article 2

Fundamental principles relating to freedom of expression

This Framework Decision shall not have the effect of requiring Member States to take measures in contradiction of fundamental principles relating to freedom of expression, in particular freedom of the press and the freedom of expression in other media as they result from constitutional traditions or rules governing the rights and responsibilities of, and the procedural guarantees for, the press or other media where these rules relate to the determination or limitation of liability.

Article 3

Implementation and report

1. Member States shall take the necessary measures to comply with this Framework Decision by 9 December 2010. In the implementation of this Framework Decision, Member States shall ensure that the criminalisation shall be proportionate to the legitimate aims pursued and necessary in a democratic society and shall exclude any form of arbitrariness and discrimination.

2. By 9 December 2010, Member States shall forward to the General Secretariat of the Council and to the Commission the text of the provisions transposing into their national law the obligations imposed on them under this Framework Decision. On the basis of a report drawn up from that information and a report from the Commission, the Council shall assess, by 9 December 2011, whether Member States have taken the necessary measures to comply with this Framework Decision.

Standing of victims in criminal proceedings—Council Framework Decision 2001/220/JHA

Council Framework Decision of 15 March 2001 on the standing of victims in criminal proceedings (2001/220/JHA)

THE COUNCIL OF THE EUROPEAN UNION,

Having regard to the Treaty on European Union, and in particular Article 31 and Article 34(2)(b) thereof,

Having regard to the initiative by the Portuguese Republic[1],

Having regard to the opinion of the European Parliament[2],

Whereas:

(1)   In accordance with the Action Plan of the Council and the Commission on how best to implement the provisions of the Treaty of Amsterdam on an area of freedom, security and justice, in particular points 19 and 51(c), within five years following entry into force of the Treaty, the question of victim support should be addressed, by making a comparative survey of victim compensation schemes and by assessing the feasibility of taking action within the European Union.

---

[1]   OJ C 243, 24.8.2000, p. 4.
[2]   Opinion delivered on 12.12.2000 (not yet published in the Official Journal).

(2) The Commission submitted a communication to the European Parliament, the Council and the Economic and Social Committee on 14 July 1999 entitled 'Crime victims in the European Union: reflections on standards and action'. The European Parliament adopted a Resolution on the Commission communication on 15 June 2000.

(3) The conclusions of the European Council meeting in Tampere on 15 and 16 October 1999, in particular point 32 thereof, stipulate that minimum standards should be drawn up on the protection of the victims of crimes, in particular on crime victims' access to justice and on their right to compensation for damages, including legal costs. In addition, national programmes should be set up to finance measures, public and non-governmental, for assistance to and protection of victims.

(4) Member States should approximate their laws and regulations to the extent necessary to attain the objective of affording victims of crime a high level of protection, irrespective of the Member State in which they are present.

(5) Victims' needs should be considered and addressed in a comprehensive, coordinated manner, avoiding partial or inconsistent solutions which may give rise to secondary victimisation.

(6) The provisions of this framework Decision are therefore not confined to attending to the victim's interests under criminal proceedings proper. They also cover certain measures to assist victims before or after criminal proceedings, which might mitigate the effects of the crime.

(7) Measures to assist victims of crime, and in particular the provisions regarding compensation and mediation do not concern arrangements under civil procedure.

(8) The rules and practices as regards the standing and main rights of victims need to be approximated, with particular regard to the right to be treated with respect for their dignity, the right to provide and receive information, the right to understand and be understood, the right to be protected at the various stages of procedure and the right to have allowance made for the disadvantage of living in a different Member State from the one in which the crime was committed.

(9) The provisions of this Framework Decision do not, however, impose an obligation on Member States to ensure that victims will be treated in a manner equivalent to that of a party to proceedings.

(10) The involvement of specialised services and victim support groups before, during and after criminal proceedings is important.

(11) Suitable and adequate training should be given to persons coming into contact with victims, as this is essential both for victims and for achieving the purposes of proceedings.

(12) Use should be made of existing contact point networking arrangements in Member States, whether under the judicial system or based on victim support group networks,

HAS ADOPTED THIS FRAMEWORK DECISION:

Article 1
Definitions

For the purposes of this Framework Decision:

(a) 'victim' shall mean a natural person who has suffered harm, including physical or mental injury, emotional suffering or economic loss, directly caused by acts or omissions that are in violation of the criminal law of a Member State;

(b) 'victim support organisation' shall mean a non-governmental organisation, legally established in a Member State, whose support to victims of crime is provided free of charge and, conducted under appropriate conditions, complements the action of the State in this area;

(c) 'criminal proceedings' shall be understood in accordance with the national law applicable;

(d) 'proceedings' shall be broadly construed to include, in addition to criminal proceedings, all contacts of victims as such with any authority, public service or victim support organisation in connection with their case, before, during, or after criminal process;

(e) 'mediation in criminal cases' shall be understood as the search, prior to or during criminal proceedings, for a negotiated solution between the victim and the author of the offence, mediated by a competent person.

Article 2

Respect and recognition

1. Each Member State shall ensure that victims have a real and appropriate role in its criminal legal system. It shall continue to make every effort to ensure that victims are treated with due respect for the dignity of the individual during proceedings and shall recognise the rights and legitimate interests of victims with particular reference to criminal proceedings.

2. Each Member State shall ensure that victims who are particularly vulnerable can benefit from specific treatment best suited to their circumstances.

Article 3

Hearings, and provision of evidence

Each Member State shall safeguard the possibility for victims to be heard during proceedings and to supply evidence.

Each Member State shall take appropriate measures to ensure that its authorities question victims only insofar as necessary for the purpose of criminal proceedings.

Article 4

Right to receive information

1. Each Member State shall ensure that victims in particular have access, as from their first contact with law enforcement agencies, by any means it deems appropriate and as far as possible in languages commonly understood, to information of relevance for the protection of their interests. Such information shall be at least as follows:

   (a) the type of services or organisations to which they can turn for support;
   (b) the type of support which they can obtain;
   (c) where and how they can report an offence;
   (d) procedures following such a report and their role in connection with such procedures;
   (e) how and under what conditions they can obtain protection;
   (f) to what extent and on what terms they have access to:
       (i) legal advice or
       (ii) legal aid, or
       (iii) any other sort of advice,
          if, in the cases envisaged in point (i) and (ii), they are entitled to receive it;
   (g) requirements for them to be entitled to compensation;
   (h) if they are resident in another State, any special arrangements available to them in order to protect their interests.

2. Each Member State shall ensure that victims who have expressed a wish to this effect are kept informed of:

   (a) the outcome of their complaint;
   (b) relevant factors enabling them, in the event of prosecution, to know the conduct of the criminal proceedings regarding the person prosecuted for offences concerning them, except in exceptional cases where the proper handling of the case may be adversely affected;
   (c) the court's sentence.

3. Member States shall take the necessary measures to ensure that, at least in cases where there might be danger to the victims, when the person prosecuted or sentenced for an offence is released, a decision may be taken to notify the victim if necessary.

4. In so far as a Member State forwards on its own initiative the information referred to in paragraphs 2 and 3, it must ensure that victims have the right not to receive it, unless communication thereof is compulsory under the terms of the relevant criminal proceedings.

Article 5

Communication safeguards

Each Member State shall, in respect of victims having the status of witnesses or parties to the proceedings, take the necessary measures to minimise as far as possible communication difficulties as regards their understanding of, or involvement in, the relevant steps of the criminal proceedings in question, to an extent comparable with the measures of this type which it takes in respect of defendants.

313

Article 6
Specific assistance to the victim

Each Member State shall ensure that victims have access to advice as referred to in Article 4(1)(f)(iii), provided free of charge where warranted, concerning their role in the proceedings and, where appropriate, legal aid as referred to in Article 4(1)(f)(ii), when it is possible for them to have the status of parties to criminal proceedings.

Article 7
Victims' expenses with respect to criminal proceedings

Each Member State shall, according to the applicable national provisions, afford victims who have the status of parties or witnesses the possibility of reimbursement of expenses incurred as a result of their legitimate participation in criminal proceedings.

Article 8
Right to protection

1. Each Member State shall ensure a suitable level of protection for victims and, where appropriate, their families or persons in a similar position, particularly as regards their safety and protection of their privacy, where the competent authorities consider that there is a serious risk of reprisals or firm evidence of serious intent to intrude upon their privacy.
2. To that end, and without prejudice to paragraph 4, each Member State shall guarantee that it is possible to adopt, if necessary, as part of the court proceedings, appropriate measures to protect the privacy and photographic image of victims and their families or persons in a similar position.
3. Each Member State shall further ensure that contact between victims and offenders within court premises may be avoided, unless criminal proceedings require such contact. Where appropriate for that purpose, each Member State shall progressively provide that court premises have special waiting areas for victims.
4. Each Member State shall ensure that, where there is a need to protect victims—particularly those most vulnerable—from the effects of giving evidence in open court, victims may, by decision taken by the court, be entitled to testify in a manner which will enable this objective to be achieved, by any appropriate means compatible with its basic legal principles.

Article 9
Right to compensation in the course of criminal proceedings

1. Each Member State shall ensure that victims of criminal acts are entitled to obtain a decision within reasonable time limits on compensation by the offender in the course of criminal proceedings, except where, in certain cases, national law provides for compensation to be awarded in another manner.
2. Each Member State shall take appropriate measures to encourage the offender to provide adequate compensation to victims.
3. Unless urgently required for the purpose of criminal proceedings, recoverable property belonging to victims which is seized in the course of criminal proceedings shall be returned to them without delay.

Article 10
Penal mediation in the course of criminal proceedings

1. Each Member State shall seek to promote mediation in criminal cases for offences which it considers appropriate for this sort of measure.
2. Each Member State shall ensure that any agreement between the victim and the offender reached in the course of such mediation in criminal cases can be taken into account.

Article 11
Victims resident in another Member State

1. Each Member State shall ensure that its competent authorities can take appropriate measures to minimise the difficulties faced where the victim is a resident of a State other than the one where the offence has occurred, particularly with regard to the organisation of the proceedings. For this purpose, its authorities should, in particular, be in a position:
   – to be able to decide whether the victim may make a statement immediately after the commission of an offence,

– to have recourse as far as possible to the provisions on video conferencing and telephone conference calls laid down in Articles 10 and 11 of the Convention on Mutual Assistance in Criminal Matters between the Member States of the European Union of 29 May 2000[3] for the purpose of hearing victims resident abroad.

2. Each Member State shall ensure that the victim of an offence in a Member State other than the one where he resides may make a complaint before the competent authorities of his State of residence if he was unable to do so in the Member State where the offence was committed or, in the event of a serious offence, if he did not wish to do so.

The competent authority to which the complaint is made, insofar as it does not itself have competence in this respect, shall transmit it without delay to the competent authority in the territory in which the offence was committed. The complaint shall be dealt with in accordance with the national law of the State in which the offence was committed.

Article 12
Cooperation between Member States

Each Member State shall foster, develop and improve cooperation between Member States in order to facilitate the more effective protection of victims' interests in criminal proceedings, whether in the form of networks directly linked to the judicial system or of links between victim support organisations.

Article 13
Specialist services and victim support organisations

1. Each Member State shall, in the context of proceedings, promote the involvement of victim support systems responsible for organising the initial reception of victims and for victim support and assistance thereafter, whether through the provision of specially trained personnel within its public services or through recognition and funding of victim support organisations.

2. Each Member State shall encourage action taken in proceedings by such personnel or by victim support organisations, particularly as regards:
    (a) providing victims with information;
    (b) assisting victims according to their immediate needs;
    (c) accompanying victims, if necessary and possible during criminal proceedings;
    (d) assisting victims, at their request, after criminal proceedings have ended.

Article 14
Training for personnel involved in proceedings or otherwise in contact with victims

1. Through its public services or by funding victim support organisations, each Member State shall encourage initiatives enabling personnel involved in proceedings or otherwise in contact with victims to receive suitable training with particular reference to the needs of the most vulnerable groups.

2. Paragraph 1 shall apply in particular to police officers and legal practitioners.

Article 15
Practical conditions regarding the position of victims in proceedings

1. Each Member State shall support the progressive creation, in respect of proceedings in general, and particularly in venues where criminal proceedings may be initiated, of the necessary conditions for attempting to prevent secondary victimisation and avoiding placing victims under unnecessary pressure. This shall apply particularly as regards proper initial reception of victims, and the establishment of conditions appropriate to their situation in the venues in question.

2. For the purposes of paragraph 1, each Member State shall in particular have regard to facilities within courts, police stations, public services and victim support organisations.

---

[3] OJ C 197, 12.7.2000, p. 1.

Article 17
Implementation

Each Member State shall bring into force the laws, regulations and administrative provisions necessary to comply with this Framework Decision:

regarding Article 10, 22 March 2006,

regarding Articles 5 and 6, 22 March 2004,

regarding the other provisions, 22 March 2002.

Article 18
Assessment

As from the dates referred to in Article 17, each Member State shall forward to the General Secretariat of the Council and to the Commission the text of the provisions enacting into national law the requirements laid down by this Framework Decision. The Council shall assess, within one year following each of these dates, the measures taken by Member States to comply with the provisions of this Framework Decision, by means of a report drawn up by the General Secretariat on the basis of the information received from Member States and a report in writing submitted by the Commission.

INDEX

Printed and bound by CPI Group (UK) Ltd, Croydon, CR0 4YY